ONE NATION, AFTER ALL

ONE NATION, AFTER ALL

ALAN WOLFE

WHAT

MIDDLE-CLASS

AMERICANS

REALLY THINK

ABOUT: GOD,

COUNTRY,

FAMILY,

RACISM,

WELFARE,

IMMIGRATION,

HOMOSEXUALITY,

WORK,

THE RIGHT,

THE LEFT,

AND EACH OTHER

VIKING

VIKING
Published by the Penguin Group
Penguin Putnam Inc., 375 Hudson Street,
New York, New York 10014, U.S.A.
Penguin Books Ltd, 27 Wrights Lane,
London W8 5TZ, England
Penguin Books Australia Ltd, Ringwood,
Victoria, Australia
Penguin Books Canada Ltd, 10 Alcorn Avenue,
Toronto, Ontario, Canada M4V 3B2
Penguin Books (N.Z.) Ltd, 182–190 Wairau Road,
Auckland 10, New Zealand

Penguin Books Ltd, Registered Offices:
Harmondsworth, Middlesex, England

First published in 1998 by Viking Penguin,
a member of Penguin Putnam Inc.

10 9 8 7 6 5 4 3 2 1

Publisher's Note
The names of the individuals represented in this book have been changed.

LIBRARY OF CONGRESS CATALOGING IN PUBLICATION DATA
Wolfe, Alan, 1942–
    One nation, after all: what middle-class Americans really think about: God,
country, family, racism, welfare, immigration, homosexuality, work, the right, the left,
and each other / Alan Wolfe.
    p. cm.
    Includes index.
    ISBN 0 670 87677 1 (alk. paper)
    1. Middle class—United States—Attitudes.   2. Social values—United States.
3. United States—Moral conditions.   I. Title.
HT690.U6W65   1998
305.5'5'0973—dc21   97-36925

B&T

This book is printed on acid-free paper.

Printed in the United States of America
Set in 11/14 pt Stempel Garamond
Designed by Ann Gold

ACKNOWLEDGMENTS

My greatest debts are to two people. Eric Wanner, president of the Russell Sage Foundation, not only encouraged me to undertake this work, but also provided the funds necessary to do so. And Jon Westling, president of Boston University, took an interest in the book from the moment I mentioned its subject matter to him and backed up his belief in my ability to carry it out in ways for which I shall always be thankful.

The research I undertook in three communities outside of Boston demonstrated to me that there exists a national community of social scientists willing to contribute time and effort to another's project. Jean Blocker of the University of Tulsa responded to a phone call from a stranger and made available the facilities of her department and university. Frank Lechner took the lead in making life comfortable for Maria Poarch and me during our stay in Atlanta, and his colleagues at Emory, especially Rick Rubinson, John Boli, Steven Tipton, and Alex Hicks, were helpful as well, as was Melvyn Fein of Kennesaw State University. In San Diego, Tim McDaniel made possible our visit, and Richard Madsen, Tanya Luhrmann, and Michael Schudson went out of their way to be of both intellectual and practical assistance. All of these people are collaborators in the best sense of the term.

My debt to Maria Poarch, my first research assistant, ought to be obvious from the text. Maria proved to be a wonderful interviewer; her energy, enthusiasm, and derring-do were indispensable to the project's completion. Less obvious to the reader, but equally important to me, was the work of my other research assistant, Julie Plaut. Julie reorganized the transcripts of the interviews in ways that made possible the interpretations I gave to them and responded to every request I made of her with alacrity and support. Dan Monti and Mette Sørensen, sociologists at Boston University, were more than willing to answer questions that had stumped me. Michael Goodman helped with census data. Peter Marsden made available to me the facilities of the Harvard University Sociology Department, providing just the right atmosphere for writing the book. The assistance of Nancy Williamson and Cheryl Minton was indispensable.

On the editorial side, I want to thank my literary agents Glen Hartley and Lynn Chu. Jane von Mehren's suggestions (and commands) improved the book greatly. I also benefited from the comments of Marion Maneker.

From the moment I met her fifteen years ago, Jytte Klausen has been my strongest supporter and best critic. And my children are getting to the age where they can understand and argue about the things I write. This one is for them.

Alan Wolfe
Wellesley, Massachusetts

Contents

I MIDDLE CLASS AT MIDDLE AGE

As the middle class goes, so goes America. And why not? From the yeoman's suspicion of aristocracy in the eighteenth century to the working man's disdain for socialism in the twentieth, Americans, whatever their accomplishments, have been persistently middle class in their aspirations. Trying to account for what makes America different from other prosperous liberal democracies, the sociologist Seymour Martin Lipset once wrote that "America has been dominated by pure bourgeois, middle-class individualistic values." Even as a debate has begun on whether the United States is being polarized between rich and poor, for many people around the world becoming American and being middle class are the same thing.

Nothing captures better the love affair between America and middle-class status than the propensity of Americans to define themselves as middle class whether or not they are. Polling on this point is voluminous: here are just two examples. According to the General Social Survey, at no time between 1972 and 1994 did more than 10 percent of the American population classify themselves as *either* lower class or upper class. And, in 1992, despite reports of economic hard times, a CBS News/*New York Times* poll indicated that 75 percent of the American people responded positively to this question: "When presidential candidates talk about the middle class, do you think they mean people like you?"

Such polls not only tell us whether people think they themselves are middle class, they also contain an implicit definition of what it means to be middle class. Americans love to debate that question. Is Zoë Baird, President Clinton's first nominee for attorney general, whose name was never mentioned without note of her $500,000 income, middle class? Are Reagan Democrats? Is a former executive struggling to start a business, but in reality living on his wife's income as a social worker? Is anyone without health insurance, whatever his or her income? Korean grocers? Divorced mothers of small children? An assistant professor of anything? When President Clinton in 1995 proposed his "Middle-Class Bill of Rights Tax Relief Act," a national debate was launched about where the boundaries of the middle class should be drawn, with Republicans proposing that a middle-class tax cut be extended to those who made up to $200,000 a year. This was an easy target to ridicule, but, at least in places such as New York and Los Angeles, it represents a solid, if not extraordinary, annual family income for two middle-level professionals who have not yet been downsized. Yet, it also makes little sense to leave out of the middle class a family in the heartland earning $45,000 a year, even if by their hands rather than their heads, so long as they work hard for whatever material goods they can afford, aspire to a good life for their children, and believe in the American dream.

Wherever we choose to draw the economic lines that define the middle class, most Americans have an expansive view of the concept. Asked in 1993 how much income you would have to make before you would be considered too rich to be middle class, 19 percent said $50,000 to $75,000, 17 percent said $75,000 to $100,000, 29 percent said $100,000 to $200,000, and 15 percent said over $200,000. The general feeling in America is that you are middle class if you say so. And, truth be told, that is not a bad way to treat the matter, for while the economic definitions of middle-class status shift all the time, what tends not to change are the moral and cultural meanings of middle-class life. Unlike being poor, being middle class means earning enough to have some choice about where and how to live; middle-class people strive to practice a sense of personal responsibility by owning as much of their home as possible and by protecting themselves as best they can from the whims of employers. Unlike being rich, to be middle class is to believe that what one has achieved is due not solely to family advantage—although within reason that is never to be spurned—but to one's own hard work and efforts. We are best off thinking of middle-class status as what the French would call a *mentalité*—a cluster of attitudes, beliefs, practices, and lifestyles that defines what it means to live in a way not too poor to be considered dependent on others and not too rich to be so luxuriously ostentatious that one loses touch with common sense.

By that definition, Judy Vogel, who lives in Cobb County, Georgia, near Atlanta, would certainly be middle class. Thirty-nine years old and a mother of two, Mrs. Vogel is a homemaker; her husband, who runs his own management consulting company, makes a six-figure income. A Republican and an active member of her Methodist church, Mrs. Vogel, like most of those who identify with her political party, feels that government programs such as welfare are responsible for the problems faced by poor people. She thinks we ought to say, "Look, this isn't working. . . . It's misguided. Let's go back and reevaluate it in a different way." Problems such as inner-city poverty cannot be solved, she believes, "by trying to come from the top down." The reason inner-city people become drug addicts or get involved with gangs is because they lack "a sense of moral rightness and wrongness." We aren't tough enough with them. Most disturbing of all to her is the complete breakdown of the family structure in inner-city neighborhoods: "In an effort to be politically correct and kind and good, we call it every kind of thing in the world," she says, "but I think somehow you've got to stand for something. You've got to believe in something, and you've got to live your life to some level of quality. I think that's been stripped."

The strong support Mrs. Vogel gives to the idea that a person should be responsible for his or her own fate is also linked, in her view, with the idea that people have a personal obligation to improve the life of their community. Selfishness bothers her. "I think that there are a large percentage of people in this community and all over America who don't see themselves as a part of any bigger picture, who don't have a commitment to anything bigger than themselves," she says. "I feel fortunate to have that. I have a sense of myself as part of a bigger world." Part of that world outside herself involves her family. Holding a master's degree in marriage and family therapy, Mrs. Vogel is a dedicated mother and a firm believer in family values. Indeed, her husband recently made the decision to begin working out of their home—restructuring, the Vogels call it—so that he can spend more time with their five- and six-year-old children. Deeply involved with the Parent-Teacher Association in her community, Mrs. Vogel is concerned that the schools are assuming too many responsibilities once the preserve of parents, and she makes it very clear that, in her family, it is she and her husband who teach their kids basic moral beliefs about God and obligations to others.

This sense that she belongs to a larger world does not stop with her family. Mrs. Vogel sees the world as composed of concentric circles that start at home and gradually expand to the nation as a whole: "We are part of this neighborhood. We are part of East Cobb. We are part of the city of Atlanta. We are . . . Georgians. We are Americans. We have enjoyed many of the benefits of that, and for that we have many responsibilities." For her, those responsibilities begin with the voluntary organization Habitat for Humanity. "We do drives for various things. We do missions in all kinds of places all over the country. . . . We just did some stuff for the Russian area." Morality for Mrs. Vogel means setting an example of the right way to live so that other people will follow: "I just believe that we were put here by God to love and care for each other and to make a difference in this world." That is why, although proud of being a Republican, she cannot bring herself to agree completely with the way "these tough, right-wing talk show hosts" talk about the poor. And she also has some reservations about the man who represents her in Congress, Speaker of the U.S. House of Representatives Newt Gingrich. It bothers her that the gap between rich and poor in America seems to be increasing. Her response is to "struggle within our own family as to how to create a sense of social values and responsibilities in our children." Because she does, it is impossible for Mrs. Vogel to attach too much importance to the conviction of conservative preachers that America is going to hell; religious fundamentalism, she says, "is the easy road.... I have high hopes for America," Mrs. Vogel concludes. "I will never give that up."

To understand what it means to be middle class in America, it is far more important to find out how many people there are in this country who hold opinions like Mrs. Vogel's than it is to find out how many have annual incomes within some predetermined range. Mrs. Vogel's opinions offer a succinct introduction to middle-class morality. I use the term "middle-class morality" to characterize the values of those people in America who strive to earn enough money so that they feel that their economic fate is in their own hands, but who also try to live by principles such as individual responsibility, the importance of family, obligations to others, and a belief in something outside oneself. Do Americans who make middle-class incomes and live in middle-class suburbs still believe in middle-class morality? Have they maintained their faith in those ideas despite the economic and political transformations taking place in their society? How many of them are there? Has middle-class morality changed? In what ways? The future of America as a middle-class nation has more to do with questions like these than with how many management jobs will be created or how many new homes will be built.

THE MIDDLE CLASS AND ITS DISCONTENTS

The adage that America is a middle-class nation, long taken for granted in self-perception, came about as close to reality as it ever would in the years after World War II. No doubt far too many Americans during those years faced poverty and indefensible racial and gender discrimination, but it is also true that unprecedented economic growth, an expansion of home ownership, inflation-proof contracts between companies and their workers, the democratization of higher education, successful Keynesian stabilization policies, social and geographic mobility, and impressive technological accomplishments allowed an astonishing number of Americans to make plausible claims for middle-class status. A level of physical and psychological security unimaginable to all but the very few a hundred years ago seemed within the grasp of the overwhelming many. Under those conditions, the promise of middle-class life—independence from the whims, blessings, and ill designs of others—seemed a reality.

How distant those years after World War II seem from the American mood in the last decade of the twentieth century! Now, according to a large number of critics, journalists, and social scientists, the middle class acts as if it has reached middle age. Those who take the pulse of the American middle class these days find the patient on the one hand lethargic, sunk into civic apathy and private withdrawal, and on the other hand hyperactive, loudly protesting its condition in support for populistic anger and collective revenge. Emerging from all corners of the political spectrum comes a rather depressing story about recent middle-class experience. The story runs roughly as follows.

First and foremost, we are told, the middle class is getting smaller. Writing during the 1980s, economists Bennett Harrison and Barry Bluestone noted with alarm that the "deindustrialization of America" was bound to depress wages, shrink managerial positions, and eventually result in a pattern of income distribution tilted toward the extremes rather than the middle. Given the importance of the charge, others challenged the data, pointing to the emergence of new jobs, as well as the ability of two-income families to make up for any losses experienced by once highly paid male workers, which in turn prompted a criticism of the critics' data and interpretations. Debates of this kind are rarely ever resolved, including this one. Nonetheless, sorting carefully through the passions involved, Frank Levy and Richard Murnane, economists at MIT and Harvard, concluded that a "hollowing out" of middle-class jobs produced "larger percentages of workers at the top and bottom of the distribution and a smaller percentage in the middle. At least for men, it is now clear that there were fewer middle-class jobs in the mid-1980s than a decade earlier." A more recent study, focusing on the distribution of overall wealth rather than income, demonstrated a pattern in which the extremes of rich and poor have grown in America at the expense of the middle. That conclusion has also been challenged by conservatives. They point out that the years in which the distribution of wealth allegedly became more polarized were also years in which significant amounts of new wealth were created.

However the statistics are interpreted, the story of middle-class shrinkage received a major boost when it was picked up by a conservative Republican, Patrick Buchanan, who made it the theme of his unsuccessful effort to win the Republican nomination for president in 1996. At a time when politicians of both parties were searching in vain for ways to strike a responsive chord in the electorate, Buchanan single-handedly launched a national discussion of whether American corporations, to meet global challenges, should be allowed to "downsize," no matter what the effects of such efforts on American jobs and communities. Devoting an unusually large number of pages to the subject, the *New York Times* published a series of stories that, in personalizing the experience of middle-class Americans suddenly finding themselves with neither income nor moorings, left the clear impression that the dream of middle-class security was fading fast in the United States.

Even those lucky enough to protect their middle-class lifestyles in the 1990s, analyses of this sort continue, found the meaning of their accomplishment ambiguous at best. The seemingly endless economic growth of the 1960s and early 1970s had led a generation of Americans to believe that middle-class status was like academic tenure: once you got it, no one could ever take it away. But in the 1990s that picture changed dramatically and those who remained in the middle class found that the price for their success was a speeding up and intensification of just about everything. Both spouses now worked to keep up, as did some of the children. Long commuting hours became routine, child care emotionally complicated and an additional source of time pressure, and public schools no longer the bargain they once were.

Under these more competitive conditions, critics argued that changes in the moral and political outlook of the middle class were inevitable. Whereas middle-class Americans were once characterized as forward-looking, optimistic, even (according to the social critics of the 1950s) too comfortable and complacent, now they were increasingly pictured as self-interested to the point of selfishness. Americans in general, and middle-class Americans in particular, had entered what *Newsweek* writer Robert Samuelson called "the age of entitlement," relying on expanded governmental programs to subsidize their housing and transportation, for example, while protesting the taxes involved in paying for them. No longer living within their means as a nation—Samuelson called this tendency of government to overpromise things "suicidal"—they also were financing their personal lifestyles, not through their earnings, but by using expanded forms of credit and speculative investment. Their lives, the critics charged, were premised on illusions; as the realities of economic downturns and the limits to government subsidies hit them, their response would be one of anger and frustration.

There are polling data available to support the proposition that Americans are indeed angry, especially about their public life. Indicative is a 1995 poll that asked whether "the American dream of equal opportunity, personal freedom, and social mobility has become easier or harder to achieve in the past 10 years"; 67 percent responded that it had become harder, while 31 percent said easier. Surveys from a wide variety of sources revealed a sense of deep hostility to American political institutions. For example, 66 percent of the American people told a 1995 Gallup poll that they were dissatisfied "with the way things are going in the United States at this time," compared with 30 percent in 1986, while a *U.S. News & World Report* survey of 1994 indicated that 75 percent of Americans believed that "middle-class families can't make ends meet."

Interpreting the mood of the middle class means finding a plausible story to explain its discontents. One such story dominates the discussion taking place among social and political theorists. The key characters in this story are large-scale social and political forces that sociologists call tradition and modernity. In a world characterized by tradition, people believed in God and considered God's commands as binding standards for right and wrong, not only for themselves, but also for others. The family was viewed as sacrosanct: divorce was highly unusual and children were expected to be grateful for the sacrifices that parents, who postponed their own gratifications in forming a family, made on their behalf. Patriotism was a strongly inscribed value in a more traditional society; people not only served in the armed forces when called, but were expected to support their country without reservation, for America, one of the world's truly successful democracies, was worthy of such support. Hard work and upward striving, virtues often identified with the Protestant ethic, were considered important in a traditionalist world. So was active civic involvement, taking pride in the voluntary ties one formed with neighbors and friends. The moral rules of a traditional world, according to its defenders, were clear, unchanging, and accepted by most people as fair.

Around the turn of the twentieth century, although the exact date cannot be specified, as this story continues, something called modernity entered, and ultimately threatened to destroy, the world of tradition. When sociologists use the term, "modernity" is often a slippery concept, sometimes referring to the ways people think, sometimes to the ways they act, and sometimes to anything that takes place at the present time. Still, the term is an important one, because something did happen to upset the world of traditional middle-class morality. We are best off thinking of that something as a very powerful idea, so powerful that it was capable of changing the way people act. Modernity means freedom, but not in the narrow sense of voting for candidates of one's own choice. The freedom associated with modernity is the freedom to construct one's own life as one best sees fit. Concretely, that means not accepting God's commands regarding right and wrong, but developing one's own personal ethical standards. It means thinking of marriage as a union of consenting equals to be dissolved when it oppresses one or both of the parties involved. A modern person loves his or her country but reserves the right to criticize it. In the modern world, we recognize the importance of working hard but also understand that work may not be available to all, requiring government involvement to insure that the gap between the rich and poor never becomes too great. Finally, modern people are mobile people, no longer sufficiently tied to their neighborhoods that they become "joiners," always ready to lend a hand building the neighbor's barn. The moral rules of modernity cannot provide the security of fixed standards, but, as those who justify them understand them, they recognize that people in the modern world are determined to choose what's best for them.

If this story of how modernity is replacing tradition is generally accepted by sociologists to be true, its implications are subject to heated debate. Around the story have developed two accounts, one that prefers traditional society and views modernity as suspect and one, not surprisingly, that reverses the evaluation. For lack of better terms, the first account can be called conservative, the second liberal.

The middle class, in contemporary conservative theory, is the moral class. As conservatives see it, middle-class Americans are ordinary people trying to live by traditional rules of working hard, saving for the future, and being loyal to family and country. As early as 1972, the neoconservative social theorist Irving Kristol wrote that "it is only the common people who remain loyal to the bourgeois ethos." Not that Kristol was completely enamored of that ethos; its lack of appreciation for the spiritual and heroic virtues rendered it inappropriate for answering deep questions about man's role in the universe. Still, the common-sense values of the working and lower-middle class had "an intimate and enduring relation to mundane realities that was relatively immune to speculative enthusiasm," he wrote. The middle-class ideal of the common good, "consisting mainly of personal security under the law, personal liberty under the law, and a steadily increasing material prosperity for those who apply themselves to that end," is not all that bad, Kristol concluded, especially when compared with the pretensions of intellectuals.

Kristol's formulation of the issue was enormously important for contemporary American politics. So long as conservatism is understood as the defense of the rich, it will always be a minority taste in middle-class America. By arguing that conservatives needed to respect the power of middle-class ideas among lower-middle-class—and even working-class—Americans, Kristol was outlining a path toward majority status for the conservative view of the world. Contemporary American conversatism can literally be defined as the defense of middle-class morality, an effort to protect the traditional neighborhoods, family ideals, religious beliefs, work ethic, schools, love of country, and security concerns of the lower-middle class, no matter how impolitically expressed, from the welfare state on the one hand and the liberal defense of modernity on the other. From such a perspective, middle-class morality is good; the only thing that is bad is its continual decline.

For liberals, by contrast, a world without fixed moral guidelines is one that offers individuals greater choice. True of everyone, liberals believe, such expanded choices are especially true of those whose needs were ignored by traditionalists. As conservatives rallied to a defense of the middle-class morality they associated with hardworking sobriety, liberals responded by finding traditional neighborhoods hostile to excluded racial minorities, traditional religiosity intolerant of nonbelievers, and traditional families first oppressive to women and later to homosexuals. Because they identify so strongly with those who were outsiders in the world of tradition, American intellectuals and activists on the left have never had much sympathy for the middle-class morality praised by the right. The left tends to believe that middle-class morality is bad, and the only good thing is that it might become obsolete. Yet, since so many Americans view themselves as middle class, by dismissing middle-class morality so blithely, the left moved rapidly toward dismissing itself as a majority force in American life.

After the Reagan administration came to power, however, liberals found a way to shift the discussion from morality to declining incomes and a lack of middle-class jobs. Economic polarization suggested that the middle class was splitting into two wings. One, the liberal theory held, was composed of comfortable financial analysts, real estate brokers, and Yuppies driving expensive cars and purchasing summer houses, while the other contained economically insecure midlevel employees and well-paid, if anything but rich, union members. If true, this split in the middle class offered liberals, like conservatives, a plausible way to talk about why middle-class Americans, including those in the lower ranks, were fed up: the left could prevent the right from monopolizing the loyalties of the lower-middle class, not by praising its moral outlook on the world, but instead by criticizing the way the upper-middle class led its life.

"The nervous, uphill financial climb of the professional middle class accelerates the downward spiral of the society as a whole: toward cruelly widening inequalities, toward heightened estrangement along lines of class and race, and toward the moral anesthesia that estrangement requires," wrote social critic Barbara Ehrenreich in this vein. Left to its own devices, critics from the left concluded, well-off Americans separate themselves physically, emotionally, and politically from the less fortunate. Using one of the most emotionally laden terms in American history, Robert Reich, before he became secretary of labor in the Clinton administration, wrote that in the new world economy that came into being in the 1980s, upper-middle-class people "are quietly *seceding* from the large and diverse publics of America into homogeneous enclaves, within which their earnings need not be redistributed to people less fortunate than themselves." Let's call this phenomenon the "middle-class withdrawal symptom." From a liberal perspective, no cultural change in America was more important than this effort by those with means to detach themselves from their obligations to those without them. Since liberals believe so strongly in a society in which everyone should have an equal capacity to determine how best to lead their lives, the conservative insistence that middle-class morality needs respect is seen by liberals as an effort to detract attention from what liberals believe to be the *real* problems facing America: economic polarization and the increasing conservatism of upper-middle-class selfishness.

Conservatives and liberals, then, disagree about the causes of middle-class anger, but in their description of the empirical reality of that anger, all agree that the middle class is in a severe state of discontent, either because it has lost jobs and income (liberals), religious belief, moral bearings, and physical safety (conservatives), or both (populists). It is what one is angry about, and not whether one is angry, that seems to define positions on America's political spectrum. Rather than picturing the middle class as unified in its disdain for the way both the poor and the rich led their lives, which is historically how the middle class understood itself, critics from both ends of the political spectrum focused instead on what seemed to be a radical split within the middle class, each identifying in some way with one side or the other. The name that came to be given to this split was the "culture war."

It has by now become something close to an accepted fact, due in no small part to the foresight of conservative writers such as Irving Kristol, that a wide gap exists in the United States between people who retain strong religious beliefs, adhere to the traditional family, possess unquestioned loyalty to their country, dislike immigration, denounce pornography, and are suspicious of cultural relativism and those—often called a new class or a cultural elite—who have accepted the basic axioms of feminism, support principles of multiculturalism, express cosmopolitan values, and place a high priority on civil liberties. At one level, such a culture war represents nothing new: the Scopes trial, battles over immigration, and McCarthyism were earlier encounters in what has been a very long conflict. But such earlier encounters took place between classes: those on the conservative, and eventually the losing, side in those battles represented forces—

fundamentalist faithful, displaced farmers, segregationists—seemingly on their way to economic and cultural obsolescence.

Now the cultural conflict alleged to be spreading through America is understood to be taking place within just one class: those in the middle. Upper-middle-class people who have prospered in the speculative 1980s and 1990s appear to be disproportionately represented on the liberal side, and those lower-middle-class Americans who still believe in savings accounts and family-oriented neighborhoods find themselves on the traditional side. Or so, at least, argues Christopher Lasch. The culture war, in his view, represents an alliance between the inner city and the outer city against those caught in between: hard-pressed Americans earning enough to move to the outskirts, but not so much that they can escape the costs of liberal experiments in social justice. In a similar way, Michael Lind views the culture war as an alliance between the overclass and the underclass, both of whom support multiculturalism, against the forgotten Americans in the middle. Scholars have been writing about the "radical center" of American politics for some time, and what they generally have found is that such middle Americans lean toward cautious support of the welfare state on the one hand and toward equally cautious cultural conservatism on the other, a sociological insight put to great use by politicians such as Richard Nixon in his appeals to the "forgotten" American. This time, what seems to be at stake in debates over the radical middle is the very future of middle-class morality: will middle-class Americans such as Judy Vogel shift toward that part of their worldview that emphasizes dismay at the character of people on welfare or toward that side that emphasizes a generous conception of membership in a larger social world? Divided between the abstractions of its upper end and the nitty-gritty realities of its lower, the middle class faces its most serious rupture of all: disappearance as a cohesive set of values in the face of simultaneous pulls and pushes from all directions.

If even part of this story about middle-class decline and fracturing is true, the implications could not be greater. The issue is simple to state: an angry, inward-looking, and hopelessly divided middle class is not a middle class at all—not in the way Americans have traditionally understood their aspirations. To be middle class in this country is to believe in the future; asked whether a person who works hard has a chance to become rich, Americans respond very positively, while Britons respond very negatively. Strip away the vibrancy, the sense of expectancy, the open-ended character of middle-class life, and America becomes more like Europe—even at a time when Europe becomes more like America. Other countries in the world, it is generally believed, experience castelike immobility, bitterly contested ideological politics, class envy and resentment, and support for parties of nostalgia—not the United States. If middle-class America is as morally divided as so many accounts from all across the political spectrum would have it, we all lose. For then, our future as a nation will be marked by incessant conflicts between irreconcilable worldviews, raising the prospect that the democratic stability that has kept the country together since the Civil War will no longer be attainable.

BUT IS IT TRUE?

The trouble is that we do not know for sure whether any of these accounts of middle-class discontent are true. Even the seemingly obvious idea that middle-class Americans are angry and frustrated as they watch their economic prospects shrink, and are shrinking their sense of generosity and obligation along with it, suffers from a number of problems. Although Patrick Buchanan made downsizing the theme of his 1996 campaign for the Republican nomination, the question disappeared from the general election; if anything, President Clinton's reelection was due to the fact that so many Americans believed the economy was moving along fine and did not need the stimulus offered by the Republican challenger. Furthermore, the 1996 presidential campaign was not marked by cultural and moral conflict over such issues as abortion and affirmative action, in large part because Americans made it clear that they do not like extremism and polarization in their politics. And Ross Perot's third-party efforts to capitalize on populist frustrations made little splash in 1996 compared with his showing four years earlier. Whatever may have motivated voters in 1996, anger was conspicuously missing.

Nor is it true, as the left perversely tends to insist, that the right has won the battle for the mind of the middle class. Americans did not became more conservative during the 1970s and 1980s; on questions of race and the acceptance of feminist goals, they moved to the left, just as on crime or immigration they moved to the right. It is also incorrect to say that, in their newfound conservatism, Americans turned against government and liberal social programs such as welfare; instead, what their mood registered, in political scientist William Mayer's words, "was simply a few modest adjustments within the present system: a little less domestic spending (or perhaps a slower rate of growth), a slight relaxation of environmental regulations in order to produce more energy, a little more reliance on individual initiative in dealing with the problems of poverty." As Mayer's sophisticated reading of three decades of polling data suggests, Americans may not be withdrawing from a sense of obligation so much as they are trying to find more effective ways to express it.

Less angry than they are often taken to be, Americans may also not be quite as engaged in a culture war as intellectuals claim. A number of books by distinguished sociologists have appeared, demonstrating, with the use of polling and other kinds of data, that there is a culture war taking place in the United States. But, then again, other studies have appeared, based on equally (if not more) impressive evidence suggesting that, with the possible exception of abortion, no such culture war exists in America. To be sure, a society divided by race and gender, dealing with such issues as immigration and welfare, and undergoing a revision of its constitutional principles on church and state, is experiencing some kind of cultural conflict. But how much conflict is simply part of the basic disagreement essential to a democracy and how much represents a country literally at war? No one has yet provided a satisfactory answer to that question.

Like many of those whose views are discussed in this chapter, I was drawn to the idea that a deep divide existed in America between upholders of traditional cultural and moral values and those attracted to more modern themes of personal or group identity; I even published an article in *The Wilson Quarterly* in 1993 arguing the point. The only problem was that when I wrote this way, like many of the others who contributed to the debate, I had not talked to Americans, many of whom might like to have a say in the ongoing conversation about what was taking place inside their heads. Why not, I asked myself, hear what they think before pronouncing further? Is it, in fact, the case that Americans are hopelessly split into competing moral camps or that morality, like the old neighborhood, is part of a world we have lost? The questions are compelling; indeed, I can think of no more important questions involving how the public thinks than these. The issue is how to go about answering them.

When sociologists and political scientists try to uncover what people are thinking, they use one of two contrasting methods. Ethnographic reports concentrate on one particular town or neighborhood: Levittown and Canarsie are two well-known examples. The theory behind this approach is that only very close observation can tell us anything important. The observer has to live in a community. He must share in its sorrows and triumphs and get to know its people. Only then can the full complexity of people's attitudes and behaviors be understood. Ever since a team of sociologists went to Muncie, Indiana, renamed it Middletown, and came back again to restudy it, such ethnographic studies of changing American economic and social realities have been undertaken, and they provide an important source of data for what has been taking place within the middle class. But these studies contain two important limitations. One is that they are not, by definition, representative of the country as a whole, since they concentrate on particular communities, a defect particularly significant when regional variations in economic dynamism and political culture are an obvious fact of American life. In addition, it is often difficult to interpret what one finds. In her examination of the residents of one New Jersey suburb experiencing economic downsizing, for example, the anthropologist Katherine Newman stresses how people live with "a vague sense of dissatisfaction" about their lives, but also "are quick to point out that in an absolute sense they have much to be grateful for." Ethnographic messages, like this one, are often mixed, which means that the reader relies not only on what the subjects have to say, but also on what the ethnographer has to say about them.

Worried about the subjectivity and selectivity of ethnographic research, other social scientists turn to "harder" data: survey research conducted after careful random sampling of the entire U.S. population or fine-grained statistical analysis of election returns. These efforts—the General Social Survey, the National Election Study, Gallup polls, frequent (indeed, possibly too frequent) polling by the media—provide valuable information about what is on the minds of Americans. They have, furthermore, been supplemented in the past few years by newer surveys that focus specifically on the moral and cultural issues presumed to be dividing Americans, such as the Pew Research Center for the People and the Press's survey on the religious beliefs of Americans and the University of Virginia's Post-Modernity Project's report on American political culture. But all such surveys, no matter how sophisticated, have their limits. In order to gain the precision that makes statistical analysis possible, surveys have to drop the way people qualify and rationalize their opinions. And election returns are notorious for their volatility at a time when Americans swing back and forth from one party and its ideological claims to another. In trying to find out what is on the minds of Americans, especially with respect to emotionally charged topics, we are best off not relying on surveys to provide definitive answers to questions about moral worldviews.

In an effort to bring quantitative and qualitative approaches closer together, my research assistant Maria Poarch and I, with funding from the Russell Sage Foundation, conducted the Middle Class Morality Project, upon whose findings I will be relying for the bulk of what is reported in this book. Any attempt to investigate what Americans are thinking, whether qualitative or quantitative in nature, involves making decisions about who gets included and who gets excluded. This is true of the Middle Class Morality Project, as well. Before it could proceed very far, it had to answer this question: To whom should one talk if one wants to talk to middle-class Americans?

My first decision was to focus on American suburbs, even while recognizing that not all middle-class Americans live in suburbs and not all suburbs contain only middle-class Americans. Clearly, as any resident of Manhattan's Upper East Side knows, well-off people have not completely deserted American cities. It is a less known fact that 36 percent of Americans in poverty live in suburbs (compared with 42 percent in the cities and 22 percent in rural areas). Still, there were reasons to focus only on suburbs when the subject is middle-class morality. For purposes of understanding the changing moral and political outlook of the American middle class, the suburb is an indispensable symbol. When social critics and social scientists write about the battle over middle-class morality America is presumed to be experiencing, their focus unconsciously shifts directly to the suburbs: conservatives find in suburbanization support for the importance they attach to beliefs about property, physical safety, and economic independence, while for liberals, suburbs represent a retreat from the problems of the inner city. The American suburb is the physical location for middle-class withdrawal symptoms.

This is especially true when the subject concerns race, as in America so many questions involving morality seem to do. "Racial prejudice played a role in the evolution of overwhelmingly White suburbs surrounding increasingly Black cities," writes David Rusk, the former mayor of Albuquerque. "How strong a role is debatable, but the demographic, social, and economic consequences have become clear over the past forty years." Other writers believe that the matter is not all that debatable. For the Berkeley public policy specialists David Kirp, John P. Dwyer, and Larry A. Rosenthal, suburbanization symbolizes "a deep antagonism toward the nation's poor and minority citizens." Herbert Gans, a sociologist at Columbia University who once provided a marvelously empathic explanation of the attractions of Levittown for its early residents, seems to have lost much of the sympathy for the middle class whose aspirations he once so movingly evoked; although he attributes much of the demonization of the underclass in a recent book to journalists and conservative intellectuals, Gans also writes of the need for "mainstream culture," "the more fortunate classes," and "the better-off classes" to scapegoat the poor and the different—terms that surely would include those suburbanites who long ago moved to Levittown to pursue the American dream.

In their account of the moral failings of suburbia, Kirp, Dwyer, and Rosenthal used the example of Mount Laurel, New Jersey—close by to Gans's Levittown—which was ordered by the courts to permit low-income housing among its middle-class single-family homes. However exclusionary Mount Laurel may have been in practice, it was also in theory open to all. But even that theoretical openness is not true of another kind of suburb—what real estate planners call a private interest or planned unit development. These communities, ensconced behind closed gates that keep in the comfortable and keep out the undesirable, intensify the middle-class withdrawal symptom. Residents of planned suburban communities, critics point out, not only pay for their own services, they also argue against paying for the services of those outside the gates as a form of double taxation. Self-protective suburban communities, writes city planning specialist Evan MacKenzie, are a form of "privatopia," in which "the dominant ideology is privatism; . . . contract law is the supreme authority; . . . property rights and property values are the focus of community life; and . . . homogeneity, exclusiveness, and exclusion are the foundation of social organization." There, according to liberal critics, the middle class is free to be as selfish as it wants; there also, as conservative journalist Tom Bethell has written, people who believe in the old-fashioned moral values can retreat as they watch liberals win the major battles in the public arena. And there, I decided, at least some of my interviews ought to be conducted.

Once the decision was made to interview suburban Americans, the next question involved which ones. My choices were designed to test the hypothesis that middle-class Americans no longer share a common moral worldview but are bitterly divided into traditionalist and modernist wings. If, indeed, there is a fight over middle-class morality taking place in America—in which liberals are engaged in a moral battle with conservatives over such issues as the family, religion, welfare, and gay rights—we would expect people in different kinds of suburbs to differ over these issues, since Americans invariably choose places to live based on the expectation that their neighbors will be like them in outlook and behavior. If, on the other hand, suburbs quite different in ethnic, racial, religious, geographic, economic, and cultural composition nonetheless reveal similar attitudes and sentiments, reports from the cultural battlefield may be exaggerated. The best way to explore this issue, in short, is to examine suburbs that on the surface would be as different from each other as possible, especially those that vary by income and lifestyle. A finding to the effect that there are sharp differences between people living in different kinds of communities would suggest that we may be experiencing deep divisions over middle-class morality. But if one discovers the opposite—that middle-class Americans, regardless of income and lifestyle, have more in common rather than less—we should be prepared to take a less apocalyptic view of America's future.

To test this hypothesis, I chose one urban area in each of the main geographic quadrants of the country: East (Boston), South (Atlanta), Midwest (Tulsa), and West Coast (San Diego). If there was a bias in these choices, it was deliberate: I made a conscious effort to overrepresent conservative and Christian communities in the South and West, so as to avoid the possibility that highly educated people who are interested in public affairs, and who tend to be more liberal, would dominate the interviews. I then selected suburbs around each area that would be as distinct from each other as possible on economic, racial, cultural, ethnic, and job-related criteria.

For the purpose of studying middle-class morality, however,

it is important that the communities chosen, no matter how diverse, are primarily inhabited by middle-class people. Given the intensity of the debates over where the lines between classes should be drawn, categorizing communities as middle-class is no easy matter. Magazines such as *Worth* rely on average housing prices to list the wealthiest suburbs in America, but housing costs may not be the best measure, for many homes in the suburbs, depending on how long they have been owned by their occupants, are worth far more than what people originally paid for them. 1990 census data are preferable, but even that data present problems; one can easily obtain median family income for communities in the Boston and Tulsa areas, for each community is also a distinct town, but there are no census tracts in California and Georgia that correspond exactly with the names people use to describe the suburbs in which they live. Finally, even if we did have census data that reflected how people actually live, one cannot use the same cut-off point in all regions of the country; a $100,000 income on the two coasts is effectively far less than the same income in the middle of the country.

Given these constraints, I chose the communities I studied in the following way. In the Boston area, I excluded communities in which 1990 median family income was above $100,000 as too wealthy and those in which median family income was below $45,000 as too poor. This means that I did not study Weston ($108,751) and Sherborn ($104,591) on the one hand and Revere ($37,213) and Quincy ($44,184) on the other. (A similar procedure was followed in Tulsa, except that the cut-off numbers were lower: communities were excluded whose 1990 median family income was under $30,000 and over $50,000.) In California and Georgia, I talked to local experts, including real estate brokers and academics, in order to rank communities in terms of their attraction to the middle class. Based on those discussions, I included Rancho Bernardo, for example, but excluded Rancho Sante Fe, once the temporary home of the Heaven's Gate cult.

When all these factors were put together, it made sense to focus on the following eight communities:

1. *Brookline, Massachusetts.* When Herbert Gans asked the superintendent of schools in the newly created Levittown what kind of education he had in mind for the suburban explorers of 1960, he said, "I won't stand for a Brookline education." Brookline, home of the first country club in the United States, is one of the most highly educated communities in America. Strongly Jewish and considered very liberal in outlook, Brookline was the scene of two battles in the culture war: a bitter fight over Western civilization in the high school and (during the course of our interviews) the murder of two women at an abortion clinic. (In early 1997, two of the remaining three cities around which we conducted interviews, Tulsa and Atlanta, also experienced abortion clinic bombings, well after our interviews were finished.) In their book *The Bell Curve,* Richard Herrnstein and Charles Murray, citing Robert Reich, argue that there has emerged a cognitive elite in the United States, a class of intelligent people who want to associate only with others like themselves. If they are correct, such a cognitive elite would live in a place like Brookline, whose 1990 median family income, by the way, was $61,799.

2. *Medford, Massachusetts.* The Boston area contains a number of communities that are formally suburban, in the sense that they are not part of Boston (never having been annexed at the time when Brooklyn was incorporated with Manhattan), but which are like the city in that they contain a heavily working-class, Catholic, and ethnic consciousness. Medford, otherwise the home of Tufts University, is such a community. The "urban villagers" once studied by Herbert Gans in Boston have moved to places like Medford. Sixty-five percent of our Medford sample was Catholic. Many of them experienced the busing controversies that dominated Boston in the 1970s, as well as racial conflicts in Medford High School in the 1990s. The home of many policemen and firemen, Medford stands for the kind of no-nonsense cultural conservatism we tend to associate with the bypassed lower-middle class. (Medford's median family income, $45,532, places it just inside my bottom cut-off point.) That

class, in turn, is often viewed as providing the key swing voters that determine elections: Medford residents are very much like the former New Dealers who became Reagan conservatives that pollster Stanley Greenberg found in Macomb County, Michigan, or the children of immigrants who turned to the right, a movement the reporter Samuel Friedman so brilliantly brought to life in his book *The Inheritance.*

3. *Southeast DeKalb County, Georgia.* The suburbs to the south and east of Atlanta within DeKalb County have experienced the largest increase in black suburbanization in America, more even than Prince Georges County in Maryland; 84 percent of our sample from this area was black. These communities received national attention when, on April 1, 1992, the U.S. Supreme Court ruled by an 8 to 0 margin that DeKalb County could be excused from further efforts to integrate its public schools. The result was cheered rather than criticized by many of the economically successful black parents living in the area, who saw no reason to bus their children elsewhere in the county, either because they sent their kids to private schools or because their predominantly black public schools were just fine, thank you. Southeast DeKalb contains many successful black middle-class Americans who have moved there from the rest of the country—unlike other parts of the county that are home to African-Americans native to Atlanta who grew up in the segregated South. Southeasterners tend to be in search of opportunities available to black professionals, although a significant number of them were disappointed by what they found. Interviewed at the height of the O. J. Simpson trial, the people to whom we talked were outspoken in their understanding of what it means to be both black and middle class in America.

4. *Cobb County, Georgia.* Cobb County, where Judy Vogel lives, wrote the *New York Times* in 1994, is the most conservative county in America. That distinction was conferred upon it when county commissioners voted (in a nonbinding resolution) that a homosexual lifestyle was incompatible with the county's

values, leading the International Olympic Committee to move volleyball preliminaries out of the county and to have the Olympic torch relay bypass it. One year after its resolution on homosexuality, the county also made national news when it voted to cut off all funding for the arts if they violated community standards of decency. The electoral base of Newt Gingrich, the suburbs of East Cobb County represent the "new South" of prosperous professionals, many of whom have moved to the area from other parts of the country, but who generally appreciate the religious and moral values of the South. Our sample in Cobb included by a large margin the richest people with whom we spoke; 60 percent of them claimed incomes over $100,000 and only one less than $50,000. If the Republican Contract with America has a cheering section, one would think it would be in Cobb County.

5. *Broken Arrow, Oklahoma.* Tulsa, described by many of our respondents as the buckle on the Bible Belt, is the home of Oral Roberts University. The Tulsa area has been considered by marketing companies the most average city in the United States, a perfect place to find out whether Americans will use a new mouthwash or breakfast cereal. Although people who live in the Tulsa area consider it a refuge from the problems of the East Coast, Tulsa has a substantial black population and was the scene of one of the most violent racial disturbances in American history. Broken Arrow, in which sits Rhema, one of the largest charismatic Pentecostal megachurches in the United States, is a generally prosperous suburb, fueled by the growth of energy companies and the success of American Airlines, even though it has experienced some of the downsizing that has affected corporate America. Interviews were conducted in Broken Arrow (and nearby Sand Springs) a few months after the bombing of the Alfred P. Murrah Federal Office Building in Oklahoma City, 120 miles to the southwest. We expected to find in Broken Arrow successful midwestern Americans with strong religious and patriotic sentiments; 68 percent of our sample were Republicans, the same as in Cobb County.

6. *Sand Springs, Oklahoma.* Sand Springs, on the other side of
Tulsa from Broken Arrow, has experienced the economic hard
times that have affected the industrial heartland in an era of
deindustrialization far more than its neighbor; its 1990 median
family income, $34,073, was lower than that of Broken Arrow
($40,233). Sand Springs is worlds apart from a place like Brook-
line; 52 percent of those to whom we talked had a high school
diploma or less (the exact proportion of Brookliners in our sample who had graduate degrees). People in Sand Springs, although
they tend to work in Tulsa, think of it not as a suburb, but as a
small town on the outskirts of a city. Founded by a philan-
thropic steel baron in the early 1900s—the Sand Springs Home,
an orphanage now operating as a service center, still dominates
the community—Sand Springers are a generation away from the
farm (as many in Medford are a generation or two away from
European peasantry). Nonetheless the American middle class
should include a place in which people, while not highly paid,
think of themselves as middle class because they work hard and
play by the rules, which people in Sand Springs very much do.

7. *Eastlake, California.* The American dream of middle-class
success has always proved attractive to immigrants, as much at
the end of the twentieth century as at the end of the nineteenth;
the fact that recent immigrants come from Asia and Latin America rather than Europe has barely dented the pattern. California
has been the battleground over recent immigration; it was the
site of Proposition 187, a 1994 measure designed to deprive immigrants of various public services, strongly supported by those
who believe that immigrants are invariably poor people who
make good candidates for the welfare rolls. But immigrants in
general and Mexican-Americans in particular tend to think of
themselves not as a racial group held down by discrimination,
but as an ethnic group about to make its first steps up the ladder
of success. Despite the fact that poverty among Latinos has increased in recent years, there has also been a rapid growth
among Americans of Hispanic origin in achieving middle-class
status; by one estimate, half of the households of Latinos born in

the United States have made it into the middle class and one-fourth of the middle class of Southern California may well be of Hispanic origin. Eastlake, a subdivision of Chula Vista located just six miles from the Mexican border, is one of the places they live. A relatively new master-planned community of single-family homes, condominiums, and spacious apartments especially attractive to immigrants from Asia (primarily the Philippines) as well as Latinos—40 percent of our interviewees were Hispanic and 12 percent were Asian—Eastlake is one of the places in America where the American dream is most vibrant. The border is omnipresent in the lives of Eastlakers: some of our respondents worked in Mexico and others sent their children to private religious schools in Mexico; one was a citizen of Mexico residing in the United States. Interviews with Eastlakers were generally among the friendliest, most interesting, and longest-lasting of all those we conducted.

8. *Rancho Bernardo, California.* A city created by developers to resemble a Mediterranean seaside resort, Rancho Bernardo is composed of Spanish-style houses and apartment complexes that, because they conform to strict codes, blend together in patterns of harmonious neatness in which its residents take pride. Rancho Bernardo is not just typical of the kind of gated communities that worry critics of the American middle class; it is the actual community to which they frequently point when making their complaints. Richard Louv was one of the first writers to use Rancho Bernardo to embody a new American ethic of withdrawal, and Evan MacKenzie's *Privatopia*, the most thorough criticism of this phenomenon, also points to Rancho Bernardo as a perfect illustration. In addition, Rancho Bernardo is primarily a retirement community; when Louv wrote about it in 1983, half of its residents were retired, which is what we found twelve years later: thirteen of the twenty-five residents with whom we talked were over sixty-five, one was closer to ninety. Themes of generational selfishness are as common as themes of residential segregation in accounts of contemporary America, a further reason to study a place such as Rancho Bernardo.

Once the suburbs were chosen, the next question involved identifying the people with whom we would talk. Searching for a number that would provide enough interviews to move beyond smaller-scale ethnographic accounts, but not so many that the in-depth character of those accounts would be lost, I settled on a total of two hundred interviews, or twenty-five in each suburb. Within each community, a random sample of residents was compiled and letters were sent out (on the stationery of the local university with which we were cooperating), followed by phone calls and requests for an interview. The response rate was roughly 25 percent. Most of the interviews were held in people's homes, but some were in their offices and a very few at the local university or a nearby coffee shop. If spouses or older children wanted to participate, they were invited to do so. Each person was asked questions about racial and economic justice, the family, religion, obligations to the country, work, and civic participation. The format was designed to encourage them to respond at length and in any fashion comfortable for them, but at the end of each interview, we also administered a short survey containing twenty-three statements with which our respondents were asked whether they agreed (or agreed strongly) or disagreed (or disagreed strongly).

Based on the information our respondents provided about their lives, it is possible to offer a collective portrait of who they were. Since my decision was to interview within middle-class communities rather than to search directly for middle-class people, some of those with whom we spoke, even by the very imprecise ways in which Americans think about middle-class status, were not middle class: our sample turned up a welfare mother living in a Brookline housing development, for example, and wives of corporate executives in Cobb County and Rancho Bernardo. Still, the overall sample does seem to capture the more comfortable, if still not rich, sector of the middle class about which so much has been written. As table 1.1 shows, the typical respondent to our study was between forty and sixty years old, Catholic or Baptist, had a family income of between $50,000 and

Political Party Preference

Republican	33.5
Democrat	33.0
Independent	32.0
NA	1.5

Family Income

Less than $15,000	1.5
$15,000–$29,000	14.5
$30,000–$49,000	16.5
Over $50,000	28.5
Over $75,000	18.5
Over $100,000	19.5
NA	1.0

Education

Less than B.A.	41.5
B.A. or B.S.	30.0
Graduate Degree	26.0
NA	2.5

Religious Identification

Catholic	21.5
Baptist	15.0
Other "Christian"	15.0
None	8.0
Methodist	7.0
Jewish	6.0
Pentecostal	3.5
Episcopalian	2.5
Presbyterian	2.5
Jehovah's Witness	1.5
Unitarian	1.0
Other	16.5

Age

20–30	12.5
31–44	29.0
45–59	38.5
60–74	12.5
75+	5.5
NA	2.0

Gender

Female	55.5
Male	44.5

Occupation

Professional/managerial	39.5
Service sector	16.5
Retired	12.5
Housewife	8.0
Proprietor	7.0
Clerical	5.0
Clergy	2.5
Manual worker	2.5
Student	1.0
Unemployed	1.0
NA	4.5

Race/Ethnicity

White	71.5
Black	12.0
Hispanic	5.5
Asian	3.5
Native American	1.0
NA	6.5

$75,000 a year, worked in a professional capacity, was equally likely to be a Democrat, Republican, or Independent, and was about 10 percent more likely to be a woman than a man.

It is not enough to make decisions about where and whom to interview; one must also decide how to do so. In the one and a half to two hours we spent with each person, we probed into why they believed what they did about the leading moral issues facing the American middle class. We tried to be somewhat confrontational with them, asking them to reconcile what they said here with what they had said there or asking them to explain in greater detail how they reached the opinions they were expressing. The point was to get underneath and around sound bites and bumper-sticker slogans, to give people an opportunity to explore at whatever length was comfortable for them their feelings about their duties and responsibilities to themselves and others. (The bulk of these interviews were conducted by Maria Poarch, who lived in each community for between three and six months; I visited each community for a shorter period of time and conducted five to ten interviews with her in each location.) At first, we wanted to break with a common sociological convention by identifying the individuals with whom we spoke by their real names, and we therefore asked them whether we had permission to do so. More than 80 percent gave such permission, but after analyzing what they had to say, I made the decision—and informed all our respondents—that I would prefer to protect their privacy by inventing new names for each person. Most of our respondents will recognize their thoughts in this book. Other readers should know that the names given are not the real names of the people interviewed.

Once all the interviews were completed, they were transcribed. Each of the two hundred interviews ran to between fifteen and twenty-five pages of text, for a total of 3,886 pages of transcript. First, I read through each interview from beginning to end, taking notes on the main themes raised by each respondent. Each interview was then broken up by subject—religion, family values, poverty, and so on—and those sections from each interview were culled, producing a series of loose-leaf books on each major topic.

To report on the respondents' views, I used two general methods. One, based on the short survey we administered at the end of the interview, simply records the degrees of agreement or disagreement with the statements we presented to them. The other, based on more in-depth conversations, required an exercise in "coding"—the process by which a sociologist reads empirical data, in this case transcripts, and decides on criteria for classifying them into different categories. In trying to make sense out of so much material, coding is an essential tool. It cannot, when all is said and done, be a substitute for interpretation, for coding is not an exact science: different investigators may code the same material in different ways. But nor is coding completely subjective, for the investigator is bound by professional norms to let the words of his subjects, and not his own preconceptions, determine how someone ought to be classified.

From all this material, I have tried to draw a picture of middle-class morality at century's end. This picture is not conjured up out of my imagination but is based on what people told me. The voices one hears in this book represent the direct words of middle-class Americans; other than dropping pauses and the occasional circumlocutions which enter speech but seem awkward when transcribed and reprinted, I have quoted them as they spoke. And what did people say? When people agreed with each other, my role was to give their voices a hearing, to tie together in one place the essential, rock-bottom moral outlook of the American middle class, those commonsense presuppositions and justifications they offer for their views. When people disagreed with each other, I acknowledged that disagreement, but I also asked whether, in their disagreements, people appealed to common principles and arguments, differing only over how they are to be applied. And when people disagreed so much that there were no common principles that could unite them, my obligation was to report that as well.

I make no claim that the Middle Class Morality Project is

representative of America as a whole. For one thing, my focus is on the middle class, even more narrowly on the suburban middle class, (and even more narrowly than that on specific middle-class people in specific middle-class suburbs), and not on all Americans regardless of class. And, despite what, for an ethnographic account, might seem like a relatively high number of interviews, two hundred is far too low a number for any kind of survey, especially when that number is divided by eight to obtain a sample for each community.

Nor is my focus primarily on how opinion is distributed on particular issues. These are two reasons for this. One is that surveys are frequent enough, and the questions asked interesting enough, to provide sufficient information about the distribution of opinion over moral matters. In reporting the results of this study, I am less interested in knowing, say, what proportion of the American population believes that respect for homosexual lifestyles should be taught in public schools than I am in reconstructing the moral visions of people who believe one way compared with people who believe another. Second, I pay less attention to reporting the distribution of opinion than surveys because I cannot always do so. Every respondent agreed to answer our survey, which means that I can examine the distribution of opinion on those questions. But for the more qualitative parts of the project, I made the decision early on not to spend equal time with every interviewee on the same question. Middle-class African-Americans in Atlanta wanted to talk about race more than Medford Catholics, for example, while more Oklahomans wanted to talk about God than Brookliners, and it seemed to me more important to try and capture the full complexity of what mattered to them most than to fit every interview into a general schema for purposes of statistical comparison. Furthermore, some questions, such as the one about teaching respect for homosexuals, were not in the original schema at all but emerged from the interviews themselves. The Middle Class Morality Project, in short, while trying to combine ethnographic and survey methods, leans toward the ethnographic: its purpose is depth more than breadth.

Despite my unwillingness to make claims about representativeness, however, I do think that, as pictures go, the Middle Class Morality Project offers an important one to consider. There is, for one thing, a great deal to be said for learning about the ways in which middle-class Americans, as opposed to all Americans, think about the world. From Benjamin Franklin's autobiography, to interpretations of the Protestant ethic, to musings about the organization man and what feminist critic Betty Friedan called the suburban concentration camp, a concern with middle-class values has been central to an appreciation of American culture. To study the American middle class is not to neglect other classes; on the contrary, it is to focus on what other classes often desire, fear, or pretend to be.

In addition, the middle class, for all its importance, has not, since the 1950s and 1960s, been the object of all that much investigation. Only one important study of middle-class morality was published during the 1970s and 1980s, and it was in Polish. There are at least three reasons for this failure to write in a sociologically informed way about both the middle class and about morality. First, many sociologists now in midcareer were born in the suburbs but grew to maturity at a time when the New Left criticized suburban materialism and middle-class greed. To study the suburbs was to return home, a difficult journey for so many of this generation (my generation) who vowed that, whatever happened to them as they grew up, they would never live in Great Neck or Skokie. Second, as part of their rebellion against their upbringing, sociologists of my generation chose for their object of study people far removed from their own experience: urban dropouts, racial and ethnic minorities, the marginalized and alienated of every size and shape on the one hand and upper class "ruling elites" on the other. The result was a deluge of sympathetic treatments of outcasts and condemnations of the wealthy, combined with an ignorance of, if not a disdain for, the hardworking, the child-rearing, and the religious believer. Third, the study of morality was suspect for many of the same reasons that led so many to examine the lives of the dispossessed: to study morality was a step toward imposing morality, many sociologists believed, and it was therefore a subject best left untouched. As a result of these forces, the number of concrete sociological studies of American suburbia conducted in the last twenty years is less than a handful—and this at a time when suburbanites have become the largest group of voters in the country. In the great debates over middle-class morality, social scientists have been largely absent, either because they do not think morality is important or because they do not know what to make of it.

Granted that it is important to hear what the middle class has to say, can the method I have used yield reliable answers to what is on its mind? It is important to stress that in a statistical sense, the answer to that question must be negative; I have not undertaken a representative national sample. But I think it also important to emphasize that this is not one of those studies that generalizes from only one neighborhood, firm, or family to the country as a whole. After talking with two hundred Americans from all walks of middle-class life, I feel confident that I will be reporting a sense of what is on the minds of enough middle-class Americans to make it worthwhile to take their views into account.

Committed in equal parts to a version of social science that believes in the use of empirical methods to uncover social realities, including those that run contrary to my own views, and to a version of the intellectual life that strongly affirms normative argument on behalf of personal political and moral beliefs, I have tried in this book to balance those two roles. There is a subjective dimension to this book. For in choosing to study middle-class morality in American suburbs, I was coming to terms with the rejection of middle-class suburbia that I, along with so many sociologists of my generation, opted for in the wisdom of my youth. Writing this book was in that sense a way of revisiting, now that I am a parent, the world my parents made. Yet, there is an objective dimension as well, for a confession of bias with respect to the subject one studies is not the same as a confession of bias with respect to how one studies it. Reading and listening to what people had to say, I tried my hardest to separate their views from my own. I just hope that the reader trusts my presentation and recognizes that, as opinionated as I may be, my primary duty in this book is to report on what others think, not on what I do. Neutral I am not; objective I try very hard to be.

The American middle class, once you start to look for it, is certainly not very hard to find, despite both its alleged shrinkage and disputes over how to measure it. The people to whom we spoke were by and large comfortable economically. They lived in suburbs that ranged from the trolley-car extensions of Boston to the freeway-connected homes lying in the desert around San Diego. Like the rest of America, our suburbanites found themselves turning conservative on some issues over the years, but on others they were still touched by the 1960s. They were concerned about the state of American society, but their primary preoccupations were with finding the time to manage busy lives. Most important of all, they wanted to talk; a significant number of respondents agreed to be interviewed when they learned that they would be expected to express their opinions at length, rather than to check off boxes in a survey. Thrilled by the idea that their thoughts might be included in a book, they thought long and hard about the questions we asked, interrupted their answers to ask if we were following their reasoning, and expressed great interest in seeing the product that would come out of the interviews. One of the most significant findings of the Middle Class Morality Project is this: At a time when Americans are increasingly viewed as selfish, preoccupied with personal safety, and quick to retreat into the privatism symbolized by closed doors, two hundred Americans invited perfect strangers into their living rooms, offered them something to eat or drink, and proceeded to discuss controversial and touchy subjects, often with profound thoughtfulness and nearly always with a deep sense of concern for their society.

MORALITY MATTERS

What is right and what is wrong? How far do my obligations to others extend? Do I have duties as well as rights? How should I balance my own needs with the needs of others? Why am I here? Does God exist? If He does, what does He want me to do? Are His desires commands or suggestions? If he does not exist, does morality? Is affirmative action fair? Does dependency on others corrupt one's character? My country, right or wrong? Who should be allowed to settle in America and who should not? Does it really take a village to raise a child? If so, then should it be the nation? Is divorce always wrong? Can other people be trusted? How much time should I give to civic affairs? Are we obligated to recognize people's native languages? Do companies have obligations to those who work for them? To those who live in their neighborhood? Does morality matter? Indeed, what is morality in the first place?

Questions about morality are, or rather should be, at the heart of sociological inquiry. There is, in fact, a moral revival taking place in American academic life. But unlike the kinds of moral reasoning used by many philosophers, theologians, and humanists, the Middle Class Morality Project sought to add the discussions and opinions of real people to quite lively debates about right and wrong, good and evil, and all the other topics that have been central to traditions of moral reasoning in the West.

Is morality a proper subject to discuss with perfect strangers? Surely, there must have been some people who received our letter and concluded that their feelings about God, sin, intimacy, marriage, and charity were too personal to be shared with academic visitors from Boston. To them, we stressed that the aim of our project was to learn about public morality—questions involving one's sense of obligations to those with whom one shares a society—and not about whether people have had extramarital affairs or how often and in what ways they pray; public confession à la daytime television was the last thing in the world we wanted to elicit. Others may well have felt that even though the subject was public, not private, morality, it would violate their religious convictions to participate in a study whose origins were so academic and secular. (One of our respondents, a Jehovah's Witness, requested permission from her church's spiritual mentor before agreeing to the interview.) Yet I am not persuaded that such reactions might have unduly biased our sample. For one thing, many deeply religious people did want to talk with us, if for no other reason than to share their joy at discovering the power of Jesus. For another, many Americans were concerned that researchers had called them about their favorite television shows, toothpaste, or voting intentions, but never to ask about the things that really mattered to them. And Americans of all kinds want to explain themselves, to figure out, with the help of someone curious enough to ask, what they really believe about matters that are important to them, but to which they feel they have not devoted sufficient attention.

Even if people are willing to talk about the morality that is on their minds, not everyone believes that we ought to listen to them. The great moral philosopher Immanuel Kant thought that the moral existed on a plane well beyond ordinary experience and subjective opinion; his reaction to a study such as this one surely would have been a resigned "So what?" Many, but not all, religious traditions would react in a similar way; if abortion is wrong, it does not matter how many women have them, how they justify their actions to themselves, or whether they act out of desperation. Some contemporary liberals and conservatives also believe that the thoughts and opinions of ordinary people about moral issues are not especially relevant to a discussion of morality. Conservatives who are convinced that welfare is corruptive of character are probably uninterested in the stories of women who have been on welfare. In a not dissimilar way, liberals who insist that the U.S. Constitution offers women a fundamental right to control their bodies also insist that their position be the law of the land no matter how strong the expression of majority opinion to the contrary.

In contrast to all these positions, I believe that we need to listen to the voices of ordinary people speaking about matters so central to modern morality. In reporting their views, I will not only be guided by what they had to say about important topics, but also by what topics they thought were important. "What matters most to you?" we asked the people with whom we spoke. One of them replied, "I first believe in God, family, and country—in that order." And that is the same order I will follow, adding to the list their thoughts about poverty and our ability to trust each other.

One should not conclude that once we learn more about how Americans think about moral matters, their opinions should end the discussion. Like William Buckley, I might trust the moral views of the first hundred names in a telephone book over the collective wisdom of the Harvard faculty, but I am not sure that I would want them to impose on me their conception of right and wrong. (Nor am I sure that, if he were to read this book, William Buckley would want them to have a say over his moral views.) My purpose in conducting this study is neither to praise nor condemn middle-class morality, but to understand it. When the appropriate time comes, I will offer my own thoughts on what I take to be the strengths and weaknesses of the ideas people expressed to me. But before offering opinions, it helps to know what we are talking about. The problem is not so much that social scientists and social critics have ignored what middle-class Americans believe; it is that we do not know what they believe. Listening to the way middle-class beliefs are so often treated, especially by those who subscribe to one or another version of the culture war, we get the impression that America is rapidly dividing into two nations, one fiercely upholding traditional values, the other enthusiastically welcoming modernity. We need to know whether we remain one nation, after all.

II   QUIET FAITH

"I usually don't have religious discussions with people," Jesse O'Donnell, a Navy wife living in Eastlake, California, informed us when we asked her whether those who are not religious can still be good people. Like Judy Vogel, the Cobb County, Georgia, homemaker whose views seem to define the quintessence of middle-class morality, Mrs. O'Donnell is a Methodist and a Republican. As she sat in a coffee shop one evening not far from the stucco condominium in which she lived with her husband and two young children, still wearing the dark blue business suit she had put on for her job placing temporary workers, she reflected on how she was brought up in the 1960s. "We were always taught that you don't discuss religion," she said, before pausing to add, "No politics or religion."

Mrs. O'Donnell's upbringing, if we consult what sociologists and historians say about American religious belief in the years after World War II, was anything but unusual. From the moment suburbanization began to expand exponentially in the 1950s and 1960s, critics wondered whether strong religious commitments could be sustained among middle-class Americans. All religions are different, and, despite ascetic origins, nearly all of them have made their accommodations with material things, but across the religious fault lines that divided America in the 1950s, one could hear the ubiquitous lament that suburbanization might not be good for the soul. For Will Herberg, the leading writer on these questions at that time, people's willingness to go to church was not due to their inner convictions but to what their neighbors might think if they did not: "The vogue of Van Gogh and Renoir reproductions in the suburban home and the rising church affiliation of the suburban community may not be totally unconnected," he wrote. "Both may ... be interpreted, in part at least, as the consequence of the craving for adjustment and conformity involved in other-direction."

Each of America's major religions pondered the question of suburbanization in its own way. Protestant concerns, like Protestantism itself, were split: liberal Protestants such as Chicago Divinity School theologian Gibson Winter worried that suburban middle-class status would disconnect individuals from a larger social conscience, while more conservative Protestants— one thinks of the eminent sociologist Peter Berger—simply could not imagine how suburban churches, given over to primarily social tasks, could wrestle with the deep theological concerns that lay at the heart of religious traditions. Jews, the most upwardly mobile of America's ethnic groups in the years after World War II, moved from the city to the suburbs—or the "frontier," as it was called—in ever-increasing numbers, but not without questioning whether the effect, especially among the young, would be to encourage intermarriage, always a threat to minority religions. For the first generation or two after they arrived in this country as immigrants, Catholics tended to live in tightly bound city parishes; heavy investments in the creation of those parishes slowed Catholic out-migration from cities, resulting in substantial conflict with African-Americans moving into northern cities from the South. But suburbanization eventually did come to American Catholicism. While there may not have been a direct cause and effect, the fact that the period of suburbanization was also a period when the rates of those leaving the church doubled, the number of men entering the priesthood declined, and parochial schools lost large numbers of both teachers and students indicated just how much suburbanization, in the words of historian Jay Dolan, constituted a "mighty challenge" for the church.

Fears that suburbanization would produce a religious decline were confirmed by the fact that church membership reached its peak in 1958 before beginning a steady decline until the 1970s, a trend that was particularly true of Catholics. But in retrospect we know that the decline did eventually stabilize. What was more important for the period of rapid suburbanization in the twenty years after World War II was not how many people would attend church, but what kind of churches they would attend.

The kind of religion that turned out to be most compatible with suburban growth was very much like Jesse O'Donnell's religion. Making religion a private matter to be discussed only reluctantly with others seemed to be appropriate for the way people wanted to live in these new communities outside the city. Suburban housing developments, no matter how vigorously they tried to attract people of the same faith, simply could not be organized with the same sharp religious boundaries as were the urban neighborhoods people were leaving. Children were finding the more orthodox religious views of their parents a hindrance to their acceptability in school and with friends. Commuting to the city during the day, men were available to their church only on weekends, reinforcing trends by which religious activity during the week was increasingly feminized. In such a world, one did not talk about religion for exactly the same reason one did not talk about politics: there were too many diverse views that might lead to conflict, and conflict, in turn, would interfere with the imperative of building a new life in the suburbs.

Like Mrs. O'Donnell's family, the U.S. Supreme Court, in the decades after World War II, also fashioned an understanding that held that the American belief in belief was essentially private: in your home, with your coreligionists, and in matters involving your own children, you were free to believe anything you wanted, but once you entered into public institutions, you accepted that such institutions would be neutral in matters of religion—indeed, in later manifestations of the understanding, that they would be neutral between religion and nonreligion.

No longer did Supreme Court justices claim, as Mr. Justice David Brewer did in a 1904 speech, that America was a Christian nation; soon after he spoke, "Judeo-Christian," became the preferred expression, and even it would come to seem exclusionary when significant numbers of immigrants who were neither Christians nor Jews began to arrive in America in the 1970s. Unlike other countries, in which religion and politics were blended, we would uphold the principle of separation of church and state and maintain our belief in tolerance among faiths. These tenets were compatible with the broad contours of what sociologists called "civil religion," the use of the religious imagination to uphold and reinforce national traditions and institutions.

By the 1990s, however, when the Middle Class Morality Project went out to talk with suburban Americans about the role religion played in their moral understanding of the world, this solution of relegating religion to the realm of private life seemed to be breaking down—both in the views of people themselves and in the decisions handed down by courts. America, in most accounts, was experiencing a return to tradition, one no longer content to accept that questions of faith were best kept out of the public realm. Not all Jews followed what had once been seen as an all-but-inevitable path from Conservative to Reform to Unitarian; orthodox, even ultraorthodox, movements blossomed, some of them in the very suburbs that were only recently believed to be hostile to such expressions of faith. In the years after Vatican II, Catholics surpassed Protestants in both educational attainment and socioeconomic status, with the consequence that "white Catholics are now very much a part of the established American middle class and upper-middle class life," as sociologists Barry Kosmin and Seymour Lachman wrote. But even as third- and fourth-generation Catholics intermarried and became more secular, religion in the suburbs was revitalized by the presence of Hispanics, many of whom, arriving as immigrants, skipped over the city and moved directly to the outskirts. The most public manifestation of the return to religion, however, was the huge growth in conservative Protestant sects that

took place not only in the South, but throughout America. As
the religious schism became not the one between Protestants,
Catholics, and Jews, but the one between the orthodox of all
faiths and the reformers of all faiths, what most marked the
differences between the two sides was the insistence by strong religious believers that unless religion became a more public force
in American life, the country would slide into moral anarchy.

While all this was happening, the Supreme Court began to
tinker with earlier versions of its privatistic formulation, allowing the formation and funding of religious groups at public universities, for example, as some justices made fairly explicit their
desire to seek new constitutional understandings on this question. No sharp line between politics and religion could be found
anymore: the Christian Coalition was formed to influence
American politics primarily by gaining influence within the Republican Party, with the predictable consequence of leading
some on the left also to claim religious backing for their political
ideals. Nor was it possible to draw a sharp distinction between
tolerant and secular America on the one hand and a religiously
charged Third World on the other, as immigrants from the latter
brought their faith with them to the former. At the turn of the
twentieth century, America's first culture war—which involved
such issues as whether Catholic schools could be supported by
government funds or whether communities could pass "blue
laws" that prevented Jewish shops from opening on Sunday—
was fought *over* religion. In the new culture war that observers
found brewing in America, the battle seemed to be taking place
with religion, as each side mobilized (or questioned) God in
support of its positions on poverty, abortion, pornography, and
school prayers.

Once it may have been enough for the faithful to have had
their own niches: Mormons had Utah, deeply devout Protestants the South and parts of the Midwest, and Jews and
Catholics New York City (the secular elite had Cambridge and
Berkeley). But questions about religious faith have become na-
tionalized: the Supreme Court, in making sweeping rulings on

such controversial matters as abortion that applied to everyone everywhere, opened the door to a response seeking public affirmations of faith for everyone everywhere. No wonder that the ways in which social scientists and social critics discuss religion at century's end is quite different from the terms used to characterize the emergence of suburban middle-class America a generation or two earlier. Worried that religion was losing its texture, critics now began to fear that people would take the word of God too literally. Accused just a few decades ago of excessive privatization, now religion was seen as invading the public sphere. Sectarianism replaced ecumenicalism as a dominant concern. A people who had trouble finding the time to pray now seemed to want prayer in schools. It is as if the social critics of the 1950s finally got middle-class Americans to take something seriously only to discover that, when they did, they took it far too seriously for the critics' comfort.

As a result of these changes, Jesse O'Donnell is not the only middle-class American talking about religion and politics in ways quite different from those taught by her upbringing. Religion has once again become a public issue in America. And because this country is a democracy, the public will, one way or another, have the final say on how public that issue should be.

VARIETIES OF RELIGIOUS BELIEF

Compared with other prosperous liberal democracies, Americans stand out for the depth of their religious belief; a 1991 study by Andrew Greeley found that 94 percent of Americans said they believed in God, in contrast to 70 percent of Britons and 67 percent of West Germans. Indeed, polling data regularly yield results that suggest that Americans are among the most faithful people in the world: 82 percent believe that the Bible is the actual word of God (although only 35 percent say that the Bible should be taken literally), 80 percent believe in the afterlife, 70 percent believe in the existence of heaven (compared with 57 percent who believe in the existence of hell), 79 percent say that God guided them in making decisions or that prayer is very important in their lives, and 63 percent think that religion can answer all or most of today's problems. When they respond to questions about their religious activities, twice as many Americans say that they go to church regularly as those who say they do not, 51 percent claim to pray every day, and 45 percent watch or listen to religious programming on television or radio. Even if we accept the well-established point that more Americans tell pollsters they attend church than actually do—and that televangelists claim more viewers than they can possibly have—there can be no doubt that church attendance is higher in America than it is in, say, Great Britain.

The Middle Class Morality Project, in keeping with its focus on public rather than private morality, was reluctant to probe too deeply into people's personal views, but we did ask respondents, so long as they were comfortable doing so, to tell us about their religious beliefs. I then coded their answers depending on how strong those beliefs were. One coding category was relatively easy to establish: those who considered themselves nonbelievers.

One hundred sixty-eight of the two hundred people interviewed in the Middle Class Morality Project talked about their religious beliefs, and only twenty-two of those were prepared to use terms like "agnostic" or "atheistic" in describing themselves (see table 2.1). "I don't think anyone would accuse me of being religious," said one of the respondents in Rancho Bernardo (where, perhaps reflecting something about California, close to half the nonbelievers lived), but he was the exception. More often, people who talked about their lack of belief in God did so hesitantly, even defensively, rather than as self-proclamation. Ian Dodson, also of Rancho Bernardo, said, "We're not particularly religious in this house . . . we're atheists, probably," at which point his wife broke in, "Oh, Ian . . . good grief, I am not." The Drakes, who live nearby, call themselves atheists. "Most of the things that people believe in, like the Supreme Being and the power and all that, I never see any real example of it," as Mr. Drake put it, before adding that "we believe that the Ten Commandments make pretty good sense." Militant atheists—those who insist that reason and rationality constitute the only sensible guides by which to live—are very hard to find in America.

But what about the other end of the spectrum: people who take their faith in God extremely seriously? In the way they respond to survey questions about heaven, God's existence, or the importance of church and prayer, Americans give every indication of being deeply religious. Comparative survey data reported by the political scientist Ronald Inglehart bear this out: asked whether morality was absolute or relative to specific circumstances, more people in Britain, France, West Germany, Italy, Sweden, and Canada said circumstantial rather than absolute; only in America was there a higher percentage for absolute (50 percent) rather than circumstantial (45 percent). Results such as those were confirmed by our survey, taken after we completed our more in-depth interviews, with each of the people with whom we spoke; half of them, the same percentage as Inglehart's believers in absolute morality, agreed or

TABLE 2.1
DISTRIBUTION OF RELIGIOUS BELIEF

	Absolutists	Strong Believers	Quiet Believers	Non-Believers	Insufficient Information
Brookline	0	2	12	4	7
Medford	2	2	15	3	3
Broken Arrow	3	4	14	0	4
Sand Springs	2	2	18	1	2
DeKalb	4	3	14	0	4
Cobb	2	0	17	2	4
Eastlake	1	1	13	3	7
Rancho Bernardo	0	5	10	9	1
Total	14	19	113	22	32

TABLE 2.2
"AMERICA HAS BECOME FAR TOO ATHEISTIC AND NEEDS
A RETURN TO STRONG RELIGIOUS BELIEF"

	Strongly Agree	Agree	No Opinion	Disagree	Strongly Disagree
Brookline	2	5	2	11	5
Medford	2	7	2	12	2
Broken Arrow	7	7	5	4	2
Sand Springs	5	12	4	3	1
DeKalb	4	13	2	6	0
Cobb	6	7	1	11	0
Eastlake	2	10	1	11	1
Rancho Bernardo	1	10	4	8	2
Total	29	71	21	66	13

strongly agreed with the statement that America has become too atheistic.

One of the questions that we hoped the Middle Class Morality Project would be able to answer is whether America is experiencing a deep religious revival equivalent to the earlier "awakenings" that have been so much a part of American history. If such a revival is indeed taking place, then the solution worked out in the years after World War II of privatizing religious belief should no longer have strong support in middle-class America. The fact that there are so few nonbelievers among our sample—and that so many insist on the importance of faith—suggests that this question should be answered in the affirmative. Yet, just because people think that faith is important does not necessarily mean that they think America has slipped into the hands of secular humanists and requires more public affirmations of religious belief. The compelling question is not whether they think religion is good for them—nearly everyone thinks that it is—but whether they think it is good for others.

It should come as no surprise to discover that, in a country that prides itself on its religious heritage, there are Americans who believe that God provides an absolute sense of right and wrong binding on all people. The McLaughlins of Broken Arrow, Oklahoma, are among them. Jim McLaughlin thinks that a nation that believes in humanism—"the religion of academia," he calls it—will be in serious trouble. As the country gets "further and further away from God, then we replace it with whoever's morals are in force at the time, and God is out of the picture. Then you have no absolute laws, you have nothing but relativism." Mr. McLaughlin uses a metaphor from golf to explain his point. If you slice your drive, it will continue to fade farther and farther off course. America is also off course, moving inexorably away from its proper target. "This nation was not formed by Buddhist framers of the Constitution; it was formed by Christians," he continues. That is important to him because "our whole nation was founded on the principles of God, and God's principles are absolute, not relative." Mr. McLaughlin wanted to bring prayer and the Bible back into the schools, "not just as literature," he emphasizes, "but as a way of study." One of the problems with education today, he said respectfully but firmly to Maria, my research assistant, is that schools teach more sociology than religion. "If you went into the field of sociology," he asked her, "how much training have you had in religion? I don't really think that you've got a good foundation in that if you've gone through the typical educational process in sociology."

The Middle Class Morality Project purposely selected the Tulsa area in which to conduct interviews because we wanted to hear from people whose ideas resonated with the revival of the conservative Protestantism that has, in recent years, driven American politics, especially the Republican Party. In one sense, we were not disappointed; people in the Tulsa suburbs talk about their faith with more certainty than, say, people in Brookline. But, in another sense, we were quite surprised, for as religious as the residents of Tulsa may have been, they were not as comfortable as Jim McLaughlin in expressing themselves in the language of absolutes. Being born again was important to at least one of them (although she also said that she did not regularly attend church). Another felt that groups like the Moral Majority had done some good for America. Yet, very few of them—indeed, very few of the two hundred people to whom we talked around the country—used words like "sin," "moral rot," "decay," or "Satan," terms that, whether fairly or unfairly, are usually identified with revivalist preachers, talk show hosts, and conservative Christians.

How many of our respondents think like Jim McLaughlin? Clearly some people take their belief in God more seriously than others, and the coding procedure involves finding the appropriate criterion separating the one from the other. An obvious method would be to group together all those who believed, as Mr. McLaughlin did, that there is one proper set of moral commandments: those established by a Christian God. Based on surveys, we would expect the number of such people to be high. But there is a problem with such surveys: expressions of absolutist principles cost the respondent nothing to express, since a survey format allows people to insist that only one set of moral rules is binding on everyone without having to worry about the consequences of that insistence for those who do not share their beliefs. We instead asked those who told us of their deep faith whether they also believed that people who held to other faiths were just as moral as themselves. Many of them responded the way Julie Skinner, a Mormon mother of six living in Medford, did. Clearly a strong religious believer, Mrs. Skinner also thought that "Most religions share the same basic values. . . . I don't feel good about one church coming out and saying, 'You're all wrong, and you're all bad,' I don't believe in telling everyone else that they are wrong."

It is more in accord with the way middle-class Americans understand their religious commitments to posit the existence of two different kinds of deep faith: one which is genuinely absolutist in its insistence on one way to the truth and one which, while equally sincere, is welcoming of all faiths. The latter category would include those, like Mrs. Skinner, who talked enthusiastically and with deep conviction about their specific faith and how it served as the guideline for their moral conduct, even if they did not think that anyone who did not share their convictions was sinful or misguided. Based on that distinction, there are, as table 2.1 indicates, more nonabsolutist people of strong faith in our sample (19) than absolutists (14).

So centrist are most Americans that answers to questions about political belief often take the form of a bell-shaped curve, with roughly equal small groups at either extreme and the large majority in the middle. Much the same is true of religious belief. Even if we combine our two categories of strong believers, the result still resembles a bell-curve, with 33 strong believers at one end and 22 nonbelievers at the other. For the largest number of our respondents, not only does the category of "absolutist" not apply to them, but neither does the category of "strong believer." Given that so many Americans believe in God—after all, 146 of the 168 who indicated something of their beliefs are religious in one way or another—the question that concerned me is why so many middle-class Americans are not even remotely like Jim McLaughlin. What is it that makes so many middle-class Americans say that, no matter how religious they are, they are unwilling to adopt Jim McLaughlin's absolutist sense of Christian right and wrong, or even Julie Skinner's equally faithful, if less absolutist, sense of religious commitment?

One answer to that question became clear in the interview conducted immediately after the one with the McLaughlins. Barbara Tompkins, a retired piano and organ teacher, is the daughter of a Southern Baptist preacher who ultimately became a district supervisor responsible for thirty-six churches. If Jim McLaughlin spoke for that part of Oklahoma that holds to strong faith, Mrs. Tompkins spoke to that part that is still frontier country dominated by an ethic of individualism. Without mentioning any names, Maria told Mrs. Tompkins about her interview with Mr. McLaughlin the previous evening, especially about what he had said about homosexuality not being merely an alternative lifestyle. "That's his right to his belief," she responded, "but he cannot make a broad statement that that's wrong. . . . Why is it wrong for them? I mean, do we all have to have the same color hair?" People who insist that there is only one way to morality, in her opinion, have "stopped preaching and gone on to meddling." Well, Maria continued, his point was that we had to have absolutes. Yes, Mrs. Tompkins agreed, we do. But "people don't [have to] choose the absolutes." For her, insistence on the priority of absolutes for everyone violates people's freedom. "Tend to their business," she says, "I'll tend to mine. . . . Where their nose starts is where my fist should end."

Mrs. Tompkins views herself as a religious person. "I think everyone inside has their own persona of God," she comments. "You don't have to accept anybody's dogma whole. Live with the concept of God as you perceive it." The difference between the way Mrs. Tompkins thinks about the relationship between religion and public morality and the way Mr. McLaughlin does is important to emphasize. For Mr. McLaughlin, if something is right and true for one person, it ought to be right and true for all; as he put it in our interview with him, "There's only one spirit," which for him means that if you don't believe in God, or even if you believe in a God other than the Christian one, "you're gonna be reading out of the wrong book." In his view, then, a virtuous person is one who does what is right, not what he happens to think is right.

Mrs. Tompkins, by contrast, would also claim to be a virtuous person, but one who thinks about virtue in a different way. Her outlook on God illustrates what can best be called "quiet belief." Because she is religious, Mrs. Tompkins believes that there are right and wrong ways to act. But because she is quiet about her beliefs, she also thinks that however strongly one applies principles of right and wrong to oneself, one ought to hesitate before applying them to others. In his study of the way Americans think about the moral dimensions of their lives, the Princeton sociologist Robert Wuthnow quoted a respondent who said, "I tend to be quietly religious." Kenneth Easterbrook, a black software consultant living in Cobb County, told us much the same thing: "I would say that we choose to practice our religion quietly in the sense that I don't go to others and try . . . to convince them that my religion, my approach to life, is best for them. It's an awareness you have to reach on your own. You cannot mandate religion." Quiet faith, as both Mr. Easterbrook and Mrs. Tompkins understand the idea, follows from a commitment to individual freedom; if we proclaim our religious ideas too publicly, we run the risk of interfering with the rights of others to believe in God as they want to. That is what distinguishes those who I classified as quiet believers from those I classified as strong believers: the latter, like Julie Skinner, thought there was more than one way to God but also felt that religion should be viewed as a public good, reinforced by America's communal institutions. The former, by contrast, no matter how deep their faith, viewed religious commitments as private: no one should tell them what is right, just as they should not tell anyone else.

There is a further argument on behalf of quiet faith, and it was made by another resident of Broken Arrow, Joyce Umber, a Baptist. Her point involved humility: something about religious absolutism strikes Mrs. Umber as presuming too much, not only about others, and not only about ourselves, but also about God. Mrs. Umber certainly does not like the secular drift she sees in America and hopes that a return to church will correct it. She also worries about her own commitments: "You know, everyday you have to seek God's guidance. . . . You drift away from God once in a while and you don't stay close to him. You know, you can be caught up in another world if you stray." Surely as religious as Jim McLaughlin, she would, however, be put off by his certainty; for her, we need God's forgiveness because we are imperfect. And because we are, how can we be certain that there is only one true way? To condemn others for lacking the proper way to God is to substitute one's own evaluation for God's.

For the overwhelming majority of middle-class Americans with whom we spoke, the sticking point, the aspect of loudly proclaimed religion that bothers them most, is the idea of excluding others who may not share one's particular religious commitments. To the question of whether Muslims or Jews are immoral because they do not accept Jesus as the one true way, one African-American woman in Georgia responded that, yes, there is only one answer to our problem: Jesus. Pausing as she said this, she looked at me with dawning self-revelation and said, "Now I don't know if you are Jewish," before recovering to add, "but if you are, hopefully you will be a Messianic Jew." Her response stood out for its uniqueness. Overwhelmingly, again and again, and in every region of the country, middle-class Americans believe that people of religious faiths other than their own are moral people. "I mean, gosh, I have all kinds of friends," we were told by Anne Harding of Sand Springs, "and they have all kinds of beliefs. I think that they're all good people." "I know an awful lot of people who are not Christian, and I respect the hell out of them," added Nancy Elliott of DeKalb. The important thing for both of them is that people believe in something.

And nonbelievers? Here, again, a reluctance to exclude turns out to be as powerful, if not more powerful, a moral force as a requirement to believe. It is not the beliefs of others we ought to respect, some of our respondents felt, but the person who holds those beliefs. Like so many others in Tulsa, Fred Jones, a jet engine mechanic and the man who, in that order, believes in God, family, and country, thinks that we made a mistake in turning away from God: "I think the reason we are in the shape we're in today is that we have excluded God instead of including God in our lifestyles," he told us. But precisely because of his religious beliefs, "I would kill my own testimony by putting someone else down." Mr. Jones works with different kinds of people every day: "I take the individual and respect him for who he is and for his beliefs." Two of his best friends never go to church. "I think they're both good, spiritual, moral people, but they do not honor God by coming to his House. I respect them. I like them." Americans understand that their belief in God does not foreclose the possibility of a belief in human beings. Their deeply held and strongly expressed faith in people prevents them from a disposition to accept the proposition that a large number of their fellow Americans are Godless sinners—even when they do not believe in God.

To exclude, to condemn, is to judge, and middle-class Americans are reluctant to pass judgment on how other people act and think. Peter Strong, a white man living in a primarily black section of DeKalb County, was one of the most conservative people to whom we talked, an enthusiastic supporter of Newt Gingrich and someone not afraid to express politically incorrect views. A Baptist, Mr. Strong believes that "the church does a lot of good," and that the country's decline can be attributed to people's lack of faith, but at the same time, he said, "I don't go around preaching to people." His opinion was widely shared. A. C. Stewart, a retired football coach in Oklahoma, quit going to church because of "the self-judgment, the 'I'm right, you're wrong'" attitude. Talking about religious leaders who would presume to judge others, Patricia Bates of DeKalb County pointed out that

> the Bible also says you cannot judge. . . . The Scripture says "Only my father can judge which is heaven." So all of you are playing God here. I think we need to step outside that. Step outside of self. Look at self. Get a mirror. Are you that great? Don't throw rocks at my house because it might shatter. . . . If everybody would step back and look at themselves, take a mirrored view of themselves, and then ask, "What is my purpose? Where do I fit this puzzle," then we'd be much better off.

Middle-class Americans have added an Eleventh Commandment, best formulated by Dolores Wales of Sand Springs, Oklahoma: "Thou shalt not judge."

Our respondents can name what disturbs them about passing judgment on others' religious convictions: such a move politicizes religion, taking it out of the private realm where it belongs and placing it in politics—a realm of human activity for which people have relatively little respect. For Tommy Fasano, a Jehovah's Witness living in Rancho Bernardo, and one of those we classified as a strong religious believer (but not as an absolutist), judgmentalism leads to politicians like Patrick Buchanan, whom he considers extremist. Mr. Fasano illustrates his point with the question of abortion: "Abortion is a moral issue. It has nothing to do with politics. You don't like it, don't get one. I am not a proponent of it. [But] I'm not about to tell you, 'Hey, you're a sinner because you're getting one.' That's not me. I am not here to judge anyone." Many would not object, and some would be quite pleased, if a pastor or rabbi advised a woman, in private, that abortion was wrong. To do so in public, and in a way not directed toward a particular person but as a general moral injunction to all, whatever their circumstances, that strikes of poking your nose into other people's business. "I would be the first one to go down with my church and stand in front of an abortion clinic. This is something that I've evolved into believing that I think is wrong," said Trent Tartt of Broken Arrow. "But," he continued, "I also wouldn't be the one to stand up and say it's wrong in every single case. Because my church would say, 'Well, you haven't grown to that point,' but I would say, 'That's maybe what you call it, but I don't think it's right that if a woman was raped, she shouldn't have a choice.'"

From the interviews we conducted, an answer to the question of whether a new religious awakening is taking place in the United States can be given. Clearly, most middle-class Americans take their religion seriously. But very few of them take it so seriously that they believe that religion should be the sole, or even the most important, guide for establishing rules about how *other* people should live. And some, if even fewer, also would distrust such rules for providing guidelines about how they personally should live. Despite the attention that conservative Christians have commanded in the political realm, there is not much support out there in middle-class America, at least among our respondents, for the notion that religion can play an official and didactic role in guiding public morality.

Standing in the way of a religious revival that would undermine the privatistic solutions that have governed American approaches to religious obligations since World War II is a strongly held belief in quiet faith. People who adhere to such a creed think the best way to fulfill our obligations to others is not by lecturing them about right and wrong, but rather by personal example. They do not believe in absolutes but in balancing what is right with what is practical. They distrust extremes, even those views they consider correct but that are asserted with too much finality. And they feel that one has to do one's best to understand, even when one does not agree with, those who think otherwise. Quiet faith, in their opinion, does not make headlines or win medals. It tends to get drowned out by the brash blaring of the media, the self-interest of groups and organizations, the certainties of ideologists, the indifference of social scientists, and, when it comes to religion in particular, the rantings of fanatics.

Our interviews were conducted at a time when questions of fanaticism, religious or otherwise, were very much in the news: a number of those to whom we spoke brought up the incident in which federal agents raided the headquarters of David Koresh in Waco, Texas, and killed him and a large number of his followers, not as an example of oppressive government, but to illustrate the dangers of religious fanaticism. Fanaticism, moreover, was not some distant phenomenon for them: for the Brookliners with whom we talked, John Salvi, who shot and killed two people at an abortion clinic in their suburb before taking his own life in prison, represented everything that could go wrong with literal absolutism. And our interviews in Oklahoma, conducted shortly after the largest act of domestic terrorism in American history, were certainly influenced by that event. Still, the degree to which middle-class Americans expressed a distrust of religious extremism is worth emphasizing.

So deep is this distrust that it extends well beyond violence-prone extremists to include revivalist preachers. During the 1980s, as a result of the televangelist scandals of 1987 and 1988, the proportion of Americans who believed that television evangelists could be trusted with money went from 41 percent to 16 percent; those who believed they were honest decreased from 53 percent to 23 percent with roughly similar declines among those who believed that they cared for people or had a special relationship with God. Our interviews indicate that little had changed by 1995. Broken Arrow disc jockey Jim Stone, a deeply conservative man with a proclivity toward conspiracy theories, certainly had little respect for them: "Oral Roberts has been ready for the butterfly net since he discovered television," he told us, before going on to make sarcastic remarks about Jimmy Swaggart—"He can't keep his pants up"—and Jim Bakker. Preachers who meddle too much in public affairs are, simply put, too loud: the very public character of their utterances is what leads people to distrust them. Political religion is to be found in other countries, especially the Middle East, not here, we were frequently told. Indeed, among the most moving thoughts on the subject came from an Iranian woman living in Broken Arrow for whom religious fundamentalism represents everything from which she fled—and for whom American religious tolerance represents freedom in a very palpable sense.

A consistent theme running through the large majority of our interviews was that religion is too important, too much a matter of personal identity, to be forced on people. DeKalb's Jamie Willis believes that "religion is the backbone of your morals and values and it teaches you a great deal of yourself," but, she added, "I've never tried to force religion on anyone." Religion is fine, said James Alexander of Brookline, but "don't push it in someone's face." Bob Cameron of Sand Springs has backed off from his once strict religious views, since he now realizes that "you can't force religion on people." "I don't like the extremism on either side of the thing," said George Slade of Cobb County, with respect to the debate over the role of religion in American life. "I have good morals. I'm not hurting anybody. . . . I'm not doing things that are wrong. I don't like the trend toward 'If you're not a Christian, or their definition of a Christian, then you're just not worth it.' "

As Mr. Slade's comments illustrate, efforts by organizations like the Moral Majority and the Christian Coalition to mobilize

Christians around specific political positions were not very well received by those middle-class Americans with whom we spoke. A case could be made that this distrust is not merely the result of revivalist preachers being arrested for sexual and financial peccadilloes: politicized Christianity is everything that an inclusive, nonabsolutist, modest, and nonjudgmental religious mentality is not. Jake and Molly Sandford, a semiretired couple in Sand Springs, worry about the decline of religion in America, but they worry even more that, as Mr. Sandford put it, "the fanatics took over. They drove away people like us. . . . The God I believe in," he continued, "is a God of love." But the kinds of people attracted to the Seven Hundred Club (a television program on Pat Robertson's Christian Broadcasting Network), "them's the meanest people. They talk mean." Sociologists believe that levels of education are the most important determining feature in accounting for the fact that some Americans hold to very conservative theological notions while others tend to be liberal. Because our sample was middle class and relatively well educated, we have no way of testing this hypothesis. But examples like that of the Sandfords—and there were many of them— illustrate that in places like Sand Springs, where many of our respondents did not attend college, there are just as many people who fear a linking of religion and politics as in places like Brookline.

Listening to so many people express a distaste for efforts to politicize religion, I was at first convinced that there must be something unrepresentative about my sample. The year of our interviews in Oklahoma and Georgia, 1995, witnessed triumphant attempts by the Republican Party to pass its Contract with America. Nearly all political commentators believed that the election of the previous year was a watershed event, one that marked a long-term transition to a conservative majority in America. The Christian Coalition had played a major role in that triumph, symbolized by Patrick Buchanan's speech at the 1992 Republican convention proclaiming the existence of a culture war in America and carried forward by the Republican electoral victory in 1994. As I watched the Republican Congress begin to carry out its agenda, even to the point of shutting down the government, I began to think that they had to be right and my data had to be wrong: after all, they could afford surveys of far greater depth and technological sophistication than my two hundred conversations.

Events since 1995, however, shed a very different light on the matter. More popular within the Republican Party than Patrick Buchanan was Colin Powell, a man who symbolizes moderation in everything he does or says. Even more important, the Christian Coalition struck a new note in its political presentation of self. Under the leadership of Pat Robertson, the organization had developed an extremist public image; one 1996 survey gave Robertson an approval rating of 29 percent compared with a 45 percent favorable rating for the Christian Coalition, while another showed that Robertson's name evoked roughly the same percentage of negative reactions as Oliver North's (and more than Jesse Jackson's). With Ralph Reed, a politically savvy leader, in charge, the Christian Coalition began to present a softer face to the general public. It clearly realized something about American political sentiment: while it is undoubtedly true that the number of evangelical Christians is increasing, and while it is also true that white evangelicals tend to support Republicans, and while it is even the case that the percentage of Americans who think that religion does have a role to play in politics has gone up, none of that translates into automatic support for those who might, in their excessive zeal, violate deeply held beliefs about fair play, second chances, and tolerance. There are more conservative Christians in America, but among them there is anything but consensus. America is, simply put, not poised on the brink of a religious counterrevolution; more Americans disagree with the statement that the federal government is hostile to religion, for example, than agree with it.

Further evidence that conservative Christian leaders realize how badly a harsh version of their message is generally received

was provided by an incident that took place while we were in
Georgia. In Atlanta, I wanted to attend services at a primarily
African-American church, and I was directed (by one of our respondents) to the Cathedral at Chapel Hill in suburban Decatur.
Its preacher, Bishop Earl Paulk, I was told, although white, has
great rapport with his primarily black congregation. When we
arrived, we discovered that he was not to give the sermon that
day; it would be offered instead by the Reverend Jim Bakker, the
very evangelist, and former prison inmate, about whom so many
of our respondents had negative feelings.

"I don't deliver sermons anymore," Bakker began. His
"message," as he called it, would be based on Proverbs 17:17—
"A friend loveth at all times"—and would be devoted to the
theme of forgiveness. At first cynical—he has a lot to be for-
given for, I thought—I was unprepared for the degree to which
Bakker's thoughts resonated with the nonjudgmental, inclusive
way most of our respondents talked about their relationship
with God. Denouncing preachers who wanted to fill up the jails
and throw away the keys, Bakker told his audience that "those
people in prison are just as real as you are—you just didn't get
caught, that's all." Being in prison had taught him, he said, that
his former approach to preaching was wrong. (One year after we
heard his message, Bakker would publish a book called *I Was
Wrong*). "Many of the churches today, they leave you when you
have a divorce or take drugs, if you go to prison, or if you had an
abortion. They abandon you in your moment of crisis," he told
his audience. A church that walks away from young women
who have children out of wedlock or those suffering from AIDS
is not a church of mercy, and Bakker, like Jesus, would rather
have mercy than religion. To thunderous amens, Bakker's talk
seemed little different from one President Clinton might have
delivered to the same group, except that Clinton, when he did
address a black congregation in the South, was more willing to
pass judgment on self-destructive behavior than Bakker. Perhaps
Jim Bakker was converted to a new worldview while in jail; perhaps his message was always directed at reaching as large an au-

dience as possible; more likely, he, like other Christian preachers, realizes that a language of meanness wins few hearts in America. When even Jim Bakker, however loudly, becomes a convert to quiet faith, it must be very powerful in America indeed.

By softening their tone, conservative Christians are trying to undo the damage of their original intransigence. If our interviews are any indication, they have their work cut out for them. The now disbanded Moral Majority left a bad taste in the mouth of middle-class America, one that a chastened Christian Coalition led by Ralph Reed's successors may never be able to neutralize. "I personally think that when the world comes to an end, there will be people that have lived well, that have tried to be good to each other," said Cathy Peterson, a Cobb County housewife.

> I feel like there will be all religions there. I feel like there will be Buddhists there—if they believe that in their heart and soul and that's the way they're taught and they live a good life. I feel like there'd be all different religions there. . . . No, I don't think those people are bad, if you say they don't go to church. It's a personal thing for me.

REAL DIVERSITY

America has become a far more religiously diverse society than anyone could have anticipated in the decades when suburban expansion took off. The trend began when more and more Americans found themselves marrying outside their faith. It picked up as Americans began to choose for themselves the faith that fit them best rather than relying on the religion of their upbringing. Then immigration brought with it a large number of old religions, which, in characteristic American fashion, were called "new" ones, eventually reaching into the very heartland of the country. That was accompanied by multiculturalism and, with it, an effort to teach about all the different roads to God, including the faiths of Native American peoples. Comparative religion, an exotic subject when I went to college in the early

1960s, has become something of a staple of public school cur-
ricula throughout the country.

According to the survey we took at the end of our interviews, middle-class Americans have accommodated themselves
rather easily to America's religious diversity. A very small
number of our respondents—nineteen out of two hundred—
disagreed with the statement "There are many different religious truths and we ought to be tolerant of all of them," while
quite a larger number—167—agreed or strongly agreed with
it. Considering how many lives have been lost in the religious wars that have characterized Western history—as well as
how much violence remains associated with conflicts over
religious beliefs in today's world—this tolerance is quite remarkable. As much as they admire religion, it would seem,
middle-class Americans dislike doctrinal strife and sectarian
conflict more.

By downplaying denominational sectarianism in favor of
tolerant acceptance, middle-class Americans redefine religion to
make it more suited to their tastes. For religious diversity to

TABLE 2.3
"THERE ARE MANY DIFFERENT RELIGIOUS TRUTHS AND
WE OUGHT TO BE TOLERANT OF ALL OF THEM"

	Strongly Agree	Agree	No Opinion	Disagree	Strongly Disagree
Brookline	10	13	2	0	0
Medford	13	9	0	3	0
Broken Arrow	3	15	3	1	3
Sand Springs	7	13	3	2	0
DeKalb	9	11	0	1	4
Cobb	10	10	4	1	0
Eastlake	11	10	1	2	1
Rancho Bernardo	12	11	1	0	1
Total	75	92	14	10	9

work, all religions, even public ones, many of them believe, have to transform themselves into private ones, for if you permit Christianity to be the "official" religion of the United States, what are you going to do about the others? "My wife has a fit because they can't hold Christmas programs up here in school," Stephen Jackman of Sand Springs informed us. To which he responded, "Well, what if they demanded that they observe Rosh Hashanah? How are you going to feel then?" Religious tolerance in America bears a distinct resemblance to laissez-faire economics: you can do what you want so long as you let me do what I want. This is especially true now that there are others here besides Christians and Jews. "If you are a Hindu and you grew up being a Hindu, keep it to yourself," said Jody Fields, an unemployed social worker in DeKalb County. "Don't impose your religion, and don't make me feel bad because I do this and you do that." You come here and practice your faith, Americans implicitly tell those outside the Judeo-Christian tradition, but you cannot practice your faith the way it is done in theocracies abroad.

This message that everyone should leave everyone else alone might strike a strong believer as odd, since many religions have contained an obligation to convert nonbelievers. Most of our respondents have a way to deal with that history as well: they simply ignore religious sectarianism. "All religions have basically the same common good things," we were told by Joti Mehta, a substitute teacher in Rancho Bernardo who emigrated from India. "Whether it's the Koran or the Bible or Gita or whatever, they have these ten commandments or eighteen commandments or twenty commandments. . . . All these things are there, you know, brotherhood and all, that's everywhere." Carmen Tosca of Eastlake is aware that in the Middle East, people kill each other over questions of faith, but, because they do, people over there cannot be truly religious: "I don't think any religion really teaches you to hate others and to be mean to others," she argues. "I think most religions really teach you to be spiritual and to be compassionate and all that, and I think religion is good, or almost any religion is good." Aaron Feldman, a physician in Cobb

County, spoke to us the day after his office celebrated its "holi-day" party. Although all the doctors in his office are Jewish, nearly all the staff are not, a situation that led everyone to agree that the party would celebrate neither Christmas nor Hanukkah. One could interpret responses like these as involving a form of deep denial: eternally optimistic, middle-class Americans are re-luctant to acknowledge the tragic dimension to religious strife. On the other hand, perhaps these people know that life in America will have a bigger impact on people of orthodox faith than people in orthodox faith will have on life in America. If so, then the way they think about religious accommodation, while insufficiently appreciative of religious conflict today, may fore-shadow a period of increasing religious pluralism tomorrow.

Although laissez-faire religious norms are widely shared in middle-class America, they are not shared by all. For the most devout among our respondents, those who believe that religion's commandments are absolute and binding on everyone in our so-ciety, confining religion to the private realm itself violates a core belief: that one should proudly proclaim one's faith and help others seek the truth. Because those who hold to this view argue that privatizing religion does not permit them to be true to the commandments of their religious faith as they understand them, their insistence that religion be given more of a public role in America upsets liberals, such as members of the American Civil Liberties Union, who hold strongly to the principle that church and state should be as separate as possible. Devout religious be-lievers have forced Americans to deal with a question that, for most of the post–World War II period, has been kept somewhat underground: can we still find ways to get along if we not only hold deep beliefs about the nature of morality, but also think that those beliefs should be operative for society as a whole?

One answer to this question has been offered by the political theorists Amy Gutmann and Dennis Thompson in their book *Democracy and Disagreement.* They argue that citizens in a de-mocracy have an obligation to reason their way to mutually ac-ceptable decisions on controversial matters—a process they call deliberative democracy. Not only is such an ideal desirable, they claim, it is also possible. On questions such as welfare and affirmative action, positions exist that can respect the views of deeply divided antagonists.

A possible objection to deliberative democracy is that it is the kind of solution that academics, who like to deliberate, would prefer, but that would have little relevance for people at large. Yet, we found that a small but eloquent number of suburbanites believed that religious diversity was valuable in precisely the way Gutmann and Thompson suggest: to enable those of different beliefs to argue out their differences in public. Consider what Rachel Benjamin, a Brookline dentist, had to say on these themes. Like so many others in her community, she was appalled when two women working in an abortion clinic were killed by someone claiming to be carrying out the will of God. Yet despite her distaste for John Salvi, she nonetheless realized that the entire conflict over abortion "really highlighted the fact that people are allowed to have different views." The only way to live with such conflict is "to talk out these issues," since "people need to understand that we see things in different ways." Her views were seconded by Bea Cohen of Cobb County. Religious diversity, she said, is a good thing "because there is no one right and no one wrong and the greater the exposure you have to different ideas ... more tolerance, I would think, grows out of that." Mrs. Duncan, a white woman in a primarily black section of DeKalb County, put the same point this way: "Even if you disagree with someone's politics, it doesn't hurt to communicate. 'Don't you see my point? Can't you see my point a little bit?' "

What one hears being expressed here is something more than laissez-faire. Rather than emphasizing a negative—no one should interfere with anyone else's beliefs—this way of thinking seeks a positive: How can another's beliefs strengthen and broaden my own? The more views we have, the more resources on which we have to draw. The resulting common morality may be thinner than the religious beliefs of one particular church, but it will also, in Dr. Benjamin's terms, constitute a set of "civilization morals" around which people of many different faiths can agree. That's why Paul Kemp, a minister in Medford, can say that religious diversity is a "blessing for this country. . . . I think people will recognize that there is value and truth in Hinduism, in Buddhism, in Judaism, in Catholicism, in Protestantism. There is a kernel of something in each of them that I think contributes to a wider vision of reality and how we need to relate to one another."

Yet, deliberative democracy is not just a process that can be used to evaluate ends: it is also an end in itself. Just as there are Americans for whom communication is important, there are others for whom faith lies beyond deliberation or argument of any kind. To ask them to enter into a dialogue with skeptics is to ensure that the skeptics win by default. What to liberals seems like a perfectly reasonable way to argue about difference to a person of faith seems like a way of taking the liberal position against the conservative one. Their reasoning can be illustrated by examples involving such charged issues as prayer in the schools or the constitutionality of allowing public displays of faith in America. For the deeply devout to whom we spoke, there is no escaping the ironclad logic of either/or: if, in the interests of fairness, prayer is not allowed in school or crosses in public places, the rights of atheists have simply trumped those of believers. On issues such as these, they believe, there simply is not much to discuss.

But it would be wrong to conclude that people who think this way are necessarily illiberal or undemocratic. A script exists for debates over religion in the public square, and each side in the debate is expected to recite its lines. Those who want prayer in school or crosses in public places are said by their opponents to be engaged in an effort to impose their religion, the majority religion, on the beliefs of minorities. Those who favor banning all religion from the public sphere are held by their opponents to be atheists intent on having the world run their way. There is, however, something amiss in both positions. People who believe in public displays of religion often fail to recognize that not all those who support religious neutrality are atheists; some are sincerely devout people protecting minority religions against majority ones. But adherents of strict neutrality misunderstand the points made by deeply religious believers as well, for the latter see themselves as most definitely *not* trying to impose their Christian beliefs on an increasingly diverse society. However wide the gap between the secular and the orthodox sides in debates of this sort, those who want religious symbols to be allowed in public do so in support of the very religious tolerance and diversity praised by many who do not. That may be why, for all the rhetoric generated on the issue by the American Civil Liberties Union on the one hand and the Christian Coalition on the other, at the local level, in places such as Springfield, Massachusetts, most such controversies are settled relatively peacefully by informal agreements among all the groups involved.

If once in America the question of religious toleration was raised in defense of nonbelievers who dissented from religious orthodoxy, today it is raised by believers who feel excluded from a predominantly secular public world. Jen Morgan of Cobb County, like Jim McLaughlin, is a strong believer and is one of the many Catholics in this country attracted to the ideas of the Christian Coalition. "Our country was founded with Christian principles in mind," she pointed out, "and when the public school system started, they were allowed to pray. . . . A Christian teacher could teach from her Christian perspective to the kids, because that was what society was like. Now, our society is atheistic or agnostic . . . and the Christians are being pushed aside." Mrs. Morgan elaborated her beliefs in ways indicating how long and hard she had thought about the issue:

> The separation of church and state was put into our laws because the people that came here from Europe wanted to be allowed to have religious freedom. . . . Now it's been twisted around to use it to suppress religious freedom. . . . They probably never foresaw that was going to happen. It was actually put in so that you would be free to profess your faith without the government interfering. Now the government is intervening and not allowing us to profess our faith.

For a significant group in the San Diego area, Mrs. Morgan's concerns were shared in the context of a real-life example. Our interviews in Eastlake and Rancho Bernardo took place when local residents were debating whether a cross that had long stood on top of a local mountain should be taken down because the land on which it stood was public property. A few of our respondents were indifferent to the question. The others who talked about it did so with a tone of bewilderment. Don't Christians have rights too? they wanted to know. Karen Calingo, born and raised in the Philippines, feels, like Jen Morgan, that the atheists are winning all the battles over the public square. "They are catering to these people," she says of the atheists. "They are winning. . . . We don't say Merry Christmas anymore in the public school. We say Happy Holiday because Christmas denotes God, denotes Jesus. There are a lot of Roman Catholics in the schools. There are a lot of Protestants. They still believe in God. . . . But here comes along people who are atheists and who are only a certain portion of the population, and they are the ones being heard."

Because they see themselves as a victimized minority, people such as Mrs. Calingo and Mrs. Morgan believe they have more in common with dissenting and minority religions than they do with establishment, monopolistic ones. Like many Christians to whom we talked, Mrs. Calingo would much prefer to have more devout Muslims and Buddhists in the country than agnostics who may have been born Christian. (As one respondent in Oklahoma put it, "Any religion is probably better than no religion at all.") And even Mrs. Morgan, who strongly believes that America was born as a Christian country, when pressed on her views about religious diversity, said that "there's ways to talk about God that wouldn't offend Moslems and Buddhists. . . . There's common ground in all of the faiths that you could talk about God and do some prayer without it offending anyone except the people who don't believe in God." In the wake of a Supreme Court ruling allowing the state of Oregon to prohibit the use of peyote in religious ceremonies, constitutional scholars have begun to question whether the Court is sufficiently protective of the free exercise rights of minority religious believers. Although they do not use legal language, Mrs. Calingo and Mrs. Morgan were essentially arguing that the free exercise clause of the First Amendment, which says that everyone has the right to practice their religious beliefs as they see fit, contradicts the establishment clause, which prohibits government from naming one church as the state's official religion. For them, a constitutional prohibition on the establishment of a religious symbol in a public space violates their First Amendment freedom to put into practice their religious beliefs.

With their arguments rooted in notions of free exercise and support for diversity, these advocates of a more public recognition of faith understand themselves as trying to be accommodating to all faiths, not seeking to impose one of them. There was a time when Protestantism was the dominant religion in America, and people of other faiths needed the protection of the Constitution to carve out space for their own religious practices, most of our devout respondents recognize. But this condition, they argue, no longer applies. For them, public displays of religious symbols or prayer in school, even if rooted in Christianity, are meant to stand for all religions, which is why they should be as broad and inclusive as possible (without, of course, losing their religious character). If Christians were out to convert everyone to the cross, such a broad symbolic meaning would not be possible. But, they claim, they are not out to make everyone Christians; they want public symbols of religion to encourage everyone from every religion to believe whatever they prefer to believe. Although many of those who want to see more public displays of religion believe in absolutes, their arguments on behalf of their position are contextual, based on an understanding that what may have been true when America was overwhelmingly a Christian nation needs to be rethought at a time when the country has become so religiously varied.

In a diverse religious climate, the proper way to treat conflicts between one religion and another is to give space to them all, or so many of our believers argued. "Everybody ought to have a turn," said Sand Springs fireman John Pollan. "It doesn't take very long to say a prayer for anybody. And you could have a Muslim prayer, a Hindu prayer, and a Catholic prayer, and a Baptist prayer. You know, you could have all four of those in the span of five minutes and then go on about the day's chores."

"When I heard all of this nonsense about how we can't have Christmas carols in the schools because the Muslims will be upset," added Cathy Ryan of Brookline, "well, excuse me, let's teach Muslim songs too. . . . Don't wipe out all the culture, add to it. . . . Do Hanukkah songs. Let's find out what a dreidel represents. Let's find out what Muslims do." In a fashion not fully appreciated by their opponents, this way of thinking puts people like these on the side of practitioners of minority religions. One need not accept their point that atheism has become the new established religion to agree that deep believers are a kind of dissenter in an increasingly secular American culture.

But if religious conservatives have accepted in their own fashion the principle that the state should be neutral among religions, they do not accept the proposition that it should be neutral between religion and nonreligion. No neutrality between believers and atheists is possible, they argue, and as a result, the only proper choice in a democracy is to side with the majority, which happens to be people of faith (all faiths, let us recall, not just one). This, of course, is exactly the kind of reasoning that leads liberals to argue for the need to protect minorities even at the cost of sacrificing a democratic principle such as majority rule. Perhaps I should make clear that, on this question, I am on the liberal side: as I listened to conservative Christians make their arguments, I could not help but feel that this country remains sufficiently religious—and sufficiently Christian—that one needs to worry about the rights of nonbelievers. Yet, I heard something else in their views as well: conservative Christians are often more willing to acknowledge the degree to which America has changed since the battles over fundamentalism earlier in this century than are those adherents to the American Civil Liberties Union who act as if religious intolerance, rather than nonjudgmentalism, is still the dominant tone of the country's religiosity.

Just as conservative Christians believe that the question of religious establishment is a different question under conditions of religious diversity rather than religious monopoly, they also feel that minority rights look different when adherents to a religious point of view no longer practice the kind of violence and intimidation once used to reinforce their dominance. The most striking aspect of our interviews on this subject is what they lacked: no one at any time, not even the strongest believers, used the word "infidel." In a way similar to the general acceptance by whites that racism against blacks is wrong (see chapter V), Protestants no longer argue that Catholics and Jews serve the interests of Satan. A group as nonjudgmental as middle-class Americans cannot be intolerant. Whether this means that we can override the rights of atheists is another matter. But the Middle Class Morality Project does suggest that middle-class Americans are not ready to replay the Scopes trial. The conflict between believers and nonbelievers is as deep as it ever has been in America, but it is no longer a conflict between know-nothings and an enlightened elite. Those who want prayer in schools or crosses on mountains are anything but know-nothings: they have arguments on their side and, even more important, those arguments are lodged not in blind acceptance, but in a liberal language of inclusion and accommodation.

For the American middle class, religious diversity is here to stay; as Barbara Odessa of Cobb County put it, "We've just got a more diverse society, so we're gonna get more diverse religions." Diversity being a fact of life, one might as well make the best of it. When we consider how many people have died in the name of religion over the years, the acceptance of so many different kinds of belief in America is remarkable. One is tempted to call it real diversity, not because the idea of diversity is inappropriate to race, gender, or sexual orientation, but because religion claims to speak to what really and truly matters in life. I confess that at some level I did not fully understand the nonjudgmentalism of middle-class Americans. I wondered why, if people were so libertarian, they were as religious as they claimed to be and why, if they were so religious, they were so unwilling to speak of sin and Satan. But those who have qualms about nonjudgmentalism ought at least to recognize what comes along with it: a strong commitment to the principle that a wide variety of religious views ought to be allowed to flourish.

THE ULTIMATE TEST

Moderation and tolerance—an appreciation of the modest virtues—are the bedrock moral principles of the American middle class: on most controversial issues, Americans instinctively try to find the centrist position between two extremes *and* attempt to carve out private spaces in which people can do what they want so long as others do what they want. But these two principles can contradict each other. If one believes in tolerance for everyone under all conditions, one is hardly moderate. And if one prizes moderation, one should look for a position that combines respect for privacy with the need to adhere to common public principles that can occasionally overrule not only private rights, but the tolerance that goes along with them. How are middle-class Americans likely to react when their two "default" moral positions come into conflict?

No other issue taps into such a potential conflict more than the issue of homosexuality. The question of gay rights is important to a discussion of religious toleration, for it is over this question that the more liberal and more conservative religious believers have had their most persistent clashes. From specific congregations to whole denominations such as the Episcopalian Church, which recently experienced a formal trial over heresy involving a decision to ordain a gay minister, a seemingly unbridgeable gulf has opened between those who believe that the Bible's condemnation of homosexuality as an abomination must be taken as a moral injunction versus those who believe that Christianity requires the love and acceptance of everyone.

Secular America has also been transformed by this clash: controversies involving gay rights in Colorado, President Clinton's response to the conflict between the military and gay advocacy groups, the frequent denunciation of homosexuality by adherents to the Christian Coalition, and highly publicized efforts to teach about homosexuals in New York City public schools demonstrate the degree to which issues involving gays have begun to dominate American politics. For conservatives, here, more than anyplace else, is where the line should be drawn: if Americans are unwilling to condemn sodomy, they would presumably be unwilling to condemn anything. For liberals, the test is the same but the results different: tolerance means little until it includes what the majority dislikes the most. The question is easily posed: Are middle-class Americans so non-judgmental that public recognition of homosexuality is fine with them or so religious that they still believe that what the Bible condemns must remain a sin?

The debate about gay rights taking place among intellectuals and academics often focuses on whether homosexuality is a choice or is determined by the biological, neurological, or genetic makeup of an individual. Americans are divided on this point; according to the Post-Modernity Project's poll, 38 percent agree that "a person is born either a homosexual or a heterosexual, and there is little they can do to change that" compared with 47 percent who disagree. Although the middle-class Americans to whom we spoke think differently from the cultural elite on many issues, on the question of gay rights they pose the issue in much the same way. Those who believed that homosexuality is a choice were more likely also to believe it was a sin. "I just don't think people are born that way," said Mavis Wright, a Jehovah's Witness in DeKalb County. "So I wouldn't want that taught to my child." On the other hand, those who believed homosexuality to be a condition would apply the same reasoning to gays that they would to any other group born different. Included in the latter group is Karen Calingo, the devout Christian from the Philippines who believes that atheists have too much power. "I think it is something we have to accept because it's part of their nature," she said about gay people. "It's not to their own making that their genes are like that." When we followed up by asking her explicitly if she was saying that homosexuality was not a sin, Mrs. Calingo emphasized that it was not. What are we going to do, she asked sarcastically, get into "gene alteration"?

For the American public as a whole, Mrs. Wright's position has more support than Mrs. Calingo's. According to the General Social Survey, roughly 70 percent of the American people believe that sexual relations between members of the same sex is wrong. But it is one thing to believe that homosexuality is wrong and another to believe that people should not be allowed to do whatever they want in the privacy of their own homes. There will always be those who treat the question of gay rights in the same laissez-faire way they would treat any other issue involving matters of privacy. "I don't care what you look like, what you're wearing, what your hair color is, what sexual preference you have," said Katherine Mullins, a Broken Arrow businesswoman with decidedly libertarian views on most questions of the day. Others are willing to show respect to gays and lesbians because, they believe, nonjudgmentalism implies that one should show respect to everyone. "You know, there are a lot of people out there that I totally disagree with, I disagree with their lifestyles," said Anne Harding of Sand Springs. "I disagree with their viewpoints, but I respect them as an individual, as a human being. I think that needs to be taught. You know, you can't judge another person. . . . You need to be fair to everybody no matter how you feel about that person." And then there are those who, making use of the same distinction between public and private that applies to religious belief, argued in favor of the right of gays to do "whatever they wanted behind closed doors in the privacy of their homes," as one resident of Broken Arrow put it, but not to bring "it out in public, like if you're in a restaurant and I have my little small children and then two men are sitting there kissing each other."

In making sense of this issue, it is important to distinguish between respect for privacy and respect for what takes place in private. The question is whether people would be willing to go beyond expressions of "negative" liberty to the "positive" position that homosexuals are deserving of public respect *as* homosexuals. This is not the same issue as whether homosexuals should be permitted to teach in colleges and universities; it is clear from General Social Survey data that Americans not only think they should, but that the percentage who think this way has increased since 1973 from 50.1 percent to 73.2 percent. That support can be explained on the grounds of respect for rights; in endorsing the right of homosexuals to teach, people are not necessarily endorsing homosexuality.

To get at the more positive issue of acceptance of gays in general, we asked instead whether people would support teaching respect for homosexuality in public schools. We cannot report distribution of opinion on this issue across our entire sample, because our question was not in our original interview schedule; it evolved out of the responses we were getting to questions about teaching values in public schools. Had we included it, especially in Brookline, our national data might well have shown the same kind of bell-curve distribution we have seen on most issues. Still, the curve would surely have had a different shape. For in the rest of the country outside of Massachusetts, especially in Oklahoma, but also in California, the tilt of opinion, compared with middle-class tolerance on other issues, leans firmly against the idea of teaching respect for homosexuality in public schools.

The coding scheme I developed to classify opinion on questions involving homosexuality was designed to distinguish between "positive" and "negative" tolerance. Easiest to classify were those who believed that because homosexuality was a sin or was unnatural, schools should avoid teaching about homosexuality entirely; such condemnatory attitudes usually were expressed unambiguously. Somewhat harder to classify were those who did believe that schools had an obligation to teach about homosexuality but who differed in their reasoning. Nonetheless, there were two relatively distinct ways of arguing in favor of teaching about gays in the schools that emerged from our interviews. Some respondents have already made clear, on the "negative" grounds of toleration, that they were not necessarily condoning homosexuality, but felt that we ought to teach respect for gay people because all people deserve respect. Others argued on more "positive" grounds. On the one hand, gay people have experienced discrimination, so we should go out of our way to treat them with dignity; on the other, they may, because they have had different experiences from most of us, have something important to say to which we need to listen.

Once our respondents were divided into these three categories, the middle category—tolerance without condoning—was, as is true of all bell-curve distributions, larger than those who condemned gays on the one hand and those who sought their positive acceptance on the other. But, in this case, the distribution of opinion on the ends of the bell curve is not even close to being equal: nearly three times as many respondents condemned homosexuality as accepted it. For those who admire tolerance, the good news in these data is the still relatively large number of people who take a nonjudgmental position on homosexuality. But for those who believe that right and wrong still exist—and that homosexuality is wrong—there is also good news. The best that can be said is that support for public acceptance of homosexuality is negative rather than positive, rooted

TABLE 2.4
POSITIONS ON TEACHING RESPECT FOR HOMOSEXUALS

	Teach Positively	Tolerate	Condemn	Insufficient Information
Broken Arrow	0	10	13	2
Sand Springs	3	12	6	4
DeKalb	6	14	5	0
Cobb	3	18	4	0
Eastlake	2	14	2	7
Rancho Bernardo	1	10	12	2
Total	15	78	42	15

more in a liberatarian appreciation of privacy than in active acceptance of homosexuality per se.

Not only is the shape of the bell curve different on this issue, but, just as significantly, the intensity of opinion on this question was quite different from discussions about most other subjects: those who opposed teaching about homosexuality expressed their views in a very determined manner. Many were clearly made uncomfortable by the topic and did not want to speak about it; one flat-out refused to discuss the subject, while others responded with nervous laughter, confusion, or expressions of pity. A large number of our respondents, while reluctant to condemn people of a different faith or even atheists, had little trouble condemning gays. Among the characterizations of homosexuality that popped up in our interviews were: "abnormal," "immoral," "sinful," "unacceptable," "sick," "unhealthy," "untrustworthy," "mentally ill," "wrong," "perverted," and "mentally deficient." Both the size of the group willing to condemn homosexuality, and the vehemence with which they did so, indicated that here is indeed the ultimate test of American tolerance: the line separating gay America from straight America is a line that an unusually large number of middle-class Americans are unwilling to cross.

If so many people feel so strongly about the issue, how do they reconcile their rejection of homosexuality with their otherwise strong support for moral individualism? Our follow-up questions to the issue of teaching respect for homosexuality in public school shed some light on this. Because homosexuality is viewed by its opponents as a choice, it is, some of them believe, possible to reject the choice without rejecting the person who made it. "I hate homosexuality," said Herbert Almond, a black minister in Georgia, but "I love a homosexual. I don't hate him, I hate what he's doing." "God didn't ever say to hate people," added Jen Morgan, the conservative Christian from Cobb County. "He said to love everyone, so you love everyone but hate what they're doing. You can hate the sin but love the person." Gays, for whom sexual preference defines precisely that aspect of their identity that makes them different, would view such comments as hypocritical at best and would doubt the genuineness of the love being offered them. Would they be correct to do so? Yes, I think, they would; the tone and body language of many who spoke this way convinced me that it was intolerance, and not love, I was hearing. One might be tempted to admire those middle-class Americans who have not become so taken with inclusive tolerance that they are willing to pronounce definitive judgment on what others do, but one cannot also deny that, when they do so, they are, in effect, condemning the person and not just how he acts.

A second prominently asserted reason to oppose teaching respect for gay lifestyles in the schools had to do with the meaning of the word "respect." "You earn respect, you just don't get it," said Luis Garcia, a hairdresser in Eastlake. "You don't just get it because you're a homosexual. . . . I don't get it because I am a Mexican." For Winston Cobb in Rancho Bernardo, respect is reciprocal: you are entitled to get it if you are willing to give it, but homosexuals, by their very nature, do not give respect to the majority's sensibilities. George Slade of Cobb County believes that everyone should be treated with respect, but, he continues, gays are divisively asking for special rights: "I see it as the type of thing where . . . you're trying to force something on people rather than some other way of educating people." Just as he would oppose forcing people to believe in one religion—Mr. Slade is among those who dislikes the Christian Coalition—he would also oppose forcing anyone to show respect for a lifestyle of which they would otherwise disapprove. While arguments such as these were hardly models of tolerance, they at least represent an attempt to find a theoretical, primarily secular, justification for the position they are supporting. In that sense, they are open to counterargument, which is not true for those who claim to love the person but not the sin.

A third way of justifying opposition to public school teaching of respect for homosexuals involves making a distinction between personal rejection of same-sex orientations and an equally heartfelt rejection of extremism in defense of heterosexuality. Trent Tartt of Broken Arrow, who said he would protest in front of an abortion clinic but would never apply absolutist moral reasoning that condemned abortion under any and all circumstances, does not want his children exposed in school to ideas about gay people, but he is also afraid that such an attitude could lead to gay-bashing, the thought of which appalls him. Reflecting on his dilemma, he admits that he might be narrow as well as wrong; maybe, he muses, he ought to explain such things to his children. "But," he continues, "I don't think morally I am obligated to do that. What I am obligated to do is to teach them what the Bible teaches: 'A man and a woman will become as one and create God's gift.' "

In explaining the different rationales by which a number of middle-class Americans try to reconcile their belief in freedom with their condemnation of homosexuality, I am not suggesting that they share enough underlying moral precepts to imagine possible agreement. It is true that some of those who believe that homosexuality is a sin, like Mr. Tartt, say so, in the spirit of their moral sensibility, quietly, as if too vehement a condemnation of homosexuality would stigmatize too severely. But there is no doubting the matter: the question of homosexuality reveals two genuinely different moral camps in America, which disagree profoundly about the fundamental nature of what they are contesting.

At the opposite end of the spectrum from those who condemn homosexuality unambiguously are those who argued in favor of teaching respect for homosexuals in public school. Many of the reasons they offered were practical, based on the simple grounds that homosexuality is a fact of human life that cannot be ignored. As Mrs. Behzadi, the Iranian woman living in Broken Arrow, put it, "I mean, I'm not approving or disapproving any kind of lifestyle, but if I know my kid is going be taught that . . . there is this fact, there are homosexuals, there are bisexuals, they don't go away by not knowing about them." Others cited the existence of AIDS, which demands, if for no other reason than self-interest, that young people learn about how diseases are transmitted; large majorities in America support the idea of using sex education classes in schools to teach children how to avoid getting AIDS. In fact, according to polls, far more were in favor of teaching about AIDS than supported refusing children with AIDS from attending school or quarantining people with AIDS at home. For a small number of those with whom we talked, such support spilled over into teaching respect for those most at risk for getting the disease.

Because they tend to be deeply devout, African-Americans in Georgia ought not to be especially tolerant of gays, both because southern blacks are more likely to believe that homosexuality is wrong than southern whites (by 92 percent compared with 82 percent, according to one poll) and because there has long existed a history of condemnation of homosexuality by black preachers. That is not what I found. The middle-class blacks to whom we talked overwhelmingly understood gays as a group that, having suffered discrimination like them, was owed respect. "Black people are more sensitive to everybody because we know how it feels," Laurie Shepard said. "If you're going to teach heterosexual behavior, why not teach homosexual behavior?" added Anna Stevens's husband, Gerald. "I'm not homophobic at all," said Vaughn Hyde. "Schools are supposed to prepare. If that's the world we live in, prepare your children." "If you're gonna respect someone or disrespect someone because of their sexual orientation," asked Todd Smith, "where does it end? Next, you can disrespect someone because of the color of their skin or the way they walk." The strongest statement—and the most surprising, given that he is a Baptist minister—came from Martin Wolcott:

> Well. I'm a preacher. My wife's a teacher. So we've taught our children to respect other people. Of course, if a person is a homosexual, it doesn't mean you have to be a homosexual, but you owe it to show respect to that person. . . . I've had some very close friends that were homosexuals. I cherish their friendship. I know they're homosexuals . . . I don't preach to them about it.

Not all the African-Americans in Atlanta were quite as accepting of homosexuality, but only a very few were condemning. Their views were remarkably like two other groups in

America especially sensitive to discrimination: Hispanics in Eastlake, who, despite a culture presumably stressing machismo, nonetheless found parallels between discrimination they had experienced and discrimination gays had experienced; and Jews, who also tended to support gay rights on the grounds of past discrimination.

Views such as these represent something of a minority position on the question of homosexuality, but they do exist. The question is whether they will remain a minority position. At the present time, Americans strongly oppose the right of gays to marry: 65 percent are against it to one degree or another, while only 28 percent support the idea. Yet, one could imagine a situation in which, like the once controversial issue of miscegenation, such opposition will also wane over time on the grounds that any marriage is better than no marriage at all. On the other hand, it could also turn out to be the case that the line drawn over homosexuality will be dug even deeper; fed up with cultural relativism, Americans may well conclude that if the distinction between right and wrong is to be applied anywhere, it should be applied here. Some differences cannot be talked out. This may well be one of them.

CAPACIOUS INDIVIDUALISM

When it comes to matters of religious faith, a libertarian stand in American thought is likely to guarantee that a strong believer like Jim McLaughlin will be keeping his beliefs to himself and will not have much success insisting that they apply as well to others. But if America avoids the problem of coercing belief, does it open itself up to the problem of believing nothing, or at least nothing worthwhile?

It certainly has not escaped the attention of conservative writers that although Americans say they are religious, they tend not to be religious in a deeply devout way. American religion, in their view, has lost all the important things religion can offer: a sense of the tragic, wonder in the face of powers higher than human beings, necessary constraints on hedonism. Faced with a choice between submission to a power outside (and greater than) themselves and a focus on their own particular needs, American individualism guarantees that the former will rarely triumph over the latter. In one sense, such critics are correct: middle-class Americans are very individualistic in outlook. When we talked to her in the Eastlake coffee shop, Jesse O'Donnell gave us a reason for discomfort with public discussions of religion. For her, religion is ultimately an individual experience. To be sure, faith in God "gives you a guideline, you know a foundation to start off with," she said. But it is not God who tells us what is right and wrong, but we ourselves. "It's just right to do certain things," Mrs. O'Donnell affirms. "You know in your gut that something is wrong, so you have to listen to what's inside."

So deep-rooted is religious individualism in America that it led a number of our respondents to make sharp distinctions between their religion and their morality. When I included a question in our interviews about the relationship between morality and religion, I assumed that most people would equate the two. To my surprise, I found that a significant number did not. "I consider myself a moral person. I don't consider myself religious," said Marion Kates of Eastlake. "Having morals can exist without believing in God," was the way Maria Kowalski of Brookline made the same point. "One doesn't need a religious structure in order to have morality," as Joseph Palumbo of Medford put it: "There are loads of behavior which are mutually beneficial which we would call moral. It is not good if we go around murdering each other over cutting each other off at a red light or something like that."

"I think morality is a kind of personal decency you have about you," added Ms. Sinclair of Sand Springs. "I think it's kind of more personal as to whether you can respect yourself." Americans are not comfortable being told what to do, even if, perhaps especially if, the teller is a supernatural force whose words are meant as commands.

It is this strong strain of individualism that helps explain why, as religious as Americans are, they also distrust organized religion: in 1990, as few as 23 percent of the American population expressed a great deal of confidence in religious institutions. The notion that Americans would be more comfortable living next to blacks than to religious sectarians is not just an apocryphal story; a 1987 Gallup poll discovered that 44 percent of Americans were hostile to the idea of a religious sectarian living next door compared with 13 percent who said blacks. We found similar sentiments; one of our survey questions stated that "there is such a thing as being too religious," and we found, again to my surprise, overwhelming support for that proposition. A situation in which every individual finds their own way to God is one that a large number of Americans find more comfortable than one in which highly organized institutions fight with each other both for members and for truth.

Americans, it has been said, like marriage so much that they constantly get divorced so that they can do it again. Much the

TABLE 2.5
"THERE IS SUCH A THING AS BEING TOO RELIGIOUS"

	Strongly Agree	Agree	No Opinion	Disagree	Strongly Disagree
Brookline	6	13	0	4	2
Medford	8	15	0	2	0
Broken Arrow	2	19	1	3	0
Sand Springs	7	17	1	0	0
DeKalb	3	13	0	8	1
Cobb	2	16	2	1	4
Eastlake	5	15	2	2	1
Rancho Bernardo	4	15	4	2	0
Total	37	123	10	22	8

same applies to their attitudes toward churches: they appreciate them to the point of constantly quitting one and joining another. "In today's society," Adam Grant of Sand Springs told us, "you know, you can go shopping; you can find anything you want out there. You can find anything that fits your beliefs and how you've come to interpret certain things." What's your religious affiliation? we asked Iris Schneider of nearby Broken Arrow. "We've gone to Catholic churches, Lutheran churches—my husband went to a Methodist church. Went to a Church of Christ in St. Louis, which is nothing like the Church of Christ down here. And we know a lot of Baptist people, a lot of Jewish people." No wonder that Rhema, the megachurch in Broken Arrow, which dominated Iris Schneider's area, provides such wonderful day care centers and soccer leagues; without them, it might lose the competition for parishoners. As a sociologist, I am not a great fan of "rational choice theory," the notion that human beings make decisions based on calculations of self-interest. As middle-class Americans talked, not about their faith, but about their churches as institutions, I came to believe that rational choice theory was a good way of understanding which ones they joined and which ones they left. Americans are free-agent churchgoers. As they do with marriages and with jobs, they leave situations that they find uncomfortable for ones that promise more happiness. When it comes to religious affiliations, short-term contracts are better.

One reason religion is seen by so many people in individual terms has to do with personal experiences of religious sectarianism. Pedro Govea, a Catholic, while dating his wife, went to a Baptist meeting with her only to hear it turn into an attack on Catholicism. Joanna Cage, an accountant in Broken Arrow, attended a number of different churches and was repelled by their sectarianism before finding one that made her and her husband comfortable. Rancho Bernardo's Henry Carter grew up as an active Methodist, joined the Army, discovered how sectarian Protestants could be, and doesn't consider himself very religious any longer. A common *rite de passage* among middle-class Americans brought up Catholic is to relate a story about how the strictness of the church eventually caused them to leave it, or at least to tone down their allegiance. There is a widespread feeling in middle-class America that religious belief, which is personal, is more important than religious affiliation, which is organizational. It is churches and sects, not people, that cause discord. By getting around the churches in the middle, individuals and God can come to know each other better. But before concluding that Americans are so committed to individualism that they lack genuine faith, it is important to understand what they remain faithful toward.

A generation ago, Will Herberg wrote that Americans put their faith in faith. Now it would be more correct to say that they put their faith in people. A deep-seated belief in people's goodness enables middle-class Americans to accept the principle that people should be free to choose their God, or even not to choose God at all, without worrying that the consequence will be anarchy, for good people will always make the right kinds of choices. Americans are not dissatisfied with the moral fiber of their fellow Americans. Is this country becoming Godless? we asked our respondents, and they overwhelmingly replied that it was not. Relatively few Americans think that the world is filled with evil and sin compared to those who believe that, as the General Social Survey phrases one of its questions, "there is much goodness in the world which hints at God's greatness." America, its citizens believe, is too good a place, and the people who live here too good a people, for jeremiads to have all that much credibility.

"Religion is a big, binding thing," we were told by Samina Hoque, a physicist in Medford from Bangladesh. "Good religions, you know, not the cult thing. Good religions teach you how to care for each other, how to have faith in life, faith in things . . . and be happy with what you have." If people are reasonable, the existence of many competing religions need not be an obstacle to finding a common morality, many of those with whom we spoke believe, and can even be an advantage. "I don't think we're all gonna read out of the same Bible," says Joyce Umber of Broken Arrow, "and I don't think we're all gonna read the same things if we did. I think there's good people and I think we are all striving for the same place. And I'm not gonna say that their religion is wrong because they might hate my religion." Compared with religious absolutists like Jim McLaughlin, who fears that without one true faith moral anarchy is inevitable, believers in quiet faith are convinced that liberal democracies must make room for people of faith, but must also insure that such room is never so confining that it excludes people of different faiths.

If the American belief in individualism were focused only on the self, there would be reason to fear that the separation of religion from one God, and then the separation of morality from religion, would lead to a situation of moral anarchy. But when Americans talk about their faith, their individualism is meant, not only for themselves, but also for others; the individualism that guides their beliefs is a capacious one meant to apply to all. Religious individualism as they understand it is a compromise position between immoral selfishness and coercive conformity; a selfish person cannot be religious, while a believer in religious absolutism cannot be individualistic. That is why it can even include people who have no religious beliefs, so long as all of them share the same faith that others can be trusted to do the right thing.

"The way I like to picture things," Judy Dropkin of Eastlake, a volunteer coordinator, summed up, "is that God is at the top of a mountain and there's a whole lot of sides to him and there are a whole lot of roads to the top. I think we all struggle to get there, and you got to find your own way." Bostonians use a different metaphor; one compared religious diversity to a rotary—everyone else in America calls them traffic circles—that different drivers enter and leave at different points. The fact that so many Americans, when searching for metaphors to discuss religion and morality, turn to transportation—wheels, highways, roads up a mountain, traffic circles—suggests that, like good liberals, they are always going somewhere but also that, like good communitarians, they expect to arrive at a destination.

In the years after World War II, critics worried that Americans were not religious enough. Then, convinced that a new religious revival was taking place in America, other critics began to believe that Americans were becoming too religious, suppressing, in turn, the rights of non-Christians and nonbelievers. And critics from all sides of the debate understand that there will always be conflicts between the liberal-democratic commitments that govern public life and the need for the faith that enriches private life. None of the questions raised by any of these critics is easy to answer. But because the first person cited in this chapter shall be the last, let me once again offer the views of Jesse O'Donnell:

> My general belief is that people are inherently good and they can make the right decisions based on what's right and what's wrong, not necessarily because that's what their religion taught them. If you don't have religion, there's still right and wrong. I think religion gives you the hope that no matter how bad things get, something is always there to make it better and that there's a reason for things. I think you almost have to believe that there's a higher [power].

As the country tries to negotiate its way through the question of the right public role for religion, people like Mrs. O'Donnell, who organize their thoughts around quiet faith, are likely to help us find if not the right answers in some ultimate sense, then answers we can live with for the here and now.

III THE CULTURE WAR WITHIN

Katherine Mullins lives in a fairly expensive subdivision of Broken Arrow, a suburb of Tulsa, Oklahoma. Besides space, proximity to an airport is an important factor in where she chooses to live; she works for a company in Atlanta, having negotiated a deal in which, since she was going to be traveling most of the week, she could work out of her home. (Her husband, who is in the air-conditioning business, also travels frequently in his work.) Although she never went to college, and has no particular desire to send her sixteen- and eighteen-year-old sons to college either, Mrs. Mullins has had great success in the business world. Her income is considerable, her responsibilities great. Talking with her, one senses exactly why she has done so well. She is articulate, determined, opinionated, feisty, and, most of all, likable.

"You know, it's tough," she explains about her decision to pursue a career. "I know in Tulsa—I can't think of any friends or acquaintances that I know that both members of the family don't work full-time jobs." In recent years, according to her, downsizing has made it even tougher: "You did one job a year ago, now you do the job for three people." It's not nine-to-five anymore, especially for someone at her vice presidential level. Asked whether it was a hard decision for her to spend so much time at her job, she responds primarily in economic terms: "No, it was not. I had to do what I had to do to continue to make the money I needed to help support this family." As she shows off her comfortable and well-furnished home, she takes pride in herself as well as her family; look, she seems to be saying, if it were not for *my* income, we would not be living nearly as well as we do.

Still, it would be incorrect to view economics as the only reason Mrs. Mullins chooses to work. After all, she was once a child and, like most children, thought a great deal about the moral choices made by her own parents:

> My mother never worked, the whole time.... And quite frankly, until I was a teenager, [I led] pretty much a sheltered life, because Mother was always there and she was involved in everything. I don't necessarily think that's a good idea. I think it's better that the parents do work, and the kids have an opportunity to experience other people in life and situations, so when they grow up, it's not so tough. I've seen that, I've been there, I've done that.... So I disagree totally with the staying at home. I really do personally.

Clearly, Mrs. Mullins has been influenced by the social changes of the past thirty years, especially those that go under the heading of "feminism." Unlike her mother, she had a choice about what to do with her life; given her personality and ambition, it was not a hard one to make. She was born to be a career woman and knows full well that if, by force of tradition, she were not allowed that option, she would never have been comfortable in her own skin.

If Mrs. Mullins can be viewed as part of the world that feminism helped define, however, she is also anything but a feminist. Not a shred of bleeding-heart liberalism exists in Katherine Mullins's outlook on the world; whether the subject is crime in the inner city or welfare, she responds in a world-weary, it's-a-tough-world-out-there kind of tone. On economic matters in particular, it is not the women's movement that defines her outlook, but the conservative firebrands within the Republican Party. Mrs. Mullins worked for a Houston energy company in the late 1970s and had to lay off forty people before the company went bankrupt and she found herself out of a job. "Got a U-Haul truck, drove back to Tulsa," she continues. "Had no place to live, had about five bucks in our pocket." As Mrs. Mullins tells it, she and her husband did yard work and scraped by—no welfare for them—before things finally improved. In her view, it's all a question of attitude: you have it or you don't, and, luckily, she has it. Were Mrs. Mullins a man, everything she says about success, hard work, and rewards would sound like classic American entrepreneurialism; the only thing that makes her language even a bit unusual is her gender, not her words. Here is an American who believes that if government would just get out of the way, America would come to respect merit and individual initiative far more than it currently does. Katherine Mullins speaks in the language of classic American libertarianism.

And how does a libertarian raise her children? Conservatives, who would presumably like what Katherine Mullins has to say about the economy and personal responsibility, would not be pleased to hear what she has to say about family values or religion. For Mrs. Mullins, work comes first and family after: "When there's a job to be done, you don't get just to quit at five because you think you've got to come home to help the kids or bathe," she asserts with some finality. "The kids would have to understand that's what it's all about, and that working just a little harder gets you something just a little more."

"Did you ever think of quitting because you were not paying them enough time?" I ask her.

"No, absolutely not. No," she responds.

"Well, what about coming home a bit early from time to time to make dinner?"

"Absolutely not."

"And your husband? Does he support you in your decisions?"

"Like he has a choice," she laughs.

Since she believes that communication is very important, Mrs. Mullins stays in touch with her kids through a pager. But it has not been easy. Her youngest son is hyperactive and has had difficulties in school, where they have had to make special arrangements for him. But not even this comment is made in a way that indicates any doubt or insecurity about her priorities as she understands them. When you come home from work, no matter how exhausted you might be, you just have to do the best you can. That's the way the world is, and, although Mrs. Mullins does not reflect directly on this, it is clear that from her point of view this is the way it ought to be.

Mrs. Mullins's views on religion also might make conservatives uncomfortable. Mrs. Mullins is one of those who, while not condoning homosexuality, also believes that it is no one's business what anyone does in private. When we asked her about matters of faith, she proved herself quite skeptical, if not downright distrustful, of any kind of organized religion: "I don't like structured, organized religion. I think that it's an incredible waste of money that we build these churches and pay for . . . preachers and . . . priests who drive better cars than I ever thought of driving, live better than I ever thought of living, you know, belong to country clubs and golf clubs," she said. Religion, in her view, is a personal thing and any public display of its features bothers her:

> I'm very saddened that . . . people think that you have to leave your home and go to another place that you're helping to pay for the electricity, the gas, and that guy's salary to have a spiritual experience that should start in the heart and not because you all come together in a group. And some of the biggest bigots I know are just so incredibly into religion; . . . all of that just kind of just sickens me, too.

"I think you really have to believe in yourself strongly," concluded Mrs. Mullins, reflecting her deeply libertarian outlook on the world. People who believe in God instead strike her as "emotionally weak."

Mrs. Mullins's choices and beliefs illustrate a great deal of what is happening in America in the area of family matters. Of all the human groups to which modern people belong, none is more important than the family. To the degree that people give of themselves for others, the others to whom they make their offering are either loved ones chosen by themselves or those to whom they are tied by near mystical forces of blood and belonging. Families, which connect us to the past and the future, are societies in miniature. As alienated as Americans may be from politics, they tend to have high hopes for the family, or at least for their own; well over 60 percent of Americans routinely say that they are "very happy" with their marriages and over 70 percent think that being married is better than being single. Roughly similar percentages find their roles as husbands and wives satisfying, and the proportion of those who believe that married people are happier than unmarried people is in the same range. Yet, with the possible exception of the church, no other institution has faced such intense criticism and nonetheless emerged in still-recognizable form as the modern family.

When those who write about family matters turn to this institution, which has engaged the best philosophers of the Western moral tradition since Aristotle, they seem to have no better language with which to express their disagreements than that of television. Two popular situation comedies, one from yesterday and one from today, define the American debate over family values. On the one hand, there is *Ozzie and Harriet*, praised by defenders of the traditional family as the way things ought to be, condemned by others as unreal, hypocritical, and unrecognizable as a model for how adults and children should and do relate to each other under conditions of uncertainty and ambiguity. On the other hand, there is *Murphy Brown*, lambasted, with counterproductive results, by a vice president of the United States and upheld by his critics as a refreshing look at how families actually are in this "postmodern" age. Even when social scientists mobilize data and arguments around the question of whether the modern family is in decline, images of these two television programs lie behind the numbers and the theories.

The questions in the debate about the family are clear enough: Should women seek careers as well as men? How many children represent the ideal number? Are two parents necessary for the happiness and success of the children? Indeed, which is more important: happiness or success? Should parents who are unhappy with each other stay together for the sake of the children? How much does divorce constitute a social problem or is it the price we must pay for women's autonomy and freedom? Are the best interests of the children still the appropriate question in determining custody? Who is hurt more by divorce: men, women, or children? Should we make divorce harder to obtain? Has marriage lost its symbolic and ritualistic meaning? How important is religion in the upbringing of children? What faith should children be taught if their parents are of different religions? Does geographic and occupational mobility encourage freedom or destroy the bonds necessary for extended families? As passionate as the debates over such questions still are, surrounding them is a sense that the horse has already been stolen; economic and political transformations already had produced new family forms in post–World War II America before intellectuals and policy analysts were able to assess their consequences.

Nevertheless, contentious debate about the family is part and parcel of American political life these days. One one side, if we listen to the left, stand religious conservatives, defenders of male privilege, upholders of discipline, and homophobes, while on the other, if we listen to the right, can be found radical feminists, secularists, misguided idealists, and cultural relativists. So familiar have these images become that they turn into caricatures: rural Mississippi versus urban Manhattan, the angry husband confronting the working wife, the hardworking family struggling to protect its children versus kids lost to the lure of drugs and sex. Where, one wonders, does Katherine Mullins fit into such images? Equally contemptuous of bleeding-heart liberals and conservative Christian preachers, Mrs. Mullins, who is never going to be an actor in a morality play written by someone else, wants to lead her life according to principles chosen by herself. If we are ever to break new ground in the moral debate taking place over family values in the United States, it will be by hearing from those—not only Mrs. Mullins, but others who made very different choices from hers—who are trying to find their own ways to be faithful both to themselves and to others.

FAMILY OPTIONS

Katherine Mullins spends less time with her kids so that she can spend more time on her career. The Middle Class Morality Project also found a number of men who are spending less time on their careers so that they could spend more time with their kids—a potentially significant development if, as has recently been asserted, fatherhood is central to the raising of children. Pedro Govea, a forty-nine-year-old second-generation Cuban, has an M.D. degree and a doctorate in biochemistry. Living in Brookline in close proximity to the largest concentration of scientific and medical institutions anywhere in the world, Dr. Govea, who at the time of our interview held a fellowship in hematology at one of the prestigious medical schools in the Boston area, would seem to be the kind of person for whom success and recognition would be driving forces in his moral accounting. Although ostensibly a member of the cognitive elite, Dr. Govea is close enough to his upbringing in a more traditional environment—his Cuban-born mother lives part of the year with him, his wife, and their three young children—to worry about the effects of modernity on the family. Just before we interviewed him, Dr. Govea had read an article in the *Atlantic Monthly* entitled "Dan Quayle Was Right," and its themes resonated with him. For Dr. Govea wants to do the right thing, and, for him, the right thing means sacrificing in work to spend more time at home.

"You have to make choices in this world," says Dr. Govea, sounding very much like Katherine Mullins. "You have to decide what is the ultimate goal." His goal, however, is the opposite of hers. "Whereas some of my single colleagues are still

working at the hospital or working in the laboratory on research, I come home instead of doing the extra experiment. And
I think it does have some detrimental effect on what academia
and the 'type A personality' . . . looks at. . . . Well, that's life, I
guess. You know, I've made that choice." Dr. Govea's values extend in two directions, for he laments not only the lack of time
most parents spend with their children, but also the time they do
not spend with their own parents, which seems to him so different from what he hears about the old country. "I get the impression from a lot of my senior patients that they get the feeling
that their offspring don't appreciate them and their value," he
tells us, which strikes him as not only inhumane, but also as bad
from a medical point of view. Fortunately for Dr. Govea, his
choice of career enables him to find that balance, even if the
price is an income far lower than the ones commanded by his
"type A" colleagues. If he has any regrets about this, they do not
show. Pedro Govea simply knows what is important to him and
organizes his life accordingly.

Not everyone has Dr. Govea's choices, of course; some men
to whom we talked stayed home with the kids because they had
lost their jobs, in many cases while their wives continued to
work. The economic insecurity captured in the word "downsizing" has caused tremendous amounts of worry for many
Americans, yet few have written about the other side of the coin,
especially the way in which unemployment forces so many men
to get to know their children. J. W. Cotton had worked for a defense contractor in the Tulsa area for twelve years before being
laid off in response to cuts in the defense budget. Mr. Cotton,
thirty-nine, has experienced what sociologist Judith Stacey calls
"recombinant families." His mother divorced at an early age,
and Mr. Cotton found his stepfather, a truck driver, a phantom
presence in his life: "He'd come in, deposit the money, say,
'Gotta go; see ya,' and off he'd go." In his own life, Mr. Cotton
has a grown child from an earlier liaison and currently lives with
his wife and ten-month-old baby. "That's one thing about [de-
fense contractor] closing," he emphasizes. "I've been able to

spend a whole year with my son of his life . . . I love it, I love it.
I love it. He's my one, he's the most, best asset I've got." As uncomfortable with feminist language as Katherine Mullins, Mr.
Cotton is not completely thrilled that his wife works outside of
the house; he wishes she could work from home. But there's
little doubt in his mind that it would be wrong for both parents
to work full-time at the expense of the children. One of the parents ought to stay home, and, if it has to be him, then he is going
to make the most of it.

In raising the examples of Pedro Govea and J. W. Cotton,
and in contrasting them with Katherine Mullins, I am not making the point that there is a major reversal of gender roles taking
place in the United States. It is certainly true that in the United
States, the public, both men and women, have accepted the fact
that women are now full-time in the labor force. Of those surveyed by the GSS in 1988, 49.5 percent agreed with the statement that "having a job is the best way for a woman to be an
independent person," compared with the 31.5 percent who disagreed. In addition, the Post-Modernity Project's survey on
American values indicated that 90 percent of Americans believed
that "the changes in the role of women in society" are good or
mostly good compared with 9 percent, who thought they were
bad or mostly bad. Such attitudes have produced changes
worldwide that have profoundly altered the ways in which
people live. Still, for every woman who was as committed to her
career as Mrs. Mullins, there were others in our sample who resolved pressures between work and family more in favor of their
families, just as far more men held views about the need to provide for the family that were more traditional than Dr. Govea's
and Mr. Cotton's. The views of these three individuals are important for another reason: they underscore the degree to which
decisions about how to raise families are the result of strategic
picking between various available options.

In order to discuss those options, it is important to distinguish between the kinds of families in which people actually live
and the kinds in which they ought to live. Because the Middle
Class Morality Project interviewed in suburbs, which are gener-

TABLE 3.1
FAMILY CHARACTERISTICS
MIDDLE CLASS MORALITY PROJECT

Marital Status		Children	
Married	153	No children	43
Single	19	1 child	38
Divorced (not remarried)	19	2 children	65
Separated	2	3 children	32
Widowed	7	4 or more children	22
Total	200	Total	200

ally viewed as family-friendly places, it should come as no surprise that a little more than two-thirds of our respondents were married at the time we interviewed them. Three-quarters of them, moreover, had children; slightly more than 10 percent of them had four or more children. Although we did not ask our respondents questions about their own sexual preferences, two of them—one explicitly, the other implicitly—told us they were gay. In their actual family choices, in other words, the respondents to the Middle Class Morality Project were relatively conventional.

Whatever kinds of families people live in themselves, America's debate over the family involves public rather than private questions. Both those who defend conventional families and those who seek alternatives to them are concerned with the moral question of how people *should* live, not just the empirical question of how they actually *do* live. It does not follow that because people might live in conventional families themselves, they would conclude that everyone else should as well. I wanted to know what our respondents thought about the larger public debate taking place over family values in the United States. When I coded their responses, one position became clear very quickly: those who can be described as *traditionalists*, convinced of the goodness of nuclear family they associate with simpler times, wary of the changes that have taken place since, and persuaded that as many people as possible ought to be encouraged to return to it.

Forty-three of the two hundred people with whom we spoke could be classified as traditionalists (see table 3.2). The history of what happened to the traditional family was succinctly narrated by an insurance accounts representative in Sand Springs, Oklahoma: "Women got liberated, and the men quit respecting them. Boom, 'bye went the family." With more seriousness, Adam Grant, also of Sand Springs, a graduate of the U.S. Naval Academy working as a quality control consultant, believes that our society is far too materialistic, so when women work to gain extra income, too often the money is used to buy a boat or a bigger house—unnecessary luxuries, when he thinks about it, that add little to the quality of family life. Nor, in his view, does America, for all its talk, really respect the family:

> Quayle spoke up for family values; look what happened to him. So I think we talk a good story, but we don't live it. Now, naturally, I'm gonna have a little stronger moral fiber, being a Christian, and [believing in] right and wrong. And this "Do what you want to do, don't bother anybody else and it's okay," I mean, that doesn't cut it.

Divorce, single parents—these are what follow when Americans put their selfish needs first, in Mr. Grant's opinion. The result is a kind of relativism he finds chilling: "So the family unit, mother, father, children; no, I don't think that unit is valued any more today than the single parent."

Adam Grant's themes echoed throughout a number of the interviews we conducted. Jen Morgan, the conservative Christian who had strong views on questions of separation of church and state, was especially upset by efforts of homosexuals to claim family values:

Now society wants us to think that two women are just as qualified to raise children, or two men are just as qualified to raise children. All of the . . . wrong morals that go along with that sort of a lifestyle and all . . . because of that, the whole definition of the family is changing. . . . It all is breaking the family down, because God wanted it to be man and woman raising a family. He must have had a reason for that.

Henry Pearson, who once taught history at a major midwestern university but now works as a risk management specialist in San Diego, told us: "It's so much a matter of . . . to use the current coin of the realm phrase, shifting the paradigm. Well, we've shifted the paradigm all right." He continued:

And we've shifted society right into the trash can along with it. The simple truth of the matter is this: commitment today is transitory. . . . When it is convenient for us to be committed we are to another person. When it becomes inconvenient . . . the other person gets dumped along the way. I'm gonna get in trouble for this, but families work when there's a way to make sure that children, particularly until they're ten or eleven or twelve years old, are well cared for, are well directed, and are the prime focus of the family as a social unit. That doesn't happen when both parents work sixty-five hours a week.

Others felt the same way. "I think we're catering a lot to . . . nontraditional families," added Julie Skinner, the Mormon mother of six living in Medford, Massachusetts. "I'd like to see people saying that it's important that men and women marry before they have children, and raise their children, and treat them well and do the best that you can for them. Just the basics . . . you know? . . . I think it's important that the mother be at home when the children are young."

By the very nature of their views, people like these would not see their attachments to traditional values as a choice: for them, God created a preferred family form and those who live

TABLE 3.2
ATTITUDES TOWARD THE FAMILY

	Traditional	Post-Modern	Realist	Ambivalent	Insufficient Information
Brookline	4	2	6	11	2
Medford	6	1	2	15	1
Broken Arrow	5	0	3	12	5
Sand Springs	7	1	2	14	1
DeKalb	5	0	7	9	4
Cobb	5	0	8	6	6
Eastlake	4	0	5	14	2
Rancho Bernardo	7	0	4	9	5
Total	43	4	37	90	26

by its rules no more choose to do so than they choose to believe that God exists. Still, what was once the common pattern is increasingly becoming the exception; even though the Middle Class Morality Project interviewed only in the suburbs, where we presume that there are more women who want to stay home with their children, less than one-quarter of those with whom we spoke were traditional in their family outlook. On few other issues in America has public opinion experienced so profound a shift over so short at a time as over the acceptance of new family forms.

Diametrically opposed to traditionalists are *postmodernists*, a kind of family form whose emergence has been announced, sometimes with enthusiasm and sometimes with an air of inevitability, by feminist writers. As a result of a simultaneous collapse of the economy and the culture, the postmodern family form is ruled by an absence of rules: both spouses go in and out of the labor market; children are not necessarily the biological offspring of the adults with whom they live; sexual preference is polymorphous; and extended kin are not necessarily related by blood. According to their advocates, postmodern relationships in the family, especially contrasted with traditional ones, bring positive benefits to individuals: women are freer because they work, gays are treated with respect because their sexual preferences are acknowledged, and children are not punished because their unhappy parents mistakenly stay together for their sake.

The Middle Class Morality Project uncovered only four individuals who would advocate something like the postmodern vision of the family—and three of them lived around Boston. Alexandra Onafri, a Brookline resident who is a physical plant director at one of the universities in the Boston area, believes that families are the best venue for raising children, but, she continues, "I don't know that we've defined what family structure really means. You know, what is a family? Family is, you know, more than one person living together and what it entails." A committed feminist, Ms. Onafri believes that too much talk of strong families is an excuse for getting women back into the home. And would society be better off for that? Not at all, in her opinion. After all, active women not only work for a wage, but they also donate their services to the community: "Volunteer organizations were responsible for achieving an awful lot in the 1950s and 1960s and even the 1970s," Ms. Onafri points out. "And, you know, a tremendous amount of work was accomplished by spouses and women who were at home and who had a lot to offer, and were offering it in the nonpaying, nonprofit sector."

Robert Smithson, a minister in one of Brookline's more liberal churches, voices similar views. "I think the social order no longer has the ability to dictate what shall and shall not happen. . . . And parents are in some way caught in between," he says. "They are both expected to pick up the slack and also are the ones screaming that somebody has got to pick it up. Presumably other than themselves. So I see everybody under stress at this point on this one. And almost nobody is taking the larger responsibility for the public order." Finally, Susan Medina, a Medford interior designer, thought very much along the same lines: "I think if women can stop hanging on to the guilt of leaving their children to child care, I think that children can develop—I think for the most part, they may get brought up more professionally than they would at home—because, again, professionally, those people have been trained."

Not only is the postmodern family form an extreme minority taste, its affinity with a city like Boston suggests that it may be one of those phenomena more popular on the coasts than in the heartland. Our survey questions dealing with single-parent families and gay marriage confirm the notion that those who have the strongest sympathy for nontraditional marriages are concentrated in particular places in America: no one strongly supported the rights of gays to marry in Georgia and California, for example, and only four did in Oklahoma. Similar results were found on the question of single-parent families, modified by the support for such families given by a number of African-Americans in DeKalb County.

The relative unpopularity of an "anything goes" approach to family life discovered by the Middle Class Morality Project is in accord with national survey data. Most polls show that a taste

TABLE 3.3
"PEOPLE OF THE SAME SEX SHOULD BE ALLOWED TO MARRY"

	Strongly Agree	Agree	No Opinion	Disagree	Strongly Disagree
Brookline	5	10	4	4	2
Medford	3	11	4	4	3
Broken Arrow	2	5	1	5	12
Sand Springs	2	4	4	6	9
DeKalb	0	5	5	6	9
Cobb	0	9	4	7	5
Eastlake	0	10	3	7	5
Rancho Bernardo	0	7	4	3	11
Total	12	61	29	42	56

for individual choices in family life is by and large confined to questions of working women and acceptance of divorce, but does not include the view that any family form is as good as any other. Here is an area in which Americans like to make distinctions: over 80 percent of the American population, according to the Roper Organization, recognizes an unwed or divorced mother living with children as a family, but only between 20 percent and 30 percent recognize gay couples with children or unrelated adults as a family. And even if single-parent families are considered families, they are not considered particularly good ones: 49.5 percent of GSS respondents disagreed that single parents can raise kids as well as two parents together compared with 36.1 percent who agreed. As they do on so many other issues, Americans split the difference on the question of the family: women should work, but not anything goes.

Perhaps the most important conclusion to be reached with respect to the question of the ideal family is that when we add the number of traditionalists and the number of postmodernists

TABLE 3.4
"FAMILIES WITHOUT FATHERS ARE JUST AS
GOOD AS ANY OTHER KIND OF FAMILY."

	Strongly Agree	Agree	No Opinion	Disagree	Strongly Disagree
Brookline	4	10	3	7	1
Medford	3	5	2	10	5
Broken Arrow	2	10	1	5	7
Sand Springs	1	11	1	10	2
DeKalb	4	8	2	11	0
Cobb	0	9	1	9	6
Eastlake	2	8	2	11	2
Rancho Bernardo	2	6	1	10	6
Total	18	67	13	73	29

together, we shall have not reached 25 percent of our sample. Clearly, some other category is necessary to capture the essence of their views. I therefore added a third coding category, which can be called *realist*. These are individuals who may not be cheerleaders for a new, and decentered, form of family life, but who nonetheless feel that women ought to work and that access to divorce should be available when a marriage becomes unbearable, since both developments promote greater equality between the genders. The realist temperament is practical rather than ideological; instead of glorifying gay marriages or stepfamilies as a move away from the oppression of the nuclear family, people of this temperament acknowledge that changes have taken place in the family, and one simply has to adjust to them.

There are, as one might expect, people who conform to this definition in middle-class America, but once again their number is surprisingly small; only thirty-seven of our two hundred respondents were coded as realists. Interestingly enough, I found the largest number of them in the South. Among whites, Cobb County contained a number of men and women whose economically libertarian outlook, which supports the idea that women should work, overcame their conservative and Christian ideal that they should not. "If a mother can work full-time and have everything under control at home, more power to her," said Frances Warren, who herself did not work and thinks she would become "a basket case" if she did. "Women working—that doesn't always hurt the family," added George Slade. "Naturally, it's rough on the children," as Jeremy Toole put it. "But . . . I don't think that today's children notice any difference because their parents have always worked. . . . As society grows, women grow, life grows. . . . My wife wants to work. She's bored if she's just at home doing gardening."

In nearby DeKalb County, where most of our respondents were black, we heard very similar themes. "I don't think you should have to sacrifice," Jamie Willis said. "If you want a career, I think you should go after a career, but you've got to learn to juggle the two," she added with reference to bringing up a family. African-American middle-class families, often dominated by strong women or by the absence of a man, were generally organized with the sense that a-person-has-to-do-what-a-person-has-to-do to get by in the modern world. Indicative of this spirit was Vivian Teller, a forty-five-year-old woman living in DeKalb County, Georgia, who was in the process of obtaining a divorce when we talked with her. A mother of two, Ms. Teller had a strong opinion when asked whether, in the best of all possible worlds, women should stay home to raise their children:

> No, I would not like to see mothers . . . necessarily stay home more, because I find my work very fulfilling. I've been home. I stayed home for about five years, and it was great the first three. Those last two years were quite . . . they were awful. [Laughter.] I feel a lot better about myself now than I did then. I don't know. I think if somehow we can continue . . . in our careers and how somehow manage more quality time with our children . . . it would be a big help. That comes down to good time management. I found that, like myself, a lot of people are not good time managers.

Ms. Teller works as a nurse manager and has earned enough to send her teenage boy to a private school in the hopes of giving him a good start in life. Like many of the African-Americans to whom we spoke, she was a strong religious believer (Seventh-Day Adventist), but her faith in God, however important to her personally, could not in the final analysis determine her choices about marriage and work; economic realities did that, and Ms. Teller was determined to make the best of it.

Realists can be found in all sectors of American society and among men as well as women. "I think it's great that women are working and having a career. Personally, I would let my wife decide what she wanted to do. . . . I mean, I think it would be very hard to be at home all day. You just have to get out there," we were told by Robert Hertzo, a border patrol agent living in Eastlake, California. "If you have a woman who chooses to be in the workforce and really doesn't want to be at home with the kids ever, and participate any way in their lives, well, of course that's gonna hurt, but you can have a woman staying at home who approaches that in the exact same way. The issue of love and involvement . . . is, to me, the crucial family issue, not where the time is spent," added Bea Cohen, a Jewish liberal in Cobb County. Timmy Sands, a landscaping business owner in Sand Springs, Oklahoma, was equally as practical: "I don't think having the mother and father working is a real problem as long as they work it out to where they're able to spend time with their kids and take care of everything that needs to be taken care of at home. Like I said, my mother and father worked and I think I turned out okay. But they balanced it out. I was able to play sports, do what I wanted to, there was always somebody there."

For all their reliance on pragmatic themes, however, even when the number of realists are added to those of both a traditional and postmodern orientation, they still constituted only eighty-five out of the two hundred individuals with whom we talked. That is one way of expressing the point that the single largest category into which our respondents can be divided when it comes to family values is not really a category at all; nearly half of those with whom we spoke—ninety out of two hundred—were so divided between traditional and modern conceptions of the family that they can only be described as *ambivalents.* The most striking aspect of the way ambivalents responded to the questions we asked about family values was to express their simultaneous faith in positions that, at least in the way the public debate over the family frames the issue, are impossible to reconcile.

"I love to work," says Louise Duffey, a twenty-nine-year-old credit marketing vice president in Rancho Bernardo. "I do like to work," she repeats herself. Then she pauses: "I don't know if that's really true. I mean, yes, the quality of time is a lot more important than the quantity, but when a child knows that when they come home after school that their mom is gonna be there and it's a lot different than . . . when the mom comes home she's so frazzled, the dad's so frazzled that they scramble up for dinner and they sit down in front of the TV for an hour and it's bedtime." Mrs. Duffey is the mother of one, with another on the way. When the conversation turns to how she personally would resolve the dilemma, she is equally ambivalent. She thinks of herself as "career-oriented," would prefer to work part-time, feels that a lack of maternal supervision has affected society in a negative way, but has yet to quit her job or reduce her hours. As she wrestles with all the thoughts she has on the subject, it becomes clear that Louise Duffey's views simply do not fit the categories we generally use when we think about how families ought to be organized—or, to put the matter slightly more accurately, her views fit many of them.

Men felt this ambivalence as strongly as women. "Is this a problem?" asks Ronald Klaus, a downsized executive working as a self-employed stockbroker, to the question of women working. "Maybe it is. Is it wrong? No, it isn't." Karl Johnson, a retired construction foreman in Sand Springs, admitted to being old-fashioned on the question: "It's kind of nice to have Mom home and supper on the table." But his personal experience contradicts his preferences: "Of course, both my first wife and this wife, they both worked all the time and all five of those boys turned out well." Todd Smith feels that life would be more secure and the economy more healthy if women did not work, but the idea that women should stay home smacks of discrimination against them that, as an African-American, strikes him as unfair. Ambivalence—call it confusion if you want to—can be described as the default position for the American middle class; everything else being equal, people simply cannot make up their minds.

One possible response to this ambivalence is to suggest that middle-class Americans want incompatible things; their views about the family, by this account, are very much like their desire to see taxes reduced while their favorite governmental programs are expanded. If people were more attuned to tough choices, conservatives in particular suggest, they would understand that if they want women to work, they must accept family decline; whereas if they want to stop family decline, they will have to accept less of a role for working women. While Americans are quite adept in asserting seemingly contradictory beliefs with equal fervor, if one looks at the moral reasoning that undergirds ambivalent responses, the picture begins to look more consistent. Middle-class Americans, for all their uncertainty about the family, are nonetheless fairly certain about what moral principle should guide it: families should be organized to fit the needs of the individuals who compose them, rather than fitting the needs of individuals to some preestablished family structure. Given that there are many kinds of people and many kinds of families, the best way to fit the one to the other is to let people make those decisions that best fit themselves.

This notion that people ought to decide for themselves what kind of family form is appropriate for them emerged so persistently in our interviews that it can be illustrated through the respondents of one suburb. Asked what she thought about women who sacrificed their children for their careers, Mrs. Tartt of Broken Arrow, who sacrificed her career for her children, said this: "That's great. That's great for them." When it comes to herself, however, she made a different choice: "I did what was right for me and my family, my children." "It depends on the person," added her neighbor Stacey Williams. "I think everybody should evaluate what they think their capacities are." "You have to do cost-benefit," reflected Stephanie Proctor, an accountant. "I think it's all how you take care of your family," added Mr. Curry, a nearby neighbor. His thoughts were seconded by Mrs. Behzadi, born and raised in Iran: "I don't think it's necessarily just being home that qualifies you for being the best mom or having the best family values or standards. . . . I chose to stay home because I really do worry about my kids." Find out what kind of person you are and organize your family values accordingly: that is the advice these middle-class Americans would give to others.

The idea of putting the individual first and the family form second seemingly confirms the viewpoint of those critics who believe that Americans have become too focused on themselves to understand the need for commitment and loyalty essential to stable families. But before reaching that conclusion, a few caveats should be introduced.

For one thing, while Americans have embraced the idea that individuals must choose the kinds of families in which they will live, they have not done so enthusiastically. Arguing that two-career families are "happier, healthier, and better-off," Rosalind Barnett and Caryl Rivers describe situations in which both parents work in gushing terms. There are, of course, some middle-class Americans, such as Katherine Mullins, who made a decisive and unblinking choice in favor of her career, understanding that, as a result, her children would pretty much have to fend for themselves. But the very unambivalent nature of her reflections makes her position a minority one among our sample. For most others, ambivalence is an indication that Americans are reluctant choosers when it comes to the modern family. As much as they expect to make individual decisions about how to balance career and family, they did not necessarily want to have that choice; changing circumstances, matters over which they have little control, such as the need for two incomes, imposed freedom on them. As a result, they feel not so much liberated by opportunity as weighted down by obligation. Both parents have obligations to themselves as individuals and to the economic well-being of the family to which they belong. And they have obligations to their children, whose demands on their time are inexhaustible, when not irresistible. "If I knew the answer to that, I would run for God," responded Jesse O'Donnell of Eastlake, to our question about how people should divide their time between career and family.

Middle-class Americans seek not to do the right thing, but to do the workable thing; as Lisa Andrews, a paralegal in East-lake, responded to a question about working women: "I don't think there's a hard and fast line on that." Some try to fit their work schedules to their life cycles: many women stay out of the labor force when their kids are very young, move up to part-time as they start school, and work full-time as the kids get older. Others obtain flextime, either from corporations sensitive to the needs of working parents or simply by taking it. Sometimes, men help out (and sometimes they don't). The point is to find the right balance. "I think that there has to be some kind of balance and some kind of compromise from both the standpoint of the father and the mother to try to make sure that things get done for the children and that there's some kind of supervision," Pedro Govea said in representative fashion.

What is most noticeable about the way middle-class Americans discuss family matters is that guilt is rarely an issue. Most people are reluctant to pass judgment on the choices other people make, religious injunctions play little role, and questions of how things ought to be take second place to how they actually are. The language of family life in middle-class America is profane rather than sacred, surely a disappointment to those who invest significant meaning in the family, as well as to those who believe we should pass judgment on the choices made by others.

Having heard from so many middle-class Americans about their feelings on the family, we are in a position to answer a question at the heart of the debate over the family: Is there a split in America between traditionalists who lament all the changes that have taken place in this country since *Ozzie and Harriet* and modernists who welcome the world of *Murphy Brown* as a refreshing advance for personal freedom? Based on the interviews we conducted, my answer to that question is yes. Two very different models of family life exist in America: one that longs nostalgically for a world in which families stayed together, three generations lived in proximity to each other, children obeyed their parents, women remained at home, and everyone believed in God; and another in which both parents are free to pursue careers, children are anxious to escape the home and give themselves over to the attractions of a consumer and entertainment culture, grandparents try to avoid either being burdened by or dependent on their grown children, and the language of rights and self-fulfillment comes to play as much a role as the language of obligation and duty. There is little question, in other words, that America is furiously divided over the family.

Still, there is one thing very much out of focus in this picture: *These divisions over the family do not take place between camps of people; instead, they take place within most individuals.*

The fact that the largest cluster of attitudes we found on the question of the proper family form was the ambivalent category suggests that the culture war lies within: middle-class Americans believe in both the traditional and the modern version of the family simultaneously. Longing for a world that no longer exists but having no intention of giving up the one that does, they are torn between nostalgia and necessity. As much as they lament the passing of the family meal, and they lament its passing mightily, they are too American not to appreciate the benefits that flow from both the material benefits of an additional salary and the political and social advantages of greater equality and personal liberty. Deep ambivalence, not ideological or religious certainty, characterizes the views of most Americans on family matters. What the sociologists Peter and Brigitte Berger called "the war over the family" may not be a war at all, but an inevitable, and perhaps even healthy, conflict between two different sets of needs, both of which have compelling reasons to exist. In theory, people cannot satisfy both needs at the same time; in practice, they are trying their hardest to do exactly that.

THE MORAL SQUEEZE

Although middle-class Americans spend as much time debating the question of how families ought to be organized as social critics and social scientists, they approach the subject in a radically different way. The debate over the family, as it takes place among intellectuals, is really a debate about whether women ought to work—and whether children are harmed if they do. For conservatives, the fact that women who once stayed home now go to work is the cause of the family's decline, a syndrome that has only one cure: women should give up their jobs and careers for the sake of their children. Children, those of this persuasion believe, are shortchanged as it is, whether by the sheer hormonal and psychological difficulties of growing up or by the tendency of society to respond to the needs of the elderly before they turn to the needs of the future elderly. When women work, some believe, they make the lives of their children even more difficult than they ordinarily would be. Feminists accept the same analysis but reject the conclusion: to be sure, women are now working who once stayed home with children, but this is good for the women and could, if our society only cared enough to spend the money on day care, be good for the children as well. Families have not weakened, people who think this way usually add, they have merely changed. Needs are not organized by zero-sum principles, they conclude: when a mother fulfills her own needs, she can also fulfill the needs of her kids.

Whatever their other differences, both parties to the debate over the family link together the question of working women, the fate of children, and the question of family form. In so doing, the temperature of the debate is inexorably raised. Jon Katz, a writer of suburban mystery stories organized around moral dilemmas, has devoted one novel, *The Last Housewife*, to the bitter conflicts between mothers who work and mothers who do not, as if the question of family values is capable of producing murder. In the suburb outside of Boston in which I live—not Brookline—no one has died over the issue, but there is an intense debate about an afterschool program for elementary school children: working women want it, those who choose to stay home do not, and both claim to speak for the needs of the kids themselves. Prepared by my own experiences to find similarly charged disputes elsewhere, I was surprised to discover that the middle-class Americans whose views I sought did not understand family life in these terms at all. So overwhelmed were they by the sheer difficulties of bringing up children under modern conditions that they had little time and less tolerance to fight with each other over the best way to do it.

As they talk about these things, middle-class Americans search for ways to separate the question of what's best for the women from what's best for the children—and to separate both from the question of what is the best form of family. Women do work, which for some is a good thing and for others is a necessary thing. Although they often do not use feminist language about equality, most women who work discover something about themselves through their jobs and would feel less than whole if they had to give them up. And rarely do their husbands view the jobs held by their wives as a threat to their privileges or masculinity; most of them like both the extra income and what their wives become as they resume responsibilities outside the home. A large number of middle-class Americans feel ambivalent about the fact of working women, but even when they acknowledge that the absence of one parent may be harmful to children, most add the qualifier that, as Brian Fischer of Cobb County put it, "we're not going to go back and women aren't going to have pearls around the house during the day and long skirts." Even women whose religious beliefs discourage working women tend to work. Nancy Ammerman's study of a fundamentalist church revealed that "although the 'ideal' Christian home has a full-time mother . . . nearly half of all the mothers at Southside are employed full-time outside the home." Ammerman argues that "sometimes . . . economic realities overshadow Fundamentalist ideals," but one could also argue that if the ideal is strong enough, people will just have to find a way to make do.

Women's entry into the labor force, and with it the development of new family forms, is one of those developments that has become all but irreversible; as survey researcher Daniel Yankelovich expresses popular sentiment:

> Majorities may claim in the abstract that they want to return to the family life of the past, but when it comes to specifics, only one out of five (21 percent) has any hankering to go back either to traditional standards of sexual relations, to the "spic and span" housekeeping norms of the past, or to the male monopoly on working outside the home.

All of which suggests that the conservative nostrum of returning to the nuclear family would be dismissed by most middle-class Americans as unrealistic and impractical.

But the fact that people have accepted the economic and cultural changes associated with working women does not mean they are satisfied with the ways families function in America. Most Americans, who know better than conservatives the positive benefits of having women work, also know better than feminists how the family is weakened by it. It is simple common sense that if both parents are out of the house most of the day, children will suffer. Day care is not an option to be celebrated, but an unfortunate necessity of life. Watching television is not the same as having stories read. It is easy to caricature the absence of family meals, but the unease around the subject conveys the truth that eat-and-run is hardly the best way to share stories and enrich life together. Things might be easier if there were more fathers like Pedro Govea and J. W. Cotton spending time with their children, but for all the men who indicated they helped with family chores, our sample revealed even more women frustrated by their responsibility for the "second shift." There is little in the views of those to whom we talked that expresses a blithe confidence that the family is simply responding to challenges and will emerge in new, and even strengthened, form.

If there is a positive consequence of separating the question of whether women should work from the question of what is good for children, it is that people on both sides of the divide have an easier time recognizing the difficult choices and impossible dilemmas faced by those on the other side. "I'm a stay-at-home mom," said Marcie Lankford of Rancho Bernardo. "I've got as many problems as those who don't.... I don't think there's any big difference in those who stay at home and those who don't." Cathy Peterson, a homemaker in Cobb County, thinks that "every woman should have a right to work . . . if she chooses to work, have a career, then I am all for it." Being a parent, Judy Vogel of Cobb County points out, has "always been a tough job." Mrs. Vogel chose to be a full-time mother: "If it costs me several years out of the workforce or if it costs us some of the other things that we might do," so be it, she reasons, for she believes that her rights are "secondary to the fact that these little people don't ask to be brought into this world." It is the very toughness of raising a family, however, that leads Mrs. Vogel to empathize with women who made different choices than she did, for it is tough for them as well. "They're doing their best to be responsible for their families and raise healthy, happy children."

For every woman who stayed home but respected other women who worked, there were women who worked who were envious, rather than contemptuous, of those who stayed home. Cathy Ryan of Brookline, a voice teacher, thinks that if parents decide to spend their time with their children rather than working, "it's terrific, it's wonderful—that's the way it should be," just as Elizabeth Moore, a real estate broker in Sand Springs, would rather see women at home, even though she herself works. This tolerance that each side has for the other is a reflection of the conviction that family forms should fit people. Since each individual will make a different choice, there is little to be gained in urging others to make the same choice you make; on the contrary: it's hard enough to decide what to do for yourself, which means that passing judgment on what others should do is beyond most people's horizon. A large number of middle-class Americans look at it this way: some individuals will be selfish whether they work or stay home and other individuals will sacrifice for their children whether they stay home or work.

"I think it's just hard. It's hard. It's hard," is how Judy Vogel characterized modern family life, whether or not both parents work. No doubt, parents have always felt that it is hard to raise children. Do they feel that because families are changing so dramatically in America, it has become even harder? Not all the respondents to the Middle Class Morality Project thought so. Some middle-class Americans think their stay-at-home mothers did a pretty poor job of raising them. One Medford resident liked the fact that parents these days are more open with children, that, as she put it, "you don't have to keep anything in the closet." Diane Sveressen of Rancho Bernardo has children ranging from twenty-three to thirty-four; describing herself as "an incurable optimist," she tells us that "they seem to be more conscious of taking care of their families and seeing that their families are happy than maybe we were when we were raising our kids." Linda Clay-Johnson of DeKalb County—"I have been truly blessed," she says of herself—thought this way:

I think that we need to put a lot more emphasis on what is right about our society. All kids are not on drugs. There are a lot of kids who are striving to do the right thing, a lot of kids who are working very hard academically and are achieving. There are a lot of kids and, when you meet them, you are just blown away by their maturity, by their level of understanding of what's going on around them.

What made it such a pleasure to listen to these people speak is how rarely expressed their thoughts were. For just about everyone else besides them, the subject of children tended to bring out a language of doom-and-gloom: stress, despair, pressure, exposure—these are the words middle-class Americans use when they talk about the lives of their children.

That part of the Middle Class Morality Project that asked our respondents survey-type questions found strong support for the notion that "it has become harder to raise children in our society"; 177 of 200 agreed compared with 16 who disagreed. Kids, our respondents believed, deserve a safe haven, but arrayed against them are all those forces of modern life that make it hard to raise children the way most parents think children should be raised. Miriam Schwartz of Brookline, who works in an elementary school with special-needs kids, has no doubt about it: "The children are getting shortchanged," she told us. "I mean, I don't even think that they are. I *see* that they are."

The pessimism our respondents expressed about children is only partially about economics. For some, to be sure, economic factors were paramount. "It's really a situation where you're chasing your tail," as Peter Martland, a Cobb County lawyer, put it. Both parents work to make enough to provide the decencies of a middle-class life, only to find that the costs constantly escalate, requiring ever more work, which in turns fuels ever greater needs. And when downsizing takes place, people discover that a downward spiral makes those on the upward spiral seem lucky. Middle-class Americans are fully aware of the economic squeeze facing them. They wonder if they will be able to keep what they have. And they are fairly certain that unless their

TABLE 3.5
"IT HAS BECOME MUCH HARDER TO RAISE
CHILDREN IN OUR SOCIETY"

	Strongly Agree	Agree	No Opinion	Disagree	Strongly Disagree
Brookline	12	9	3	1	0
Medford	13	11	0	0	1
Broken Arrow	8	15	1	1	0
Sand Springs	8	12	1	4	0
DeKalb	14	10	0	0	1
Cobb	12	10	0	3	0
Eastlake	7	16	2	0	0
Rancho Bernardo	10	10	0	5	0
Total	84	93	7	14	2

children work hard, they will be unlikely to achieve the benefits their parents would like to pass on to them.

Yet, as difficult as it may be for those worried about the next meal to accept, a surprisingly large number of middle-class Americans believe that one of the problems facing their children is the existence of *too much* money. "It sounds like a contradiction to say that affluence leads to the breakup of the family, which leads to poverty," but that contradiction made perfect sense to Peter Martland. No one wants to go back to the Great Depression, but, especially among older Americans, there persists the notion that hard times strengthen character. And not just for the elderly. Modern parents with young children worry not that their kids will lack choices, but that they will have too many; reluctant choosers when it comes to their own lives, they are unambiguously upset about the number of options their kids have. Personal telephone lines, answering machines, expensive clothes, cars—these are the things kids want. For some parents, the question is not whether they can afford them—they can—

but whether they ought to satisfy the cravings of their children for material things. Whatever they decide when asked to open their wallets feels like the wrong decision. If they say yes, they worry about spoiling their children. If they say no, they worry that they will lose control over their children. "There's just so many different things going on out there," said Eastlake's Robert Hertzo. "You know, kids are so advanced now. I have a sister who is fourteen and . . . she goes out whenever she wants. If she doesn't get permission, she goes out anyway. When I was at home, if your parents said no, that was it."

Parents who talk this way are facing a moral squeeze rather than an economic one. Middle-class status for them is not defined by income but by certain values, especially the ability of parents to play a role in guiding their children to make the right choices in life. Material things, too much wealth, corrupt that moral capacity: the glitter and attractions of expensive goods will always win out over the seemingly old-fashioned values of the parents. That is why parents worry about television; it is not just the sex and violence that bother them, but the glitz and the hard sell. It is also why so many of the middle-class Americans to whom we talked think that wearing school uniforms is a good idea—anything that detracts from the pressure of peers to buy more things would be welcome. "The affluence is difficult if you are middle class," said Denise Lott of Rancho Bernardo. "The values are so skewed. I think it is very difficult to combat that. You know how kids are. They want what other kids have. They want expensive sneakers and jackets. They have to have these things."

Not only affluence but also poverty contributes to the moral squeeze. Americans like the suburbs because only there do they feel that their children are (relatively) safe. As they watch stories on television about the conditions of inner-city life, what bothers them most is how poor kids are introduced to sex, violence, and drugs long before they have the emotional and physical capacity to understand their attractions and dangers. Now, to their astonishment, they find their own children facing these same choices.

"Well, I think when you have so much choice, it's tough," Joyce Slone of Brookline told us: "When you hear what's going on in the schools—kids with knives and called over to sell drugs. I mean we are trying to minimize and erase these situations. But with all the different choices and so forth . . ." Mrs. Slone illustrated her concerns by telling us about two of her friends

> that are in my social strata, who are raising sons. One of them—I mean, these are upper-middle-class kids—one of them gave his friends his parents' credit card, and they went up to [an outlet mall] and charged two or three thousand dollars before they were apprehended. A second one, the son gave his friends the key to his apartment when his family was away for the weekend. The friends robbed and cleaned out the apartment. This is a son!

Her concerns did not just reflect an urban, East Coast perspective. "I don't think you have to be poor to commit crime," pointed out Dolores Gaffney, a retired nurse in Eastlake. "I mean, you can come from a very affluent home." "I think kids always fought. There were always bullies. Kids were always beaten up on the schoolyard. Now we've got guns. Technology has escalated the battle," said Brian Fischer of Cobb County. Both of them know full well that gangs, once associated primarily with the inner city, have become an increasing presence in suburban high schools. As have drugs. Surveys undertaken by the Monitoring the Future Project at the University of Michigan report an increase in drug use among secondary school students in America in 1994 and 1995, and most parents are aware that drugs are available if their children really want to find them; as Foster Rice, also of Cobb, put it, "I don't want to throw one word out too often, but there's no question that the proliferation of drugs in this society has had a terrible detrimental aspect. And drugs are in all communities. They're not just in the inner city." Asked in 1994 what was the most important problem facing teenagers in America today, 37 percent said drugs and 22 percent said crime and violence, compared with only 9 percent who said peer pressure, 6 percent who said pregnancy, and 4 percent who said sex.

That does not mean, of course, that teenage sex is a nonissue for middle-class American parents; 84 percent of the American people think that teenage pregnancy is a very serious problem. A feeling that parents have lost control over their children's sexuality is one of the deepest currents in American public opinion; according to a 1985 poll, only 3 percent of those surveyed thought that parents had a great deal of control over the sexual activity of teenagers compared with 46 percent who thought they had very little control. Even if there were not life-and-death issues involved with sex in the age of AIDS—our respondents are certainly aware that there are—middle-class parents are more perplexed about sex than ever. "I have a niece who's fourteen," said Karen Hamilton, an assistant in a Medford interior design shop. "I swear she knows about sex. I know she knows about sex. But, I mean, when I was fourteen, I was singing Mickey Mouse songs. I was . . . I mean, and Annette Funicello, that was big, or watching *American Bandstand.*" Once her niece asked Mrs. Hamilton when she first had sex. When Mrs. Hamilton responded that she was twenty-three and engaged, "she looked at me like I had two heads." Suddenly, it seems that kids cannot be kids anywhere, and few things make middle-class Americans more unhappy.

Sociologist Kristin Luker, studying sexual behavior, could just as easily be discussing drugs and violence when she writes, "What parents . . . seem to want is some measure of control over how their children behave in the world of sexual freedom that opened up in the 1970s." And control is precisely what most Americans think they may never obtain. Middle-class moral pessimism stems not from the fact that raising children is difficult—as Judy Vogel noted, it has always been hard—but from the powerlessness of parents to instill middle-class values. When such values work, our respondents believe, they can protect kids against their own temptations, delaying the moment of choice until children are mature enough to face them. But middle-class values, they also believe, rarely work. The citadel has been invaded, and the lure of pleasure is impossible to resist.

Like populists in America who view the middle class as squeezed between those below them and those above, middle-class Americans find all kinds of parallels between the world of wealth and the world of poverty. Television in particular provides those parallels for them: "It's like America is divided into two things," said Diana Hamilton, a day care worker in Sand Springs. "Either everyone lives like *Beverly Hills 90210* or they are living like people on *Roseanne*. I don't know anybody that lives like either one of those groups of people." One thing that seemed to be on the minds of a significant number of our respondents was sneakers; if a symbol were required to mark the spot where ghetto culture, fabulous wealth, threatening images of violence, and the media all came together it would be where expensive basketball shoes are advertised. Americans are not surprised that when the media chose to discuss a problem they associate with the underclass—unwed mothers—they did so through the character of a member of the overclass, Murphy Brown.

Against the twin threats of immoral wealth and immoral poverty, what is a parent to do? For some, love is the answer; Carmen Tosca of Eastlake believes that only an "I love you, I would kill for you, I will die for you" approach to her kids makes sense, and even though her kids are grown up, she still smothers them with as much love as she can. For others, faith is essential. Jim McLaughlin and his wife, the strong religious believers who put their faith in absolutes, are active in their local church and have a son who attended nearby Oral Roberts University. If most parents would instill respect for God, they believe, all the kids would be better off. But most parents around them do not, with the consequence, predictable to them, that kids are "gonna test their parents to their limit." A third approach, one that resonates particularly strongly among conservative Christians, emphasizes discipline, what Stephen Jackman, a retired steelworker in Sand Springs, calls "three hours of close-order drill a day." That might sound "ridiculous" to some, but, he continues, "close-order drill teaches you one thing: Do what you are told."

Under the right conditions, all three can work: we were left in no doubt that Carmen Tosca's love for children was genuine or that the McLaughlins were able to transmit their values to their children. But even for those who choose them, love, God, and discipline are limited in the face of realities of modern life. Not everyone was as convinced of the power of love as Carmen Tosca; many middle-class parents worry that love can turn into giving kids everything they want, when sometimes a little discipline might be necessary to go along with the love. And for all the attraction that discipline may have in theory, in practice, most parents have come to accept its limits. Even those in our sample who would prefer to discipline their children more found it difficult to administer in the right way; Dolores Wales of Sand Springs believes in spanking her children and does not like the fact that the government tells her not to do it. "I think the parents have more or less backed off," she notes, and "therefore the children rule the parents instead of the parents taking over the children." But even Mrs. Wales, as did others who shared similar views, realizes that too much discipline could step over "a fine line" into abuse. Confusion about discipline was particularly apparent among middle-class Americans with close ties to an immigrant past; many of them commented on how, back in the Philippines, Mexico, or Italy, parents were willing to say no to their kids, but here in America, it seems both futile and old-fashioned to do so.

Most poignant of all were the responses of those who wanted to instill religious values in their children but felt powerless in the face of a materialistic onslaught. Vaughn Hyde of DeKalb County is a religious believer: "I want to see a recognition of a power greater than you. Now you do it any way you want to do it, but you better understand that something greater . . . something made you, and it wasn't Mom and Dad." But no matter how hard one tries to teach children respect for that power, they do not learn it: "Children these days have no concept of life or death, no concept of respect, no concept of God." Even if God were not in competition with television, many middle-class parents feel torn between their own religious faith and what their kids need to get by. The McLaughlins, for example, among the most devout people we talked with, strongly considered a Christian academy for their sixth-grade child. But, Mrs. McLaughlin explained, "we chose to keep them in the public school, because we felt that they couldn't be sheltered, we didn't want them sheltered, and hopefully what they learned at home, their values, and at church, would help them make decisions not to take drugs or not to drink or not to get in the car to go wildly down the street." As they see it, parents like them "are at a real dilemma": their faith is enormously important to them, they want it to be just as important to their children, but they are also concerned about protecting their children too much, as if the world around them requires a touch of Godlessness for sheer survival.

There is one way to solve the problem of how to raise children properly: one parent, usually the mother, can decide to stay home and give the children the attention they need. For the forty-three people in our sample I have called traditionalists, that solution was so obvious that they would not consider anything else. "There's so much more going on, particularly in the high schools now, particularly from the standpoint of morality and looseness of character and drugs and all that sort of thing. . . . That's gotta make it tougher for parents than it was," we were told by Winston Cobb, a retired executive in Rancho Bernardo. Mr. Cobb, one of the most thoughtful people to whom we spoke, was under no illusions about what parents should do. "All things considered, I think a family, any family, is far better off with a mother at home and a father doing what he has to do to provide the living for the family and the guidance for the children." Working women—that's simply not a good idea. Kids need "a mother, a nurturing, caring, someone-to-be-there-when-they're-needed kind of person."

Mr. Cobb's thoughts raise an important question: If middle-class Americans could, in one fell swoop, considerably reduce the anxiety they feel about uncontrollable children, why don't more of them do it? Defenders of the traditional family have an answer to that question: Such parents lack the courage of their convictions, wanting to be more involved with their children yet selfishly refusing to make the sacrifices, easily within their power, to bring about such a result. Everything I have said in this chapter may well give support to that conclusion; after all, if people can choose their own family form, they certainly can choose the one that puts kids first. Should we, therefore, respond to parents' fears for their children by reminding them that a substantial number of those fears would be reduced if one parent, usually the mother, were to put her interests second and the needs of her children first? It is a fair-enough question: social critics do have an obligation to give advice about how people ought to lead their lives. When we listen to people themselves, however, we simply cannot ignore the ambivalence that characterizes so much of the reaction of middle-class America to the dilemma of the modern family. Even Winston Cobb, for all his traditional ideas, went on to say that "I can understand why a lot of women want to work, want to become something better than 'a housewife,'" which, nonetheless for him, "is the greatest occupation in the world and the most seriously needed."

Many middle-class Americans, unwilling to return to the traditional family of their parents' generation, live with considerable frustration. Caught between the needs of their children and their own economic and psychological reasons for working, they feel under incredible time pressure. "When you are working and the children are small," said Eastlake's Jason Cooper, "it's like speed-reading a great novel and you can never get the novel back." The rewards of hard work, including higher incomes, turn sour if they wind up spoiling the kids. Means of escape, especially the mass media, entrap them in worlds they would prefer to avoid. If their problems could be solved by returning to the traditional family, they would not feel themselves to be in such an impossible moral squeeze. The fact that so few of them are as optimistic about the prospects for their children as they are about other features of American life indicates just how pressing that moral squeeze is.

MODEST VIRTUES

Wherever there is frustration, there are likely to exist efforts to mobilize it behind one political cause or another. Unhappy with the impact that the modern family has had on their children, middle-class Americans might seem susceptible to those who would blame the problems facing children on larger social and moral forces dominant in the society. Conservatives in particular sense in middle-class anger about children a possible avenue of mobilization: in the last few years, bad schools, a loss of parental control over children, the decline of discipline, sex education, gay rights, and the seeming contempt for middle-class morality on the part of teachers and social workers have formed the basis of campaigns to assert "parental rights" and have been taken to justify home schooling or the use of vouchers for religious education, a conservative version of the middle-class withdrawal syndrome. At the same time, however, attempts in states such as Colorado, Kansas, North Dakota, and Virginia to win passage of "parental rights" legislation have failed.

Conservatives blame such failure on the power of education lobbies, but my interviews suggest a different explanation. For all their sense that children are harmed by the demands on the modern family, it runs against the grain of middle-class sensibility to politicize family issues. Dana Mack, a conservative writer on this subject, sees in the fears of middle-class parents for their children, and especially in the actions taken by some of them to provide their children with more religious and tradition-based educational alternatives, the emergence of "two distinct political cultures in our nation." Since educational professionals, in her view, represent a "culture of conformity, of homogenization, collectivization, peer-orientation, and a dictatorial vision of political activism," those who opt for such remedies as home schooling "are barely aware of the more sub-versive implications of their choice," for they are asserting a counter political vision "that values individualism, pluralism, privatism, intergenerational interaction, and grassroots political activism."

But the middle-class Americans with whom I spoke would be reluctant to view themselves as heroes in a struggle against il-legitimate authority. The reason has a great deal to do with their approach to morality in general. In a fashion quite similar to the quiet ways in which they express their religious faith, middle-class Americans believe in what I propose to call modest virtues. Adherents of the modest virtues would agree with those conser-vatives who suggest that Americans need to pay more attention to virtuous behavior. Our society too often rewards the cynical and the selfish, they believe. We do not appreciate nearly as much as we should those who try to lead their lives by such time-honored principles as respect for authority, faithfulness to spouses and friends, and selfless devotion to the public good. That is why children seem to be in trouble. In our narcissistic preoccupation with ourselves, we are ignoring the important duty of transmitting to the next generation respect for virtues that will enable it to lead, not just self-fulfilling lives, but also meaningful ones.

Yet as important as virtues are to middle-class Americans, it is just as important that we realize them modestly. Non-judgmentalism holds that the pursuit of virtue ought not be taken to the point of condemning others as lacking goodness be-cause they make a mistake. It is important to pay homage to such classic virtues as courage, perseverance, honesty, loyalty, and compassion, but nothing should ever be taken to extremes. One should always be wary of those who preach virtue too in-sistently, for who knows what personal failings they may be covering up? Above all else, virtue, like religion, cannot be equated with politics, for that would lead to division and dis-cord. This belief in modest virtues explains why, as sympathetic as middle-class Americans are to complaints that we have failed our children, they would be as unhappy with conservative plans to turn that failure into a political agenda as they were with liberal efforts to transform the schools to serve such goals as greater equality or support for bilingualism. Of course children should be taught right from wrong. But, just as important, they should not be taught in ways that immodestly insist that one person, institution, or ideology has all the right answers. The whole point is that children should be children, not actors in anyone's grandiose, and more didactic, morality play.

Anyone seeking to transform anger over the family into a conservative—or liberal—cause will have to deal with people like the Carltons of Sand Springs, Oklahoma, who, perhaps because they are grandparents, have a long-term perspective on questions involving families and children. Mrs. Carlton thinks that "children need security" and that "a mother missing the growing-up phase has missed a terrific amount"; for her, both parents and children suffer when women work. Still, the Carltons are too optimistic about life in general and their country in particular not to see that most parents are trying to do their very best: most parents, Mrs. Carlton continued, "are well prepared. They study up on parenting skills and they . . . try to do the right thing by their children." As a result, in spite of time pressures, materialism, the availability of drugs and sex, and all the other negative influences on the modern family, "I don't have any fear that these children aren't going to grow up to be probably a lot better than we were." Nostalgia for the old days is a bit misplaced, she concludes: "I'm positive I've made a world of mistakes with my children. They were honest mistakes, but I made mistakes. The young people today will too, but . . . I think today's children are on the whole most of them polite and good. I just think they're better. I do." Such nonideological, practical, and—above all—modest ways of treating these issues simply deflate any attempts to use people's private sense of what's best for their children to support someone else's public sense of what we ought to do about it.

MIDDLE-CLASS
MORAL PHILOSOPHERS

While many of the middle-class Americans to whom we spoke
lack the language and concepts of academic philosophy, their
thoughts about the family overlap with one of the most important philosophical debates taking place in America. John Rawls's
1971 book, *A Theory of Justice*, started the discussion. Situating
himself in the social contract tradition, Rawls, in a fascinating
thought experiment, asked us to evaluate the justice of various
actions or policies as if we were behind a veil of ignorance, unable to judge the eventual effect those policies would have on us
as real people in the real world. Although Rawls did not concern
himself directly with gender issues—the family plays relatively
little role in his original formulation of the problem—his work
is as relevant to questions of justice within the family as it is to
questions of justice in society at large. Arguing from a position
roughly within the Rawlsian tradition, Susan Moller Okin
claimed that family forms that do not respect the autonomy of
the members of the family fail the test of justice. The traditional
nuclear family, in which women subordinated themselves to the
careers of their husbands and the needs of their children, would
certainly count as unjust by this criterion.

Rawlsian liberalism quickly met opposition. The most detailed criticism came from Michael Sandel, who pointed out that
a self unencumbered by membership in a community is too
poverty-stricken a concept upon which to build any viable social order. The very idea of a self presumes that a person will be
cognizant of his own ends, but if such a person is understood to
be cut off from others in the way Rawls's thought experiment
implies, how can he or she know what those ends are?

Sandel's point quickly became identified as a "communitarian" response to Rawls's "liberalism." At stake in the debate
was the question of the degree to which the virtues of individuals were fashioned by themselves in relative isolation or in what
Sandel called "embedded" relations with others. Taking on the
question of the family directly, Alasdair MacIntyre, another

critic of liberalism, argued that individuals are shaped by narratives of belonging that make possible the search for the good. Nuclear families, because they provide for continuity between the generations, are, in his view, one of the most important institutions of tradition; without them, individuals would be hopelessly lost, unable to believe in anything, even individualism. The importance assigned by MacIntyre to traditional institutions, in turn, aroused the suspicions of many liberal critics such as Okin, who quickly pounced on the idea as evidence that communitarian philosophies contained, as part of their agenda, the subjugation of women.

As fascinating as the debate between liberals and communitarians became, it also became a frustrating one, since it seemed to set in opposition two goods, both of which are essential to modern human beings: autonomy on the one hand and membership in groups on the other. Not surprisingly, given the nature of debates of this sort, a middle position began to emerge, even from those who could be said to belong to one camp or the other. Philip Selznick's *The Moral Commonwealth,* while not directly addressing the family, concluded that people need both a conventional or pietistic morality, which respects moral traditions, and a critical morality that asks whether traditional institutions continue to serve individual goals. Even John Rawls himself moderated his views by making a sharp distinction between political liberalism—which was restricted to matters of government—and a broader moral liberalism, which would include questions of meaning and purpose.

A large number of the middle-class Americans with whom we spoke reached a similar middle position in this debate, based, not on theory, but on their own experiences trying to live in a world without fixed rules. Any family that prevents a woman from working, *so long as she herself wants to work,* would be viewed by them as unjust in ways not dissimilar to those in which Susan Okin understands the nuclear family to be unjust. But it does not follow from this understanding that every woman has a *right* to work. The fact that so many of those with whom we spoke were ambivalent on the question of the modern family suggests that women ought to work for practical reasons, not principled ones. Some women, moreover, will not want to work, and that decision should be respected as well, even though, from the viewpoint of liberal theory, a person ought not to be easily permitted to renounce a right that belongs to her. Moreover, the language used to justify women entering careers was not a language of rights but one of self-discovery. The difference matters. For the individualism so strong in American culture is not, to borrow from Rawls, political individualism; it is not an assertion of a zone of sacred autonomy against the claims of the state. It is rather a generalized belief that people should find themselves and suggests, as a distinct possibility, that they will find themselves by working together, rather than against others around them. The kind of individualism that Americans want family forms to respect is not seen by them as a threat to the family. Structured the right way, the family can, in fact, protect it.

In very much the same way, Americans understand communal institutions, including the family, as ones structured tightly enough to allow for tradition, but not so tightly wound that they disallow for personal autonomy. The communitarian critique of Rawls would make sense to them, for the family, in their view, is a place in which people are formed; unformed people, including those whose upper-class or lower-class family backgrounds prevent a proper socialization, are no good for anyone. There is no necessary conflict, in the opinion of those with whom we spoke, between forming people and allowing them freedom of choice; the whole point of the family is to get people ready to leave it. At one time, those who left were children after they had grown up. Now the people who are leaving it, or at least leaving its traditional form behind, are women. The question is not whether women should but whether they are ready. And the answer is that when they decide they are ready, they should do what fits them best, without anyone telling them that, in the name of tradition or hierarchy, they are wrong to do so. "It's almost as if the family has to break apart to survive," said

DeKalb's Jackie Stevens. Mrs. Stevens was talking about families on welfare, especially those in which men are asked to absent themselves so that women can collect their checks. But in some ways her comments apply to all families in a culture marked by individualism: the family has to break apart to some degree so that each person can discover things about himself or herself, but then it is obligatory on the part of those people, most of our respondents believed, to do their best to put the family back together again.

The middle position that middle-class Americans have discovered in dealing with this issue may turn out to be an unstable one. After all, as ambivalent as Americans tend to be on most issues, they seem even more ambivalent on family issues, appreciating the gains that have come from family transformations, while worrying about its effects on children. But some of them recognize that the moral principle implicit in their understanding—people should be free to choose the right family form, not to fit into family forms given by history or God—contains one possible benefit. The modern family, as it has evolved in America, is not very old; most people compare the way they have formed their own families with the way they grew up in quite different families formed by their parents. A moment's reflection indicates that if it has changed so much in one generation, perhaps it will change equally as much in the next. For all their belief about how hard it is to live by the right values, these kinds of things tend to run in cycles, some of our respondents felt, and the next cycle may well turn out to be one in which family values are once again respected. "In the last couple of years," Jane Sargent of Cobb County told us, "I started to see a trend where I think it's becoming more acceptable for people to begin to value family more. I mean even in myself and my friends I've seen where it's become more acceptable not to work weekends, because you just want to vegetate, cocooning or staying home and being together." What do you think about a term like "family values"? we asked another working woman in Rancho Bernardo. "I think it's coming back," she replied. "I don't think it's as bad as it used to be. From what I see with my own children—I have children ranging from thirty-four to twenty-three—. . . they all seem to be more conscious of taking care of their families and seeing that their families are happy and content than when we were raising our kids."

If the cycle in America does swing back to a more family oriented society, it will be with a difference. Given how deep are the roots dug by the changes in the American family, it is highly unlikely that the idealized nuclear family of the 1950s suburbs will ever return to America: women are too committed to working and children too accustomed to independence for that ever to happen again. At the same time, few of the middle-class Americans with whom we spoke, women or men, would proclaim their independence from family ties as assertively as Katherine Mullins. But suppose that individuals, of their own free will, decide to find ways to incorporate what they appreciate about strong and binding families with the idea that people within families, and not just families themselves as units, deserve respect? Such an ideal best characterizes what middle-class Americans are searching for, and while they may never find it, they are aware that without some attempt to do so, they will never be able to resolve the problem of how to be an autonomous person and tied together with others at the same time.

IV MATURE PATRIOTISM

Shortly after that terrible time known as the McCarthy period, when charges of treason filled the American air, one insightful sociologist pointed out how unusual it was to have something called the House Un-American Activities Committee. What other nation, Seymour Martin Lipset wondered, would charge an official body of its legislature with determining who was and was not a legitimate member? The notion of an Un-French Activities Committee, he pointed out, would strike Parisians as absurd.

The fact that questions of loyalty assume such a prominent place in the American identity could be taken as an indication of the degree to which patriotism is a strongly inscribed American moral value. Most of those who live here certainly think so. Americans, we have traditionally believed, not only love our country, but also love our country more than the people of any other country love theirs. This disposition was brought out in polling data that asked whether, if free to do so, you would permanently leave your country: 38 percent of Britons, 30 percent of Germans, 21 percent of French, 19 percent of Canadians, but only 11 percent of Americans said yes. But the same fact is also subject to a countrary interpretation, one favored by Lipset: that we needed to create a committee to investigate who is American suggests a deep insecurity about American patriotism, a sense that loyalty to the country is in question, or why else bring the matter up? From this point of view, Americans are not necessarily more or less patriotic than people in other countries, but they are patriotic in a different way. Our patrimony is not a given: since we are a country formed by immigration, we have to ask questions about membership all the time because they have not been settled by birth, race, or language.

We have never been able to furnish definitive answers to the question of who is an American, but in recent years, the uncertainty of who belongs here and who does not has taken on an added dimension and has been exacerbated in two unprecedented ways. One is the power of global capitalism. Trade, to be sure, has always existed on a world scale, but most Americans remember a time when certain companies were specifically and identifiably American, while others were Japanese or German. Now, as "American" companies downsize in the heartland to expand with labor abroad, and as "foreign" companies pick up the slack by building branch plants in the heartland, no one knows to whom they should properly give their loyalty. Recent trends in international capitalism, it has been suggested, foreshadow the end of the nation-state. While that may be an exaggeration, Americans are beginning to discover that their government, which compared with other countries never had that much power to regulate the economy, now has even less.

Threatened from outside its borders, American identity is also challenged within its borders: at the moment capital moves there, labor moves here. Immigration, like global capitalism, is anything but a new phenomenon; previous periods of American history, especially the decades around the turn of this century, witnessed far more migration to the United States than the present one. But since the passage of the 1965 Hart-Celler Act, which abolished quotas that discriminated in favor of Europeans, this immigration is different. For one thing, it is less white: the great bulk of the new immigrants are Latino and Asian. Unlike the Irish, they rarely speak English as their first language. Once here, they are, if they choose to be, eligible for social benefits that did not exist when earlier immigrants came and can even qualify for affirmative action programs and diversity initiatives denied to some whose families have been here for a long time. And whatever the change in legal immigration, the past twenty years, most Americans believe, have seen a dramatic increase in illegal immigrants, especially from Mexico, who come to work in low-wage industries in California and Texas. For middle-class morality, already threatened by the exposure of children to the simultaneously seductive temptations of the overclass and underclass, this undermining of the meaning of America on both the labor and the capital front is doubly disturbing.

In this atmosphere of uncertainty, the whole meaning of loyalty is up for grabs: engaged with the issue of how to make a family, Americans also find themselves in the process of making a country. It is no longer enough to say that every American ought to be a loyal patriot. The questions now are more complicated: loyal to what? patriotic to whom? in what way? at what cost? with what benefits? Times of uncertainty like the present are particularly appropriate for asking people questions such as these. Were we living at a time when borders were tight, the Internet did not exist, only the very rich could get to Europe, and economic decisions were primarily local, we would not need to spend much time talking with Americans about their country because we could assume that the meaning of America was pretty clear to them. Should we come to live in a world beyond the nation-state where citizenship is irrelevant and boundaries nonexistent, we also would not need to know much about how individuals understand their country because they would not comprehend the question. But because we live in neither kind of situation— because America is experiencing rapid changes in its meaning while still meaning something—the Middle Class Morality Project would have gone amiss if, in talking with people about God and family, it did not extend the discussion to country as well.

THE GOOD IMMIGRANT

The transformation of the United States into a society no longer characterized by European roots has not quite caught up to the sample of Americans interviewed by the Middle Class Morality Project. More than three-fourths of our respondents (152) claimed to be of European background. When the twenty-three African-Americans, who have very deep roots in this country, are added to them, fewer than twenty people in our sample were of ethnic backgrounds such as Asian or Latin American, which resonate with recent patterns of immigration to the United States. (One of the black respondents in DeKalb was a Latin American from Panama.) Fifteen of those with whom we spoke were immigrants themselves. They came primarily from the former Soviet Union, Mexico, Iran, India, China, and the Philippines. As might be expected, most of them lived in California and on the East Coast; only one of our Oklahoma sample was a recent arrival to the United States. Furthermore, the number of second-generation Americans, twenty, was only marginally higher than the number of immigrants.

Since the bulk of America's recent immigrants have found themselves living in cities, the ethnic backgrounds of our respondents are probably typical of those found in suburban communities around the United States. Our objective, however, was not to

TABLE 4.1
ETHNIC BACKGROUND
MIDDLE CLASS MORALITY PROJECT

	Europe	Africa	Latin America	Asia	Other	Not Available
Brookline	22	1	1	1	0	0
Medford	24	0	0	1	0	0
Broken Arrow	22	0	0	0	1	2
Sand Springs	21	1	0	0	0	3
DeKalb	4	20	1	0	0	0
Cobb	24	1	0	0	0	0
Eastlake	12	0	9	3	0	1
Rancho Bernardo	23	0	0	1	0	1
Total	152	23	11	6	1	7

talk with people about their own ethnic background and immigrant status but about their views on what the border represents:
Should it be kept open to allow more people from around the
world to come here or should it be closed, or at least severely restricted, because there already are too many immigrants in the
United States? Immigration has become such a powerful issue in
American life because it raises, in the raw and unavoidable form
of real people, the question of how far-reaching people's obligations should be. Without some borders in place, it is not clear
that there is a distinctive country to which Americans can pledge
their loyalty. But without some immigration, the America that
people have known and respect would no longer exist.

By definition, borders divide those on one side from those on
the other: they exclude, therefore they exist. For those for whom
exclusion suggests stigmatization and inequality, borders will
always be suspect. Under conditions of economic uncertainty,
they would argue, Americans will be tempted to reinforce
their borders. The popular support for Proposition 187 in

TABLE 4.2
IMMIGRANT STATUS
MIDDLE CLASS MORALITY PROJECT

	1st generation	2d generation	3d+ generation	Not Available
Brookline	1	4	19	1
Medford	1	6	18	0
Broken Arrow	1	0	11	13
Sand Springs	0	0	8	17
DeKalb	2	0	21	2
Cobb	0	2	13	10
Eastlake	6	6	10	3
Rancho Bernardo	4	2	16	3
Total	15	20	116	49

California—a 1994 measure to deny social services to illegal immigrants—suggests that this is indeed the case. Just as middle-class people are believed to be withdrawing to gated communities and retreating from the inner-city poor, anti-immigrant sentiment could be interpreted as a turning away from those who suffer economic deprivation and political persecution outside America. Those who hold to this view suggest that what we are seeing is the middle-class withdrawal syndrome gone global: America is the "suburb," restrictive immigration policies are the "gates," and the rest of the world is the "inner city," all of which would explain why there is so much popular sentiment to solidify Fortress America.

There is good reason to conclude that Americans, to protect what they value about their country, are rethinking the porousness of their borders. The results of Proposition 187 are backed up by public opinion data that suggest why politicians might choose to make opposition to immigration a "hot button" issue to gain votes. According to a 1995 Gallup poll, a measure like Proposition 187 was actually more popular outside California than inside: 63 percent of those in other states said that they were in favor of such a measure for their state, compared with 52 percent in California. Historically, Americans have always been somewhat suspicious of immigrants, a sentiment that thawed considerably in the 1950s and 1960s, before undergoing a resurgence in recent years. Persistent patterns of anti-immigrant sentiment over the past ten to twenty years led Congress to pass the Immigration Reform and Control Act of 1986, designed to make illegal immigration into the United States more difficult. At best, the new act had mixed results in deterring new arrivals. If anything, polls since the passage of that act indicate a hardening of the line against immigrants. By one account, 63 percent of the American people believed that immigration should be decreased or reduced in 1994 compared with 39 percent in 1985. No matter what the question or the pollster, roughly twice as many Americans are skeptical about immigration as are sympathetic to it: polling for the Pew Research Center for the People and the Press in 1994 found that 63 percent thought that immigrants are a burden on the economy, compared with 31 percent who said that they strengthen the country through hard work. A Gallup poll found that 57 percent believed that immigrants cost the taxpayers too much compared with 36 percent who believed that they would become productive citizens, and the General Social Survey of 1994 found that two-thirds of Americans believed that immigrants should not be eligible for public services, in contrast to one-third who thought they should be. Despite efforts by social scientists to show that levels of immigration, even of the illegal variety, are neither especially high nor especially hurtful to the economy, what once made Americans proud is increasingly a source of concern. The atmosphere is such that thoughtful commentators speak of "a widespread populist backlash against immigration" as a defining characteristic of the present political mood.

The Middle Class Morality Project did discover indications of that backlash. Some of those to whom we spoke were "tired of being sucked dry by all these people" or exclaimed, "For crying out loud, haven't we got enough?" while others believed that "we're bursting at the seams" or that "you've got to draw the line somewhere." Overall, however, we found that it would be a mistake to conclude that our respondents are now ready to shut the doors of their country. On this point, both our survey and our in-depth interviews are in accord. Our survey, for one thing, revealed that our respondents were more likely to disagree that we should shut the doors than to agree that we should. And when we probed deeper to find out whether people's opinions would change when challenged, we discovered that hostility toward immigration declined even further.

To try to capture some of what our respondents had on their minds with respect to this subject, I coded their responses to the more qualitative parts of our interviews into three categories. Some people clearly wanted to restrict immigration—the sooner, the better. If they recommended closing the doors, or even starting to close the doors, I classified their views as "restrictive." If they talked about the benefits that immigrants brought with them to the United States, and spoke of how much the country would lose if they were to be denied entry, I classified them as

TABLE 4.3
"THERE ARE TOO MANY IMMIGRANTS IN AMERICA AND
WE OUGHT TO BEGIN TO CLOSE THE DOORS"

	Strongly Agree	Agree	No Opinion	Disagree	Strongly Disagree
Brookline	1	5	3	12	4
Medford	1	6	4	14	0
Broken Arrow	1	8	6	9	1
Sand Springs	3	10	3	7	2
DeKalb	1	7	3	11	3
Cobb	2	5	4	12	2
Eastlake	0	10	2	10	3
Rancho Bernardo	1	12	0	10	2
Total	10	63	25	85	17

"welcoming." And if they supported immigration under some conditions but not others—for example, and most frequently, by making a distinction between legal and illegal immigrants, but also by suggesting various reforms designed to improve the process—their opinions were classified as "qualified." Table 4.4

TABLE 4.4
ATTITUDES TOWARD IMMIGRATION

	Welcoming	Qualified	Restricted	Insufficient Information
Brookline	7	12	3	3
Medford	4	11	8	2
Broken Arrow	3	8	5	9
Sand Springs	2	11	4	8
DeKalb	7	6	5	7
Cobb	2	14	1	8
Eastlake	4	16	2	3
Rancho Bernardo	3	10	9	3
Total	32	88	37	43

presents the by-now-familiar pattern of opinion in which the middle category dominates and the two extremes are smaller and roughly equal in size.

A number of conclusions can be drawn from this distribution. One is that immigration is an issue that depends very much on geography; we found that Brookliners were most in favor of welcoming immigrants and residents of Rancho Bernardo most against. Our Brookline sample contained a large number of Jews, who will never forget how hard it was for those who managed to escape from Nazi Germany to enter the United States; our Rancho Bernardo sample contained many people proud to announce their support for Proposition 187. Because education is invariably associated with less restrictive attitudes toward immigration, we also found more hostility toward immigration in our Oklahoma communities and in Medford (both of which contained disproportionately large numbers of non-college-educated individuals) than we did in Cobb County, where our respondents were frequently highly educated (and relatively wealthy) professionals. Despite evidence that blacks tend to be hostile toward immigration because of direct competition with immigrants for jobs, the middle-class black Americans in DeKalb County with whom we spoke tended to be very divided on the issue, some quite hostile to immigration, while others, reflecting the importance they attach to protections against discrimination, were quite supportive.

The existence of a large group of people whose opinion was qualified between the two extremes, furthermore, suggests that it is the meaning people attached to borders, and not just whether they are open or closed, that is most important to them. Anthropologists have long been interested in borders—not necessarily those between nation-states, but boundaries of any kind—because processes of transition from one side to the other generally become infused with symbolic meanings that help a people define what is important to them. In the way they discuss who has a right to belong in the country and who does not, middle-class Americans deal with basic philosophical ideas about altruism and self-interest. They know full well that

Americans are fortunate to have bountiful amounts of what a good deal of the rest of the world wants, especially political freedom and material prosperity. The question for them is a simple one: Should others be allowed to share in their good fortune?

Altruistic answers to that question were offered by some of our interviewees—more than one might expect from public perceptions of this issue. Those who wanted to keep the borders open did so for one major reason: as Henry Pearson of Eastlake succinctly put it: "I think that anybody who denies immigrants ultimately denies America." The cliché that America is a nation of immigrants has remarkable staying power in middle-class America; it was repeated over and over again by those with whom we talked. As they saw it, to call for closing the borders is to give up on one important meaning of the American dream: "Without it," Marion Kates, also of Eastlake, told us about immigration, "I don't know what kind of country we would be." It is not an exaggeration to say that open borders, rather than having the effect of diluting what it means to be an American, define, for a sizable portion of the American middle class, what America is all about.

The notion of America-as-refuge is a demanding one, requiring, as it does, that those who face persecution abroad still have a right to come here, even under conditions of tight employment. Some were willing to meet those demands. Stephen Jackman of Sand Springs was in the process of making an argument *against* immigration when he said this: "Every time I start saying I believe in tighter immigration policies, somebody else will be a pitiful case, like the boat people, and I don't see how you possibly can turn your back on them." His thoughts were seconded by Lena Parker of DeKalb County: "When people flee their country, it's usually for a reason. Visually, what I've seen on television and places like that, any time someone will get on a boat and risk their lives to come across for a better opportunity, I say go for it." "They are human beings, so let them come in," added Cobb County's Cathy Peterson. "That's how I feel. I don't want them taking jobs away from us, but ... they flee these countries, so they must be awful." For people like these, the notion of America as a country of immigrants is more than a cliché. Some country has to take in those who have nowhere else to go, and God, fate, or destiny has determined that such is America's duty.

Humanitarianism also extends to the immigrants who are already here, even among those who have qualms about their entry in the first place. Despite the widespread unpopularity of illegal immigrants in America, almost as many Americans oppose denying them access to hospitals and schools (45 percent) as favor such measures (50 percent), and in California, the two groups are equal (48 percent). When they think about the extent of their obligations to those already here, our respondents often brought up the same example of hospital emergency rooms and whether they should turn illegal immigrants away: the general sentiment was that, as Victoria Carter-Smith of Rancho Bernardo, put it, "you don't just deny humanitarian aid." Similar sentiments apply to the children of illegal immigrants, who are viewed as innocent and therefore worthy of support. To deny kids hospital care or schooling because their parents are here illegally, "That's like the dumbest rule I've ever heard," Chad Noone of Brookline said. Explicitly altruistic rationales for extending one's obligations to noncitizens are not foreign to the American middle-class vocabulary.

But nor are they common. There are nonaltruistic ways to express altruistic sentiments, and middle-class Americans, perhaps reflecting a distrust of too much idealism, frequently rely on them. Among those sympathetic to immigration, the most commonly cited reason for wanting to keep the borders open is that most immigrants share the same middle-class morality on which Americans pride themselves. Indeed, some of those to whom we talked took an even stronger position, arguing that middle-class Americans, no longer living by the moral precepts they preach, require immigrants to remind them of the importance of values they are increasingly spurning. One example of this position involves the family. Just at the moment when Americans are experiencing ambivalence about the family form most appropriate to them, immigrants are seen offering a welcome alternative to postmodern pressures. Peter Hamilton, a Brookline health care data analyst, was one of those men who took time off from his own career to spend more time with his children; he likes immigrants from Mexico and Asia because they "have very strong family values. . . . People set up a family business and everybody will work together in a store." A second example involves God. Immigrants are widely perceived to be more devout in their religious beliefs than Americans who have been here some time; "Their moral upbringing," as Dan Charette of Broken Arrow expressed it, "has been great." Many middle-class Americans prefer strong religious values of any kind to relativistic and atheistic ones and recognize that immigrants provide them. Jim McLaughlin, the conservative Christian whose faith in moral absolutes is unshakable, is the kind of patriotic Oklahoman that East Coast liberals associate with xenophobia and intolerance. Yet, Mr. McLaughlin appreciates immigrants for the religious devotion they bring with them: "The people that I taught that came over here from Vietnam or Thailand or any of those countries, they were so happy to be here that they were willing to become Christians. And when they did become Christians, they really understood. They were better Christians than we were," he concludes.

Kenneth Roberts is the immigrant from Panama. "We black foreigners," he told us, "not all of us, but the majority, have worked hard for what we want to accomplish. Some of us work two or three jobs at a time to accomplish 'the American dream.'" Many of the nonimmigrants in our sample would share his perception. Mrs. McLaughlin followed her husband's comments about the religious faith of immigrants with her own idea that "they are hard, hard workers. They have a real work ethic. And most of them that I've been around, they're very honest with you." Those are qualities deeply appreciated in middle-class America and play a large role in America's positive attitudes toward immigrants.

"We've hired a pretty good number of Asian people here," said George Slade, the general manager at a tool production facility in Cobb County:

We've hired some people from other countries, too. Those
people . . . they come to this country, and man, it's the American dream. They go to work. These people will give you six-
teen hours a day. Not that I'm looking for that, but I'll tell you
what. They train themselves. They teach themselves. . . . And
why? Because they left a war-torn country, or they left where
the opportunities weren't there for them. What that is going to
show other Americans I would hope eventually is that, jeez,
this ain't all bad.

Immigrants not only work harder than native Americans,
David Butte of Brookline commented, they are probably also
smarter. Joseph Palumbo, a physicist in Medford, had lots of
reasons not to like immigrants, since they compete directly with
him for jobs. Still, he could recognize that "it's the people who
come to this nation with very little and worked their butts off
which have created . . . the greatest economic benefit for us all. I
have nothing but admiration for these Vietnamese boat people
who came over here in rags, couldn't speak a word of English,
and now own chains of restaurants." From this perspective, the
notion that immigrants are taking jobs away from Americans
seems wrongheaded. Americans no longer want to work in jobs
that demand long hours and offer low pay, so it's a good thing
that someone does. Maybe we can even learn from them. "These
people hustle," as Tommy Fasano of Rancho Bernardo put it. "I
think they're a good example."

What all these sentiments add up to is a picture of what
could be called "the good immigrant." These are people who
have experienced violence and disruption, usually in places both
far removed from the United States, and, in the case of Vietnam,
people to whom we have a special responsibility because we created the conditions of havoc from which they are escaping. Good immigrants ought to have little trouble adapting to
America when they arrive here because they are seen as having
the discipline and devotion necessary for success. The distance
they traveled to America and the difficulty they had getting here
not only remind Americans of their own grandparents' passage,

but also insure that their numbers will be finite. By welcoming them, Americans receive the best of two worlds: confirmation of their humanitarianism and a steady source of labor for necessary, but not pleasant, jobs.

Good immigrants cannot exist without bad ones. If good immigrants bring the work ethic, bad ones bring welfare. "With all the people that come in from Mexico, they can immediately get on the welfare rolls. Yours and my tax dollars is paying for that, and that is absolutely ridiculous," said Steve Reardon of Sand Springs. Bad immigrants deal in drugs, form gangs, and have a propensity toward crime. Like the urban underclass, they are also sexually promiscuous; it is not welfare that encourages them in this behavior but, as Lydia Radchenko of Rancho Bernardo noted, when they have "their babies here, the baby is automatically American." In addition, our respondents often noted, they never learn English. Worse, according to Jake Sandford, also of Sand Springs, they "want . . . their schoolchildren taught in their native language. They never get to participate." The major points were all summed up by Vaughn Hyde of DeKalb: "I don't think it's fair [that] somebody . . . sneaks into my country, uses the welfare system, uses hospitals, takes jobs, undermines pay scales, okay, in my country. You might as well come into my house and open my refrigerator. That's a button of mine. I don't like it at all, at all. I see them crossing the border, laughing."

Disrespectful of America, bad immigrants, according to those who felt this way, make no move to become citizens, longing for the day when they can go back to their homes enriched by the generosity of American taxpayers. Because there are so many bad immigrants in America, many of our respondents believe, we ought to be careful about subsidizing them too generously. "Charity begins at home," said Caroline Carlson of Brookline. "I think we've gotten to the point where we have to start taking care of our own first," added Anna Stollini of Medford. Not very many people were for sending immigrants back, although at least one was, but many wanted to slow immigration down, to regulate it more, and, above all, to make distinctions.

"I'm for legal immigration, and the reason I am is that there are a lot of smart people out there that need to come to this country if we can get them," as Rancho Bernardo's Fred Richards put it. "But these people come illegally into the country. I want to build that fence just as high as I can."

The distinction made by Mr. Richards is one of the most tenaciously held distinctions in middle-class America; the people with whom we spoke overwhelmingly support legal immigration and express disgust with the illegal variety. In that, they are in accord with public opinion data; although Americans divide roughly evenly between those who would deny health and educational assistance to illegal immigrants, 73 percent of them would oppose cutting off such benefits to legal immigrants, compared with 24 percent who would favor it. Illegal immigrants come from everywhere—they arrive at Kennedy Airport just as they cross the Rio Grande at night—but most middle-class Americans associate illegal immigration with Mexican immigration; indeed, for some in our sample, especially among the Californians, there was little difference. The obvious conclusion is that legality, for them, is not really the issue. What is the issue is an effort to single out one group, Mexicans, for reasons that resemble racial discrimination: they just do not like them or are made uncomfortable by them.

"I know this sounds terrible," said one resident of Rancho Bernardo, "but I resent living in a neighborhood like this and having homeless Mexicans just walking up and down the street ... wandering through the neighborhood which they really have no business in." "You know, first off we have to put all these signs up for the Mexican people and we have to put everything in their language," added another resident of the same community. "We even have to go to the bank and it says do you want this in English or Spanish? Well, phooeeey. This is America, you want to live here, you speak the language." Yet, despite such sentiments, the ways in which middle-class Americans, including Californians, invested the distinction between legal and illegal immigration with moral meaning suggest that such borderline racist attitudes are atypical.

For Judy Dropkin of Eastlake, for example, the distinction between legals and illegals is not about immigrants but about law. "I am against illegal immigration whether it comes from Mexico or Asia," she said. "I am one of those persons who firmly believe in law. If you don't have law or if you flaunt it, you go into chaos." Mrs. Dropkin, who described herself as a sixties person, illustrated her point with an anecdote. Like many of her generation, she opposed the war in Vietnam. She remembers that some of those who objected to the war and who left to go to Canada were later prosecuted while others were not, a degree of arbitrariness in the way laws are enforced that strikes her as criminal. Standards have to be consistent, she believes, and America's immigration policy is not. "If you don't like the law, get it changed, which is one of the reasons why I'm against illegal immigration whether it's from Europe or whatever. You just have to have law, you have to have a system."

Who, then, is breaking the law? To my surprise, a very large number of Americans who do not like illegal immigration blame not the immigrants, but the employers who hire them, which also tends to undermine the notion that their dislike of illegality is really just a covert form of racism. "If you are going to penalize anybody in California, penalize the business people that are paying them," argued Pedro Govea of Brookline. "Make it illegal to employ them," said the same community's Norman Wolfson. Added Eastlake's Carmen Tosca:

> I have a problem with [California's governor] Pete Wilson and all the Republicans who are against immigration, because they turn a blind eye when it's to the advantage of the United States. . . . I think that when he talks about Proposition 187 and arresting the illegal aliens, he knows where they're at. Everybody knows where they can be found, and yet it depends if it's to his advantage or not. If it's the agricultural season, he's not going to go to the fields and arrest all those illegal aliens.

The same point was made by Eastlake's Henry Pearson: "It's the white American businessman who lives in La Jolla and Rancho Santa Fe who knowingly employs these people in their companies or who picks them up on the street corners in Pacific Beach every day to give them a job as a gardener for five bucks a day" who ought to be held responsible for the problem. "It's the folks that are creating the demand. That's where you fix it."

If one should not blame the immigrants but their employers for the plight of illegals, it hardly makes sense to scapegoat the former. The harsh-toned xenophobia that one would associate with racist responses to illegal immigration was generally missing from the language of those with whom we spoke. Instead, the very humanitarian language used by those who thought of America as a refuge for the downtrodden was also used by those who had qualms about illegals. Mexican-Americans who come to work in American fields make more than they ever could in Mexico, which is clearly why they come. But not all Americans realize this. And even if they do, they would make a distinction between exploitation abroad, which is outside their moral purview, and what Kenneth Easterbrook of Cobb County calls "the exploitation that occurs through the immigrant system" within the United States. In Mr. Easterbrook's opinion, there is suffering enough already in the United States, and he cannot understand why we should deliberately create more.

Mr. Easterbrook, who is black, spoke in ways quite similar to other African-Americans who had qualms about immigration. Polling opinion data consistently show that black Americans support such programs as Social Security, Medicare, federal aid to education, and government assistance to the poor by anywhere from 10 percent to 30 percent more than whites. Not surprisingly, then, the language used by those among our black middle-class respondents who had reservations about immigration was a humanitarian language in defense of the welfare state. "I can't understand us, that we will allow immigrants to come in and receive funding—never paying in—and then I have to catch hell getting funding for something that I . . . have a right to," as Patricia Bates put it. Ms. Bates implicitly understands that there is a tension between expanding immigration and expanding the welfare state, even though people on the left generally tend to support both (and further support high-wage work, which also conflicts with open borders). "Like you are going and taking care of the poor and hungry in another country and you got poor and hungry, black and white, living right here, but you'd rather see them die of the disease, decay, and the rot than to acknowledge the fact that it's here, to stick your chest out and go take care of it over there," she continued. For Patricia Bates, white Americans will go to great lengths to deny their obligations to the inner-city black poor; supporting foreign aid abroad and immigration at home are two of them.

The fact that individuals on both sides of the immigration divide expressed their opinions in humanitarian language contains an important implication for America's debate over this issue: left and right positions on immigration do not exist. Americans are not divided between conservatives who are suspicious of foreigners and unwilling to pay benefits on their behalf and liberals who welcome the oppressed from abroad and want to help them while they are here. Nothing in the history of immigration has ever supported a division between left and right: business, which is usually considered conservative, has supported it, while labor and African-Americans, generally thought of as liberal, have tended to oppose it. Our respondents are just not easily classifiable into recognized political camps on this issue. In some ways, the most traditional people in our sample— those who believed most firmly in the ideals of God, country, family, and work—were the ones most anxious to have immigrants arrive and kick-start those values, while those who most strongly wanted a caring government that would take a special interest in the unfortunate were skeptical about admitting whole new categories of people in need. So while the opinions of those interviewed by the Middle Class Morality Project reveal divisions over immigration, what divides them is not politics, but differences over how best to reach goals—a society that respects law, a society that takes care of people, a society that is open to opportunity—upon which most people agree.

The results of the Middle Class Morality Project suggest that politicians may be making a mistake to assume that they can ride a backlash against immigration into office. That very mistake, interestingly enough, was made by the Republican candidate for president in 1996, Senator Robert Dole. In his campaign, Dole, who previously had no particular history of opposition to immigration, endorsed policies designed to tighten the borders and denounced the Democrats for supporting the right of illegal immigrants to obtain welfare, moves to shore up his base among conservatives. Such a stance proved costly in an electoral sense, swinging the usually Republican state of Florida to the Democrats and contributing to a larger-than-usual loss in California. What the 1996 election revealed is that it makes little sense to talk about "American" opposition to "immigrants" when so many Americans are immigrants. In particular, Republican flirtation with xenophobic themes cost them support among a natural ally: Hispanic voters, who tend to be devout Catholics with solid bourgeois values, yet who were concerned that anti-immigrant measures, even ones they support, would contribute to discrimination against them. It is also plausible that harsh anti-immigrant sentiments contributed to a nationwide perception that the Republicans were "harsh" and "extremist," thereby widening the already significant gap between men and women in support for the Republican Party.

Because they do not see immigration as a "political" issue that divides left from right, middle-class Americans search for a practical way to deal with the issue. For them, the solution is obvious: since they make a distinction between good immigrants and bad ones, America should, as Rancho Bernardo's Yuri Kozlof, himself a Russian immigrant, put it, "allow good people to come in and not allow the others." Aware that this might be interpreted as anti-Mexican, Mr. Kozlof, without prompting, quickly added that "it has to be the same for everybody, for Mexicans, for everybody." "You should have to pass some tests before you become an immigrant in this country," said one of our respondents in Broken Arrow. Middle-class Americans like the idea of a selection mechanism—a kind of middle-class morality exam—which would help them sort out who belongs and who does not. Even if such a test were impractical, its objectives could be met in other ways. By their conduct once they are here, immigrants provide an ex post facto justification for their entry. If they are willing to learn English, to work hard, to transform themselves into good immigrants, then we were obviously right to have admitted them. If they persist in isolating themselves from the rest of America, then we were wrong to have admitted them.

As ways to regulate the flow of immigration, such solutions, of course, make little sense. Part of the frustration expressed by those with reservations about immigration lies precisely in the impossibility of devising some ordered system to regulate it. But immigration is also a moral issue, one that divides philosophers between those who believe that a country such as America has a moral duty to keep its borders open and those who believe that, in a Hobbesian world, a nation has a contrary duty to preserve its way of life. In contrast to both positions, the idea that immigration in itself is neither good nor bad but depends on the kind of immigrant makes considerable sense. Middle-class America is long past the time when the definition of the "good" immigrant would have been a European; these days, bourgeois values can be associated with people of many races and languages. The identification that middle-class Americans make between good immigrants and legal immigrants is furthermore based on the proposition that those who follow the law in coming here will be more likely to obey the law after their arrival; citizens who worry about lawlessness are not going to be sympathetic to illegal immigration whatever their views about race or poverty.

But the most important reason that the distinction between legal and illegal immigrants is so deeply ingrained in middle-class America is that such a distinction itself constitutes a border, a way of marking off two different kinds of people. There is a school of thought that, suspicious of distinctions, believes that all demarcations represent arbitrary attempts by one group to maintain its power and status over another. From such a perspective, commitments to universal or cosmopolitan values ought to take preference over national identity. Whether or not this is true, it is also the case that people have a propensity to

make distinctions in order to give a sense of order and control to
the world. Particularly for something so difficult to control as
immigration, creating a border between those we want to allow
in and those we do not helps ease the anxiety of living with
an open border between this country and the rest of the world.
Unable to control the country's actual border, in other words,
middle-class Americans do their best to put another in its place.
Rather than representing a racist effort to keep out "bad" Mexicans while allowing in "good" Asians, the distinction between
legal and illegal immigration has the opposite intention: to shift
the question of boundaries from one marked by country of
origin to one marked by deservingness. That way, America can
be open to people from everywhere without being open to
everyone.

The "middle-class morality test" that Americans would like
to administer to potential immigrants thus represents an attempt
to balance realism with humanitarianism: the only way it makes
sense to uphold the altruism involved in welcoming others is to
combine with it what is good for the self-interest of the nation.
"I think any country has the right to determine at some point in
time what its population can stand," Nancy Elliott of DeKalb
County believed. "I guess what it comes down to is that I believe that everybody needs to contribute. If you're contributing,
you come to work here, then you're going to pay some tax or
whatever. If you come here illegally, you're not on the roster.
You're not really contributing any 'pay,' but you're reaping the
benefits of what's there, and I think that's not fair." Views like
hers surely underestimate the contributions both to the
economy and the tax rolls made by illegal immigrants, most of
whom do not match the stereotypes that middle-class Americans have of them. But Mrs. Elliott also understands something
that is just becoming clear to economists and policy-makers,
which is that, in economist George Borjas's words, "the most
important lesson is that the economic impact of immigration
will vary by time and place and can either be beneficial or harmful." Middle-class Americans extend the same notion that immigration is not a univocal phenomenon from the economy to

citizenship: some immigrants strengthen the nation, others dilute it. Common sense suggests that if one believes in both a strong country and an openness to the rest of the world, making distinctions between those who are worthy of coming here and those who are not is a more appropriate moral response than keeping the borders completely open or completely closed.

BENIGN MULTICULTURALISM

Regardless of whether they want the border more open or more closed, middle-class Americans would be reluctant to cut off benefits for immigrants already here, even if they came illegally. It is, however, one thing to say that people's rights should not be denied and another to say that their identities should be respected. Once we turn from the "negative" issue of whether immigrants should be punished to the "positive" question of whether their differences should be celebrated, are middle-class Americans as welcoming as they like to think they are? What has come to be called multiculturalism is hotly contested terrain in American life. In the way multiculturalism has been debated in America, particularly among intellectuals and university professors, it appears to pit two important principles against each other: American respect for tolerance and pluralism suggests that we ought to welcome cultures from all over the world, while American ideals of loyalty and patriotism suggest that such differences should be blended into support for America and its way of life. It would be helpful to know how middle-class Americans choose between these principles. Do they appreciate diversity, as they do with the great variety of religious beliefs in this country, or do they condemn those who are different, as they do with respect to homosexuality?

One conclusion emerges in sharp clarity from our interviews: If support for multiculturalism means support for bilingualism, middle-class Americans are against it. Americans place great store on English as the language of the country: when given a series of statements about the obligations of citizenship—voting, keeping informed, serving in war—being able to speak and understand English placed second in importance, behind only reporting a crime that one has witnessed. That helps explain why, according to the 1994 General Social Survey, 62.9 percent of the American people favor making English the official language of the United States compared with 27.6 percent who do not. Groups such as U.S. English, which promote the notion of one official language for the United States, have had some political success: while their efforts to pass a constitutional amendment requiring English as the official language of the country failed, state measures, such as California's Proposition 63 in 1986, have generally passed. Indeed Proposition 63 passed by 73 percent of the vote and won a majority in every county in the state. English, it is clear, matters.

Middle-class Americans, it would seem, think about other languages the same way they think about homosexuality—and not the way they think about minority religions. Our respondents were strongly opposed to bilingualism, no matter where in America they lived, and, overall, the percentage of those unsympathetic to the rationale behind bilingualism was four

TABLE 4.5
"PEOPLE WHO DO NOT SPEAK ENGLISH WELL SHOULD BE
TAUGHT IN THE SCHOOLS IN THEIR NATIVE LANGUAGE"

	Strongly Agree	Agree	No Opinion	Disagree	Strongly Disagree
Brookline	0	6	2	13	4
Medford	0	4	0	13	8
Broken Arrow	0	2	1	13	9
Sand Springs	0	5	2	11	7
DeKalb	0	4	0	19	2
Cobb	1	4	0	15	5
Eastlake	1	7	0	5	12
Rancho Bernardo	0	1	0	11	13
Total	2	33	5	100	60

times greater than the proportion that was sympathetic. This finding suggests that the deviation from a normal bell-curve distribution is even greater on the issue of bilingualism than it is on the issue of homosexuality.

What accounts for this opposition? Although many of those with whom we talked insisted that their opposition to bilingualism was meant to help immigrant children get along better in their new country, in fact, hostility to bilingualism is primarily symbolic in nature. Bilingualism is one of those issues that generate passionate research, each side claiming empirical support for how much such programs can work or how little they achieve. But even if they were persuaded that bilingual programs worked effectively, our respondents would still be likely to oppose them. For them, a willingness to learn English is one of the marks, if not the most important mark, of the good immigrant. It is a test: pass it and you belong; refuse to take it and you don't. To a considerable degree, public policy has had to accommodate itself to such sentiments, as have the debates over bilingualism; increasingly, defenders of such programs emphasize not the political imperative of protecting minority languages, but how bilingualism, when done right, can help smooth the transition to English.

Because insistence on English is seen as a test, it is likely to be resented by those being tested. But middle-class America did not invent the symbolic dimension of bilingualism: it has been part of the arguments made *for* these programs. Some claim that bilingualism is a political challenge to a dominant culture, an argument likely to lead those who uphold the dominant culture to dig in their heels. Others suggest that all immigrants will eventually learn English anyway, so that we ought to allow bilingualism to show respect for those who came here under such trying conditions. Our respondents simply turn that symbolism around. We all know they are going to learn English anyway; therefore, the sooner they do, the better off they will be. Respect for immigrants is important, but respect for the country is more important. On this issue, for most of our respondents, the idea that we are one nation clearly takes precedence over the idea that difference should be celebrated.

Despite the large proportion of people who expressed hostility to bilingualism in our survey, however, it would not be correct to conclude that these attitudes represent an intolerance comparable to, or greater than, the way our respondents thought about homosexuality. For one thing, the intensity of the language they used when discussing bilingualism was not the same as the language they used when respect for homosexuality was the issue: people do not think of those who want to preserve Spanish as perverted or immoral. For another, despite strong support for making English the official language of the United States, the General Social Survey also discovered that there are majorities in America behind both bilingualism in schools and multilingual ballots. As much as they like the idea of English as the official language of the country, it would seem Americans want those who speak other languages to preserve them: a 1987 poll taken just about the time that Proposition 63 in California passed discovered that a substantial majority of the state's residents thought it was "a good thing" for immigrants to keep their languages and traditions. Opposition to bilingualism and support for the preservation of original languages sound as if they are in contradiction to each other, but the more one listens to how people express themselves, it becomes clear that they are not. As most Americans grapple with these issues, they support the principle that groups within the United States ought to be allowed to retain their distinctiveness, but only so long as they do so within an official culture that insists on the priority of the national community over subnational ethnic groups.

This is certainly the way our respondents thought about the conflict between the larger nation as a whole and the specific nations that make it up. On the one hand, they had little doubt that group loyalties had to take second place to national ones; table 4.6 presents data from our survey question dealing with this issue. While one can detect some racial polarization in their responses—primarily, black respondents in DeKalb County

TABLE 4.6
"THERE ARE TIMES WHEN LOYALTY TO AN ETHNIC GROUP
OR TO A RACE SHOULD BE VALUED OVER LOYALTY
TO THE COUNTRY AS A WHOLE"

	Strongly Agree	Agree	No Opinion	Disagree	Strongly Disagree
Brookline	0	6	4	12	3
Medford	0	7	2	12	4
Broken Arrow	0	3	2	14	6
Sand Springs	0	4	2	14	5
DeKalb	0	11	4	9	1
Cobb	0	6	0	13	6
Eastlake	1	2	1	20	1
Rancho Bernardo	0	2	3	12	8
Total	1	41	18	106	34

were more sympathetic to the claims of ethnic and racial groups than those elsewhere—the overwhelming majority sentiment across the country not surprisingly puts the nation first.

Yet, there is also another side to the story, one that revealed itself to me in an unexpected way. As a college professor and writer, I have been deeply involved in debates over "multiculturalism," the idea that we have a strong obligation to emphasize the differences and special characteristics of the groups that compose the American mosaic; my position in those debates generally has been unsympathetic to multiculturalist claims, preferring instead an assimilationist position that I identify with my own familial and ethnic experiences. Because the middle-class Americans with whom I spoke were so hostile to bilingualism, I naturally assumed that they would share my personal distaste for multiculturalism. They did not. When we asked people how they felt about taking special steps to recognize and celebrate specific cultures, most of those with whom we spoke put aside their opposition to bilingualism and indicated strong sympathy with multiculturalism.

Often there was some confusion in people's minds about the two. When we asked people whether they supported multiculturalism, a number of them responded by denouncing bilingualism. When we explained that we were not asking about language but culture, many said that was different: of course, we ought to respect other cultures. Teaching children respect for the many cultures brought to this country was variously described by our respondents as "very good," "real good," "important," "fine," "great," "really great," "neat," "superb," "helpful," and "necessary"; only a few said it was "harmful" or an example of "political correctness run amok." Even when challenged—on this question, we tried to be very challenging—people rarely backed down from their enthusiastic support for the idea. "Spend a week on this and a week on that, that way the person is full-rounded," said J. W. Cotton of Broken Arrow. Well, Maria intervened, some people say we need to stress the basics. "Like I said," he responded, "a week or two on each. I mean when you've got four or five months in school, I am sure you can sneak in a week or something. . . . There's room for fluffy stuff." Although survey researchers have demonstrated that support for multiculturalism is stronger in the Northeast than in the other regions of the country, we found strong support in each region, perhaps reflecting the fact that multiculturalism is also more popular among better-educated Americans.

The middle-class African-Americans with whom we spoke were the most unabashedly enthusiastic about multiculturalism. "You should automatically respect someone when you first meet them," Gerald Stevens pointed out. "It's almost like unconditional, until maybe that person does something to make you lose respect." The same rule, he believes, applies to groups. Black people like him ought to have the benefit of the doubt for their culture unless or until that respect is lost. "As a young child," Vaughn Hyde added, "I knew far more about Europeans than they could ever possibly know about me. That's not fair." Over and over, African-Americans brought up the example of Christopher Columbus, proving, in passing, how controversies over historical symbols have real cogency in the country at large.

How could he have discovered America, they wanted to know, when people of color were already here? Latinos in California shared the same point of view. Their enthusiasm for multiculturalism ranged from the practical—"I would be out of a job" without it, as an educational training coordinator laughingly put it—to such idealistic reasons as the "need to expand ourselves."

White Americans, although sympathetic to multiculturalism, were not quite as enthusiastic. For one thing, even those who support multiculturalism have qualms about forcing it on people; they think about cultural diversity in the same laissez-faire way they think about religious diversity, as a good thing as long as no one tries to impose their views on others. Multiculturalism, William Fahy of Cobb County argued, should be, "low key," which to him meant that "you don't take it to extremes." Searching for the right word to characterize his feelings, he finally found it: multicultural education is all right so long as it is not "political." Whether he knew it or not, and I think he probably did, Mr. Fahy was trying to support the idea of multiculturalism without supporting the agenda of the activists behind it. He would object to multiculturalism as its most passionate defenders understand it. They believe we should teach respect for all groups as a means to achieve equality among them, whereas he would teach respect for all groups because they exist here in the same country with us.

Multiculturalism usually is identified with particularism. To its supporters, the majority culture tends to overlook the accomplishments of particular cultures, requiring an emphasis on the singular achievements of special groups, while to its opponents, multiculturalism represents a splintering of society into its ethnic and racial fragments. One reason that multiculturalism can be so popular in middle-class America is that many of those who support it do so for universalistic rather than particularistic reasons. Just as they believe there is only one God, despite myriad ways of worshipping him, they also believe, as Samina Hoque, a Medford physicist from Bangladesh put it, that "people are not very different. Deep down, they are all the same." They even look the same, according to Sand Springs's Diana Hamilton: "When was the last time you saw a kid in Egypt dressed in a linen thing wrapped around their waist?" she asked us. "They look just like the rest of us. . . . So if you could really have a multicultural curriculum that . . . explained people's differences and then showed how we're all the same, that would be good. But a lot of the ones I've observed don't do that at all. Like I said, it serves to point out all the differences, and say 'Oh, isn't that weird.' "

Multiculturalism that is tailored to be compatible with the more universal values of America can be described as "benign." To do it right, as Eastlake's Jason Cooper put it, "you don't institutionalize the celebration of those differences. You let people celebrate those differences by association and by civic groups and by public interest organizations. You don't have to institutionalize that in society by saying that on this day we're going to celebrate Cinco de Mayo in public schools to recognize that there is a group among you that happens to be affiliated with that heritage." Benign multiculturalism is informal rather than official, soft in its particularism rather than hard, and assimilationist in its objectives; it is, in short, an example of a modest virtue. The national culture, like middle-class morality, requires occasional revitalization, which particular identities can provide. But those particular identities can only do so by subsuming themselves under the broad umbrella of Americanism.

There is, along these lines, a generally unrecognized conservative set of arguments in favor of multiculturalism, ones that the more conservative among our respondents were quick to make. Brian Fischer, a conservative resident of Cobb County, dislikes multiculturalism vehemently: "To predicate an educational environment on stressing dissimilarities so people can understand where they came from, I think is the greatest load of crap," he said in no uncertain terms. But, he also noted, in the South, individuals "need to know who their people are." He would have all students sit down with a tape recorder and talk to their parents and grandparents, getting a sense of their struggles and hopes. In that way, he believes, multicultural education "gives a person a sense of worth and a sense of tradition." A number of our respondents thought that learning about your background gives you roots, anchoring you in the scheme of things in a way that strengthens your sense of place in the society. Taking pride in your group is a way of taking pride in yourself: "I mean, there's nothing wrong with heritage-type education, you know, like a background," said Alex Molinari. "For example, my heritage is Italian. Hey, there's nothing wrong with a little Italian in school. That's great." Everybody should learn something about their heritage, even if, as José Velasquez put it, "you should be American and then something else, not the other way around." Even African-Americans, who supported multiculturalism more strongly than our other respondents, did so in essentially conservative ways. Kenneth Easterbrook sees nothing wrong with black students at university having their own dorms and congregating with each other. "That's not because I want to separate, that I don't want to deal with you," he added. "It just says that at times I just want to touch base with who I am."

Benign multiculturalism has one additional advantage: it is practical. If you really want to make money in mutual funds, you have to invest globally, said Jeremy Toole of Cobb County; for that reason alone, he would have his children learn more about the rest of the world. Cathy Ryan tells us that her husband would require that the president of the United States spend a year abroad, like an exchange student; if he is going to make decisions that involve other places, he ought at least have an appreciation for them. Even selling products here in the United States now requires familiarity with all the cultures and languages that live here. "I think that with the mixture of people that we have in America now too, we have to learn the languages of other people," as George Slade put it. In reality, both America and the world are changing, and multiculturalism can help with the transition.

The preponderance of conservative and practical arguments in favor of multiculturalism suggests an answer to how middle-class Americans would choose between the principle of pluralism and the principle of patriotism. By avoiding the extremes of parochialism on the one hand and particularism on the other, benign multiculturalism enables middle-class Americans to avoid making that choice. Herbert Gans once coined the term "symbolic ethnicity" to characterize the way earlier immigrant groups, among them Italians, Irish, Poles, and Jews, took pride in their group but always at somewhat of a distance from its tribalist claims on them. It is that experience with multiculturalism in the past that shapes how middle-class Americans view multiculturalism in the present. They want newer groups of immigrants, as well as African-Americans, to be able to express their ethnic diversity, but they also want them to move quickly toward what the historian David Hollinger calls a "post-ethnic" perspective. "The national community's fate can be common," Hollinger writes, "without its will being uniform, and the nation can constitute a common project without effacing all of the various projects that its citizens pursue through their voluntary affiliations." If multiculturalism is organized in such a way that it serves American goals and values, it becomes possible to respect the diversity of the groups that belong to America and to respect America at the same time.

PEACE OVER VIETNAM?

And how much should America be respected? For many, if not for most, Americans, the answer to that question is axiomatic. Country, as we were reminded by one of our respondents, stands with family and God as part of a trinity of things Americans most hold sacred. Patriotism is generally thought of as among the most important of virtues. The duty of an American is not to judge based on abstract principles of justice but to judge based on what strengthens the nation. It is not liberty that makes America possible, many of our respondents believe, but America that makes liberty realizable. There has long existed a distrust of worldly cosmopolitanism in the United States, a sense that those who believe in disarmament or global harmony are hopeless idealists; we need them, many Americans would claim, for we always need ideals, but we should never be guided by them, for they fail to understand in their heads what the common people know in their hearts: that this country is especially blessed.

If ever there were an issue on which we could expect popular opinion to be at odds with academic opinion, it would be over the question of patriotism. Perhaps reflecting Socrates' death at the hands of his own people, patriotism, as much as it is respected by ordinary people, has always been a suspect virtue among philosophers. In its concern with timeless universals, moral philosophy has rarely attributed that much importance to the parochialism, blind faith, and propensity for double standards it associates with defense of the nation. No one embodied this distrust more than Immanuel Kant, for whom nationality was one of those arbitrary real-world contingencies we needed to avoid if we were properly to understand our moral duty. But nearly all versions of liberal political theory assert that our obligations to anyone in the world are equally as compelling as our obligations to fellow citizens. From the standpoint of high moral principle, nationhood is, as the contemporary philosopher Martha Nussbaum puts it, "a morally irrelevant characteristic," one that, if properly ignored, would enable us to be as concerned with famine in India as we are with floods in West Virginia. Although there has been a rebirth of interest in the national community among political philosophers, it remains the case that intellect tends to be suspicious of country.

These two visions of patriotism—one of acceptance, the other of suspicion—crashed into each other during the 1960s. An older generation, its experience marked by the Great Depression and World War II, was especially attracted to the binding power of national unity, without which, most of its members were convinced, something frightful would have happened to American democracy. Their children, by contrast, reflecting a common experience of being the first in their families to attend college, were intrigued by ideals of liberal universalism and repelled by what they took to be their own government's violation of those ideals during the Vietnam War. Such divisions persist to this day: only 23 percent of the American people believe that Vietnam was a "just war," compared with 86 percent for World War II, 49 percent for Korea, and 67 percent for the Persian Gulf War. The Vietnam experience is alive and well in the interviews we conducted across the country: "It's almost like you can divide America's consciousness between pre-Vietnam and post-Vietnam," was how Diana Hamilton of Sand Springs put it. Generations, of course, are not solely defined by year of birth; many Americans who grew up during the 1960s shared their parents' attitudes toward their country, volunteered or were drafted to serve in Vietnam, in some cases gave up their lives, and in other cases returned to jobs and families. But the 1960s clearly marked a dividing line in the American experience of nationhood; from then to now, the country remains split between one group that longs for the parades, the holidays, and the pride in flag of a unified nation, while another swears never again to give blind loyalty to its government's version of the truth.

Yet, as we continued to talk to middle-class Americans, it became clear that the gap between these two visions of American patriotism has narrowed considerably since the 1960s. What we discovered is something that can be called "mature patriotism," formed by movement on both sides of the Vietnam divide. Twenty-five years after peace came to Vietnam, peace over Vietnam may be coming to the United States.

For those who once demonstrated in the streets against the war or, in extreme cases, left the country, the past two decades have been a process of making peace with the United States. Gone is reflexive anti-Americanism, the once deeply ingrained belief that other countries are inherently more peaceful or more just than the United States. A significant portion of the 1960s generation has learned that America, for all its flaws, is a country worthy of their allegiance. Once told to love it or leave it, they have chosen not to leave it and, if not to love it, then at least to like it.

Frank Orzos, an Eastlake pharmacist (whose father was a

sheepherder in Spain), recalled to us an interview he recently heard with the actor Peter Fonda: "It was twenty-five years since the *Easy Rider* movie had been released or something like that. His interviewer was asking him, 'What do you think now looking back on that whole era? What do you think about your generation, what you guys did?' " Fonda, Mr. Orzos recalled, responded by saying, "We blew it.... There were so many problems. The world was a mess. The country was a mess, and we turned our back. We condemned everybody we felt was responsible for it and turned our backs on them. There was so much work to be done to correct things. We wouldn't even take part. We were totally wrong." That made a huge impression on Mr. Orzos, one, he claimed, he will never forget, for it seemed to summarize his own feelings so accurately. Mr. Orzos was not alone in those sentiments. "I think that those of us who are from the Vietnam era . . . became quite ashamed of being American," Elizabeth Tyler, a real estate developer in Brookline, told us. "It's because we . . . were taught one thing and then found with a rude awakening that it was something far different" when it came to making American foreign policy. But recent events around the world—the collapse of Communism, political instability in Bosnia and the Middle East, starvation in Africa—had a strong impact on her views toward America. When we see what other countries are like, she continued, "increasingly people are feeling proud of who we are . . . problems and all." Mrs. Tyler is pleased that her daughter, who has just come back from a semester traveling around the world, sees this country pretty much as she does. The important point she wants to make is that awareness is not a threat to patriotism; to know about the rest of the world is to come to appreciate America that much more.

According to many of those with whom we talked, patriotism is different in America these days: it's no longer "Mom–baseball–apple pie stuff," "John Wayne movies and Clint Eastwood...," "Norman Rockwell..., the giant turkey and all of the family," or "the whole rah, rah, rah kind of thing." The old symbols do not quite work the way they used to. One reason is a change in gender norms that has reached into the armed services. Michelle Knight of Broken Arrow serves in the Reserves. She remembers how, when her father wore his uniform, he would get immediate respect. When she wears hers, by contrast, "there's a stigma attached . . . you are either a lesbian or you're looking for a husband." Men in particular, she is implicitly saying, have had a difficult time getting used to the fact women serve their country just like men.

There is, a number of respondents believed, no reason to lament the passing of the "my country right or wrong" attitude. America, in their opinion, has simply grown up. Once again, the inclusion of women's voices has accounted for part of this change. Women, according to Joyce Palma of Medford, are less likely to support jingoistic kinds of responses. They have, she argues, "a whole different viewpoint on everything. I think they are more peace-loving. I see it . . . everywhere; you hear the men yelling as though they are sort of scared about what is going to happen to their money and their rights and their control." Very few in our sample wanted the 1960s to return, remembering it, for better or worse, as a time of bra-burning, drugs, and violence. But a significant number also believe that, as John Liera, a Medford fireman who served in Vietnam, put it, "good things happened in the sixties. We questioned the government." Demanding that government be held to a higher standard represents, for one side of the 1960s divide, a more nuanced patriotism than blind obedience.

Furthermore, a number of our respondents believed that old-fashioned patriotism is increasingly inappropriate in a world becoming more globally integrated. "I mean, the one thing I'm proud about," said Jane Sargent of Cobb County, "is that we have a government that's lasted well over two hundred years that's really managed to pretty much deal with . . . every major crisis and conflict." But now it is time to use the confidence that comes from such pride to function more effectively in a world that has to some degree transcended national boundaries. "I think that in the coming years we're going to have to learn to let go of the ethnocentric way we view the world as kind of 'We're the center of the universe.' . . . We're going to have to learn to think of ourselves less as a superpower and more as just one more team member in the group of European states." Annette Pisano of Medford expressed the same kinds of thought. Americans are not "as overtly flag-waving or jumping up and down, you know the Fourth of July thing," she commented, but "people are becoming aware of the global world," one that is different from the world we knew as children. Both women are suggesting that, in its own way, the disillusionment with American power expressed during the war in Vietnam may have helped America reach a level of balanced patriotism relevant to a post–Cold War world.

At the same time that reflexive anti-Americanism has waned, so has reflexive pro-Americanism, producing another version of mature patriotism, but this time from those who once gave automatic support to their government during Vietnam. Victoria Ross of Medford is convinced that "Vietnam played a major role in shaping American society as we know it today." For Mrs. Ross, Vietnam stands in sharp contrast to World War II. The Smithsonian Institution, she knew, had tried to sponsor an exhibit on *Enola Gay,* the plane that dropped an atomic bomb on Japan. "That was an instance," she says, "where we did what we had to do to win. Was it right? Good question, but we did it." In Vietnam, however, we were caught between what was right and what was necessary, and "they aren't necessarily the same thing at all. . . . The division in the country as a result of it was very deeply felt by a lot of people, and I think maybe it did irreversible change to the country." America, in her view, has never been quite the same since.

It was not just Vietnam that changed the country, but the assassinations of Kennedy and King, Watergate, periodic lesser scandals, and the failure of Great Society programs to fulfill, often at great expense, the promises made on their behalf. Tempered by so many disappointments, Americans have lost faith in many of their institutions, most especially government. Since government is supposed to embody the common values of society, suspicion and cynicism are difficult to reconcile with unabashed patriotism. The result, especially for the most patriotic of Americans, is a loss of innocence. They know that governments can lie, that promises can be broken, that ideals cannot always be followed. The reaction of the overwhelming majority of deeply patriotic Americans to the disappointments of the past two decades is to continue to love their country, but in an older-but-wiser fashion. "I think that there was a naïveté that was abounding in those years," said Denise Lott of Rancho Bernardo of the period before Watergate. But there is a bright side as well: "I think there was a coming of age for an awful lot of people." Middle-class Americans are now more demanding before they give their unthinking loyalty to anyone.

The consequence of the shocks of the 1970s is that American patriotism is considerably more leavened with realism. William Fahy of Cobb County, like many Americans, likes sports, but "this thing about being number one, we're always number one, I think that's been taken way too far, way out of context. That seems to start when these little kids are about two feet tall. . . . Gotta win, boys. That's the only thing. Vince Lombardi told us how to do it." It's a new world out there, and such attitudes, inappropriate for kids, no longer work for the country. That doesn't mean you hate your country; it means that you love in a new way. Joseph Palumbo of Medford expresses this sense of mature patriotism well. "Unless you've traveled the world and been exposed to other countries, I think you may not have an appreciation for what America has achieved," he says. "The American Revolution, the Declaration of Independence, the Constitution were outstanding moments in our history. . . . The things American society has achieved, technologically, socially, I think are amazing. I have no apologies for the United States." But Mr. Palumbo is aware that his government may not have acted very wisely in Vietnam, and this gives a more realistic quality to his appreciation for his country. "I'm not saying we should teach a jingoistic American history where we are God's manifest destiny to rule. No, that's not true. But we have achieved. We have suffered. And we have done great things. I think a lot of that's lost."

For those for whom Vietnam symbolizes the failure of

American nerve, maturity means that America can no longer be expected to police the world unilaterally. That kind of sentiment has led some to the conclusion that we are witnessing a return to isolationism, especially as the Republican Party calls for cuts in foreign aid, decreased support for the United Nations, and a reluctance to commit American troops abroad unless their victory, with very few casualties, can be guaranteed. Such moves in the direction of isolationism are popular, but, according to both public opinion polls and the Middle Class Morality Project, it would be wrong to call such sentiments isolationist, at least in the way that term was understood prior to American involvement in World War II.

There has, in fact, been little difference, as far as public opinion is concerned, between support for internationalism from 1973 (68.3 percent said the United States should take an active part in world affairs) to 1994 (65.9 percent). A comprehensive review of polling data indicates that the support Americans give for their country's involvement abroad has not changed significantly throughout the post–World War II period, although there has been a decline among those who believe that the country has humanitarian or altruistic obligations to help others abroad. Most current surveys reveal that Americans remain internationalists: 66.1 percent disagree with the statement "This country would be better off if we just stayed home and did not concern ourselves with problems in other parts of the world," compared with 29.3 percent who agreed; more disagree (55 percent) with the statement "The United States should mind its own business internationally and let others get along as best they can on their own" than agree (42 percent) with it, and almost twice as many Americans think it is important for the United States to be the number-one military power in the world as think it is not important. The "Vietnam syndrome," the reluctance to deploy American troops abroad, does not translate into a sense that Americans should gaze at their own navels.

This same sense of tempered internationalism was strongly reflected in our interviews. Middle-class Americans are fully aware of how tragic is the situation in Bosnia or how needy are the orphans created by tribal wars in Africa. When it comes to helping people abroad, a strong sense of Christian duty in some cases and a feeling that America has special obligations in others combine to restrict isolationist inclinations. "If I saw a little kid getting beaten up by a man out there, I'd probably go out there and take care of the kid. The same situation [exists] on a global scale, it's our responsibility to make sure nobody gets beat up," was how John Pollan of Sand Springs put it. "Americans are the most generous, the most caring, people in the world," Peggy Carlton, also of Sand Springs, echoed; if we have made mistakes in the way we have treated the rest of the world, she continued, those mistakes are due to good intentions, not malignant design.

Certainly, middle-class Americans believe that too much is spent on foreign aid (often in ignorance of how much actually is); 71 percent want to reduce it, according to a recent Gallup poll, compared with only 27 percent who oppose reducing it. They also become suspicious if they think that politicians manipulate foreign policy crises for their own political advantage. Still, when all those things are discounted, the attitudes toward country manifested in our interviews do not so much reflect isolationism as much as a sense that America's power is limited, so that we should pick and choose our spots with extreme care. Middle-class Americans are attracted to what Jim Stone of Broken Arrow calls "a little bit of isolationism," one that would make it harder for the rest of the world to take advantage of the United States even while allowing the United States to fulfill its responsibilities outside its borders.

And it would help if others were willing to join with us; as Mr. Stone continued, "Somebody has to take the first step, but we've made too many first steps." One of the aspects of the global situation that made middle-class Americans especially unhappy was the reluctance of America's allies, especially in Europe, to share the burdens of leadership. Ronald Klaus of Rancho Bernardo, himself of Serbian descent, is outraged with the Serbian government's conduct. "I think they should be slapped down," was how he put it, "but I don't think the U.S. should be doing it all. . . . The Europeans are very reluctant to take care of the problems in their own backyard, and that annoys me no end." From his perspective, "the Serbs need to be taught a lesson," but if America teaches that lesson alone, its message will get lost. Carmen Tosca, a high school teacher living in Eastlake, like many of the Mexican-Americans to whom we spoke, is extremely patriotic. "I know I tell my students all the time that I am very proud of being an American," she said. "I'm very happy to be living in this country." For her, it is axiomatic that if America wants to be a world leader, it will have to get itself involved in unpleasant situations; it has that responsibility. She just wishes that, in a case like the Bosnian one, "the international community had been able to do something instead of just sitting there through all these years and just letting things happen."

Perhaps the most dramatic indication of how the meaning of patriotism has changed for those attracted to old-fashioned American ideals emerges from the way people reflect on incidents such as the bombing of a federal building in Oklahoma City. A propensity to distrust extremism, which leads Americans to be critical of those who conflate religion and politics, also leads them to question those who confuse their politics with their presumed love of America; the Post-Modernity Project's survey showed that more Americans had very negative feelings about militias (28 percent) than any other of the words and images proposed by the interviewers, rivaled only by the National Rifle Association (21 percent). By contrast, political correctness evoked a very negative association of 12 percent; affirmative action, 10 percent; feminist, 10 percent; and therapy, 3 percent. Even among the most dedicated conservatives, it is simply not credible to claim to love America while blowing up its buildings and killing its people. Oklahoma City played the same role for conservatives in the heartland as the Weathermen and other violence-prone groups and actions played for the antiwar left, forcing people to rethink some of their basic assumptions and moving them toward the center. Our respondents in Oklahoma like to make a distinction between America, which they love, and the government, which they distrust. After the bombing, that became very hard to do. Stephanie Proctor of Broken Arrow thinks, "It's just a scapegoat to say it's all the government's fault. The people created it. Whatever's there, we voted in." For someone like her, mature patriotism means everyone sharing in the sacrifice required by the national interest, not taking matters into your own hands in an "extreme" fashion.

Mature patriotism means that those who think globally temper their internationalism with respect for America while "my country right or wrong" patriots moderate their love of America with a recognition that its power is limited. If it is indeed true that movement on both sides of the once powerful Vietnam divide can meet around such a perspective, Americans may be able to focus their attention on what truly bothers them about their country. Although none of the middle-class Americans to whom we spoke used this term, their concern is that America, and its political institutions, lacks *gravitas*. There ought to be room for solemnity in American life—times and places designed to show respect for what is special about us. But this, many of them feel, is lacking. "Look at the ball games," said Karen Calingo. "It just bothers me when people go there and sing [the national anthem], and then afterward they just start laughing. . . . That's a shame." Edvardo Valdez made the same point by using an illustration from television. He remembers a program called *The Waltons*. On one show, the Walton family was gathered around the radio in the living room while the president was speaking and one of the children made a disrespectful remark about him. Grandpa Walton responded, "Hush your mouth, you respect your president," a scene etched into Mr. Valdez's consciousness. This has nothing to do, in his opinion, with politics, Republican or Democrat. He would not want a return to the Great Depression or World War II, but he recognizes that such crises gave his father's generation what his lacks: a sense of reverence.

Social scientists are unsure why Americans have lost respect for their country's institutions. Some of our respondents were aghast to see the president talking about his underpants or playing his saxophone on television. The media, which are universally viewed as destructive forces in American life, came in for their share of the blame. Companies are viewed as no longer interested in protecting American jobs but in serving greedier ends. One remembers black athletes who protested against America at the Olympic Games by demonstrating during the playing of the national anthem. The most common response, however, is an inadvertent recognition that the end of the Cold War has brought with it a sense of purposelessness in American life. What is it that makes you most proud of being American? we asked people, only to find that their answers were not always as articulate or well-defined as one might expect.

To be sure, most middle-class Americans will cite economic individualism and political democracy as the defining characteristics of America; the people to whom we spoke invoked those freedoms often, sometimes in eloquent, moving language, and it would be foolish to deny how important those values are to those who invoke them. Two of the black Americans with whom we spoke in the Atlanta area, both ministers, cited the right of the Ku Klux Klan, an organization they detested, to have their say as what made this country unusual. Polling data indicate that immigrants to America are strongly attracted to the ideals of the American dream. This was very much the case among the immigrants in our sample, many of whom cited not only money and good schools for their kids as reasons for their love of America, but also, as someone from the Philippines put it, "that word 'freedom' here that people take for granted, but we are without a lot of constraints that people in other countries have to deal with. We don't have a dictatorship, we're not under martial law, we're currently not having any kind of civil unrest." In a nutshell, what middle-class Americans find distinctive about America is that it enables them to be middle class. Unlike India or Japan, the very rich and the very poor are smaller classes here, and opportunity enables those with the desire and the capacity to better their lot in life.

As much as middle-class Americans appreciate economic and political freedom, however, they are also aware that, by itself, freedom is not enough: as Toni Cartwright of Sand Springs said of America, "The same things that can make it a better place can also make it a worse place." Economic freedom, out of con-

trol, leads to worship of shallow material things over deeper
spiritual values. Political freedom, out of control, results in a
country without common purpose, the splintering of America
into all the groups and individuals who compose it. Unleashed
moral freedom is even more problematic. "I think we've
stopped thinking of the other guy and only think in terms of
'I,' " was how Joyce Slone of Brookline expressed this concern.
People have become too egoistical, wanting more rather than allowing themselves to be satisfied with what they have. Preoccupied with ourselves, "We don't want to sacrifice. We've got too
much. We've been fat and laid back for some time now. . . . You
know everything is fast, fast foods, minute rice, minute everything," said Herbert Almond, one of the black ministers from
DeKalb. According to accounts such as these, we have lost the
old-fashioned sense of limiting our needs to serve God, family,
and country. This is seen as a downside to the libertarianism that
otherwise sits so well among middle-class Americans.

In this conflict between their love of freedom and their worries about its consequences, middle-class Americans find their
belief in mature patriotism a way to split the difference. Their
feelings about their country are best characterized, not as blus-
tery self-confidence, but by the emergence of a sense that
Americans are both distinctive from the rest of the world yet not
quite so different as they once believed. "I'm a flag-waving son
of a gun, okay. . . I believe America is the greatest spot on planet
earth," Ted Borrelli of Medford said. Few of our respondents
put their faith in their country in terms like his. Far more common is a quieter tone: "I very much appreciate being an American," as Barbara Tompkins of Broken Arrow put it. "I very
much appreciate living in America. But I don't go around toot-
ing many horns about it." People who think about their country
in this way are likely to believe that, having been through so
many difficult times such as Vietnam and Watergate, something
positive is bound to emerge. "The people in this country are
good," as Jesse O'Donnell expresses this point of view, "just like
any other country. I mean, granted, we have our own problems,
and we need to get together to find the solutions to all the

problems we have, but I don't think it's overwhelming. I think it can be done, you know, and I've never been much of a pessimist. It just doesn't fit my personality."

THE REUNITING OF AMERICA

The story of Americans' attitudes toward their country over the past three decades is the story of one shock after another: Vietnam and Watergate in the 1960s and 1970s, immigration and the emergence of global capitalism in the 1980s, multiculturalism and culture wars in the 1990s. And as if that was not enough, Americans have experienced a questioning of their country's sense of purpose at the same time that their faith in God and family has undergone significant change. So much has happened so quickly it is no wonder that serious students of American history have raised the question of whether the Union is falling apart. Yet, it is remarkable how few of their worries about the country's future have filtered down to most of the people who live here. In the opinion of the middle-class Americans with whom we talked, the idea of living in any other country in the world is barely conceivable.

These middle-class Americans have a message to deliver to those who worry that America might fall apart: Calm down. Yes, the country has changed, perhaps for the better, perhaps not. But everything changes all the time. The trick is not to lament what has passed but to come to terms with what is emerging. We are not facing the disuniting of America but its reuniting. This being America, it cannot be bad.

The confidence that America will reemerge as a strengthened society draws on a number of sources. Religious Americans who believe that God has always taken a special interest in this country believe that, as Mrs. McLaughlin of Broken Arrow put it, "if we get down on our knees and pray to Him, He will change, you know, change our land and help us to heal our land." Others, such as Judy Vogel of Cobb County, think that disagreement and discord offer more of a secular test. When faced with

TABLE 4.7
"EVEN THOUGH IT HAS ITS PROBLEMS, THE UNITED STATES IS
STILL THE BEST PLACE IN THE WORLD TO LIVE"

	Strongly Agree	Agree	No Opinion	Disagree	Strongly Disagree
Brookline	9	11	3	2	0
Medford	12	11	1	1	0
Broken Arrow	16	9	0	0	0
Sand Springs	18	4	2	1	0
DeKalb	11	11	3	0	0
Cobb	12	12	0	1	0
Eastlake	18	6	1	0	0
Rancho Bernardo	19	5	1	0	0
Total	115	69	11	5	0

political conflicts and different versions of the meaning of the country, "I think we need to listen with our hearts a little better and try somehow to find answers," for "this country has a strong foundation," one that enables it to struggle through until we find the right thing to do. Over and over again, people stressed two things about the country that, in their view, will never change. One is that the people here are too good for bad things to persist too long. The other is that the history of America is a history of generosity and caring; Americans are the kind of people who help out when times are tough. If things get bad enough—they have not quite gotten to that point yet—the way in which Americans pull together when facing floods and earthquakes will help them move beyond their political disagreements and controversies.

The most significant source of national regeneration, however, stems from what many middle-class Americans see as an inevitable cycle: our freedoms make us special; taken to extremes, they cause us problems; but when we experience those problems, our very freedoms will help us find a way out. This whole cycle of distinctiveness, decline, and possible rebirth was expressed in one sentence by Rancho Bernardo's Megan Graff:

> I think the obvious freedom of speech that we have, I think when we compare ourselves to the other countries, we are definitely the best, that when you try to run a country of this size with all the ethnic diversity, you're going to have major, major blowups and problems, but we do try to sort them out and I don't think a lot of other countries put as much effort into keeping everything on a smooth keel.

As that cycle works itself out, the country will move toward what Elizabeth Tyler of Brookline called "some sense of shared purpose and commitment to continuation of our culture, some sense of survival of the next generation, some sense of things living in a proper way ... and some sense of living in a country that is free with free choice and some measure of leisure and some measure of economic freedom ... fairness, and correct moral and ethical values in the way we treat one another and the world."

Compared with the McCarthy period, when questions about a changing national identity were also very much on the minds of the American people, the present period—for all its occasional turbulence over Vietnam memorials, historical exhibitions, and debates over multiculturalism—is remarkably calm. In the 1950s, when charges of treason filled the air, American identity was not especially threatened; the economic and political power of the United States was unsurpassed; there was relatively little immigration; no significant domestic disputes upset a national consensus; women and children were not in rebellion; and rapid technological change was just around the corner. In the 1990s, by contrast, the power of America is weakening economically and politically, the country has become far more diverse, its ideals are challenged constantly, and new technologies seem to flower annually, yet Americans have not responded by accusing each other of lacking sufficient love for their country. Patriotism in America may have declined in one sense, but it is doubly mature in another: not only has it become more quietly thoughtful, it also has to deal with more complicated challenges. If ever there were a case to appreciate the sense of modest virtue shared by so many middle-class Americans, it would be around issues of what it means to be an American. Nationalism can embody both the best and worst of human emotions; mature patriotism is an especially effective way to love one's country without turning one's back on the rest of the world.

V SUBURBIA'S CHANGING MORAL STORY

What does one buy when one buys a house in the suburbs? That was a question much on my mind as Maria and I drove from my hotel in Atlanta out to southeastern DeKalb County for a day of interviewing. Once upon a time, I thought to myself, the South might have marked a distinct regional culture in the United States, but one would never know it from the Atlanta suburbs these days. Not that they were unattractive; on the contrary, the Atlanta area is known for its lovely trees, which gave the suburban community at which we soon arrived a distinctly "old suburb" look. The moment we left the main access roads, which were lined with more than their share of franchised outlets, we reached quiet streets with relatively few cars on them, school buses driving around to pick up well-behaved children, construction crews putting additions onto old houses and, from time to time, building new ones, a smattering of men washing the cars parked in their driveways, lots of mothers walking infants in strollers, and all the other signs that loudly proclaim, as they would in any similar community around New York or Chicago, "Beware—suburban life is lived here."

We began our interviews in DeKalb the same way we did in all the communities that were part of the Middle Class Morality Project: we asked people why they lived in the suburbs rather than the city. Formulating his thoughts about why he liked where he lives, Robert George, the owner of a construction business, said, "We like the school and the neighborhood. It's real quiet and everything." But, we challenged him, a lot of people say that those who live in the suburbs are really just trying to avoid the crime and poverty of the inner city. Even when challenged, Mr. George would not take the bait. His response was typical of those who thought as he did: a particular house, space, quiet, lack of traffic congestion—these are the kinds of things on the minds of many American suburbanites as they talk about why they live where they do.

Demographers interested in residential housing choices have long focused on pushes and pulls as metaphors for understanding human behavior. If Robert George articulates those features of suburban life that "pull" people to the suburbs, many of his neighbors spoke of factors that "pushed" them away from the city. Jamie Willis—twenty-five years old, single, working as an insurance claims adjuster—feels that urban life is simply too unsafe and unsettled: "It's kind of violent," Ms. Willis says, "and I guess the socioeconomic status in the city of Atlanta isn't really where I fit in, you know." In a similar way, Jackie Stevens and her husband, a young professional couple with a three-year-old child, moved from one suburb close to the city to one farther away with the problems of the city very much on their minds: "I wanted to stay in DeKalb County," Mrs. Stevens told us, "but I wanted to move a little farther out because I wanted somewhere that was a little quieter, and to be quite honest, to try to get away from the crime." Americans, it is commonly believed, have a Jeffersonian distaste for urban life and will, if they can, do anything in their power to escape it. Conversations with people such as these confirm that such Jeffersonian sentiments survive in contemporary America.

The question of whether suburbia lures people in search of the good life or provides an escape from the city is the central question in a moral (and legal) debate that has broken out in America as more and more individuals find themselves living in suburban surroundings. Critics of suburbia have no doubt about the predominance of pushes over pulls; in their account, mundane motives cannot be at the heart of the suburban housing decision because home ownership is understood not only as a practical but also as a symbolic decision. The particular shape and location of the suburb, its relationship to the city, its ethnic and racial composition, its density, the physical design of its houses—all these are held to be pregnant with symbolic significance. Suburban land use and housing patterns presumably tell us about ourselves; they reveal our hidden assumptions about domesticity, work, and gender, or, if we read between the lines, they delineate our fears about outsiders and aliens. "Live and let live"—that popular expression about just leaving things be—is exactly what social scientists will not let suburbanites do. Decisions about where to live are assumed to be decisions about what kind of life to lead.

On no aspect of American life does the symbolic significance of suburban home ownership assume greater importance than on issues of race and poverty. Once upon a time, the suburban ideal was held to express a longing after the kinds of small town communities that are increasingly hard to find in the modern world. Suburbia, its defenders believed, was a Tocquevillian laboratory of democracy. In this refuge from the anonymity of mass society, people became engaged in their communities for no other reason than that these were *their* communities. No doubt selfish motives were involved in the lure of suburbia: a home of one's own, a desire to be seen as successful, the two-car garage. But even with all that, the choice of suburbia was a choice in favor of a particular version of morality, one that resonated with utopian visions of the good life. The attraction of what Justice William O. Douglas called the "sanctuary" of "a quiet place where yards are wide, people few" is still viewed by many as the very definition of happiness in America.

As American cities filled up with immigrants and the very poor, the moral choice to live in the suburbs began to seem less praiseworthy. A society composed of wealthy white outer enclaves and poor black inner rings is said to create a form of racial segregation that, according to its critics, resembles South African apartheid more than a utopian sanctuary, especially when cities themselves are organized into neighborhoods that are heavily concentrated by race. Under such conditions, the mere existence of suburbanization suggests a certain immorality, a desire, above all else, to escape from one's obligations to the less fortunate. This is nowhere better symbolized than by a Connecticut Supreme Court decision that declared unconstitutional a system in which downtown Hartford's schools were primarily attended by racial minorities, while the schools in the surrounding suburbs, financed through property taxes, primarily served whites. And if this were not indictment enough, critics insist, the suburbs are also increasingly becoming old, characterized by property tax revolts and an unwillingness to support services, such as schools and playgrounds, used by the young. Suburbanization, from this point of view, represents the retreat from community, not the desire to embrace it, if community is understood to include the dependent, the needy, and the less fortunate. As David Kirp, John P. Dwyer, and Larry A. Rosenthal wrote of the Mount Laurel, New Jersey, residents they studied: "The very last thing they want to do is to assume responsibility for those whom they deliberately left behind."

Ask suburbanites themselves whether they feel a sense of obligation to help those who remain in poverty, and they invariably, at least in survey form, answer that they do. This was certainly the case when I surveyed our respondents; only four of them strongly disagreed that such an obligation existed, while forty-two disagreed in general. Yet such evidence would not be given much weight by suburbia's critics. The problem of what the better-off owe the worst-off cannot be settled by such means, they would argue. Even though there is nothing to prevent those with whom we talked from expressing their hostility to the poor explicitly if that is how they feel, many people will give what they believe to be the right answer rather than acknowledge a less pleasant truth that they happen to believe, especially when race is involved. What people do is more important than what they say, critics would maintain, and what they invariably do, when they have a chance, is to buy a house as far from the city as they can afford. From such a perspective, what suburbanites themselves have to say about the moral accounting involved in their housing decisions is less relevant than the hard reality of their housing choice.

TABLE 5.1
"MIDDLE-CLASS PEOPLE WHO LIVE IN THE SUBURBS
CAN DO AN AWFUL LOT MORE TO HELP PEOPLE IN
THE INNER CITY WHO LIVE IN POVERTY"

	Strongly Agree	Agree	No Opinion	Disagree	Strongly Disagree
Brookline	6	14	0	5	0
Medford	3	13	1	7	1
Broken Arrow	2	15	1	7	0
Sand Springs	3	13	1	8	0
DeKalb	7	13	1	3	1
Cobb	2	18	0	5	0
Eastlake	3	15	1	5	1
Rancho Bernardo	4	15	3	2	1
Total	30	116	8	42	4

The Middle Class Morality Project uncovered at least some evidence suggesting that critics are right when they claim that middle-class Americans, no matter how idealistic they sound, are fleeing from the city's problems. Even those who emphasize how attractive they find the benefits of suburban life, after all, are making an implicit judgment about how distasteful they find the drawbacks of urban life: tranquillity can be another word for absence of crime, just as space can be a contrast to poverty. The most commonly cited reason for wanting to live in suburbia—good schools for the children—is an obvious commentary not only on the poor quality of inner-city public schools, but also on single-parent families and other urban problems that might contribute to bad schooling. It may well be, therefore, that those who stress the positive aspects of suburbia are unconsciously emphasizing the negative.

One can, for example, hear criticism of the city in the words of Todd Smith, a newspaper copy editor, who was quite frank about the relationship between suburban people and suburban schools: "These are the kinds of people," he says of his neighbors, "that if you believe the demographic studies, you know they're gonna value education and they're going to push their kids to excel. These are the kids that are gonna boost these schools. I figure it's just a matter of time before that happens." For Henry Johnson, a tax auditor, homogeneity was important for him and his wife, Linda: "We wanted a neighborhood where we would feel comfortable, where we could get to know our neighbors." Patricia Bates, fifty-one, an extremely enterprising nursing-home operator, hated the neighborhood in Atlanta from which her father came: "It was cluttered, it was congested. . . . The population there was not something that I was used to." She was equally forthright in expressing her desire to live near advantaged people such as herself in suburbia: "Like I said, coming from an environment where I lived in upper-middle-class neighborhoods all of my life, I was not ready to settle for anything less. That's the bottom line. I was not going to settle for anything less than being in an upper-middle-class community."

Should we conclude from comments like these that the "middle-class withdrawal syndrome" is alive and well in suburban America? Perhaps we should, but there is also more to the story that needs to be told before we do so.

BEYOND PUSH AND PULL

As Patricia Bates's comments indicate, there will always be some individuals who will confirm the hypothesis that suburban residents are fleeing from a sense of obligation to those forced to remain behind in America's inner cities. But it does not follow that race is the driving motivation behind their decisions. Accounts of suburbia as a retreat from race are not so much wrong as incomplete. For not only is Ms. Bates herself black, but so is every single suburbanite whose views I have so far cited in this chapter.

The percentage of African-Americans living in suburbs went from 21 percent in 1980 to 27 percent in 1990 and 30 percent in 1994. Nor were these poor African-Americans who were moving out of the city: the average income of black suburban families in 1990 was $35,000, 55 percent higher than the average income of central city black families. Rates of suburbanization for nonblack minorities, especially Asians and Hispanics, were even higher during this period. Not all African-Americans and Hispanics, needless to say, are upwardly mobile, and among those who are, not all are leaving the city; indeed, research undertaken by the public policy specialist Richard Nathan points to the revival of entrepreneurial values in working-class and middle-class minority neighborhoods inside city limits. But enough minorities are moving to the suburbs, and enough of those who remain have adopted middle-class values, that the image of poverty-stricken urban and ethnic minorities trapped in the cities surrounded by whites in the suburbs no longer rings true.

Black suburbanization has not produced racially integrated suburbs; in most cases, the rise of a black middle class produces black middle-class suburbs distinct from white ones. American housing patterns, notoriously color-conscious in the past, remain color-conscious in the present; although Americans agree that blacks "have a right to live wherever they can afford to," 45 percent of them (in 1990) still favored "allowing homeowners to decide for themselves whom to sell to, even if they preferred not to sell to blacks," with the obvious consequence that "most whites prefer neighborhoods with a clear white majority." Yet, despite the persistence of racial segregation outside the city, the existence of thriving black middle-class suburbs makes it increasingly difficult to equate the decision to move out of the city with the decision to avoid blacks in general, unless, of course, one believes that middle-class blacks are just as racist and callous toward those left behind as middle-class whites. One must either conclude that racism is so powerful a force that it includes those of the very race it denigrates or that there are motives for wanting to live in the suburbs that have little to do with race per se, however much they have to do with distancing oneself from the problems of the inner city. And if one concludes the latter, then the existence of a suburban black middle class suggests that racism is one thing and wanting a good life is another.

Do black suburbanites view their choice to live outside the city in ways different from whites? The results of the Middle Class Morality Project suggest they do—but not in the way one might expect. It is among blacks that the middle-class withdrawal symptom—the tendency of middle-class people to flee from the problems of the inner-city poor—is most pronounced; one demographer has described the 70 percent increase in black suburbanization during the 1970s as "an exodus from central cities." Since the 1970s, according to one estimate, the rate of suburbanization among black Americans has, in fact, exceeded the rate among white Americans. It makes a good deal of sense to apply push-and-pull theories of suburbanization to recently embourgeoised African-Americans. On the one hand, many of them have family and friends in the city, own businesses or hold jobs there, or feel unwanted by the suburbs. On the other hand, middle-class African-Americans have firsthand experiences with ghetto conditions, want to remove their children from what they judge to be negative influences, and have either personal or collective memories of urban and rural poverty. African-Americans in our sample, in other words, are roughly similar to ethnic Americans of the immediate postwar period who faced a choice between remaining in the urban areas in which they were raised or moving to the newly expanding suburbs outside the city. For individuals of that generation, as for so many African-Americans now, there is a choice: stay behind or move. So long as there is a choice, it makes sense to talk of pushes and pulls. And so long as the city that they, or people close to them, have experienced is associated with violence and unstable families, push will nearly always win out over pull.

The fact that so many black suburbanites see themselves as making a choice in favor of the suburb and against the city raises the question of whether the middle-class withdrawal symptom ought to be viewed as quite as immoral as its critics frequently charge. The interesting thing about the responses of the African-Americans who spoke with us about the attractions of suburbia is that their words, if offered by whites, would sound racially callous—clear examples of code words designed to cover a dislike of the urban poor—but when offered by blacks, they seem much more to be expressions of racial pride. Todd Smith's belief that good people make good schools, for example, was made in the context of defending schools that were predominantly African-American; Mr. Smith went on to criticize upper-middle-class black parents for removing their kids from the public schools in favor of private ones. Henry Johnson, talking about how important it was for him to have neighbors to whom he could relate, was making a comment about his former community in Florida and how difficult it was for him as a black male to get to know the white people who lived around him there. And Patricia Bates's certainty that she is owed an upper-middle-class lifestyle is also an expression of pride that someone of her race has been so successful. In an ironic way not fully appreciated by those for whom suburbia is viewed as a refuge from racial problems, middle-class African-Americans often need suburbia as an expression of, not as an escape from, their racial consciousness. Only when black kids are organized into soccer leagues or attend book discussion groups at the public library after school—the public library we visited in southeastern DeKalb County was the most active and busy of all the public libraries we stopped into—can these black Americans feel pride in their accomplishments as black Americans.

This dislike and distrust of the city one finds among black suburbanites complicate the story of suburbia as a retreat from the problems of race. Black suburbanization changes not only who lives in the suburbs, but also how we think about them. At least with respect to decisions about where to live, class may well be replacing race as the significant motivating force. If true, that does not make for a just society; an unequal distribution of such goods as safety, education, and opportunities for children raises questions about justice whatever the criteria used to differentiate those who get more from those who get less. But it does make for a different story. Suburbanites in America may be withdrawing from something, but whatever it is, it is no longer just about race.

None of this means that the whites with whom we spoke were free of racial motives. Residents of Cobb County have a reputation for extreme conservatism, which we did not always find: our Cobb sample included a Jewish liberal, a woman who gave up a high-paying position in health care to work as a financial adviser for an inner-city nonprofit hospital, and a number of moderate Republicans. But it also included one housewife for whom Atlanta (her native city) and African-American were close to synonymous terms: "It's run by the blacks. It's run by the blacks, and there's a lot of corruption. There's a lot of crime. It's not just in downtown. We're seeing it come north into the suburbs. We basically would not move back into Fulton County."

For this woman, even the suburbs of Atlanta were problematic places to live due to the presence of African-Americans. She and her husband had moved to eastern Cobb County from Smyrna, but that was not far enough out: "We watched the city [Smyrna] decline, and it is political. All the corruption . . . we've watched the school systems deteriorate. The crime in Smyrna got so bad— Of course I know it's even worse in other parts. That's just the worst in Cobb County, right where we were living."

This woman's views were not singular: liberal Brookline has its share of people who, reflecting either a new authenticity or the collapse of old taboos, were quite up front in their focus on race. James Alexander, a forty-eight-year-old self-employed carpenter of Irish descent, asked about the problems of inner-city Boston, responded this way:

> Well, they don't seem to be helping themselves, to be honest with you. I mean, there's a lot of kids, well, you're basically talking about black kids. I go to the Brookline Library a lot. You rarely if ever see a black kid in the library. You go up to the high school to the gym and it's all black kids. They'd rather play basketball than do their homework. It's as simple as that. They don't want to work. They don't want to study. That may be overly racist but that's strictly my observation.

Talking to Mr. Alexander, one gets the feeling that his views have never changed: strong discipline, conservative values, and a faith in hard work are his most important values, and all he can see when he turns his eyes to the inner city are young black males who, he believes, hold his values in contempt.

Further evidence of white resistance to demands for racial justice is provided by another of the survey questions I included in the Middle Class Morality Project. What about *your* suburb? we asked people. Could it do more to become more racially integrated? While suburbia's critics tend to believe that the answer to such a question, for nearly all suburbs in the United States, ought to be yes, the answer most of our respondents gave was no.

Yet, if black suburbanization complicates our understanding of the suburbs as a retreat from race, so does an important change in the way whites think about their housing choices. Many of the black middle-class people with whom we spoke thought of suburbia as representing a clear choice over the city.

TABLE 5.2
"MY SUBURB OUGHT TO WORK MUCH HARDER AT BECOMING
MORE RACIALLY INTEGRATED THAN IT IS AT PRESENT"

	Strongly Agree	Agree	No Opinion	Disagree	Strongly Disagree
Brookline	1	3	4	16	1
Medford	1	6	6	12	0
Broken Arrow	0	8	4	12	1
Sand Springs	0	7	6	12	0
DeKalb	2	6	5	12	0
Cobb	0	3	1	20	1
Eastlake	0	1	2	20	2
Rancho Bernardo	1	5	2	15	2
Total	5	39	30	119	7

But what if there is no choice? Many of the white respondents to the Middle Class Morality Project grew up in the suburbs and have never lived in the city. For them, the question of why they chose to live outside the city makes little sense because they do not understand their housing decisions as a choice. Not all of them answered the way Jesse O'Donnell did when asked whether she would ever move back to the city—"I'm not sure I understand, like city as in . . . ?" was her response—but most of them seemed surprised by the question. Middle-class Californians in particular view the problem of where to live as a decision between one suburb and another; for those in the San Diego area, the choice was invariably between North County and South County, not between either one and the city in the middle. Californians may be unique in this regard. But if California is unique, it is only relatively so; suburbs have now become so central to the American experience that, for the middle class, they are the rule, not the exception.

White middle-class Americans do not choose the suburbs because they have a template of options about how to live and find the suburbs to fit one of them. Rather, they know how they want to live—with some control over their environment, with options for their children, and with a balance between privacy and community—and believe that only suburbia offers them a way to do so. They live in the suburbs because the suburbs are where they can live. Their decision, in that sense, is not a philosophical one; if they could obtain a stable and secure life in what Alan Ehrenhalt calls "the lost city"—once flourishing, lower-middle-class, ethnically homogeneous neighborhoods within the city—they might still prefer to live there. But they cannot, at least not anymore. Their housing choices can be understood as the opposite of their family choices: in the 1950s, when so many middle-class Americans did have a choice between remaining in the city and moving to the suburbs, most of them accepted on faith the ideal of the one-income nuclear family; now, when most families decide for themselves whether women should work or how many children they will have, they have relatively little choice over the kinds of places in which they will live.

Children, especially young children, are the reason for this lack of options. "Just look at how the city is structured and what the priorities of city life are," said Maria Kowalski of Brookline, a twenty-eight-year-old buyer for a major department store. "There's no place for the kids to play, to run around, to do anything. Whereas if you walk out into the suburbs, everything around here is geared toward where the children are, where the school is, you know, whatever." Her remarks sounded very much like those of Samuel Gonzales, born in Queens, New York, now living in Eastlake, California. "Downtown for me," Mr. Gonzales says, "is a more adult type of place. For me, it's not a family kind of place. I wouldn't want my kids walking around there . . . I mean, if you're single . . . it would probably be okay, but for us with kids it is not." Each of these individuals has a fairly sophisticated understanding that there are essentially two classes in America: not rich and poor, and not even black and white, and certainly not Anglo and Hispanic, but those who have younger children and those who do not. While gender and race significantly divided Democratic voters from Republican ones in the 1996 presidential election, President Clinton's pollster, in a postelection analysis, called the fact that twice as many voters thought that Clinton's election would be better for young people than Dole's "one of the widest issue gaps of the race." Having young children may establish an economic and political fault line, but it also puts into place a moral one: the choice between city and suburbs may still be a reality for some middle-class Americans with one or no young children, but for those whose children's futures lie in front of them, and who can afford the expense, suburbia has become as automatic a stage in the life cycle as having children in the first place.

And not just for them. Joanna Cage and Michelle Knight, both twenty-somethings, married, and so far childless, emphasized schools for the kids they were planning to have as a reason to leap over any urban experience in Tulsa before an eventual settlement in Broken Arrow. A nearby resident, Stacey Williams, a sales representative for a consumer products manufacturer, is single but also prefers Broken Arrow over gentrified areas of Tulsa, not, she says, because "I'm afraid of the crime or anything," but instead because of "more house for the money." If Americans want to live in the suburbs before they have children, they also continue to want to live in the suburbs after they have children. Some of those to whom we talked, especially those close to retirement, thought it might be nice to dispense with gardening, but their idea of an alternative was an apartment in the suburbs, not a safe neighborhood in town. Rancho Bernardo, north of San Diego, is a suburb for former suburbanites; people would move there from places like Greenwich, Connecticut, the suburbs of Chicago, or Silicon Valley. What was once an American ritual—accumulating enough money to buy a house outside the city—has become transformed: now it is about staking out new developments and subdivisions about to be built in a never-ending process of moving up and out.

Suburb-hopping is a response to forces shaping life outside the city, forces quite different from those that existed during the post–World War II economic expansion. Demographic shifts to the South and West, highway construction, the emergence of national retail patterns organized through shopping malls, the graying of the inner suburbs, immigration, deindustrialization, the decline of ethnic solidarity, new family patterns, and the maturing of the baby boom generation have changed the moral meaning of suburbia. Particularly in places like Atlanta or San Diego, suburb and city have become increasingly indistinguishable; there are simply highways along which houses can be found. Other suburbs are filled with people who move to a particular area to be near jobs that were relocated out of the city; a world bifurcated between city and suburb makes no sense to them because they do not commute from one to the other or even acknowledge the existence of a city around which their suburban community is supposed to revolve. If Americans no longer go the suburbs so much as the suburbs come to them, how much moral significance can be attributed to their decision to live where they do?

None of the qualifications I have introduced to the story of suburbia as a retreat from the ideal of a more racially and

economonically integrated society should lead to the conclusion
that such a story is a false one; nearly all the available evidence,
from this study as well as others, suggests that issues of poverty
and issues of suburbanization will always be intertwined. But
my findings also indicate that it is not always clear how they are
tied together. The middle-class Americans with whom we spoke
are neither heroic moralists struggling to keep alive family values and bourgeois ideals in a society crumbling nihilistically
around them, as conservatives would like to believe, nor with-
drawn resigners from the complexities of living in a multicultural world, as liberals would have it. They are rather simply
trying to lead their lives as best they can in the only way they
think they can.

Some may view it as tragic that suburbanites feel that they
have so few choices about how and where they live, but suburbanites themselves generally do not view the matter that way.
And, for America as a whole, there may be good news in this
lack of choice. If suburbia is more of a necessity than an option,
we should think twice about attaching too much moral and
symbolic significance to living in the suburbs rather than the
city. That is not a step that everyone will be prepared to take.
Charles R. Lawrence III, a law professor at Georgetown, argues
that, for purposes of ensuring racial justice, it is insufficient for
only governmental behavior to be free of discriminatory intent:
eliminating private actions from our purview "leaves untouched
the largest part of the vast system of segregation in the United
States," especially such matters as "a white family's decision to
send its children to private school or to move to a racially exclu-
sive suburb." There can be little doubt that, at the level of
theory, Lawrence is right: the cumulative effect of a series of private decisions can result in public racial segregation. But if it is
also true that such a family's decision is not so much taken con-
sciously out of racial exclusion as it is unconsciously out of a desire to lead the best life one can, the best path to racial justice
may lie neither in trying to outlaw such private decisions, nor in
hectoring those who make them for their immorality and insen-
sitivity, but rather by responding to the needs of all Americans,

of whatever race or class, to live in ways that give them some sense of protection for their children and themselves.

ALFRED DOOLITTLE'S LAMENT

Welfare—by which I mean income support for the poor, such as Aid to Families with Dependent Children—is one of those issues that define, at least in the popular imagination, the difference between urban and suburban life. If living in the suburbs symbolizes success, something has to symbolize failure, and nothing seems more appropriate for the job than the notion of people, especially young and unmarried mothers, being supported by public funds. It can hardly be a coincidence that the first presidential election held under conditions of a suburban majority produced a president, Bill Clinton, who signed into law an end to federal guarantees of welfare.

Because for so many social critics living in the suburbs has come to symbolize a retreat from a larger sense of social obligation, the pulls and pushes of suburban life are often linked to conservative and liberal political views about welfare programs. Conservatives who like suburbia usually dislike welfare. In their view, the same set of virtues that makes middle-class home-ownership desirable, especially a strong sense of responsibility for one's own fate, is precisely what makes the dependency associated with welfare undesirable. On the other hand, liberals sympathetic to welfare usually dislike suburbs. As they see it, everyone is to some degree dependent on everyone else, so those who think they can escape the city's problems by moving outside its borders are only deluding themselves.

When the right and left debate welfare, at stake is not so much public assistance itself as the moral views of those against whom one is debating. The right, in attacking welfare, is in reality criticizing the left. According to the conservative publicist Myron Magnet, welfare carries to its logical conclusion the beliefs of 1960s leftists who rebelled against discipline and traditional values in favor of a doctrine emphasizing hedonism and value relativism, only this time applied to an "underclass" for which such values can do nothing but harm. Conservative hostility to welfare is based far more on a moral view of the world than on its inefficiency or expense. As George Lakoff argues, contemporary conservatives attach great importance to discipline. That is why they focus so much of their attention not at the relatively helpless people who have to survive on welfare, but on the privileged "elitists" at prestigious universities and in the media, whose moral outlook, they believe, is soft and forgiving when punishment and tough love are required.

The left returns the right's fire. So deep is the conflict between welfare and core American values that people on the left do not so much defend welfare as attack the conservative worldview of those who could curtail it. The idea that dependency is wrong simply cannot be taken seriously, many of the left point out, when conservatives either ignore or go out of their way to justify welfare for the rich, the military, or those with political clout. If opposition to dependency cannot be the real motivation for opposition to welfare, something else must be. And that, in turn, can be nothing else but poverty itself. Just as the right charges that the left's support for welfare is in reality support for moral relativism, so, according to the left, the right's opposition to welfare is really about something else—middle-class morality. Those who want to end welfare as we have known it are trying to impose one particular version of morality on everyone else; their moral vision is a class vision, one that will not be satisfied until everyone adopts middle-class values and behavior, whether appropriate to them or not. Beware, therefore, anyone preaching virtue.

What does the public think about these debates among intellectuals? Both survey data and the responses to the Middle Class Morality Project show that Americans are not as fed up with welfare as are many conservative intellectuals, but nor are they as accepting of a fundamental right to welfare as are many liberal intellectuals. Surveys indicate that public support for welfare spending did decline between the 1960s and the 1990s, with most of the decline taking place between 1961 and 1973. Among those who oppose welfare, moreover, racial stereotypes can readily be found, despite the fact that more whites receive welfare than blacks. This suggests that opposition to welfare is often an example of "race-coding," mobilizing antiblack sentiment without using explicitly racist language. The idea that Americans are increasingly unwilling to support a welfare system, at least in part because that system they believe—incorrectly—disproportionately supports African-Americans, has an empirical basis.

At the same time, however, roughly 57 percent of the American population agrees with the proposition that government has a responsibility for the very poor, compared with roughly 40 percent which disagrees. According to the General Social Survey, 83 percent of the American people believe that welfare helps people overcome difficult times and 89 percent believe that it helps prevent hunger, even though 85 percent also believe that it makes people work less. Asked whether they favor or oppose reducing welfare benefits to people living in poverty, 48 percent were opposed to one degree or another and 31 percent were in favor. Americans make a sharp distinction between welfare in general and welfare designed to help the very poor; they want to target programs for those who deserve them while remaining convinced that those programs generally known as "welfare" do not always do so. Almost two-thirds of the American people, furthermore, say that they would be willing to have their taxes increased to provide job training that would help get people off welfare. If a different way could be found to undergird the moral principle that people are responsible for the fate of each other, they would in all likelihood embrace it. One comes away from these data either impressed by the continued strong support for the principle that people who are in need deserve support or depressed by the common practice of believing that a large number of those who obtain public support, especially racial minorities, do not deserve it.

Because survey questions depend so much on how they are worded—welfare itself being one of those words that carries negative associations—the Middle Class Morality Project

attempted to see beyond opposition to welfare in an attempt to
explore the more general question of what obligations middle-
class Americans believe they have to the very poor. Our interviews confirm what surveys show: there is very strong support
in middle-class America for the *principle* of welfare. "I think
you definitely need a welfare system," we were told by Joanna
Cage, the unmarried twenty-nine-year-old accountant living in
Broken Arrow. "I mean, I think it serves a purpose and I think
that if administered properly, it really can help a lot of people get
back on their feet." Stephanie Proctor, also an accountant and
resident of Broken Arrow, had similar feelings. One of the
women in Ms. Proctor's church is a single parent and Ms. Proctor would never think of asking her how she gets by, but if someone like this woman needed public support to help with her
kids, that would be fine with her. "You know," she concludes,
"you sit there and you almost feel guilty with what you have
just because I had the benefit of a higher education." Views like
these were not unique to women; although my numbers are too
small to make statistically significant conclusions, five of the
nine individuals who were extremely supportive of welfare were
women, but so were eight of the thirteen who were extremely
hostile toward welfare. Typical of the men was another resident
of Broken Arrow, Edward Carter, retired (although not yet on
Social Security), who, despite conservative views on most topics,
felt this way: "I'm not against welfare because it does help people get started or maintains them when they are in bad conditions of employment."

The level of support for the principle of welfare we found
exists despite widespread negative associations with teenage
pregnancy, drug use, and other common linkages with poverty
and dependency. Given our interview format, we were able to
challenge initially favorable responses defending welfare by asking about welfare cheats, the potential for abuse, or a willingness
to have taxes raised to pay for additional assistance. Not very
many people modified their opinions. Over and over again, in
every part of the country, middle-class Americans wanted it on
record that they recognize that sometimes people need help and

that they are prepared to pay for the help they need. In some cases, these attitudes were rooted in personal experience: more middle-class Americans than one might at first think have either been on welfare at some time in their lives or have close friends and relatives who were. In other cases, religious belief gave a foundation for a strong sense of altruism and obligation that no amount of antiwelfare rhetoric could extinguish. Whatever the source, middle-class Americans are not prepared to see welfare cut off, now, immediately, without a safety net.

Such support is remarkably widespread. I coded our interviews into three categories: those who opposed welfare in strong terms; those who were just as strong in defending it; and those who supported welfare in principle but had reservations about its applications in practice. As table 5.3 shows, only 27 of the 192 people who discussed the subject indicated their opposition to the principle behind welfare. "Take away the kids and put them in foster homes, or open up orphanages again," said Patricia Sullivan of Medford, Massachusetts. "It's an awful thing to say, but I think if the parents didn't have the money to blow on drugs or liquor or whatever they are addicted to, then they're not going to have these kids." What is striking is how uncommon a response Ms. Sullivan's was. Not only was opposition to the principle of welfare uncommon, but even when expressed, it was often qualified. Alfred Shoals of Sand Springs, Oklahoma, believes that welfare is "a total disaster," one that is "destroying the American way of life." But, his daughter Elizabeth quickly added, "I've seen some people that are really, really having a hard time." Just about everyone who expressed opposition to programs such as AFDC, moreover, made it clear that if by welfare we mean unemployment compensation or help for the disabled—in fact, for anyone whose life is adversely affected by forces beyond that person's control—they would be in favor of it. Opposition to welfare, finally, was strongest in DeKalb County, that is, among black Americans, many of whom were especially vehement in their denunciation of its deleterious effects. The notion that a massive backlash against welfare exists in the United States, one fueled by symbolic hostility to the poor and to minorities, does not find strong support among our subjects.

But this is not to say that the people to whom we talked liked the welfare system that presently exists. In fact, a far smaller number of people, fourteen in all, gave unqualified support to welfare as we have known it than the number expressing unqualified opposition to it. Robert Smithson, the minister of one of the more liberal churches in Brookline, pointed out, much like a sociologist, how opposition to welfare expressed "a sense of demonization of the welfare mother." Also in Brookline, psychiatrist Clark Potter was one of those who argued that the welfare system has never gone far enough in providing support; he wanted a more "user-friendly" system that would give individuals the support they truly need. But if there are people in middle-class America who think like sociologists, there are not many of them (and, as stereotype would have it, they tend to live in places like Brookline). The overwhelming majority of middle-class Americans—more than 80 percent of our sample—

TABLE 5.3
ATTITUDES TOWARD WELFARE

	Strong Support	Qualified Support	No Support	Not Available
Brookline	4	20	1	0
Medford	3	18	4	0
Broken Arrow	0	21	3	1
Sand Springs	0	22	2	1
DeKalb	1	16	6	2
Cobb	2	18	4	1
Eastlake	1	20	1	3
Rancho Bernardo	3	16	6	0
Total	14	151	27	8

express support for the idea of welfare but are very critical of the actual form that welfare has taken in America.

No one person can represent the views of all those to whom we spoke, but two of them expressed thoughts quite close to the consensus on welfare that exists in middle-class America. One, Christine Onenke, a human resources manager in Medford, had no doubt that welfare ought to exist: "I don't think I fully buy the stereotype of, you know, all welfare mothers sit around and watch TV all day and do drugs and drink. I don't believe that. I think there's circumstances out of people's control that happen where people need to be able to get back on their feet."

But that was not the end of Ms. Onenke's moral reflections, for she was quite aware that welfare, however necessary, is anything but perfect: "I know people that have struggled to get off it, but . . . a lot of times you see it perpetuate itself over and over again—and that isn't right either." Ms. Onenke has become friends with a black nurse in her company who works with pregnant teenagers and they talk frequently about what can be done to break the cycle. This woman, Ms. Onenke tells us, "knows both sides of it," how it can help and how it can hurt. Like nearly all Americans, including most members of Congress, Ms. Onenke has no idea how to make it help more and hurt less. Her bottom line on the issue is that she has no bottom line.

Unlike Ms. Onenke, who generally supports welfare but is worried about its long-term effects, Brian Fischer, a regional sales vice president living in Cobb County, does not like the idea of welfare but is also worried about those who would abolish it. "I have voted Republican every year," Mr. Fischer says. "There's part of me that says we really ought to tighten up the welfare system." And yet:

> I may have my facts wrong, but my general understanding is that when Reagan closed down a lot of the funding for the mental and nervous hospitals . . . they took people that were

not capable of functioning on their own . . . [and let them out].
That, to me . . . was the beginnings of the homeless problem.
So there's a part of me that says I don't like welfare cheats, I
don't like people that live off my tax dollars, and yet on the
other hand the Republicans haven't completely convinced me
that we're not going to have another problem like we had
when they shut down the mental and nervous institutions.

The ambivalence of Ms. Onenke and Mr. Fischer perfectly
captures the combination of support in theory and unease in
practice that defines so much of the middle-class attitude toward
welfare.

Because of their ambivalence, middle-class Americans are
not direct participants in the anything-but-ambivalent debates
between conservative and liberal intellectuals over welfare. But
their attitudes are relevant to that debate nonetheless. For if it is
true that support for the principle of welfare still exists in America,
despite decades of conservative attack and liberal defense,
one wants to know why the federal guarantee of welfare was
abolished in 1996. Liberals tend to blame conservatives for the
demise of welfare, and to the extent that conservative Republicans
took the lead on the issue, they are right; sympathy for the
downtrodden has never been high on the list of conservative priorities.
But the way our respondents talk about the issue suggests
that the left is not without blame: a defense of welfare as it
has evolved is different, in the opinions of most of them, from a
defense of the idea that people have obligations and duties
toward the poor and unfortunate. By confusing one with the
other, the left overburdened the concept of obligation until it
had no recognizable relationship to the way Americans understand
help.

One way support for the idea of welfare was undermined
was by a tendency to advocate that people have a *right* to welfare.
Rights language is viewed by many Americans as inappropriate
to welfare, not because of what Daniel Bell once called
"the revolution of rising entitlements"—Americans have no objection
to entitlements and their language is filled with the

"rights talk" such entitlements imply—but because the idea of a right to welfare constitutes an improper merging of politics and morality. Support for welfare in America is premised upon the obligation to provide, not the right to receive. This obligation has many sources: it comes from God or, for more secular people, it's just the idea of doing the right thing. It has long been apparent to people on the left, both in Europe and the United States, that charity and alms are demeaning, that people's survival should not be dependent on the good graces of the fortunate. That is a conception I happen to share, but it flies in the face of the way our middle-class Americans understood morality. The right to welfare, unlike the right to free speech, requires not protection from government, but action from government. As the right to welfare was translated into bureaucratic rules, it became harder for our respondents to recall the sense of moral obligation that gave foundation to what they believed was a helping act; for them, what ought to have been an obligation to give had been transformed into the burden of being taxed.

This does not mean that they reject a role for government in providing welfare: very few in our sample wanted to go back to a system organized by churches and private charities. It does mean that government should be a provider of last resort, however—a temporary, limited, but always reliable source of support when hard times hit, as most Americans understand they will. Recognizing a limited role for government in the provision of welfare enables those with whom we spoke to balance their idealistic principles about moral duty, which they recognize have their limits in a complicated world, with their practical recognition that sometimes more than charity is required. The notion of a right to welfare—which for them implies permanent guarantees, support irrespective of changing economic conditions, and encouragement of behavior that seems to defy common sense—upsets that balance.

Which brings us directly to the second reason why the language of the left dealing with welfare seems to leave so many of our respondents shaking their heads: the widespread support in our slice of middle-class America for making a distinction between those who deserve support and those who do not—precisely the distinction that the left has taken the lead in challenging. "I'm one of the undeserving poor: that's what I am," says the appropriately named Alfred Doolittle, in George Bernard Shaw's *Pygmalion*. "Think of what that means to a man," he further informs Henry Higgins and Colonel Pickering. "It means that he's up against middle-class morality all the time."

Ever since, liberal social critics—wanting to defend the marginalized, the alienated, or just simply the different—rarely invoke the expression "middle-class morality" without disdain. The distinction between the deserving and the undeserving poor, for scholars like Joel Handler, Michael Katz, and Herbert Gans, who believe strongly in the idea that the better off have a strong obligation to help the worse off, is the very definition of an intrusive and burdensome idea of middle-class morality. At best, the distinction between deserving and undeserving poor is misguided, they believe, for no one is truly undeserving. At worst, it is the latest chapter in America's long history of intolerance, primarily racial intolerance, directed against people whose behavior, however destructive, is the result not of their character, but of their poverty.

From the interviews we conducted, I would say that there is no belief more strongly held in America than the belief that welfare should only go to those who deserve it; it even surpasses the distinction middle-class Americans make between good and bad immigrants in its ubiquity. The ideal of personal responsibility is very deeply ingrained in the middle-class mind; three people in our sample, completely unprompted, brought up the adage that it is better to teach someone to fish than to give them a fish. "Responsibility" was a word we heard over and over again throughout our interviews. Belief in its importance lies behind the fact that most of our respondents, according to two of the survey questions we asked, were willing to pay taxes to help those who could not find work (176 agreed or agreed strongly) but were far less willing to pay taxes to help those, including mothers of small children, who do not want to find work (only 34 agreed or agreed strongly compared with 158 who disagreed or disagreed strongly). One can also get a sense of how widely the ideal of personal responsibility is shared in middle-class America from yet another survey question we asked on the matter; only a quarter of our respondents disagreed with the idea that poor people are primarily responsible for their own fate.

Because notions about personal responsibility have such resonance in middle-class America, it is important to parse the meaning of such terms as "deserving/undeserving" or "responsible/irresponsible" carefully. Critics of such terms are sure that they are code words for prejudice. Teenage mothers on welfare—presumed to be sexually promiscuous, careless, unwilling or unable to plan for the future—are especially good targets, these critics believe, for middle-class people to (inappropriately) apply their own moral values. According to the Berkeley sociologist Kristin Luker, teenage mothers make "a convenient lightning rod for the anxieties and tensions in Americans' lives." For Linda McClain, a Hofstra University law professor, talk of responsibility is a disguised form of rhetoric designed to use

TABLE 5.4

"THE PROBLEMS OF AMERICA'S INNER CITIES ARE
LARGELY DUE TO PEOPLE'S LACK OF PERSONAL
RESPONSIBILITY FOR THEIR OWN PROBLEMS"

	Strongly Agree	Agree	No Opinion	Disagree	Strongly Disagree
Brookline	6	7	4	6	2
Medford	8	8	2	7	0
Broken Arrow	6	14	2	2	1
Sand Springs	10	10	1	3	1
DeKalb	2	11	1	9	2
Cobb	4	11	2	7	1
Eastlake	4	13	1	5	2
Rancho Bernardo	6	11	4	4	0
Total	46	85	17	43	9

teenage mothers and welfare recipients as scapegoats for a conservative-led rollback of the welfare state. If these authors are correct, a category such as "undeserving" or "irresponsible" will be viewed by middle-class Americans as a demographic category linked to a behavioral category: if you are young, black, and pregnant, you will fit both categories nicely.

But this is not the way in which most middle-class Americans to whom we talked made their distinctions between those who deserved support and those who did not. For one thing, it is simply not true that they believed that teenagers who become pregnant outside of marriage forfeit the help of others. On the contrary, Americans, as surveys document, have by and large accepted the sexual revolution; roughly two-thirds of the American population supports providing teenagers with birth control pills compared with one-third who oppose it, about the same proportions as those who agreed that "the greater openness about sex and the human body" is to one degree or another good (63 percent) compared with those who thought it was bad (37 percent). Despite the fact that the 1960s have a reputation for sexual experimentation, such numbers are actually significantly higher than what the polls showed at the end of that decade; Kristin Luker is correct to conclude that "a small, fairly constant number of people still long for the old sexual order," but also that "most Americans do not." In addition, Americans tend to be very forgiving, a disposition that leads them to conclude that just because a young and single female has had an active sex life, and even become pregnant as a result, she should not be condemned. "I feel like you can just make a mistake and you shouldn't be punished for it," said Valda Sellers, a biochemistry researcher in Medford, articulating a view that was widely shared by many of those we interviewed. "I hate big blocks of judgment." Whatever middle-class morality is these days, it is neither puritanical nor judgmental; modest virtues do not allow much room for finger-pointing.

But let that same person become pregnant a second time or a third, and, middle-class people generally believe, that person has an attitude problem. "I really don't like Newt Gingrich," said

Rachel Benjamin, the Brookline dentist, "but this whole family values thing is really important. You know, you don't have to have a 'conventional family,' but you need to have people being responsible." That is why Dr. Benjamin, despite her liberal belief that welfare is necessary, also believes that "there have to be limits" when it comes to out-of-wedlock births. It is clear from her comments that people who do not live in traditional nuclear families are still deserving, so long as their underlying attitudes are responsible, but once evidence exists that a person is irresponsible in the way they think about the world—for example, by their repeated failure to limit themselves—they move from one side of the deservingness issue to the other. The same moral reasoning, for many of our respondents, holds for questions involving work. Anyone can lose their job—and anyone who does ought to have help. But if that person fails to look for work, or loses a second job or a third, once again that person has proved himself undeserving. Reactions on this point were as clear as they were consistent: you become undeserving, not because of who you are, and certainly not because you did the wrong thing, but because something is amiss in the way you think. In particular, you think you can get away with behavior that taxes the generosity of the middle class over and over again and you believe that the person paying for your irresponsibility is not going to object.

Those who question the distinction between deserving and undeserving poor are worried that Americans will look for any excuse to deny help to the poor. But what becomes clear from my interviews is that middle-class Americans believe that everyone is deserving until proven otherwise; the benefit of the doubt works to the advantage of those in need. This is how people reconcile their support for welfare with their generally favorable disposition to individualism. Given the importance middle-class people attach to responsibility, they believe that everyone ought to be capable of supporting themselves. But they know that not everyone can—at least not all the time. The way you protect the dignity of those who cannot is to help them in return for their promise to support themselves when they can. In that sense, middle-class Americans make a distinction between those who deserve help and those who do not, not to limit welfare, but to justify its existence: it is the future autonomy of the individual on welfare, and not her current dependency, that welfare programs aim to support. From the point of view of many middle-class Americans, those who would question or abolish the distinction between the deserving and the undeserving poor are not helping to sustain welfare, but working to undermine it. For if people get help even though they are not willing to reciprocate, what they are being offered is perpetual dependency—and that will eventually make them undeserving even if their original need was genuine.

So deep is the distinction between deserving and undeserving poor that it reaches to the poor themselves; "undeserving poverty is my line," Alfred Doolittle informs his daughter's handlers, and all he wants from them is a fiver for "one good spree for myself and the missus." Unlike him, Doris Casey, an unmarried mother of five surviving on welfare who lives in a public housing project in Brookline (and therefore, although not middle class, was included in our sample), wants nothing more than a little respectability. Ms. Casey has few illusions about how welfare works. Should we cut off benefits for women who continue to have children? she was asked:

> Well . . . I could almost agree with that. Because you know we all have these children for different reasons. Some of us are irresponsible, which was the case with me. When I started out having children at the age of nineteen, and I really didn't pay attention to what was down the road. You know, it's just irresponsible. And I think knowing that you have the welfare system to lean on makes it a lot easier to just produce and just not worry. . . . The welfare system makes it very easy for people to just give up. And they make it very difficult to get off. It's not really a help, it's a hindrance. Because here you have this money coming in every month and you don't have to work for it. I always tell my children I work for it, because I really work hard with my children.

Ms. Casey, a woman of great dignity and intelligence, like so many others to whom we talked, does not advocate abolishing welfare. But she also knows that her support is contingent on the generosity of the taxpayer, which bothers her. Help me, she reasons, and I will do what I can in return: go to school, give my children the attention they need. In this way, she reflects the fact that "mainstream" attitudes toward welfare are often found most strongly among those who have had experiences with the system. Reciprocity is the contract that undergirds welfare, a contract implicitly recognized by most Americans no matter on which end of the welfare bureaucracy they find themselves.

"Yes, I'm my brother's keeper," we were told by Hope Landy, an opinionated black woman in DeKalb County working as a public defender. "But I am not my brother's sacrifice." There can be little doubt that support for welfare in America is broad, but also that it is thin. Middle-class Americans are trying hard to protect their altruism from their cynicism. For some, it is a losing battle; already hostile toward politics and government, they are especially hostile toward governmental programs they identify with irresponsible conduct. Others retain their faith, not only in the principle of welfare, but in the government that offers it. Just about everyone else finds their allegiances up for grabs, swinging this way and that based on personal stories, anecdotes, or political mood. This is hardly a picture that will inspire those who believe that welfare is a right that ought to be extended to all, whatever their behavior and however long their need. But it also a picture that may make it possible to defend and preserve welfare by protecting the moral ideal it is meant to embody. Political debate will determine which of these alternatives wins. If it were up to middle-class morality, America would keep welfare—and also rediscover gratitude.

PRINCIPLE AND POLICY

Whatever may be the private motives of suburban middle-class Americans for their decisions about where to live and what to believe about welfare, publicly, with occasional exceptions, they rarely express explicitly racist sentiments. Just as Protestant

Americans no longer condemn Catholics and Jews as unworthy of salvation, whites have modified their once unfavorable views of blacks; surveys undertaken over the course of the past two or three decades record a "strong and still growing commitment to egalitarian principles among whites." Furthermore, despite negative publicity involving skinheads and racial conflicts in schools, there are no signs of decreasing racial tolerance among young whites in America. At least at the level of surveys, real progress has taken place in the degree to which white Americans have accepted ideals of racial justice and integration that, before the Civil Rights Act of 1964, were considered quite radical and, in some parts of the country, dangerous and subversive. If words were all that mattered, America would be far along toward full repudiation of its racist past.

But words can be treacherous, and because they can, social scientists have not reached a consensus that racial progress is significant and lasting. Words, for one thing, are ambiguous; in principle, Americans say that they agree with efforts to promote racial justice, but, as far as policy is concerned, the difference between white and black opinion on such questions as whether the government should promote equal opportunity in employment or take efforts to desegregate schools is so wide that it has been described as "a huge racial rift," a reflection of the fact that "blacks and whites inhabit two different perceptual worlds." No wonder then that black and white Americans, as Princeton political scientist Jennifer Hochschild has argued, look at the same American dream and come away with different visions: "African-Americans increasingly believe that racial discrimination is worsening and that it inhibits their race's ability to participate in the American dream; whites increasingly believe that discrimination is lessening and that blacks have the same chance to participate in the dream as whites."

And if there were no gap in black/white opinion, there would surely remain the gap in black/white conditions of life: what does it matter what whites say about blacks if poverty, unemployment, substandard housing, even poor health are to be found more in one group than in the other?

As with the question of welfare, one hardly knows whether to be overwhelmed by the favorable change in American opinion toward principles of racial fairness or depressed by the gap between rhetoric and reality. Surely skepticism is in order when it comes to interpreting the fact that whites, when talking about race, rarely use the explicit racist language of the 1950s South (or, if my experience is typical, the Jewish urban North); Americans have had too much experience with racial coding not to know that there are ways of signaling racism implicitly. Yet, it is also true that words are the only way by which Americans can debate the things that matter to them. If the words have changed, that in itself is significant; like the dog that did not bark, the absence of overt racism in American discourse has to be a clue about something.

Nowhere is the conviction that racism and discrimination still persist as significant forces in American life stronger than among middle-class African-Americans, no matter how successful their career trajectories have been. Although a few of the black suburbanites to whom we talked in DeKalb County believed that race relations had improved in America since the 1960s, many were angry, disappointed, and frustrated. Some, indeed, were so angry that they could barely articulate reasons, but many more were quite specific in citing evidence for their pessimism. Lena Parker, a high school physical education teacher in inner-city Atlanta, simply cannot understand why white employers fear black workers: "If you hire me you're hiring a good person," she says. "You're hiring a Christian person, one that has values, one that will stand for no nonsense and will give you an honest day's work for a honest day's pay. I will be loyal," she continues (and one fully believes, listening to her, that she will), "now see, why wouldn't you hire a person like that?" Job discrimination is the most frequently cited kind of discrimination faced by African-Americans, but not the only one. Todd Smith, the copy editor who likes the suburbs because people there value education, is disturbed that whites and blacks go to different subdivisions and rarely see each other after working hours. Vivian Teller, a nurse, takes the higher prices in grocery stores in black neighborhoods as a personal affront. A common thread that runs through the way prosperous African-Americans talk about the persistence of racism is the sheer insult of it all—the daily hurts and rude indifferences that add up to a feeling of never quite belonging in white America.

There are a number of ways in which middle-class whites with whom we spoke could respond to the anger of middle-class blacks. Significantly, denial is not one of the ways they actually do. Just as white Americans have accepted principles of nondiscrimination, they have also accepted the reason why such principles are necessary: discrimination, they are fully aware, still exists. It is interesting to compare the views of the whites in Cobb County to those of blacks in nearby DeKalb. Of the twenty-four white suburbanites to whom we talked in Cobb (one of the Cobb respondents was black), only one or two felt that racial discrimination was a thing of the past. Not very many were as liberal as Bea Cohen, the child of Holocaust survivors, for whom racism was rampant in the way her neighbors thought about crime. But most of them acknowledged that although racial progress had been made in this country, much remained to be done; as William Fahy, a retired executive, put it, "You'd probably be a fool" to argue that racism no longer exists in America. There are obvious differences between DeKalb blacks and Cobb whites; the anger about discrimination which burns so brightly in the former is replaced by optimism in the latter, an optimism that black suburbanites would surely find inappropriate. These differences are significant and lend support to those who find a deep racial divide in America.

And, yet, because of the changing language of racial politics in America, there is no counter anger among whites that racial justice has moved too quickly to match the anger among blacks that it has not moved quickly enough. The language of accusation is different between the races. For the most frustrated blacks in DeKalb that language is anger; for the most conservative whites in Cobb, it is resignation. George Slade, general manager at a tool production factory, was one of the unhappy white males to whom we talked:

> Back in the sixties it was really definable what discrimination
> was. Nowadays it's . . . it seems like there's a lot more thin
> skin. . . . It's the way words come across. It's like what you say
> instead of what you feel. I'm talking about just in general con-
> versation all of a sudden it's like you're the worst thing since
> sliced bread. . . . You could've done everything that you
> thought was right for the last twenty years, and you can be ru-
> ined over one statement that was taken out of context.

Mr. Slade's comments were similar to those of Karl Hyde, a
consultant for the Atlanta transportation system. Once Mr.
Hyde saw a sign advertising a "black circus" and that prompted
these remarks: "I see so many references to 'black' this and
'black' that. To me, it should be equal. It should say . . . if there's
a great circus in town, to use that analogy, it doesn't matter to
me if it's white or black performers. It's a circus that does this.
The subject is a circus. It's not . . . that it's a white circus or a
black circus." Both these men were clearly frustrated by having
to take notice of a black presence in American life, one they
could, years before, safely ignore. Their discomfort might be interpreted as a form of racism. But if so, it is a defensive form.
The language of equality has become the common language in
American discussions of race. Agreement in language, one has-
tens to add, does not imply that reality has changed; the gap between blacks and whites in terms of income, education, justice,
and decent housing is still very much present. The important
question is whether consensus over words yields sufficient
ground to attack the remaining disparities.

The prevalence of a solemn recognition on the part of whites
that discrimination still faces blacks at least makes a concerted
attack on racial inequality possible. Jane Sargent, a white director of billing at an Atlanta-area hospital, asked whether things
were getting better in America, said, "I think they're getting better, but they feel worse." Matters dealing with race had, in her
opinion, become an open sore on the body politic. Yet perhaps,
she mused as she talked, things had to get worse before they
could get better:

I really think . . . a lot of what came out of the Million Man
March, for example, was . . . I think more of it is being . . . ad-
dressed more openly. I think . . . for example, the O. J. Simpson trial was a great example up here. I think about 75 percent
of the people who work up here are black. It was very divisive
for two or three days after the verdict. It was uncomfortable,
but we talked a bit about how uncomfortable it was. That to
me was very healthy.

Simpson's trial told her that "it's . . . very apparent that we
can't pretend that race doesn't play a role in the way that we interact with each other. In some ways, I think it's real slow, and I
think it's gonna be hurtful. I think that sometimes it's gonna be
explosive, but I think race relations will end up . . . in a very different, much better place ten years from now than they are
now." For Ms. Sargent, the presence of angry black leaders like
Louis Farrakhan and Jesse Jackson was upsetting, but unlike
George Slade and Karl Hyde, she recognized that they were necessary. Racial progress was not going to be easy, she believed,
but if "it will bring some better understanding and finally
some resolution," no matter how long it takes, we will all be
better off.

Reading the transcripts of our interviews without looking at
the racial identity of the speaker, it is not hard to figure out
whether a black person or a white person is talking. As more
black Americans make it into the middle class, one expects a certain racial healing, and the fact that so many middle-class blacks
are so angry—according to some polls, their views are more
radical than poor and working-class African-Americans—sends
a loud and clear message that we are far from the promised land.
But as divides go, one between those who are both articulate and
angry on the one side and those who are occasionally puzzled
but at least willing to listen on the other, however wide, is not
unbridgeable. When discussing issues of racial equality, most
Americans, black or white, rely on the same words: their disagreements are about what the words mean.

Whatever agreement exists in America over general moral

principles of racial fairness is not present around specific policies such as affirmative action. Whites and blacks, according to polling data, are polarized on the question; the 1986 National Election Study showed that 4.9 percent of whites strongly favored preferential hiring, compared with 49.3 percent of blacks, and a review of nearly all the surveys ever taken on the question demonstrates that less than 20 percent of whites support preferential hiring, while black support is nearly always more than 40 percent. In general, surveys seem to indicate, whites are against affirmative action, blacks tend to be for it, and Hispanics are split down the middle.

What people say can be as important as what people are for or against, however, and as one explores the moral language in which affirmative action is discussed, polarization is not quite as prominent. For one thing, not all the whites with whom we spoke were opposed to affirmative action (and not all blacks were in favor of it). Susan Medina, a Medford resident, believes she understands minority frustration. It is, in her opinion, fair for a black person from inner-city Boston to get a job as a firefighter even if he scores lower on a test than a white applicant. Putting herself in the position of that person, Ms. Medina says, "Well, you've got to give me a handicap. You understand handicaps when it comes to sports. Why can't you understand a handicap in a life situation?" Whites have a legitimate gripe about such things, Ms. Medina argues, but because preferential hiring policies "have given people a chance where they never would have had one," she just hopes that the angry white person will become "educated" on the issue and understand why such policies may be necessary. In a like manner, David Peters, a reticent Oklahoma college student trying to become a policeman, accepts as just a fact that a woman or a minority person might beat him out even if he scored higher. "I can understand like going into minority neighborhoods, it's better to have a minority officer," he says matter-of-factly. And women? "Yeah, I've seen people, they tend to obey a woman officer better." "No reason to get angry" about such things, Mr. Peters concluded. One got the sense talking to him that he just wanted to know what the rules are; whatever they are, he will find a way to accommodate them.

But most of the middle-class white people in our sample, in contrast to Ms. Medina and Mr. Peters, do not like affirmative action and would like to see it scaled back or completely eliminated; the hesitancy about ending welfare now, today, right away, was less pronounced with respect to affirmative action. Reverse discrimination, quotas, merit—all the words one associates with opposition to affirmative action appear throughout white responses. But so do words like backfire, unbalanced, and, most frequently of all, overboard; the general response among whites was that affirmative action was once a good thing, but it has gone too far and needs to be curtailed. The reasons for this belief varied. Michelle Knight of Broken Arrow was skeptical of affirmative action because she was skeptical of government: "Like every government thing, it's overdone, it's over-regulated." Or, as José Velasquez of Eastlake, California, put it, "When anything becomes a political football, it's bad." Nancy Elliott, a white woman living in predominantly black DeKalb County, was a devotee of the humanistic psychologist Abraham Maslow's "hierarchy of needs" and believed that a quota "does nothing at all to generate love." A few individuals with detailed knowledge of the programs such as Adam Grant of Sand Springs, Oklahoma, wondered, "How long do we have to keep paying this price—you know, society as a whole—for the sins of our fathers?" But overall the most common response among whites was one of puzzlement: if the point of racial justice is to break racial stereotyping, then how can that goal be served by classifying and counting by race? Joyce Palma of Medford was saddened that "people are withdrawing into their own camps," a trend, she believed, that was furthered by affirmative action. For every white person who thought affirmative action "stinks," is "absurd" or "baloney," a far greater number felt that good intentions had been taken to an extreme they could no longer support. The default language for whites was a language of balance more than a language of rejection. Affirmative action programs have been around long enough for the abuses to be visible. "I truly believe that all systems are abused," said Edvardo Valdez of Eastlake. It is as if all programs have their moment, and the moment for this one is passed.

That language would not be well received by many of the blacks in our sample. Not all of them would dismiss white objections to affirmative action as "a crock," as did Maryann Kate Roberts, a DeKalb bank teller, but for many of them, affirmative action's time is anything but passed. For some, the notion of reverse discrimination made little sense: how could whites know the kinds of discrimination experienced by blacks on a daily basis? "We're not in a country yet where people are judged by their character," Ms. Roberts continued. "When we can totally say that this country is color-blind, then we can end affirmative action." That day, she made clear, had not yet come. "You can't ride a bicycle by looking at the picture," Clay Jones, a computer programmer, added. "You've got to get on the bicycle, you've got to fall down some, but if you can't get on . . . the bicycle then it's not gonna do you any good."

On this issue, the data one obtains from surveys and the data one obtains from more qualitative interviews are not always the same. Survey researchers have discovered that a much of the response white Americans make to questions about affirmative action depends on how the questions are worded. Even whites who say that they are strongly opposed to preferences and quotas, it has been discovered, will support job training and corporate outreach programs, so long as they believe such programs will not take away jobs from whites. I found that the way blacks responded to questions about affirmative action also depended a great deal on the way they were worded. Based on earlier survey research, which demonstrated strong negative associations with words such as "quotas" and "preferences," I tried to find another term that would substitute for them in phrasing my own survey question on the subject. The word I finally came up with was "priority," which, I believed, would be less likely to arouse strong opposition, at least among blacks. I was wrong; both blacks and whites indicated strong disagreement with the statement that African-Americans should have priority in jobs and

TABLE 5.5
"BECAUSE OF THE HISTORY OF SLAVERY AND DISCRIMINATION,
AFRICAN-AMERICANS SHOULD HAVE PRIORITY IN
COLLEGE ADMISSIONS AND FOR JOBS"

PERCENTAGE OF EACH GROUP

	Black (N=24)	Asian (N=6)	Hispanic (N=12)	White (N=158)
Strongly Agree	0	0	0	1
Agree	12.5	40	0	13
Disagree	75.0	60	67	52
Strongly Disagree	0	0	33	31
No Opinion	12.5	0	0	3
Total	100	100	100	100

college admissions because of their past experiences with slavery and discrimination. There was a difference between them—75 percent of blacks disagreed or disagreed strongly compared with 83 percent of whites—but such a difference is not very significant.

The important differences between blacks and whites on affirmative action occurred, not in the survey question, but in the way they talked about affirmative action. A few of the blacks in DeKalb thought that real racial progress has been made in the United States and that affirmative action programs were sometimes misused or out of balance. Still, said Martin Wolcott, a Baptist minister, "because there are some people who can still benefit by affirmative action, it is not a 'damnable program' as some are trying to make it." "Let me just preface this with saying that I believe that the person who is the most skilled should be the one that gets a job opportunity," began Henry Johnson, the tax auditor for whom homogeneity was an incentive to move to DeKalb County. The problem is that white males who have traditionally had the power to hire and fire might not, because of inherited racial stereotypes, recognize who is truly skilled. Affirmative action, he believes, is necessary, not to undermine a system based on merit, but to make it possible. "I'm not saying that we need affirmative action to erase four hundred years of slavery and all that," he comments. "It's just that sometimes there are people who need to be forced to make the right decision." Like many African-Americans to whom we spoke, Mr. Johnson's support for affirmative action was more pragmatic than principled. "My skin tone automatically subtracts ten percent from my merits," says Herbert Almond, who supports affirmative action because it restores to him that 10 percent. If, as Vaughn Hyde put it, we knew whose merit system we were using, we might not need affirmative action. "But I'm gonna be tested on some rules . . . that I didn't play a part in making up," he continues, and that is not fair. The bottom line for these black men, as for many of their neighbors, was that jobs were distributed based on informal networks to which African-Americans do not belong. (Henry Johnson's wife, Linda, recognizes that she was lucky, obtaining her job because the white dean of the business college she attended put in a good word for her.) Affirmative action was understood by many of them as a corrective to networking, as a broadening of the pool, not a one-on-one competition.

Such a perspective is not all that far from ways by which affirmative action could be mended and made acceptable to a number of whites. Seymour Martin Lipset argues that Americans believe in both individualism and egalitarianism but will always choose the former if it conflicts with the latter; to the degree that affirmative action is justified in ways that do not appear to contradict a rock-solid belief that people should be rewarded for their abilities, opposition to affirmative action moderates. And the way to do that is not to make a case that race in itself offers merit—that strikes too close to dreaded quotas—but to point out what almost all middle-class Americans know to be true: that networks are important and that black Americans do not have full access to them, or at least to the ones that matter. Putting affirmative action in those terms underscores the points on which blacks and whites tend to agree: both believe that the practical goal of diversity is a more important rationale for affirmative action than the principled goal of reparations for past acts of slavery or racism; both think that affirmative action may not be needed some time when the racial picture improves; and both focus more on private companies and their programs than federal set-asides or efforts to classify by race. That may help explain why the most recent survey data, including the National Election Study, show fairly dramatic drops in black support for job preferences over time, yielding "a considerable convergence in black and white opinion on this issue and a decrease in polarization." And it may also have something to do with the way the politics of affirmative action have proven resistant to polarization along political lines: Republicans did not make repeal of affirmative action a major national issue in 1996; the support of women for affirmative action makes opponents in both parties tremble about recommending its abolition; and the increasing importance of ethnic and racial groups that define themselves as neither black nor white complicates the bookkeeping.

Despite differences between blacks and whites on this issue, in other words, there is room for common ground. Christine Onenke, the Medford human resources manager whose views on welfare seemed to outline the consensus on that subject, also expresses what might emerge as an eventual common position on affirmative action. Ms. Onenke is deeply involved with hiring decisions in her company. "Discrimination—it exists to an extent everywhere," she feels. "I think I'm a little more aware of it because of what I do." She has seen cases where as a result of affirmative action policies white males have not gotten jobs, "and I've seen the reverse—I have seen the old-boy network alive and well; I've seen the glass ceiling." Affirmative action and a concern with diversity have been good for her company, she thinks, but when taken to extremes, they can turn into absurdities, such as excessive litigation: "The amount of money and time you have to spend defending crazy cases and things that have nothing really to do with the fact that someone's black or white or gay or whatever they are." Listening to her talk, I could easily imagine her in a room with Herbert Almond, the black DeKalb County resident who believed that affirmative action restored back to his qualifications the 10 percent that racism took away, starting from different places but winding up pretty close to agreement.

Anyone who examines the polling data or scans letters to the editor knows that such agreement is not yet here. Whether it will ever come is anyone's guess. But as I listened to middle-class Americans speak about the issue, one sign of optimism did emerge: agreement on the moral principle of human equality may turn out to be more important than disagreement on a policy such as affirmative action.

This runs counter to the argument of political scientists Donald Kinder and Lynn Sanders, who see in the survey data an America deeply divided by race. They believe that white opposition to a policy such as affirmative action is more significant than white and black agreement on general principles of nondiscrimination and racial equality, since it is the policies "that bear unambiguously and differentially on the fortunes of blacks and whites" that really matter. There is an obvious truth here: moral principles do tend to be consensual until applied to actual cases, when disagreement becomes far more likely. Yet, it does not follow that the division over policy must always be given more significance than agreement over principle. No policy, after all, is unambiguous, and few are more ambiguous than affirmative action, since both opponents and defenders can claim that they are striving to move toward a color-blind society. And all policies bear differentially on various groups: support for AIDS research, for example, benefits some at the expense of others, despite rhetoric efforts to argue that everyone is at risk from AIDS. Besides, Americans are *supposed* to disagree about policy, especially controversial ones like welfare, crime, or affirmative action. And when they do disagree, what they are disagreeing about may well be not race itself but more general attitudes toward activist government. Finally, as a *Wall Street Journal*/NBC News poll has shown, for all the differences between blacks and whites on some issues, there is strong agreement on others, such as crime, the amount of racial progress in America, and questions about whether integration is the right way to solve America's racial dilemma.

Principles, by contrast, are least appreciated when most ubiquitous. It does not take a historian to remember a time when significant portions of the United States did not accept the principle that everyone was a moral equal regardless of race. The fact that nearly all Americans now do is what makes it possible to disagree about a policy such as affirmative action, for a substantial portion of that disagreement takes place within reasonable interpretations of what the common moral principle means. The principle of the moral equality of all leads neither to the conclusion that affirmative action must be abolished because it fails the test of color blindness nor to the conclusion that only those who support affirmative action support the ideal of racial justice. As Americans argue over moral principles—equality, merit, fairness, racial justice—different policies aimed at realizing those ideals will command varying levels of support. Americans disagree by race over affirmative action, although not as much as we sometimes think. We are lucky that they do, not because disagreement is necessarily good, but because disagreement over policy is much better than discord over principle.

Perhaps the last word on this subject should be given by Alex Molinari, a post office manager from Eastlake, California. Recalling those religious believers who would solve the problem of separation of church and state by allowing every religion to have its say, Mr. Molinari said this: "I think affirmative action is good, but I think it should be for everybody." A bit stunned, Maria asked whether he meant that affirmative action should be class-based, as a recent book has argued. "No," he replied, "I think affirmative action should be based on the whole populace. . . . In other words, not just one segment of the population. Not, for example, just women alone for affirmative action. I think it should be for everyone, for all races, all genders, all citizens." It is not clear that Mr. Molinari understood what affirmative action was, but in his own way, he offered the commonsense remedy for polarization: let's not do away with affirmative action; rather, let's make it so inclusive that it resonates with, rather than against, the deeply ingrained sense of moral equality held by all Americans regardless of race.

LEFT, RIGHT, AND RACE

Questions of race and poverty are among the most divisive facing America. Since the Kerner Commission in 1968 warned of the emergence of two Americas, separate and unequal, there have appeared numerous books warning of the dangers facing the country if we did not begin to cross our racial divide. The titles of such books—*Tragic Failure*, *American Apartheid*, *Two Nations*, *Divided by Color*, *Faded Dreams*, and *The Coming Race War*—are meant to emphasize the seriousness of the case that needs to be made against white resistance so that black Americans can achieve social justice.

Such an emphasis is surely warranted. The conditions of life for the poorest black Americans have approached levels of desperation and hopelessness that no civilized society ought to accept and, as our interviews in DeKalb County reinforce, even well-off African-Americans continue to face unwarranted and unfair racial discrimination. But with race, as with so many other facets of social life, it is nearly always a question of interpreting data that point in two directions, not one of hammering home facts that only point in one. The story about race in America over the past two or three decades is a complicated one. Some black Americans are doing better than ever; others worse than ever. Integration and segregation seem to be increasing at the same time. Compared with where we were, there is progress. Compared with where we should be, that progress is insufficient.

This is not the place to enter the already extensive debate about whether the glass representing the question of race is half full or half empty. Nor could I do so even if I wanted to, for the research on which I am reporting involves primarily middle-class Americans, leaving out many of those whose voices have to be heard in the debate, including those of the rural poor, working-class people of all races and ethnicities, and the "streetwise" men and women of the inner city. Still, most Americans, black and white, aspire to middle-class status. When it comes to questions involving race and poverty, there may be something to be learned from the attitudes of behaviors of middle-class people of both races.

Many of the white middle-class Americans with whom I spoke had surprising things to say about the ways in which race matters to them. Trent Tartt, for example, a conservative Christian from Broken Arrow, had his world turned upside down when he attended a Promise Keepers rally at the University of Tulsa football stadium. Promise Keepers, an organization started by the former football coach at the University of Colorado, brings men together in revival meeting settings to stress to them the importance of the promises they make as husbands and fathers. Seen by critics on the left as antifeminist and homophobic, Promise Keepers also offered Mr. Tartt something he never had before: the opportunity to hear a black man preach the evils of racism. "You white people need to turn the other cheek," he recalls the speaker saying. "You need to wash a black man's feet." The audience, he continues, was stunned into silence. But when the speaker went on to say, "But every black man needs to learn the same thing and to wash a white man's feet, as Christ washed all the feet of his twelve disciples," the ideal of racial dignity and moral equality was brought home to him in a new way, precisely because it was couched in a conservative language in which he was comfortable and not in a language of liberal elites that would have been alien to him.

Joyce Slone, by contrast, is a fifty-two-year-old retired psychiatric social worker in Brookline, a self-described child of the sixties. In some ways, the liberalism of her youth remains intact. "There are good people in those communities," she responds, when questioned about Boston's inner-city black neighborhoods, noting that those who live in them "must be frightened to death every night to go out and be afraid that they're going to be the victim of a random bullet. I think it's awful, and I think we should spend some money ..." Mrs. Slone, who is Jewish, recalls the Holocaust, which gives her a special sympathy for those who are victims of the prejudice of others. Childless, she feels that she ought to pay taxes to help others raise their children. Yet, a new tone, strange even to herself, shapes her feelings about these issues: "But I'll tell you something, when I'm walking down the street and there's a black person behind me, I will often just stop and wait for them to pass. I'm afraid of them, more than anything else. Because I just don't know, and I mean ... I want them to have opportunities, I want them to help themselves."

Mrs. Slone does not think of herself as a conservative. Now, however, she feels more attracted to the values she associates with her parents' generation. Disobedient children frighten her. Her conversation continually comes back to the theme of violence. She does feel that it's better to give kids more leeway, but she also thinks that, in the name of discipline, we have to impose more control. What seems to characterize Mrs. Slone's views are a deep ambivalence: an almost instinctual liberalism, which wants to treat the very poor of the inner city just like everyone else, combined with a fear that things have simply gotten out of control, forcing her, almost against her will, toward fearful encounters with racial minorities.

Since at least the time of the civil rights movement, disagreements over racial progress have corresponded to disagreements over larger political worldviews: in general, liberals were perceived as being in favor of racial equality and conservatives were seen as resisting it. If respondents such as Mr. Tartt or Mrs. Slone are any indication, whatever disagreements middle-class Americans may have over race, they are no longer disagreements about political ideologies. When we can no longer assume that all conservatives have a monopoly on racism and liberals a monopoly on goodwill, America's dialogue over race will improve, and not just because there are more conservatives in America than liberals. For too long, race has been asked to serve as a symbolic proxy for other things; intertwined with issues like affirmative action, welfare, and urban assistance, it came to be taken for granted that anyone who had qualms about the policies also had qualms about the intended beneficiaries of the policies.

There is much to be gained by treating race as a thing in itself, not as a stand-in for other values; if there is one aspect of political discussion that distinguishes intellectuals (liberal and conservative alike) from the people with whom I talked, it is that the former like to read symbolic meaning into all kinds of things—the houses people buy, the way they raise their children, whom they have for neighbors, even what they eat and drive—whereas the latter tend to believe that mundane matters are really mundane matters. Adopting a bit more of the latter's sensibility reminds us that, when it comes to race, it is people, not policies, that ultimately matter. And at least among those people who are white, personal experience matters far more than political ideology in shaping their commitments to racial equality. The less Americans talk about welfare and affirmative action, and the more they deal with the practical realities of an increasingly multiracial America, the greater will be the progress toward a society that can begin to live up to its racial ideals.

There is also something to be learned from the black Americans with whom we spoke. Black middle-class anger over race is real, but it is also *middle-class* anger; it is not a rejection of middle-class values such as merit, recognition, and reward, but a demand that those values apply to all. Whether the subject is welfare, affirmative action, or moving to the suburbs, black middle-class Americans uphold, sometimes more tenaciously than whites, the very middle-class morality that, academic commentators often tell us, is designed to keep minorities in their place. Reading academic accounts of these issues, and then listening to black Americans, it seems as though the academic left wants to take away middle-class morality just at the moment when substantial numbers of black Americans are effectively claiming it.

If the strength with which a number of black Americans have claimed middle-class values often makes them more bourgeois than their white counterparts, it also strips from whites a way of resisting black progress. So pervasive are middle-class values in America that once the debate shifts to how and why people make it, no language exists for denying those values to anyone, whatever their race, who can make a credible claim to them. That is why the virtual disappearance of overt racism from surveys and interviews is important. Even if dark thoughts lie behind the nice words, and I am not sure how often they do, white Americans will be forced by their own professed rhetoric to accept and acknowledge the fundamental equality between them and other middle-class Americans whose race is different from theirs.

Suburban America—for people of all races—is an acquired taste. Academics tend not to like it, finding it, in the words of Homi Bhabha, a well-known professor of English at the University of Chicago, "a culture of paranoia" that is "founded on a fear of difference; and a narrow-minded appeal to cultural homogeneity . . . that draws the boundary between what is acceptable and unacceptable ever more tightly around the norm of the 'known.' " Most middle-class Americans, by contrast, tend not only to like suburbia, but to imagine no other way in which to live. There being no accounting for taste, suburbia, and the people who live there, are fair game for criticism. But before the critics get carried away in their denunciations of the middle class for its indifference and callousness toward racial minorities, they ought to hear the other side of the story from those whose motives they are interpreting. When they do, they will learn that Americans may once have moved to the suburbs to flee the black poor who remained in the cities, but now many of them, having been born outside the city, are no longer fleeing from it, and many of those who are fleeing the city are themselves black. The moral story of suburbia has changed. We ought to understand it better before we rush to judgment about it.

VI ORDINARY DUTIES

Jorge—"Call me George"—Martinez, thirty-five years old, grew up mostly in Mexico, moving back and forth to the United States as a child. Finally settling in this country, he attended San Diego State University, majoring in engineering. Maria and I met him at his office in downtown San Diego, where he works as a regional supervisor for CalTrans, the state agency that builds California's notorious freeways. Mr. Martinez's desk, behind which he was too energetic to sit, faced not only us, but also a huge map of a freeway linking the northern and southern sections of San Diego County. What, we wanted to know, was important to him? "Money," he responded, "and this is going to sound strange, money to me is not an issue." He continued:

> I don't rely on money to drive what I'm doing. It has to be something that I enjoy doing. I enjoy building highways, I enjoy going out to the communities and explaining to them why we're going to build this highway right through the middle of their community. I enjoy being in the middle of an open field that a mortar grader is coming through and we're going to plow through that to build something. I think I enjoy building something out of nothing or out of a set of white papers, putting something together like it's behind you there. A freeway. And I see that also as a greater benefit because I'm helping my community be able to be more mobile, move goods . . .

Robert Moses, the man whose plans for highways so transformed New York City, was once compared to Goethe's Faust,

Conrad's Mr. Kurtz, and Karl Marx. Mr. Martinez is far too soft-spoken for any such comparisons, but he does remind one of the time, so well symbolized by Robert Moses, when Americans were enthusiastic builders. One thing about his job bothers him, however; his roads divide communities. "I mean, if I put in a freeway, one town or one area may become more affluent than the other town on the other side. Why? I can't explain that." But although some may be hurt by his highways, others are helped. "You know one half goes away and does their own thing and the other half becomes really successful. I mean, that's why I'm doing what I'm doing."

Concerned about the impact of his work on other communities, Mr. Martinez is also active in communities of his own. "A lot of people don't know who their neighbors are and don't depend a whole lot on them. . . . We do. I mean I know my neighbors as much as I can and we have become great friends." But the most important community for him is the one that has formed at work. "I've been working here for twelve years now," he says of his experience at CalTrans. "There's folks that started at the same time I did. We grew up together I guess you could say in a lot of ways, so I depend on them, and they depend [on me] a lot." Because he is an immigrant, Mr. Martinez feels especially strongly that communal ties, whether at work or where you live, are necessary to help newcomers make adjustments: "Some of them," he says of his coworkers, "came from other places in the U.S. where they didn't know anyone but their coworkers, so they became really good friends of ours." There is no conflict in Mr. Martinez's outlook between his sense of self and the need to cooperate with others. "I think in my mind if we are to become more successful as a group, we need to learn more about each other."

Like many of the Mexican-Americans with whom we spoke, Mr. Martinez, a Catholic, personified a sense of hard work, patience, upward mobility, and reward that the great turn-of-the-century German sociologist Max Weber identified with the Protestant ethic. But unlike the dour Protestants of Weber's text, Mr. Martinez was as happy in his personal life as he was in his work life. If you could have your ideal life, what kind of life would you want? we asked him. Nothing different from what I presently have, was his response. "I enjoy what I do, and I enjoy where I live, also. I have a wonderful wife, a daughter, and good friends, good people. I'm able to do things outside of work also that I enjoy doing. So, no, I mean in some ways . . . I'm happy where I'm at, not that I want to become that comfortable, either. I mean, I always strive for more."

At first glance, Mr. Martinez would seem to embody all those characteristics that middle-class Americans have associated with middle-class status: hardworking, forward-looking, happy, and disposed to see the good in other people. Yet, it is precisely such dispositions that, according to a number of interpretations of American society, are increasingly disappearing in this country. Those interpretations take different forms and emphasize different themes, but nearly all of them are persuaded that Americans have become so selfish and cynical that they no longer cooperate effectively with each other. The most widely discussed of these accounts is the thesis, associated with the Harvard political scientist Robert Putnam, that the "social capital" of America—the benefits that flow when civic participation and trust in others are high—is in serious decline. If this thesis is true, then people who have Mr. Martinez's hopefulness and concern with community should also be disappearing.

Survey data provide support for that conclusion: 46.3 percent of those contacted by the General Social Survey in 1972 said that people could be trusted, compared with 34.4 percent in 1994. Moreover, according to the GSS for 1993, 62.6 percent of Americans agreed or strongly agreed that you had to take care of yourself before helping others, compared with 26.5 percent who disagreed or disagreed strongly. Our own survey question indicated strong agreement with such findings; 133 of our respondents thought selfishness was becoming more of a problem in America, compared with 49 who did not. By the answers they give to survey questions, Americans are indicating a belief that their fellow citizens have become much more preoccupied with their own affairs. This is the kind of warning signal that has led a

TABLE 6.1
"COMPARED TO TWENTY YEARS AGO, AMERICANS HAVE
BECOME MORE SELFISH"

	Strongly Agree	Agree	No Opinion	Disagree	Strongly Disagree
Brookline	3	12	3	6	1
Medford	4	15	0	6	0
Broken Arrow	3	13	4	5	0
Sand Springs	4	13	2	6	0
DeKalb	7	13	1	4	0
Cobb	5	14	2	4	0
Eastlake	0	15	3	6	1
Rancho Bernardo	2	10	3	10	0
Total	28	105	18	47	2

number of writers to conclude that the capacity of people to depend on others is disappearing from American life.

If so, the consequences would be serious. Trust, we have been told, is fundamental to economic performance; societies that value this quality, absolved from reinventing the wheel with each economic transaction, will be more productive in increasingly competitive global environments. And if a lack of trust has serious consequences for economic performance, a political system characterized by mistrust will generally lack the legitimacy necessary for sustained democratic performance; journalists and political commentators have begun to wonder if the level of cynicism has reached dangerous levels in American life. Although impossible to measure, the experiences of societies that lack even elemental forms of social trust ought to be enough to convince those that do have it how fortunate they are.

For many who write about this topic, the cause of trust's decline are not that difficult to understand: a diminishing sense of the voluntarism and participation that so attracted Alexis de

Tocqueville in the nineteenth century—reflected either in a falling off of membership in civic associations, a lack of concern with civic virtue, or a sense that political participation has decreased while political polarization has increased—lies behind the withdrawal of Americans into selfish, rather than civic, pursuits. There is, I believe, a good deal of truth in this observation; in my book *Whose Keeper?*, I tried to document with empirical evidence, relevant both to the United States and Scandinavia, how the texture of civil society was being thinned out by an increasing reliance on markets and states. Although the idea that civil society is in decline has been subject to considerable criticism, there does seem to me to exist fairly compelling evidence that the institutions of civic life—those forms of participation and engagement that rely on people's sense of moral duty rather than on economic self-interest or the state's coercive capacity—have constricted in recent years, with predictably problematic consequences for the ways we live together.

Yet, that is not the whole story either. Membership declines and voter apathy are objective phenomenon that, because countable, can be established either to have taken place or not. But trust, an attitude, is subjective in nature: it can exist even when civic life appears to be in decline or can atrophy even when civic life flourishes. Middle-class Americans have experienced vertiginous changes in their lives at every level of experience—from the emergence of new family forms, to new patterns of religious belief, to limits on the capacity of the American nation-state to get its way in the world. Facing transformations of this magnitude, it would not be surprising if they became less trustworthy and more skeptical, as polling data suggest they are indeed becoming. But then there are people like Jorge Martinez, who not only defies the stereotype of a distrustful America, but who spends his free time traveling around the San Diego area talking at high schools composed primarily of minority students about his love for his work.

Two arenas of American life, both important in Mr. Martinez's conversation with us, seem particularly fruitful sites for examining how middle-class Americans view the changing nature of their social ties with each other. One of them is the workplace. In the iconography of American suburbia circa 1950, work was the place you went to when, if you were male, you left the private world of the household; the picture that sticks in our mind when we think about those years is the commuter railroad station platform, filled with men who, having just gotten out of the family station wagon, were waiting to be conveyed to the highly public world of the big business corporation. These days, there are a significant number of women waiting on the platform as well; as more Americans have gone to work, the number of Americans who experience the workplace as the public arena in which they come into contact with strangers outside the confines of their private families has dramatically increased. We usually think of the "public sector" as a shorthand term for "government." But if we think sociologically, it is the workplace where most people learn about themselves, find out which values are truly important, make friends, develop their networks, eat their lunch, give to charity, fall in love, discuss television and sports, and learn what's on the minds of other people. Business may well be "private" in the sense of property rights, but from the perspective of everyday life and how it is experienced, corporations are as public an institution as one can find.

In telling us how much he loved his work, Mr. Martinez also told us something about his work. He builds freeways. Anyone looking for a symbolic representation of what has gone wrong with a sense of community since the 1950s might well choose the highway as the second symbol of social decline. Mr. Martinez's own remarks tell the story: freeways divide people from each other. They also offer people means of escape from their towns, pointing them in the direction of other places, away from close ties and obligations. The focus of much of the literature dealing with the decline of social capital focuses on the local community, no doubt why Robert Putnam picked the bowling alley, a community-based institution if there ever was one, to represent what has happened in America. Our interviews all took place in communities through which interstate highways pass, even those in the space-shy Boston area. Are the eyes of our interviewees on those highways? we wondered. Do they feel that their local communities—even emptier during the day than they were in the 1950s when the station wagon turned around and drove back home—no longer provide a source of social regeneration? Or do they cram into their evenings activities, including local educational and neighborhood issues, that once occupied full days? As middle-class Americans tell the story of how they perceive the changing nature of their ties with each other, work and community, along with church, are the arenas around which they organize their thoughts.

BALANCED CAPITALISM

When he diagnosed the organization man—that conformist employee of one of America's largest companies forty years ago who pledged his loyalty to the firm in exchange for long-term economic security—journalist William H. Whyte, Jr., was describing not only real people, but people as the leading social scientists of his day thought people should be understood. Whyte took as his texts works by Elton Mayo dealing with the firm, W. Lloyd Warner dealing with the community, and Frank Tannenbaum dealing with the union—all of which emphasized how obsolete had become the individualist of the American liberal tradition. Modern large-scale organization required belongingness, these scholars believed. Free-floating fluidity, according to then popular theories of mass society, would, in loosening people's ties to each other, make them that much more vulnerable to totalitarian leaders promising to bring them back together. People closely tied to organizations would dampen the emotional fires in which extremism spread. The social scientists of the 1950s were calling into being the very world of close ties and strong commitments that the social scientists of the 1990s see disappearing.

Of all the institutions that emphasized the benefits of belonging, none were more important than those at the workplace:

the union and the business corporation. Each is essential for a discussion of the changing nature of social trust in America.

For those Americans of working-class background raised into suburban middle-class prosperity by the economic growth of the 1950s and 1960s, union membership, as Samuel Freedman's account of some of those families in *The Inheritance* makes clear (and as our interviews confirm), was a badge proudly worn. According to many social scientists of that period, they had good reason for their pride; when they functioned properly, unions taught the skills necessary to make democracy work. That may well be why so many of the middle-class Americans with whom we spoke had a soft spot for unions. Alas for unions, however, that soft spot reflects a nostalgia for the past rather than a guide to the present, let alone hopes for the future. The decline of union members as a percentage of the nonagricultural workforce—from 16.5 percent of private sector workers in 1983 to 10.8 percent in 1994—is a well-known phenomenon, so persistent and consequential a development that the withering away of the trade union stands as an important piece of empirical evidence for making the case that the institutions of civil society are not what they were.

Given how important unions were in raising so many Americans into the middle class, what seems remarkable now is the relative equanimity among middle-class Americans as they contemplate the possibility of an economy without unions. "I think unions were very good when . . . you had child labor and twelve-, fourteen-hour days and that kind of thing," was how Broken Arrow's Michelle Knight expressed a widely held point of view. In very similar terms, Susan McCarthy of Brookline, who, like Ms. Knight, is in her twenties, argued that "unions are a great thing." Both women immediately made it clear, however, that they were not talking about the present time. "I don't think you would ever have that problem again," Ms. Knight added, referring to the era of child labor. Besides, she continued, "a lot of union-based jobs have a very poor work ethic. They're rewarded not on merit but on their time in service, their positions in the union, their whatever." And Ms. McCarthy, who thought unions were great, continued this way: "But I think unions are also a really bad thing right now, because it almost makes it impossible for you to work."

Jason Cooper and his wife, residents of Eastlake, disagree with each other on question of unions. Companies, she believes, "are getting much more efficient, maybe too efficient." "Well," interjects her husband, "unions are alive and well." "Unions are not alive," she responds. "You know I'm in a profession that is well protected, we're very strongly union, and there's a lot of deadwood. Hopefully, we will get away from that." The reason why we might be better off without strong unions, not only in Mrs. Cooper's account but many others as well, is that the very solidarity they encourage seems anachronistic in a more dynamic and competitive world economy. "Out of the unionism," argued Elizabeth Tyler of Brookline, there "came an idea that you didn't have to work very hard and you shouldn't have to work very hard," which, in her view, was the beginning of America's recent economic decline. Talking to middle-class Americans, it becomes very clear that, however much they believe that unions were important at one time in encouraging a sense of collective purpose, they are too realistic about the dynamics of capitalism not to understand that such solidarity can become counterproductive. As important as such solidarity may be, there are other things that are more important, especially the need of business to adapt to changing economic circumstances. The strongly collectivist norms of unions are still admired, but in the way museums and historical exhibits are admired: these are things that veterans are expected to explain to the young, not principles upon which people can be expected to rely in the way they treat one another.

If middle-class Americans can be described as indifferent to unions, they are also increasingly hostile to corporations; the fact that they recognize business's need to compete does not mean that they like what happens as a result. This should not be taken to mean that middle-class Americans are anticapitalist; even before the ignominious collapse of planned economies in Central and Eastern Europe, Americans have never expressed much sympathy for socialist ideals. But the capitalism they like is not the one celebrated by advocates of unfettered markets, whose one great idea is that firms, as well as individuals, ought to be able to do whatever they determine is in their own self-interest. Strong believers in the idea that people should try to act virtuously, if always in modest ways, middle-class Americans would hardly be likely to endorse the rather immodest suggestion that self-interest is always and inevitably beneficial to others. And moderate in their politics, it should not be surprising that they are also moderate in their economics, especially because, in the modern world, economics is politics. Support in America for a conception of capitalism that includes a prominent role for economic justice is remarkably broad and is as likely to be shared by conservative Christians as by East Coast liberals.

In contrast to the world of laissez-faire so admired by economists, middle-class Americans adhere to an ideal that can be described as balanced capitalism. It takes three general forms. One is that corporations should balance their self-interest with the need to consider what benefits the larger society. A second is that corporate life should be organized in ways that permit people to balance their obligations to work with their obligations to family, church, and community. And a third is that corporate executives should be compensated in ways that are not out of balance with common sense and moral proportionality. Middle-class Americans worry that on all three accounts, corporate America is increasingly out of balance, a trend that, if allowed to continue, could have negative consequences for the social fabric of their society.

Populists of both the left and right are persuaded that the new era of corporate downsizing into which America has entered will mobilize public anger behind whatever political and economic agenda they happen to support. Yet, at least in the 1996 election, the anger that seemed so apparent when Patrick Buchanan campaigned in New Hampshire had largely evaporated by year's end. One reason, surely, was that Americans were relatively satisfied with the performance of the economy.

But another reason received insufficient attention. The fact is that middle-class Americans are not opposed to the necessity for downsizing, at least in theory: they fully recognize that companies can become too overstaffed and settled in their ways for their own good. "The downsizing or rightsizing or whatever you want to use the term is something that is getting a huge amount of attention," said Rancho Bernardo's Charles Duggan. "But I must tell you in all candor that I did that sort of work for twenty years; I ran successive reductions in forces." For him, such changes are simply part of economic life in the real world: "This happens, it has to happen. You've got to shift in order to keep the organizations doing what they have to do." Mr. Duggan's explicit justification for downsizing was not typical of most of our conversations, but it is true that the world of the organization man, with its emphasis on security for life, is not one middle-class Americans necessarily admire. Paternalistic firms, like entrenched unions or even nuclear families, can be stultifying; when some of our respondents talked about the lives of their parents, what struck them most was how little mobility, freedom, and personal drive characterized the outlook of that generation.

Trent Tartt's father was a career officer in the Air Force. "He's a penny-pincher, boy, he saves a lot of money," said his son. But for Mr. Tartt, who is a district manager for a consumer products company, his father never made enough. "I want to be wealthy, I want to be rich," he told us. "You know I could have laid back and stayed with a company that was paying me a salary and just gone with the flow. But I had an opportunity to take less salary, but there's an opportunity for more commissions. . . . If you're not willing to stretch, you're not willing to grow." Mr. Tartt's comments reflect strong American commitments to individualism, mobility, and opportunity. From such a perspective, downsizing, however tragic its implications in specific cases, is not worth too many tears. And, indeed, some of our respondents, optimists like Jorge Martinez, were quick to spot the positive aspects of the phenomenon. For J. W. Cotton, the father of a ten-month-old child in Oklahoma, downsizing gave him a chance to spend more time with his baby. For Kenneth Easterbrook of Cobb County, who is no longer an executive with IBM, a somewhat involuntary retirement means more time to be active in his community. DeKalb's Steven Carpenter, another former IBM employee, became a tennis coach to adults and kids, which gave him "an opportunity to see more quickly a direct cause-and-effect kind of relationship between what you do or the information you impart and someone's ability to use it," before finding another job in the computer field. Others see changing jobs the way they see changing neighborhoods: they are simply used to moving and to making the best of each new situation they face. The lives of many middle-class Americans are organized to meet challenges, and if one of those challenges happens to mean searching for a job, that is just something they will have to do.

Yet, middle-class Americans—who support the principle of welfare without liking welfare programs—also support a company's need to become more efficient without endorsing how they do it. Companies have, in their view, simply become too ruthless, letting far too many employees go at once, relying on impersonal and bureaucratic means to convey the message, rehiring people on a contract basis, or protecting some jobs and eliminating others without sufficient justification. One of the consequences of such precipitous and arbitrary downsizing that particularly bothers them is its impact on loyalty. "There's no loyalty left," was how Adam Grant of Sand Springs put it. "I mean, I worked for IBM, and you know, when I first started, I was gonna be there for life. But . . . now . . . IBM's like any other company: layoffs, downsizing. And they were the company that never had layoffs." There is a new kind of corporation in America, described in one account as "lean and mean," and it is not one that anyone can easily love. "Nobody's looking for a gold watch anymore," was how William Fahy put the matter.

> My father owned a corporation. . . . His advice to me was "Look, you work like hell. You get the job done, be honest, and all these good things will happen to you. . . . When you

work for a guy, you give him a day's work and more." That certainly isn't the attitude today. The attitude today is that I get this job and I float—the day I get the job I start floating my résumé somewhere else, hoping for a better job.

Working in this new corporate environment has become so high-pressured, so governed by the ironclad logic of profit-and-loss, that it's hard to know who is better off: those who lose their jobs in the new corporate environment or those who keep them. "The donkeys that are left are carrying two packs instead of one pack," according to Mark Mercurio, a retired Chrysler executive in Cobb County. "The work didn't go away. They just got rid of the people." The competition that was once expected to take place between strongly organized firms now takes place within the firms themselves. Employees, said Ray Moore, a Sand Springs steelworker, "are not as dedicated to the company as they used to be because some of them get sold down the river by the company, so they don't believe in companies anymore." "People used to feel like they'd put their all into a company and they'd get it back," added Kimberly Cass, a disability benefits specialist in Broken Arrow and a conservative Christian. "They'd be taken care of by their company, not by the government. And, you know, granted, companies are having to streamline and do things to survive and compete in the national and international marketplace, but I think it's really brought down the sense of quality in work. You're just a number."

These comments suggest that middle-class Americans think of downsizing as both a moral and an economic issue. Populist platforms assume that the anger generated by corporate greed will be of a personal nature; it seems obvious that as corporations shrink, people will be worried about their own jobs and economic future. But however much corporations themselves are motivated by self-interest to reduce jobs, many middle-class Americans speak about downsizing in terms of its impact on others, not only, or even mainly, on themselves. Robert Russell, a public relations consultant in Brookline, happens to benefit from downsizing, for, as an independent consultant, he picks up the business that used to be done by full-time people on staff: "They're schlopping out the work to lechers like myself," was how he put it. Still, the whole process bothers him greatly. "My perception is that companies are running on a virtual skeleton crew." Under these new conditions, "people are still working harder and the sense of competition is, I think, more acute." Cobb County's Cathy Peterson saw things the same way: "Everybody is now out to get everybody. People are afraid," she told us. Her husband has been lucky enough to keep his job—so far. But it is hard not to notice the effect on the younger generation. "They come in and they just don't seem to enjoy themselves as much as we used to. I grew up in the 1950s. . . . It was happy days. It really was."

From the perspective of the industrial relations literature of the 1950s, company loyalty was the font of all loyalty: through the experience of belonging to the firm, one learned the requirements of belonging to any human group. Americans may not want to go back to an era of economic paternalism, but neither are they very pleased with the emergence of an economy in which employers and employees no longer take the interests of each other into account. Consider the following figures compiled by the Roper Organization. In 1939, while America was experiencing a Great Depression right out of Karl Marx's playbook, 25 percent of the American people believed that the interests of employers and employees were opposed, while 56 percent believed they were basically the same. By 1994, when unions and class consciousness were in steep decline, the percentage of those who believed that employers and employees had opposite interests had increased to 45 percent, while those who thought they were the same had decreased to 40 percent. There are, many middle-class Americans believe, no alternatives to capitalism. But a form of capitalism that sets up individuals in situations of intense conflict with each other is corrosive of the ideal of a society in which people are understood to share a common fate.

A second way in which capitalism can become seriously out of balance is if it no longer permits people to meet the many obligations they have: to their children, to their communities, to their church, to their elderly parents, to their friends, and to their political system. There is no question that, for a very large number of those with whom we spoke, the changing conditions of life in the corporate world force people to pay too high a price for economic efficiency. J. W. Cotton, the laid-off technician who, because of downsizing, is spending more time with his child, put his concerns this way: "It's like you've got three circles: you've got the family circle, you've got a work circle, and then you've got a pleasure area." Sometimes, one expands and the other contracts, he continues, and that is not a problem. But on other occasions, "business requires [its circle] to get too big; pretty soon you don't see the other two circles." Many middle-class Americans still believe in the work ethic, although, as table 6.2 indicates, the majority of them believe that the work ethic has declined. But if their comments in the more in-depth portions of our interviews are compared with their answers to that survey question, the picture that emerges is slightly different: it is not that people are lazy, but that, as Cathy Ryan of Brookline put it, they "are working like crazy." If so, then, many of them believe, the work ethic *ought* to decline because only then could people lead more balanced lives.

TABLE 6.2
"THE WORK ETHIC HAS SERIOUSLY DECLINED IN AMERICA"

	Strongly Agree	Agree	No Opinion	Disagree	Strongly Disagree
Brookline	5	5	5	9	1
Medford	4	11	1	9	0
Broken Arrow	2	12	3	8	0
Sand Springs	5	8	2	8	2
DeKalb	3	15	0	6	1
Cobb	1	11	2	11	0
Eastlake	2	9	3	11	0
Rancho Bernardo	2	6	5	11	1
Total	24	77	21	73	5

Many of our respondents argued along those lines; "Border-line workaholics," as Annette Pisano of Medford called them, "are so focused on their jobs as careers ... that people tend to marry later and are less likely to have families." Like her, Steven O'Malley, also of Medford, who works for a Japanese company, thinks that the demands of work have become so intense that other important values have been lost: "People work too much in a certain way. . . . It's unbelievably competitive, I see people who work all day and then go to school at night. And now you're seeing two people in a family working like crazy and they have no time for anything when they go home—throwing together a pizza." For at least three others with whom we spoke, Japanese capitalism was cited as a model—to be avoided. Judith Garber of Medford, a computer business analyst working for an American firm she describes as a "workaholic sweatshop," knows how efficient Japanese firms are, "but, then again, the Japanese do nothing but work and have no life. And Americans, I think have gotten to the point where they should have some life." It bothers Jason Cooper, the Eastlake lawyer who still admires unions, when Americans say, " 'I'm entitled to my salary. I've put in my time and can go home and drink beer and watch the Super Bowl' as opposed to 'I really ought to stay an extra ten minutes and make sure that bolt got tied or that document got mailed.' " Yet, when he thinks about Japanese economic success, he also recognizes that "there are costs, social costs, you know. You got a lot of real paranoid children that are not going to do well enough to please their parents." Meanwhile, George Slade wonders why we should even try to emulate the Japanese, who, in his view, put loyalty to the firm ahead of loyalty to the family. "I don't put work first," he emphatically informed us. "I would never do that."

In a book published in 1997, the Berkeley sociologist Arlie Russell Hochschild wrote of working women who, far from lamenting lost time with their family, had come to appreciate life in the corporate sector. Aside from locating the firm she studied somewhere in the Midwest, Hochschild, to protect the privacy of her respondents, tells us very little about where they actually lived. That makes it impossible to know how much in common they may (or may not) have with the respondents to the Middle Class Morality Project. I can say, however, the large majority of those with whom I spoke do not sound that much like Hochschild's harried interviewees. To be sure they felt the pressures of lack of time, but many of them believed companies that turn employees into workaholics violated the moral principle of balance, as do people who neglect their family ties for higher income and occupational prestige. Moreover in their own lives they were doing whatever they could to bring work and family into balance. As they do with just about every other virtue they admire, middle-class Americans believe the work ethic, which is important, should never become so important that it trumps everything else.

Middle-class Americans even have economic arguments to advance on behalf of this thesis. To become more efficient, Jason Cooper's wife believes, companies are justified in shedding their fat. But because they then turn to contract workers, who have little incentive to put out for someone else, the overall performance of the company may suffer. Cobb's Mark Mercurio used quite utilitarian language to criticize the ways companies treat their employees. "If I was a business owner and I had constant turnover, I would want a base, I would want a pool of people to go to, not to have to sign out three hundred sixty-five days a year and not know where I was going to get the next person or [wonder] whether the next person was going to steal from me . . . or whether I was hiring an ax murderer or whatever." Christine Onenke of Medford made the same point. As people work harder and harder, they become:

> so pressed for time that they're always looking for a shortcut. I mean, everyone does. You look for a quick way to be able to juggle, you know, because you've got a lot of things you need to do. You need to go home and clean your house, you need to get the groceries, or need to stop by the doctor's. . . . People are always trying to kind of shortcut the system. And society

has encouraged that. I mean, you no longer have to wait in line for a bank teller. So we're getting to the point where we're always looking for a shortcut. Everybody, everybody is.

As Ms. Onenke understands the world, corporate self-interest sends concentric ripples throughout all of civil society, resulting in an increasingly uncivil country. Unbalanced capitalism, in her view, carries with it the prospects of an unbalanced society; whatever tears exist in the social fabric can be—indeed, have to be—a consequence of what happens at work.

Closely related to all these concerns is a third sense in which American capitalism is increasingly viewed by middle-class Americans as out of balance: the growing gap between what top executives bring home compared with everyone else. As one might expect for a society as committed to capitalist values as America, some of those with whom we spoke believed that high salaries for CEOs were simply a response to supply and demand and were not particularly upset by great disparities in income in this country. But they were most definitely in a minority. Much were common were those, like Steven Carpenter, who said that "the disproportionate distribution of wealth and all the glamour that's attached to having it" means that "we've created a situation where that's what everybody's after. As a result of that, it's by hook or crook, any means necessary." As much as they like capitalism, middle-class Americans have little respect for the slash-and-burn tactics of leveraged buyout specialists or junk bond entrepreneurs like Michael Milken, especially when their earnings skyrocket even as the firms they take over find themselves laden down with debt. The argument by economists that people like Milken are performing a necessary economic function would strike them as morally skewed.

"I think it's criminal, the fact that the CEOs of America's corporations get multimillion-dollar bonuses while they're laying off and downsizing. . . . It's just greed," as Joseph Palumbo of Medford put it. Ronald Klaus of Rancho Bernardo was one of the angriest people with whom we spoke:

The company I worked for had one hundred twenty thousand people. When I lost my job with that company we were down to fifty-five thousand. We're down to thirty-two thousand now. That person [the CEO] hurt that company by misjudgment, and yet he got some very big golden handshakes. This is going on a lot in the corporate world and I don't think it's right.... I mean, the amount of money they make—it's not even jealousy on my part. To me, it's insanity. How can people get the kind of money they're getting—based on what? ... I don't understand it. They're laying off people left, right, and center, these companies, and they're going overseas for cheap labor, and they're still paying themselves these big compensations. Something is really wrong.

When AT&T announced forty thousand layoffs shortly before its CEO added $11 millon in stock options to his base salary of $5.85 million, it reinforced the conviction of people like Mr. Palumbo and Mr. Klaus that something is indeed seriously wrong in contemporary capitalism.

It is important to understand that conviction. From an economic point of view, huge differentials in pay could be held to violate a norm of fairness: the difference between what a CEO contributes to a firm's profits and what a manager or worker contributes, by this account, would not justify such a huge gap. But that is not quite how the matter is understood in middle-class America. Extremely high salaries and unjustifiable perks violate a moral as well as an economic ideal. Very few middle-class Americans say what Trent Tartt did: that he wanted to be rich. For the rest, too much wealth is like too much of anything else: a bad thing. People with too much money violate a deeply held middle-class belief in proportionality; their lives, however glamorous, are to be pitied more than envied. "I guess people have to pay a price sometimes to make those dollars," was how Sue Thompson of Broken Arrow described her feelings, and the price they pay is leading a life of imbalance, one that contributes especially to divorce and personal unhappiness. If that's what they want, she concludes, fine for them, but "personally, I'm not willing to make the trade-offs that some people have to make in those professions in order to have that kind of money." Her comments reflect the findings of sociologists Richard Coleman and Lee Rainwater, who discovered in 1978 that the "high-status life is not so attractive to Middle Americans. They have the impression that it is a stressful existence, full of civic obligations and social reciprocities, of striving to rise higher financially and/or politically, of desperate concern for public acceptance and personal reputation."

High corporate salaries, like the income made by professional athletes—according to a Roper poll 79 percent of Americans think that CEOs are overpaid compared with 90 percent for professional athletes—reflect, according to our respondents, a world that has lost a sense of moral grounding. In complete contrast to Immanuel Kant, middle-class Americans develop their moral philosophy anecdotally; they listen to the news and read newspapers to find stories that underscore virtuous and selfish behavior. When they hear about Aaron Feuerstein, the Massachusetts industrialist who kept his employees on the payroll after their factory burned down, they conclude that America is good. But when they hear about seeming corporate indifference to the honest folk who are laid off as companies try to right themselves, or about the exploits of professional athletes who blithely kick cameramen filming their talents, their respect for capitalism comes into conflict with their belief that America has always been a special place because people take responsibility for each other. Wide-scale differences in pay not only offend people's appreciation for modest virtues, they also undermine a collective sense of trust to a much greater degree than any number of declining bowling leagues.

If they had read the distinguished Austrian-born economist Joseph Schumpeter, middle-class Americans might come to understand that capitalism requires a certain amount of destructive energy in order to create anew. The question for our respondents is how much destruction is required. Economists who espouse a laissez-faire approach to their discipline have been inclined to argue that high CEO salaries, even when seemingly outrageous, benefit everyone eventually, since inefficient companies or underpaid executives serve no one's real interest. But from the perspective of middle-class America, high corporate salaries are more likely to be viewed as selfish, and selfish people and organizations, because they are out of balance, threaten the delicacy of the social order. William Fahy, the retired executive in Cobb County, has little love for fancy M.B.A.'s in the business world: "Those guys were trained to step on their own grandmother's eyeballs to get another rung up the ladder. I think that's actually taught in some of those better business schools." Companies do need to take account of the bottom line, Americans like Mr. Mercurio believe. But they don't have to do it in an extreme way. Alfred Shoals, a real estate entrepreneur in Sand Springs, and a man of generally conservative views, thinks that all Americans, employers and employees, have to work together. "Most companies, you know, they say five percent is a fair profit for a company. But most of the companies want thirty to thirty-five percent profits. They don't just want five percent. They don't just want ten percent. . . . If they get rid of the union, they're moving to another country. And this is very damaging to the people at work." The question on his mind was posed succinctly by his daughter Elizabeth as she listened to him talk: "When is enough enough?" People like Mr. Shoals and his daughter think that, because most people want to be loyal, companies ought to take their employees' sense of loyalty into account even as they respond to the demands of the market. They are convinced that social trust is a precious asset and that any company or country that abuses it has lost touch with common sense. Restoring the balance necessary to make capitalism both profitable but also humane, because it makes moral sense to them, also makes economic sense to them—as it does to most of those with whom we spoke.

There may well be a certain naïveté to this perspective. Since most middle-class Americans are not corporate policy-makers— nor, may I quickly add, am I—they do not have blueprints in the drawer for transforming capitalism, well-known for its imbalances, into an economic system that respects modest virtues. One could easily criticize them for their lack of realism in this area, their unwillingness to accept the fact that profit is, finally, what capitalism is about. But as one listens to them talk, what they suggest sounds anything but unreasonable. "The most important thing is to be profitable so that they can continue to provide jobs," said Kimberly Cass of American corporations. "But I think it's important for them to get out there and support the community whenever they can. And usually those functions that support the community also bring together a lot of teamwork and a lost sense of family. I think that's very important." Alisa Rice of DeKalb County, a vice president of finance in a marketing company, pointed out that "businesses owe their existence to a community. You know, I would like to see some kind of benefit, maybe tax benefit or something, come to companies who would . . . donate their talents or even personnel or whatever to help figure out some of the problems we're having." Corporate self-interest runs contrary to the moral law as understood by Toni Cartwright of Sand Springs: "Whenever you can be nice to other people, it brings out the niceness in you." The fact that socialism with a human face failed does not mean that capitalism with a human face is impossible.

Balanced capitalism, middle-class Americans believe, will help restore the sense of responsibility they see declining in America. Putting aside the empirical question of whether corporations contribute to community decline by constant downsizing or revitalize it through community investment, they know what business *should* do: it should treat the community with the same loyalty that they want to receive from it. Mary Ferrannini of Rancho Bernardo believes that the obligation of business is "to become part of a community, to support community events, to give back." Fred Richards of the same community strongly rejects the idea that business should become more politically involved in financing elections or supporting candidates, but he does feel that business should become more involved civically in nonpartisan pursuits: "But as far as community life is concerned, I think they owe the community an arts council. They owe anything that is good for the entire community: . . . better school facilities, better schools, better playgrounds. . . . I think they are tremendously important for kids, kids that are growing up to be adults. That's the reason they're so important. I think business corporations should enter into that." It cannot always be the bottom line, according to Judy Dropkin of Eastlake: "You can't keep drinking from a well unless something goes back and I think industry is going to start realizing that again. . . . You have to give back. You have to be more careful."

This deeply held sense of the moral correctness of balanced capitalism cannot be considered an end in itself; it all depends on what is being balanced with what. For most middle-class Americans, it does not seem unreasonable to think that the virtues of capitalism, which they admire, can be reconciled with the virtues of family and community, which they also admire.

INSTRUMENTAL TIES

Treatments of suburban life in the 1950s featured a sharp contrast between the world of work and the world of community. The former, populated by men, emphasized hierarchy, obedience, material rewards, and formal procedures, while the latter, dominated by women, was characterized by voluntarism, friendships, talk, leisure, and—at least in the account of feminist social critic Betty Friedan—great unhappiness. Now that the proverbial commuter railroad platform is crowded not only with men but with women, and now that the trains run earlier in the morning and later in the evening to accommodate the frenetic work schedules of a more competitive capitalism, the ties of trust and mutual dependence upon which communities rely have been as radically transformed as company loyalties and employer-employee relations.

As they talked to us about their perceptions of their suburban communities, middle-class Americans painted portraits of their community ties that give strong support to the idea that America is depleting its social capital. Here is a sprinkling of their comments:

"It's almost as if we set up our own islands. It's a street full of islands. And, you know, we would love to have a great relationship and great neighbors and that sort of thing, but it has just never evolved."

"We don't know who those people are or how they spend their time. We pass them on the street. We talk across the fence, but socially we don't do things with our neighbors to speak of."

"People are a lot more isolated."

"I've been living eight years over here and I still don't know my neighbor."

"There's absolutely no sense of community here whatsoever. I've never found it anywhere."

"Strangely enough, I am unbelievably and sadly disconnected from the community that I live in. Do I identify with Brookline? I do not."

"The way the suburbs are built today, I don't think there's a sense of backyard barbecue communities."

From comments such as these, America's suburban communities do seem to be chilly places. Devoid of people during the day, they are filled with people sitting in front of television or computer screens in the evenings, too self-preoccupied to live a Tocquevillian life of civic engagement.

Nor is it difficult for middle-class Americans to find a cause for the lack of community they feel: everyone is working too hard. "People just have less time," said Rachel Benjamin, the Brookline dentist. "When you look at the number of hours people spend at work now, the whole issue of living in the suburbs has cut time off people's days. Having dual career families cuts time out of the day." Asked why in his opinion communities seem less active, Derek Langer of Cobb said, "I think the big companies transplanting people have something to do with that. . . . A lot of executives are moved around the country. [People] were transferred every two years, no matter what. When two years came around, time to go somewhere else." If there has been an eclipse of community, the cause is the workplace. So great have become the demands of the job that the obligations of the neighborhood have had to give way.

Even among more traditional families in which women remain at home during the day, a deep feeling exists that life has simply become too busy to accommodate a strong sense of community. Ashley George of DeKalb, a homemaker, would like to interact more with her neighbors, but nobody, including herself, has the time. Cobb County's Judy Vogel remembers enough of her college sociology to offer us a short course in Durkheim's theory of anomie. Although she, too, is a homemaker, she feels special concern for her female neighbors who hold jobs: "There's nobody for backup. You're working. You're expected to work. Your child has an ear infection. There isn't a grandmother or an aunt or a cousin to call." That's why, according to her reading of the situation, "people are more isolated . . . you're into your big house with the door closed, and you're not out there with your neighbors." Suburban housewives find themselves facing demands on their time little different from the workaholic schedules of their husbands, and, as they do, something has to give. Brookline's Alexandra Onafri, who does work, wonders "how volunteer organizations in communities survive" these days now that so many women, who once staffed them, are in paying jobs.

There is one exception to this generally dismal picture of life in the local community: the church. Especially in Oklahoma and Georgia, Sunday is the day for socializing and church is the place around which it is organized. "Church is your biggest strongpoint," as DeKalb's Laurie Shepard put it. "Most people that work together really don't socialize outside of work. First of all, because you're probably living in a million different areas. They may do formal things, baby showers, weddings, and all that little stuff. Church is probably gonna be your biggest social [activity] outside of family." But even church attendance has been hit by the way life is organized in modern America. "You can go to church and then just go home," Mylene Santos of Eastlake pointed out. "I wouldn't put church too high. My impression is that those that go and attend services regularly, they probably don't have a whole lot of time to get involved."

Although comments such as these lend substantial support

to the notion that the vibrancy of American civic life is in decline, there are nonetheless important qualifications that need to be introduced. For one thing, the estimates of group membership cited by Robert Putnam turn out not to be correct; the GSS excluded memberships in service clubs and PTAs between 1989 and 1994, and when those are added back in, the recalculations show "only a slight decline over the period 1974–1994." Our experience with the Middle Class Morality Project suggests an additional reason why declines may be exaggerated. Sociologists know that Americans overestimate their church attendance. I believe, by contrast, that people often underestimate their group memberships. "I don't belong to any organizations. We don't go to church on Sundays," Dolores Wales of Sand Springs told us, before proceeding to tell us all about her enormously time-consuming experiences in a league devoted to auto racing. Cathy Peterson of Cobb County—who complained that everyone was too busy to have block parties and told us that she and her husband "don't do anything socially"—also said of her neighbors that "if I have a Super Bowl party, I invite them over . . . ; they're very good neighbors." It is quite possible that middle-class Americans, when asked about the kinds of civic organizations to which they belong, assume the questioner is interested in "serious" ones, such as the League of Women Voters or the Masons, and do not talk about the everyday groups in which they may be quite active.

We also discovered yet another reason to qualify the Putnam thesis. The notion that people are not that active in their communities seems especially inappropriate for one group of middle-class Americans: blacks in the Atlanta suburbs. Most middle-class people in this country develop their social networks at work and have fewer social contacts in their neighborhoods. But black suburbanites work with whites and live with blacks, and for them, the situation is quite different. "The majority of my social life involves social interaction with people of this community, who are predominantly black," we were told by Linda Clay-Johnson. If it is true that recent African-American suburbanization is similar to the wave of post–World

War II suburbanization among so many white ethnics, then black suburbanites are now building local ties in ways not dissimilar to the Levittowners of the 1950s and 1960s. On the slope of civic decline, they are a generation behind.

When these qualifications are added together, it should come as no surprise that, despite the oft-expressed sense of alienation from their local communities, middle-class Americans remain civically active; even if there has been a decline, it started from a high peak, which means there still is a great deal left. Sybil Ross of Cobb County has lived in her present home all of one year, so, she explains apologetically, "I don't know everyone yet. I probably won't know everybody, it's so big." But because she is a mother, involvement follows automatically:

> The people that I do know are pretty active in their children's lives and in the family as far as school involvement, after-school activities. I'm very involved as far as getting my son involved in things with other kids, gymnastics, sports, music, stuff like that. I've found that the people here are also pretty involved with setting up play groups and then we'll share sitters and we'll all go out together, throw neighborhood parties. We try to have a lot of neighborhood get-togethers.

Just as we thought she was about to stop, Mrs. Ross found a fresh breath of energy:

> I am also a neighborhood watch leader here. I'm also a block captain, which means I distribute all the newsletters to a section. God, there's I don't know how many sections we've got. I have seventeen in mine, so there's probably fifty sections. I distribute newsletters every month, and I give welcome packages to new members telling them everything we have. In the neighborhood watch, there's one coordinator that when something's called in to the police, they're notified, then they call all the leaders, and then we call everybody in our area and let them know what type of a crime has taken place. There's not many. I think I've made two phone calls in a year, and they've

been for like somebody was in somebody's garage, and the other one was a house broken into during construction. It seems to work. You'll find a lot of people involved in that.

When she reached this point in describing her community life, she still was not finished:

We also have safe houses where they paint little houses. In fact, I'm supposed to pick up my stencil. It's for people that are home . . . a pretty good amount of time during the day. They'll put a safe house on their driveway so that if any child gets off a bus or is coming home and feels threatened or anything they know there are people there to welcome them. They can go into them and not be afraid. What else do we have? We have a lot of stuff like that. . . . They have a big sale here that we get involved in where we work the sales. Some of them are charity and some of them are garage sales for the subdivision. We do a lot of family activities. Like Halloween, there's a big parade. There's a big thing at Christmas for the kids with Santa. You know, we'll make things, make contributions of food or money or volunteer, dress up.

One can only wonder what Mrs. Ross's community life will look like after she has lived in her subdivision a little longer! There really are "soccer moms"—media shorthand for civically active suburban women like Mrs. Ross—in America.

TABLE 6.3
ORGANIZATIONAL MEMBERSHIPS
MIDDLE CLASS MORALITY PROJECT

No organizations	52	Civic organizations	96
1 or 2 organizations	117	Church-related	83
3 or 4 organizations	16	Work-related	66
4 or more organizations	15	Social/fraternal	52
		Other	11
Total	200	Total	308

Mrs. Ross was clearly atypical, but she was by no means the only person with whom we spoke who was civically active. Our 200 respondents belonged to 308 organizations in all, which means an average of roughly one and a half organizations per person.

Although one-fourth of our sample indicated that they belonged to no civic organizations, the majority claimed membership in at least one and often more than one.

Among the groups in which people were active were many voluntary associations and organizations, such as Habitat for Humanity, City Year, the National Association for the Advancement of Colored People, the Masons, the Rotary, the Optimists, the American Civil Liberties Union, Black Men of Cobb, the Red Cross, the Lions Club, the American Heart Association, the American Association of University Women, the Navy League, Up with Trees, and AIDS Walk Day. Parent-teacher organizations, sports leagues, country clubs, church groups, library support groups, bridge clubs, professional organizations, ethnic associations, unions, and block associations were the focus of their social and civic engagements. Fred Richards, a retired construction company owner in Rancho Bernardo, was on the Missouri State Council for the Arts, serving as vice president, and on the Missouri historical preservation committee. J. W. Cotton is president of an association to which 185 "retired"—by which he means victims of downsizing—men belong. Even childless families in America's suburbs are civically engaged. Samina Hoque of Medford, for example, who emigrated from Bangladesh in 1972, not only works in one of the leading cancer research institutes in the country, she also organizes poetry readings in New England, started a Bengali school in her basement, and is writing a play, inspired by her experience with church after-school programs, about inner-city youth. Henry Pearson of Eastlake, the former history professor, spends considerable time "on-line" in various discussion groups, is also active in the San Diego Zoological Society, and retains his membership in the American Historical Association, besides belonging to numerous other professional and civic organizations.

To some degree, then, Americans are still "joiners." Moreover, the organizations to which they belong, as table 6.3 shows, still tend to be civic and religious rather than purely social. By themselves, these membership figures cannot answer the question of whether our respondents are less civically active than similar suburbanites a generation ago. Certainly, many of those with whom we spoke, by emphasizing how little sense of community participation they felt around them, were indicating support for the idea that some thinning out of American social life has taken place. Still, one final comment needs to be added before concluding that America's social capital has been depleted to seriously low levels. The figures in table 6.3 suggest that work-related organizations are more common in American middle-class life than social and fraternal ones. To the degree that we look at the place in which people live for evidence of the decline of social capital rather than where they work, we may be looking in the wrong place.

One of the sharpest criticisms made of the "Putnam" thesis is that it idealized a world dominated by men and left the impression that the decision of so many women to enter the workforce was responsible for the decline of civic involvement in the community. Putnam, in subsequent formulations of his thesis, responded by suggesting that no verdict could be given to the question of whether working women were responsible for declining social capital. Our interviews suggest that because women are working, they are not quite as available for civic duties in their communities as they once were. But, at the same time, like men, they are more available to engage in civic activity at work. Jeremy Toole thinks that these days people get about 90 percent of their social connections from the workplace. Most of his friends come from the office, and he thinks his wife may be jealous of that fact. Then he pauses before adding that she, too, works and 90 percent of her friends come from her job.

For every middle-class American woman who may not

be involved in a local organization, there are many more who are involved in their workplace settings. "I think people's lives revolve around their work. They make their friends at work, they do their community service through work," says Diana Hamilton of Sand Springs. Elizabeth Tyler no longer feels part of Brookline because its liberal politics conflict with her increasingly conservative sensibilities. But, she adds, "I feel very much like I belong to a community of work. I very much belong to a community with my own office, with my own company, within my own industry, and I am very much involved in community affairs in Cambridge, where my office is, and in Boston." Groups like City Year and Read San Diego work with employers to find ways in which employees can take a day off work to become involved in tutoring inner-city children or cleaning vacant lots. Caroline Carlson of Brookline was "flabbergasted" from her City Year experience to learn what it was like to live in a neighborhood without parks, while Diane Sveressen just thinks there has to be somebody to offer reading opportunities to those who have too few of them. The Hudson Institute's John Clark has written that "although most discussions of civic engagement, eroding social capital, failing trust and so on refer in passing to the workplace, no one examines closely the relationship between work and community." While the Middle Class Morality Project did not observe people at work at the close level he recommends, it did find that workplace involvement has to be taken into account in any effort to portray the state of civic America.

Work-related civic activity was also important for African-Americans. Linda Clay-Johnson, who noted the ways in which black suburbanites in the Atlanta area feel closer to their black neighbors than to their white coworkers, still found that the workplace offered her a number of white friends with whom she goes to ball games or office parties. It is at work that she spends time on the activities of Habitat for Humanity, one of the organizations to which she belongs. Her husband, Henry Johnson, uses his experience at the workplace to make a point about race relations in America:

> One of the things in my office I try and push. We sometimes
> have social get-togethers, Christmas parties, a picnic in the
> summer and so forth. I always welcome these opportunities,
> especially to bring my wife and kids to these gatherings. A lot
> of times society has a problem seeing black males as family
> men. Any opportunity I get I do that, where I bring in my
> family and say, "Here's my wife and kids."

Despite the fact that social and civic engagement continues
to flourish in America, if often in places different from where
people live, there is reason to question whether the quality of
ties made at the workplace can be compared with those we generally associate with the local community. Different spheres of
social life tend to be associated with different kinds of social relationships: family ties reflect a level of intimacy, and can promote a level of anger, that we would never expect of ties between
members of a parent-teacher organization. Of all the various
kinds of dependencies we develop with each other, economic
ties have always been the most suspect from an ethical or moral
point of view. Because we form such ties to promote the highly
secular activities of getting and spending, friendships and connections developed at work generally are assumed to have an instrumental character: we use people, and they use us, to solicit
more business, advance our careers, sell more products, or
demonstrate our popularity.

Economic ties are therefore often dismissed as not quite
real, authentic, or genuine enough. This is a point that can be
traced to the great theorist of capitalism: Adam Smith. In *The
Theory of Moral Sentiments*, Smith pointed out that the patron-
client relationships associated with feudalism, because they
were based on necessity, could not be equated with friendship, a
relationship that should be premised on sympathy. Although
the implication of Smith's point is that free-market relations
will not be characterized by feudalistic necessity, a case could
be made that modern capitalism requires that people give to
their company, and to their coworkers, not only their physical
labor, but their emotional labor as well. If so, it follows that

even if the decline of civil ties in the neighborhood is being
compensated by new ties formed at work, the instrumental
character of the latter cannot be an adequate substitute for the
loss of the former.

This may well be true: our middle-class respondents thought
of the social ties they developed at work in very instrumental
terms. Jane Kates of Sand Springs, who is now a homemaker, is
extremely down-to-earth and practical in her thoughts about
her social contacts. "I think it depends on probably where you
spend most of your time," she said. "When I worked, my
friendships were work-related. When I quit working and started
doing more schoolwork with the kids, my friendships became
school-related. . . . I can see that as I progress through age here,
that as I get into more volunteer things, that my friendships are
formed around them." Shortly after we talked with her, we
talked with Toni Cartwright, an administrative assistant. "I
think most people get most of their socializing out of their work
experience, just because it's a must situation. You have to go to
work, and it's the only place you have a group of people." For
these women, work is simply where they are, so, making the
best of it, that is where they form their connections with others.

Brian Fischer, a regional sales vice president in Cobb
County, was one of those who wondered whether such instrumental ties could ever be truly satisfactory. Asked where people
form their most important social networks, he at first responded
in a way typical of many with whom we spoke: "It used to be
the family. And then to a lesser degree residential. But it has become business." This trend bothers him. He told us:

> It has become watered down, because we have two categories
> of friends. We have real friends that you share stuff with, that
> you care about and will help. And you have all the other peo-
> ple that are friends. They're just people you know. We've kind
> of lost that . . . a real friend is someone that you bond with and
> you have a bond with two or three other people in the
> world. . . . We don't have hundreds of friends. You have hun-

dreds of acquaintances that you call friends. . . . People don't connect over their lives anymore, people's lives are so transient that you connect for times and places. Now the question is: Does that diminish the relationship because it's on a temporary basis?

Mr. Fischer has clearly answered his own question: Something has gone out of the world because so little is left in the world to make the kinds of truly meaningful ties that give life its depth and meaning.

One way to interpret Mr. Fischer's comments is to suggest that the literature dealing with civic decline has tracked something important, but not necessarily in the right way: it is not the overall decline in group membership that is crucial—for, when added up properly, there may not be that much of a decline—but a change in the qualitative nature of those ties that matters. Active engagement in social and civic life is important, not as an end in itself, but because it expresses an altruistic desire to do something for others. If, instead, people are joining groups to do something for themselves—to win friends and influence people—then society could experience a *rise* in organization memberships and still be facing a situation of depleting social capital. Only a handful of our respondents, it turns out, indicated any particular attachment to self-help, twelve-step recovery groups, often pictured as exemplifying an obsession with the self. Still, the fact that, in spite of their organizational activities, so many of them believed that selfishness in America has increased suggests that, in their view of the world, the quality of the social ties they experience are not as rich as they ought to be.

Since it is much harder to measure quality than quantity, we may never have the final word on this important subject. Still, we can be certain of how middle-class Americans frame the debate over what these qualitative changes mean. For the fact is that while people like Mr. Fischer offered eloquent statements of what is increasingly missing in American life due to its increasingly instrumental character, others took the opposite position:

instrumental ties, however "thin" they may be with respect to classic ideals of friendship and loyalty, also give individuals greater choice in fashioning their social lives in ways they see fit.

Just as a significant number of middle-class Americans lament the passing of the traditional family but welcome the new freedoms they increasingly have, they also see something positive in obligations undertaken out of individual choice. Middle-class Americans often form their community ties in ways similar to the formation of their family ties. Rather than starting with an ideal of community into which individual needs should be fit, they begin with individual needs and shape their community involvements accordingly. Joseph Palumbo, for example, would rather choose those with whom he will associate than have them determined by the fact that he lives in a particular place. Some of his neighbors are community-oriented. "People are pursuing those things because they find it to their advantage. It works for them," he comments in the spirit of rational choice theory. But not for him. "I can drive thirty miles and be in any number of different communities. My life is not restricted to Medford. The people with whom I choose to associate do not have to live in a three-block radius of my home. It's the disappearance of boundaries," he claims, and he likes it. "I have transportation. I have a telephone. I can do anything I want with almost anyone instantaneously. It's a virtual society now."

The same kind of reasoning applies at the workplace. Guided by their belief in individualism, middle-class Americans assume a kind of moral division of labor: the right balance between work and civic obligation has to be found by each individual. Some people will always want to work hard while others will not. As Cobb County's Tommy Stevens memorably put it, "If you sit there eating bonbons and watching *As the World Turns*, the world is going to turn without you." Let those who want to work "daylight to dark," as Marcus Ward, also of Cobb, put it, do so and let others do something else: "There's a place for everybody here." Alisa Rice added her thoughts: "I think people have different talents," she told us: some people have a special gift for being involved and others do not, so it makes perfect sense to encourage the former and discourage the latter. This moral division of labor may not be the most attractive vision, and it may not even be a workable one, but it is one that corresponds with strong American adherence to individualistic values.

NO MORAL HEROS

Can a nation of individualists take into account the inescapable fact that in a complex modern society, everyone's fate is related to the fate of everyone else? Social critics—skeptical that it can—are quick to find fault with the narcissism and self-absorption that clearly is part of middle-class American culture. Such critics worry whether the instinctive libertarianism of middle-class America is compatible with a strong sense of moral obligation. There is a basis for those worries. So protective are Americans of their individual freedom that our somewhat innocent question about social obligations at work yielded an occasional attack on the ways corporations collect charitable gifts from their employees, finding them too invasive and compulsory on the one hand—"I just don't like to be told what to do," as one of our respondents put it—or too supportive of groups with which they are in disagreement—Planned Parenthood came up—on the other. Middle-class libertarianism is too pervasive to be ignored.

Of course, not all middle-class Americans are libertarian in their moral outlook. Some of those with whom we spoke are very conscious of the divine origin of their duties. When we asked Sue Thompson of Broken Arrow about her duties as an American, she replied that her duties come from the fact that she is a Christian. For her, as well as for her neighbor Kimberly Cass, religion and country usually work in harmony: obligations such as voting or being responsible to others are part of both creeds. Two of our respondents, moreover, were Jehovah's Witnesses, and while they had a duty to pay taxes, they also made it clear to us that they had no duty to vote. It is not surprising to find people in middle-class America who worry that their country has become so committed to individual liberty that it has lost touch with the blessings of faith.

What is surprising is to find so many people who do not see themselves as commanded by God to do the right thing, and not just because a significant number of Americans, no matter how strong their religious beliefs, are nonetheless reluctant to tell others how to act. It is not the idea of religion that bothers these people but the idea of a commandment. Libertarianism in America can go so far as to question whether our obligations to others should be thought of as a duty at all.

Even some of the most civically engaged people with whom we spoke made it clear to us that they do not, at least as they understood themselves, act out of a sense of duty. "Paying my taxes, belonging to organizations that do good work, plus the work I do as an individual, I don't do that out of a sense of obligation," said Cobb's Brian Fischer, the man who was worried that instrumental friendships are not real friendships. "I do it because I think it is the right thing to do," he commented, echoing the freeway builder Jorge Martinez. Working hard, paying your taxes, those are not enough, Mr. Martinez said. "I think we have to try and help the less fortunate ... not by giving them money and things like that, but by trying to educate them," as he explained his involvement with high school kids. "I see that as part of the things I need to do to help people who are needy and things along those lines. Whether that's a duty—to me it's more like a belief, but I don't know if it's an American belief or if it's just mine." The strongest statement of this point of view was made by Jane Sargent of Cobb County: "I don't believe we have a duty ... I think being active in the community or helping to take actions to help those perhaps who are less fortunate is more like a developmental phase that one goes through. I don't think it's a duty, for example, of an American to be a volunteer at all."

Such comments might lead one to conclude that critics of American individualism are right when they suggest that strong individualists flourish when social ties are frail. But the people who made comments like the ones just quoted, despite their denial of duties, are quite involved in taking responsibility for others, which makes one wonder why they react so strongly against the suggestion that their morality is obligatory. One of de Tocqueville's great insights was that individualism understood as selfish behavior had to be contrasted with what he called "individualism rightly understood," in which the person takes responsibility for the larger society. Middle-class Americans would make a similar distinction between acting out of a sense of obligation to others blindly, which they generally do not like, and acting out of a sense of obligation to others wisely, which they do like.

And what is a wise moral choice? The political philosopher Judith Shklar has written about "ordinary vices," such as hypocrisy, snobbery, and betrayal. All of them are harmful, she argued, but at least one, cruelty, is more harmful than all the others. And while she insisted that her account was not meant to justify any of them, she also made it clear that different vices look different depending on whether the context in which they are practiced is private or public. If vices can be ordinary, so can virtues: middle-class Americans express a sense of what might be called "ordinary duties." Like Shklar's catalog of vices, ordinary duties refer to the experiences of daily life, in contrast to conceptions of duty emphasizing the kinds of altruistic sacrifice associated with heroes or extraordinary, once-in-a-lifetime experiences such as natural disasters or war. Ordinary duties can be defined as the obligations that arise in daily life, simple ways of relating to one another, which are carried out not because we are commanded by God, law, or tradition to do the right thing, but because we decide that the right thing is the right thing to do. In middle-class America, ordinary duties are the best duties.

Also as in Shklar's account, middle-class Americans believe that their strongest duty is not to be cruel. "I don't think you should be doing anything that's gonna hurt another human being," was how Cobb County's George Slade put a widely shared point of view. A wise chooser chooses not to inflict unnecessary damage on others. As DeKalb's Steven Carpenter summarized the point: "By 'wisely' I don't mean that you follow a particular pattern or that you follow some dictum that someone has set out for you, but you try to choose wisely just with regards to making sure that the choices that you make don't do any harm to any of those people that are choosing differently from the way that you're choosing." A large number of those with whom we spoke fear that morality, if understood as a set of moral injunctions, can lead to intolerance, an outcome unacceptable to a people as nonjudgmental as middle-class Americans: trusting people rather than duties is the best way to insure that it will not.

Because choosing wisely means respecting the choices of others, the kinds of moral commands chosen will inevitably be minimal: doing little things well is better than doing big things that can backfire—just as having a few friends chosen by yourself is preferable to living in thickly embedded communities of people with whom you never chose to associate. "Being aware, being informed, taking your civic responsibilities seriously, voting, not blindly but wisely voting, knowing what's going on, not only in your own community but nationwide . . . caring, participating in the civic and political process," these are the obligations Americans have, said Marion Kates of Eastlake. Her list was inclusive of most people's lists. "I think we have to look after each other. I think we have to care about each other. I think we have to contribute in some way," was how DeKalb's Nancy Elliott put it. "To obey the law, to pay our fair share of taxes (although I think we are overpaying). I think we need to vote. I think we need to pay more attention than most of us do to the government," was the version offered by Elizabeth Moore of Sand Springs. It is not so much what you do but the fact that you do something that matters. "Everybody was put here to do something, whatever that is," said Cobb's Lila Stich. "Whether it's menial, whether it's bagging groceries in the grocery store or building buildings, whatever. If you don't give of yourself, you get nothing back."

Listening to so many middle-class Americans either react against the notion of duty or claim for themselves ordinary ones, I wondered why I heard less about people who jumped into frozen rivers to rescue drowning children or about some American version of Mother Teresa. The answer has much to do with a strong ethic of individual responsibility. The moral ideal of middle-class Americans revolves around the notion that people are responsible for their own fate; they reserve the seventh circle of their moral hell for people like the Menendez brothers who kill their parents but claim that it was because of abuse or those—"sue happy," as one of our respondents called them—who knowingly buy a flawed product and then pursue litigation when its flaws are revealed. Of course, they think of themselves as responsible for others—but not that much. "I don't know about being my brother's keeper," as Toni Cartwright put it, "maybe my brother's helper." Too strong a sense of duty can quickly turn into an assumption of too much responsibility for the fate of another, which in turn can lead that other person to avoid taking responsibility for himself. "Everybody has to be responsible for everyone, but you have to be prepared to pay the price for what you have done. . . . You can't just go do things and blame other people, I mean it just doesn't work that way," as Sand Springs's Dolores Wales expressed a widely shared point of view.

Ordinary moral duties are the only appropriate duties for people with such a strong sense of personal responsibility for two reasons. One is that such duties reinforce a rough kind of moral equality: not everyone can be as rich as everyone else, but anyone is as capable of being decent as anyone else. By assuming that our most important duties are relatively modest ones, we set an equal standard for all. "The things I want for us," said Trent Tartt about his family, "are nothing less than I'd want for other people willing to work for them." Moral heroes, precisely because they are more saintly than the rest of us, imply a hierarchy of goodness that runs counter to the idea that we are all equally responsible for our fate. The second reason that ordinary moral duties are appropriate to middle-class Americans is that they are compatible with the pragmatic, everyday, nonutopian aspects of the American creed. Middle-class Americans recognize that if the moral standard is set too high, ordinary people will probably fail to meet it. And if they should fail to meet it, they know that some other superior force—God or government—will meet it for them, returning them to a world of strong moral commandments from which they had hoped to flee.

The modest nature of the middle class's sense of duty is likely to disappoint those for whom recent American experience constitutes a descent from a time when—guided by religious commandments, strong families, and firmer rules—Americans were presumably more likely to place altruism ahead of self-interest. Yet, before concluding that Americans ought to set their moral sights higher, one also should take seriously their fears of what might happen if they do. Believers in modest virtues would rather avoid inevitable fluctuations between angels and devils, recognizing, perhaps, that for all their other differences, moral perfectionists and moral nihilists share black-and-white attitudes with which they are uncomfortable.

Middle-class Americans can live with a certain amount of imperfection so long as it stops short of cynicism, just as they want to see moral improvement, while refusing to pass judgment on how much improvement is actually taking place. They adhere to a belief that fewer obligations undertaken wisely represent a more realistic response to the dilemmas of the modern world than more of them undertaken unthinkingly. Suspicious as they are of moral saints, they do not view themselves as moral sinners. They want morality to serve the needs of people, not for people's freedom to be sacrificed in the name of morality. Surely, that is why, as much as they share a sense that the decline of a world of tighter social ties and deeper moral obligations is to be regretted, they also feel that the emergence of a world of greater freedom is to be welcomed.

THE REASONABLE MAJORITY

When he was president of the United States, Richard Nixon, a man who had his own problems with morality, coined one of the great images of modern politics: America, he claimed, gave insufficient respect and appreciation to "the silent majority," those hardworking people who play by the rules, believe in American values, and have little patience for utopian planners and naïve idealists. The Middle Class Morality Project can be understood as an effort to let the silent majority, or at least one significant portion of it, speak. When people do, their voices in the 1990s do not register the politics of resentment attributed to them in the 1970s. American society is dominated by the ideas of the *reasonable* majority: people who believe themselves to be modest in their appetites, quiet in their beliefs, and restrained in their inclinations. They want the world to be organized in such a way that their reasonableness counts. As sociologists Richard Coleman and Lee Rainwater put the matter in a book published just after Nixon's resignation:

> It is quite clear from our research, as well as from that of some others, that a great many Americans are quite sensitive to the world around them, that they give that world a considerable amount of thought, and that they struggle to try to bring into congruence their view on the nature of the world, the worth of their fellow citizens, public policy, and a more just society. It is important both for sensible development of public policy and for more basic understanding in the social sciences that this complexity be appreciated, rather than obliterated, by our research efforts.

It is the very reasonableness of most of the people in middle-class America that prevents them from attaching the same importance to the case for social and political decline that preoccupies social critics and social scientists. This is not due to lack of knowledge. Because they directly experience them, the people with whom we spoke are aware of all the social problems that lead social scientists to question whether there is sufficient social capital in America for the country to prosper: some of them have lost their jobs, others experience their neighborhood as empty, and few of them have much faith in politicians and government. But none of this translates into a sense that the country as a whole has lost its bearings. If one asks them about

TABLE 6.4
"IF YOU WORK HARD AND FOLLOW THE RULES,
YOU WILL GET AHEAD"

	Strongly Agree	Agree	No Opinion	Disagree	Strongly Disagree
Brookline	3	12	0	8	2
Medford	2	12	2	7	2
Broken Arrow	1	10	0	12	2
Sand Springs	4	8	2	8	3
DeKalb	1	9	1	12	2
Cobb	1	14	0	9	1
Eastlake	2	20	0	3	0
Rancho Bernardo	3	13	2	6	1
Total	17	98	7	65	13

the basic fairness of American society, more of them still think it works well enough compared with those who do not. Whatever objective data exist to the effect that the rules are breaking down does not translate, according to the survey question we asked them, into subjective feelings that the system no longer works.

None of those with whom we spoke seemed to embody this sense that reasonable people make for a reasonable society better than Ian Dodson, an electrical engineer living in Rancho Bernardo, who, like Jorge Martinez, was an immigrant (but in this case from Great Britain). Mr. Dodson was another of our respondents too hopeful, too much in love with his work and his family life, to carry around any sense of resentment and anger. He appreciates America and its free enterprise system because, again sounding like Mr. Martinez, "you're talking to an engineer. In England, engineers get a terrible deal. Here you actually build things. . . . In England, engineering is a frustrating profession to be in. You usually end up working for the government and everything gets canceled. Over here, you actually work on stuff that flies."

Mr. Dodson has another reason to love his work. When we asked him whether, in his opinion, racism is a problem in America, he was quick to find it where he lived: "There's a fantastic amount of racism, buried just below the surface, and you talk to people, like our neighbors, you just talk to people, you dig a little bit below the surface, and it's most definitely there. There's a lot of deep, ingrained racial hatred, I'd say." But he did not find the same kind of racism where he worked because, in his view, "engineers tend to be very reasonable people." Give an engineer a problem to solve, and he just wants to find the best way to solve it, exactly the kind of nonideological, deeply pragmatic attitude that, according to Mr. Dodson, America needs to bring to such intractable problems as racial prejudice. Most people, he tells us, "are fairly moral." They don't need strong religious commandments to do the right thing. (Mr. Dodson was one of the few self-proclaimed atheists we found among our respondents.) Just let them be themselves and see how good people really are. All this explains why, when he was asked about his obligations and duties, Mr. Dodson responded in a typically modest way:

> To do a good job of raising my children and instilling good values in them. Trying to make them tolerant of gays and different races and trying just to make sure they grow up to be reasonable people and don't steal, cheat, or lie or do any of the things that are on my list of values.... Otherwise, to be a good citizen I just—I'm fairly conscientious in my work habits, I do the best job I can.

"I have this idea in my mind," we were told by Cobb County's Judy Vogel, that "one day I'd like to write a book or whatever. Where you talk to people ... with successful marriages, or regular people, not famous people. How do you do this? Why do you believe in this? How did this come about? I just think that would be so fascinating to hear what people would say." She does not think she would have trouble finding people to interview. "I don't want to be a Pollyanna, but there are lots of good people out there. There are people who are doing their very best." Reasonable people are omnipresent in middle-class America. "When I see TV and read the newspapers," Evelyn Goldberg of Rancho Bernardo told us, "I think this: Oh, God this is terrible, children killing children." But, then, Mrs. Goldberg continued, she looks at her own kids and friends and says, "You know, they're just good folk." Even the young ones, the kids, "I mean every generation is going to be a little different. But basically I see them as good solid citizens, and I feel much more happy when I've been with all of them." Hardworking people who take care of their families and care about their neighbors have been given a gift, said Michelle Knight of Broken Arrow. "And if you've been given gifts like that, then you have to give something back, you have to take care of people that are less fortunate than you, whether it's charity or community service or whatever. You have a responsibility, I think." The moral ecology of middle-class America is built step-by-step through ordinary acts and quiet gestures, rooted in a faith that a free people will choose to exercise their freedom in reasonable ways.

Although they may not express the point in exactly this way, middle-class Americans would insist that the solution to the problem of America's depleting social capital lies in trusting reasonable people to find the right way out. Their faith in balance is so strong that they just naturally assume that if the pendulum swings too much in one direction, it will be adjusted in the other. Many of them believe that in the last few years, America has indeed experienced serious rifts in its social fabric, reflected in the dangers facing young people, the divide between the races, and imbalances between work and family. But they also believe just as strongly that we are now coming out of that bad period and are poised to make a new start. If there is indeed less social capital, this does not represent a long-term secular decline but a cycle that goes up and down—and we are now in the process of moving up from a low trough. "Our pendulum has, or is close to, reaching its peak toward the bad end," Todd Smith of DeKalb County believes. "If you know anything about America and about the values that have shaped us over the centuries," added Henry Pearson, "you know that you get by giving. . . . I'm not sure in the last thirty years it's been the part it should be. I think the pendulum is starting to come back in that direction."

When it comes back, middle-class Americans are fairly sure they know where it will stop: as Lena Parker expressed her sense of the American creed, it was that "everybody should be obedient, you know, to the law. I think everyone should be trustworthy. I think all of us should . . . have good moral standards and be honest." She could continue this way, she said, but she wanted to summarize: every individual should try their best to be "just an overall, well-adjusted, morally sound person." Her comments, along with those of so many of the other people with whom we spoke, help put into perspective the way middle-class Americans think about what is happening to the American social fabric. From their perspective, the changes overtaking corporate America—fewer unions, more competition, corporate downsizing, women working, diminished civic obligations, less friendly neighborhoods, busy people—constitute objective evidence that it has become far more difficult these days to uphold the old virtues of loyalty and belongingness. In that sense, they agree with those social scientists who worry about declining social capital.

But not only do they also understand—often in ways more sophisticated than some of the critics of America's social decline—that all was not well at a time when organizations and individuals were much more tightly bound together, middle-class Americans also express a sense of hope that the right balance will someday be found. There is a positive side to the dramatic social changes taking place in America. More Americans are working, but that also gives more of them access to a public life once monopolized by men—as well as new opportunities to expand their civic horizons. Instrumental ties clearly do not bind as tightly as those of family, church, and community, but Americans have never liked to be bound much at all. Neighborhoods may—or may not—be quite as committed to an ethic of belongingness, but, more important, people get to choose for themselves the forms of their involvement with others. Civic America, many of those with whom I talked would probably agree, is not so much in decline as, like the rest of the country, going through changes. What comes out probably will not be Tocquevillian (just like the modern corporation is not Smithian), but, this being America, it will probably be something we can live with.

VII MORALITY WRIT SMALL

As they probe into the soul of American society, intellectuals and scholars are never quite sure what they expect to find. If they discover a people basically content with life, hopeful for the future, and willing to try to work together with those of different political views, their conclusions, healthy as they may be for the Republic, leave little role for the social critic as moralist or the social scientist as diagnostician. If, on the other hand, they reveal an angry people, bitterly divided from each other over deeply entrenched moral questions, and thinking seriously of withdrawing their allegiance from their country, they have their work cut out for them, but the society may not be able to wait until their remedies have been offered.

So it often seems with the ongoing discussion of America's culture war: no one ever seems quite sure whether it is about to break out into violent conflict or about to be subsumed under the ideals of the American creed. Properly convinced that the only way to resolve the issue is by finding out how people themselves think about these matters, the sociologist James Davison Hunter, one of the most balanced interpreters of American political culture, commissioned the Gallup Organization to conduct a major survey of the American people in 1996. Hunter found remarkable agreement, across class, gender, and even racial lines, around such crucial aspects of the American creed as the special destiny of the United States or support for the principles of American democracy. "Americans," he wrote, "do indeed share some common beliefs about their collective history and they do seem to be committed to our nation's established political system."

But Hunter did not conclude that it would be correct to say good-bye to the culture war. Americans, he argued instead, are culturally divided into five categories: neotraditionalists, conventionalists, pragmatists, communitarians, and permissivists, each constituting more than 10 percent of the population. Hence, the title of his report: *The State of Disunion*. Indeed, in the most dramatic finding of his study, Hunter pointed out that "one quarter of the population do repeatedly express the conviction that government is run by a conspiracy, and one in ten Americans strongly subscribes to this view."

I can understand why Hunter reached the conclusion he did. There are strong divisions in middle-class America—one could even, if one so desired, call them camps. On a number of important issues—respect for homosexuality, support for postmodern families, sympathy toward immigration—the Middle Class Morality Project found significant regional variations; people in Brookline clearly do not think the same way as people in Tulsa. On moral matters, there is no unanimity in America. Who could doubt that some Americans believe in God and the absoluteness of His commands, uphold the nuclear family as an ideal, are worried about a declining sense of patriotism, and find the cultural relativism implicit in such notions as bilingualism abhorrent? Nor is it wrong to suggest that others believe that a loosening of the moral rules by which society conducts its business is a healthy development, especially for women, minorities, and young people, and are pleased with open borders, gay rights, free speech, and strict separation of church and state.

Should we therefore conclude that America is experiencing a culture war? My answer is yes—*but it is one that is being fought primarily by intellectuals, not by most Americans themselves.* To be sure, in surveys and polls, Americans divide themselves up into sharply contrasting categories on important moral and cultural questions. But, then again, surveys, because they ask for a range of agreement or disagreement around those questions, are designed to divide people up. Polling not only measures the level of anger in the country, it also contributes to what it measures, giving the impression that there is more disagreement than there may actually be. What are you angry about? we asked our respondents in the Middle Class Morality Project. "I'm not really angry," one of them, Cobb County's Jeremy Toole, replied. "I'm just morally frustrated. Going back to the polls. Everyone is polled today. It's not a vote. It's polled. It's polled by the certain questions you ask. They are asked in such a way that you have to give them one extreme or another and nothing in the middle. I think America wants to be in the middle more than anything." Without capturing voices like that, no measure of American moral opinion can ever give a complete picture of the culture war.

Democratic as it is, America is rightly guided by its polls; besides the results of the previous election, which appear too late for them to be useful, politicians have little else to go on in formulating their views than the polls published in the newspapers and discussed on television. But we also need to listen to people like Jeremy Toole. Over and over again, the Middle Class Morality Project found ways in which polls do not get opinion in this country quite right and, on a few occasions, get it downright wrong. Americans are not nearly as publicly religious as the polls suggest. Had that been understood earlier, politicians might not have been in such thrall to extremist groups using religion to push a political agenda. As feminists reading poll data insist, they have accepted such changes in the family as the need for women to work, but they do not welcome such changes with enthusiasm and they certainly would not describe their beliefs as "feminist." Knowing that, politicians can surely discover ways to appeal to the gender gap without necessarily accepting all the views of feminist organizations as the final word on what women want. Nor are middle-class Americans, polls to the contrary, turning their backs on immigrants. There is enough humanitarianism and nuance in the way Americans think about membership in their country for any politician to formulate a position respectful toward America's tradition of welcoming those from abroad. The polls demonstrate conclusively that

Americans do not like bilingualism but fail to reveal their possible sympathy for multiculturalism. We are not nearly as divided on affirmative action as any poll that uses words such as "quotas" and "preferences"—or, as I discovered to my chagrin, "priority"—indicates. Finally, and perhaps most important, we would be making a serious mistake if, persuaded by surveys, we were to conclude that distrust has run so rampant that it threatens the legitimacy of our democratic order. Most middle-class Americans simply do not live their lives, nor formulate their moral thoughts, as if they believed that to be the case—even when they tell survey researchers that it is.

By moving beyond polls and surveys to more ethnographic attempts to uncover people's beliefs, I have found little support for the notion that middle-class Americans are engaged in bitter cultural conflict with each other over the proper way to live. Middle-class people are not, in their cosmopolitan liberalism, out of touch with America and its core values. But nor are they so conservative that they have turned their backs on the problems of the poor and excluded. Neither determined secularists nor Christian-firsters, middle-class Americans have come to accept religious diversity as a fact of American life. Reluctant to pass judgment, they are tolerant to a fault, not about everything—they have not come to accept homosexuality as normal and they intensely dislike bilingualism—but about a surprising number of things, including rapid transformations in the family, legal immigration, multicultural education, and the separation of church and state. Above all moderate in their outlook on the world, they believe in the importance of leading a virtuous life but are reluctant to impose values they understand as virtuous for themselves on others; strong believers in morality, they do not want to be considered moralists.

There are surely differences between more conservative and more liberal Americans, but those differences mark where a discussion of America's values starts, not where it ends. Even as a beginning, moreover, the camps into which theorists of the culture war divide people are not all that helpful in understanding them. In particular, terms such as "traditional" and "modern," which have become so central to the ways both conservatives and liberals talk about American values, are seriously limited in their capacity to express how people engage in moral accounting. The most traditional Americans have incorporated into their lives some of the social transformations both positively and negatively associated with the 1960s: more likely to send their children to integrated schools and to have them exposed to the wider world, they also know that divorce, working women, drug use, and teenage pregnancy are not the monopoly of any one group of Americans. And the most morally modern Americans, those who repudiated the middle-class morality of their parents a generation ago and have both led and benefited from a sense of individual autonomy, now live in the suburbs, fear crime, raise children, and deal with their elderly parents just like everyone else; those who criticize middle-class morality find it relatively easy to live by its tenets.

The two sides presumed to be fighting the culture war do not so much represent a divide between one group of Americans and another as a divide between sets of values important to everyone. People who adhere to such "traditional" values as belief in God, strong families, patriotism, and civic and neighborly loyalty do so because, in most cases, they choose to do so; as awkward as it sounds, they are best described as modern traditionalists. And people who insist on the importance of their own conceptions of God, who value women's autonomy, and who select their friends and neighbors based on personal taste believe strongly in the importance of religion, family, and neighborhood; they can best be viewed as traditional modernists. It is a basic truth of American society that no one is a traditionalist or a modernist, but that everyone lives with varying degrees of both.

Consider two of the Americans interviewed by the Middle Class Morality Project, each of whom could easily be stereotyped into the culture war's opposing camps. We talked with Foster Rice—fifty-one years old, Catholic, "downsized" out of one job only to find another in marketing and sales—in his office in a downtown Atlanta skyscraper. He is proud that the

Speaker of the House of Representatives, Newt Gingrich, is his congressman and likes the fact that the area of East Cobb in which he lives is, as he put it, "one of the most fundamentally Christian right communities. . . . I think the morals and values in this society have grossly deteriorated," he told us. "We've gone too far with our acceptance of all aspects of the First Amendment. Clearly, the First Amendment is probably one of the greatest things of our whole Constitution, but at some point, we're going to have to say, 'Wait a second, there is a basis for right and wrong.' " Mr. Rice fits just about every image of the conservative Christian one can find. "I happen to be adamantly opposed to homosexuality," he says, because his Christian beliefs consider it a sin. But Mr. Rice is also an American, which means he knows something about social change. "You have to adjust to societal changes," which is why, realist that he is, he also understands that "as we open our eyes to the fact that there are millions and millions within our society who have a sexual persuasion or leaning" in that direction, he has begun to change his mind. "I happen to work with some of those people. They're very gifted, the ones I've known, and I think we need to look at things and look at people with respect and as human beings." Mr. Rice, in short, believes simultaneously in a fairly strict distinction between right and wrong but also believes that "the strength of this country is its people," even, it would seem, those whose sexual preferences violate his strong sense of moral propriety.

Far away from Cobb County, in Brookline, Massachusetts, we interviewed Elizabeth Tyler, a commercial real estate developer and power broker in local politics. Because she is successful in her work and articulate in her views, it would be easy to characterize her as a typical sixties person, influenced by feminism, the civil rights movement, and other efforts to make America a more open society. Such a characterization, it turns out, would be true—up to a point. Mrs. Tyler is not the only former liberal so repelled by battles over multiculturalism in the Brookline schools that she has changed her views radically in the process.

"I am becoming a 'reactionary,' " she said, "and you can put that in quotes." Distraught by the bad consequences of good intentions, she feels that the "basic knowledge that one needs to have of writing and mathematics and science has been sacrificed on the altar of political correctness." She would have no reservations, she says, about throwing the baby out with the bathwater. The whole agenda of the multicultural left—sensitivity training, teaching of non-Western cultures, sex education—is something she can do without. We have to return to teaching moral values to kids, she concludes, giving them a much firmer sense of what's right and what's wrong, for otherwise they will go crazy "simply because they are constantly having to compromise those values."

One could interpret the reactions of these two Americans not as evidence that the culture is receding, but that one side is simply switching with the other. (In this case, the fact that Mr. Rice was born in Boston but moved to Cobb and Mrs. Tyler was born in a small town in the South and moved to Brookline might suggest that both are coming back to their roots.) That would, however, be the wrong conclusion. In the context of where they live and what they believe, both are struggling to find ways in which their core beliefs can be reconciled with experiences that seem to contradict them. They retain some of the assumptions of their original beliefs, whether liberal or conservative. But they have added to them nuances based upon an unblinking assessment of the people and practices around them.

In that, such respondents differ from a number of the intellectuals who write about moral issues. Intellectuals, attracted more often to principles than to pragmatism, generally split apart the cultural and moral opposites that ordinary people are trying to reconcile. For intellectuals, tradition and modernity do not represent two competing sets of values of equal importance, but fundamental, sometimes irreconcilable, life choices, such that any decision one way forecloses decisions the other way. When expressed as a conflict between one camp of traditional Americans and another camp of modern ones, the culture war

takes a form especially appealing to intellectuals, since, which-
ever side is taken, there is an intellectual style that can be put to
good use.

Those who like the changes that have been introduced into
America since the 1960s can call upon the intellectual's usual
sympathy toward social change. Convinced that whatever is
more modern is usually better, supporters of the more liberal
camp invoke such ideals as equality, inclusion, civil liberty,
identity, and progress in defense of a moral outlook rooted
in tolerance, the avoidance of absolutes, and a willingness to
experiment. From their perspective, the older America of unquestioned patriotism, strong religious belief, low divorce rates,
ubiquitous stay-at-home moms, loyalty to the job, and active
social involvement was a world that paid insufficient respect to
individual self-discovery. Although he is not necessarily a defender of the 1960s and its legacy, Daniel Yankelovich expressed
well what is attractive about that legacy to those who place significant importance on individual freedom:

> Throughout most of this century, Americans believed that
> self-denial made sense, sacrificing made sense, obeying the
> rules made sense, subordinating the self to the institution
> made sense. But doubts have now set in, and Americans now
> believe that the old giving/getting compact needlessly restricts
> the individual while advancing the power of large institu-
> tions—government and business particularly—who use the
> power to enhance their own interests at the expense of the
> public.

At first glance, it would appear that intellectuals defending
the traditionalists in the culture war would have fewer intellectual resources upon which to draw: people who value faith and
loyalty have not had many H. L. Menckens to poke holes in the
arguments of their antagonists. But all this has changed in recent
years, as a vigorous conservatism has developed in America in
support of traditional middle-class morality and in opposition
to the alleged relativism and secularism of the cultural elite. One
cause for that change is the very success of the 1960s social

transformations. So deeply ingrained have 1960s values become in such American institutions as schools and families that defenders of those values, who once thought of themselves as radicals, now find themselves in the uncomfortable position of justifying what exists. This allows conservatives, who oppose the values of the 1960s, to use the 1960s-like language of radical social transformation. Conservatives who believe that "large chunks of the moral life of the United States, major features of its culture, have disappeared altogether, and more are in the process of extinction," as Robert Bork states the case against "the enemy within" called "modern liberalism," find themselves occupying the intellectual's role as a dissenter from orthodoxy. From their perspective, the liberals have become the establishment, protecting their monopoly of ideas by insisting on standards of political correctness, while the conservatives are upholding such intellectual ideals as free speech or open inquiry.

The culture war, unlike the subatomic particle, is one of those phenomena whose interpretation becomes intimately tied up with prescription. Those who write about such emotionally charged topics as morality generally have well-developed moral views themselves and quite naturally expect that the people "out there" share them. And since the views of Americans tend to be moderate and, on occasion, contradictory, social scientists and critics can usually point to at least some evidence behind their assertion that the positions they defend as advocates are positions that have real support in the country.

Surely this holds for me as well. Like many of the participants in the culture war, the passionate controversies in America over such subjects as the Triple A—abortion, AIDS, and affirmative action—have swept me into their orbit; when I am not a sociologist, I write very opinionated essays for very opinionated magazines on these very subjects. Anyone who knows those essays will be aware that they argue for recognition of a common-sense middle position in debates that tend to encourage ideological extremes. Lo and behold, having studied the views of two hundred suburban Americans, I come away impressed by how they, too, long for a sensible center and distrust ideological thinking. There are obvious grounds for a skeptic to conclude that, in studying the middle class, I am projecting on to them views that I very much want them to hold, since I happen to hold them myself.

But the fact is that I do not necessarily hold the same political views of those interviewed by the Middle Class Morality Project. For whatever it is worth, I often found myself to the "left" of many of them, especially on issues involving the distribution of income and support for the poor. Yet, on other questions, especially those dealing with the cultural issues, I frequently found myself to the "right" of my respondents; their general inclination not to pass judgment runs against the grain, not only of my own judgmental temperament, but also my strongly held belief that a good society will learn how to say no to people's immediate demands.

Even more important than the political differences I had with those with whom I talked, there were also substantial moral differences. In their tolerance, their belief in morality by example, and their sometimes casual ways of practicing their religious faith, middle-class Americans have little appreciation for the idea, associated with the great Enlightenment philosopher Immanuel Kant, that morality is a duty commanded by a will that lies beyond immediate experience and personal interpretation. I do not consider myself a Kantian; such ways of thinking about morality, I believe, need to be tempered by respect for real life conditions. But one can go overboard from many directions, and as I listened to middle-class Americans speak about their fear of duties and their reluctance to judge, I could not help but conclude that a little Kant might be good for their souls; there is considerable truth in that idea that people cannot know what is right until they have a standard against which they can judge what they believe—or want to believe—to be right in specific cases. A society that reaches moral judgments through anecdotes is a society whose moral judgments will always be arbitrary.

There is, finally, an additional way in which my respondents and I disagree, and disagree strongly. If middle-class Americans do not understand themselves to be that divided culturally, they are even less likely to see themselves at war. Conflict, dissent, controversy—all of which define the tone of the culture war—are not foreign to intellectuals, for argument is in their lifeblood. What I heard as I talked to Americans from all walks of the middle class, by contrast, was a distaste for conflict, a sense that ideas should never be taken so seriously that they lead people into uncivil, let alone violent, courses of action. "I would just like for people to learn to just really seriously sit down and learn to understand—not fight, bicker, or argue, just listen and understand," was how DeKalb's Maryann Kate Roberts expressed a widely shared point of view. "I'd like to see the divisiveness stop," added George Slade of Cobb. "I'd like to see true leaders show up," by which he meant those who could inspire the country to work together instead of driving it apart. In the late 1990s, there have been attempts by intellectuals and policy-makers to refocus on the question of civility in American life: the National Endowment for the Humanities led a conversation on pluralism, the University of Pennsylvania sponsored a three-year Commission on Society, Culture, and Community, a Council on Civil Society was founded at the University of Chicago, and The National Commission on Civic Renewal, chaired by William Bennett and Sam Nunn, held hearings in 1997 on the question of American civic responsibility. If these are efforts by intellectuals to convince the general public of the need for civility, they are too late. The public is already committed to civility and needs no lectures from people who may be smarter, but who also have less sense.

This discomfort with controversy and conflict, however, is to some degree a discomfort with people like me; I plead guilty of trying to be an intellectual with a taste for opinioned debate and a desire to express those opinions in public as vigorously as I can. As I listened to people express their strong support for consensus, I wanted to join the Harvard political philosopher Michael Sandel in telling them that democracy needs controversy, that it is unreasonable, if not unrealistic, to expect that issues that have divided people for centuries can be resolved through sweet reason. Because my opinions on matters of moral controversy tend to be strong ones, part of me wants to believe that there really is a culture war in America, for if there were, I would like the side that agrees most with my point of view to win.

There is a time and a place for intellectuals to fight the culture war. This book, however, is not one of them. In reporting more on how others think rather than on my own opinions, I am suggesting that we move beyond the culture war, that we stop focusing on what presumably divides one group of well-meaning Americans from another, and instead to listen to what people from all sides of the political and cultural spectrum are trying to say about their hopes and fears for their country. For, despite their reasonableness and their optimism, there are things about this country that bother these Americans and that make them wonder about their country's future. Convinced that the middle way is the best way, they believe that the modest virtues by which they want to lead their lives are not shared by those who have the power to determine how they will lead their lives. This is especially true of those in the media and government, who, in their opinion, have lost touch with the moral truths important to them.

BELOW POLITICS

Of all the indicators that something may be seriously wrong in public American life, none has been quite so persistent over the past quarter-century as the popular dislike of government and politics. An astonishingly high three-quarters of the American population no longer believe that public officials are interested in ordinary people, up from 58.9 percent in 1973. So long has this distrust persisted, and at such significant levels, that it is no longer possible to explain it as a consequence of Vietnam and Watergate. The American political climate is a rough one these days, whether mapped by the level of anger expressed in radio and television talk shows, efforts by conservative politicians to claim status as revolutionaries, or the breakdown of comity between the political parties. Whether or not the lack of confidence Americans express in their political system represents a crisis of legitimation, such alienation from politics cannot possibly be a healthy sign for American democracy.

Yet, one thing that has always puzzled those who take the pulse of the American people is that this discontent with public life somehow coexists with positive feelings toward one's own private life. Americans are usually thought of as an optimistic people, emphasizing the positive, quick to turn away from despair. They may have become cynical about and resentful toward politics and politicians, but, by the same token, they have always been, and continue to be, hopeful about their own prospects. Hence, for all the talk about how badly they are governed, 81 percent of those surveyed by the Hudson Institute in 1994 agreed with the statement "I am optimistic about my personal future," while the same General Social Survey that shows strong distrust for government also shows that 92 percent of the American people indicate that they are very happy or fairly happy with life today, compared with only 8 percent who say they are not very happy or not at all happy. The often-noted paradox that Americans tend to be pessimistic about their country but optimistic about themselves led the Pew Research Center for the People and the Press to create an "optimism gap," the difference between people's understanding of their prospects for themselves compared with those for their country; in 1996, that gap was higher than at any time since polling on the subject began in 1959.

We found evidence for such an optimism gap in the more qualitative sections of our interviews. Some of our respondents *were* quite angry about politics. "I like Rush," said Broken Arrow's Kimberly Cass of one of talk radio's angrier hosts, although she also was worried that in putting down government so much, he was also putting down the country. "A lot of our problems are with politicians," added another of our Oklahoma respondents. "They go up there and do great for the first year or two until they get knocked down by all the corruptness that's already there." DeKalb's Peter Strong contributed his thoughts:

"We've got too much government, too many bureaucrats, too many lobbyists in Washington, too much money." One simply does not have to dig very deep before discovering that the common perception that Americans are fed up with politics is widely shared.

Yet, most of the Americans with whom we talked, no matter how critical of politics and government, were upbeat about their personal prospects and overwhelmingly satisfied with their private lives. When we asked people what kind of life they would like to lead if money were no object, nearly all of them responded that their perfect picture would be very much like their actual lives. This is a country, after all, that has something called an "Optimists Club"—in which Peter Strong, whose anger I just cited, was very active. Optimism is so pervasive in middle-class America that many found it unimaginable that "our society is going to continue to decline and decline," as one of them put it. "I call myself the proverbial optimist because I think nothing will ever go wrong," Jesse O'Donnell told us. "I've heard the voices of doom sounded repeatedly recently because of the things going on around us," said Steven Carpenter of DeKalb County, "and I don't know if it's just me being naïve or just hopelessly optimistic, but I don't believe that things are quite as bad or gone as far as most people have the tendency to believe." As Mr. Carpenter's remark illustrates, it was common in our interviews for people to assume that they were being optimistic while everyone else was pessimistic, when, in fact, very few of our respondents expressed the kinds of strongly pessimistic views one would be inclined to associate with a society facing some kind of crisis of values. And one final indication of how optimistic our respondents were is provided by one of our survey questions. Despite their concerns about their economy, and quite in contrast to their concerns about the dangers facing their children, more of them, according to the survey question we asked them, were optimistic about their children's prospects than were pessimistic.

Faced with a gap between people's relative contentment with their own lives compared with their anxiety about society at

TABLE 7.1
"THE PROSPECTS FACING MY OWN CHILDREN ARE WORSE THAN THEY WERE FOR ME WHEN I WAS A CHILD"

	Strongly Agree	Agree	No Opinion	Disagree	Strongly Disagree
Brookline	5	11	3	5	1
Medford	9	9	0	5	2
Broken Arrow	5	7	3	10	0
Sand Springs	5	6	1	11	2
DeKalb	4	8	1	12	0
Cobb	2	13	1	7	2
Eastlake	2	11	0	10	2
Rancho Bernardo	2	8	2	11	2
Total	34	73	11	71	11

large, the common response is to suggest that political cynicism and anger are dangerous for the society. There are indeed dangers, but such a perspective can also get the relationship between public and private backward: people's hopes about their private lives may be more important in judging the future trend of the country then their fears about public life. Political scientist Eric Uslander, responding to the question of why America's social capital may be depleting, refuses to blame television; one of the strongest predictors of why some people join civic associations, he argues, is their optimism about the future. Such a finding suggests if not a satisfactory explanation of the optimism gap, then at least a way to think about it. Instead of first trying to discover why people are pessimistic about their public lives, we ought first to understand what they have hopes for in their private lives. Then we might be in a better position to tease out the implications of their alienation from the political system.

Intimate worlds composed of family, friends, and an occasional neighbor have one obvious advantage over distant worlds such as Washington, D.C.: there, in familiar surroundings, people are likely to feel that a sense of modest virtue is appreciated. The American preference for the local—usually expressed by terms such as "Jeffersonian" or "grass roots"—is well known, but it often suggests more of a longing than a description of an actual reality. Especially in the realms of economics and politics, Americans have long lived with arrangements quite un-Jeffersonian in scope: large-scale monopolies—once national, now international—dominate the production of the goods they consume and, despite periodic efforts to balance the budget and cut taxes, their government has not decreased in size since the Great Depression and World War II. While Americans frequently worry that too concentrated an economy and too big a state mean that things are out of control, they have found ways to live with a political economy staggering in its complexities.

But if middle-class Americans are no longer Jeffersonian political economists, they want very much to be Jeffersonian moralists. Most of the people with whom we talked are not philosophically articulate or self-conscious in their moral outlook, but they do subscribe to a general theory of moral obligation. It would seem to run something like this: Because people attach so much importance to virtues modestly expressed, the best moral relations, they believe, are between those closest to each other. We can call it morality writ small: not only should our circles of moral obligation never become so large that they lose their coherence, but morality should also be modest in its ambitions and quiet in its proclamations, not seeking to transform the entire world but to make a difference where it can.

Morality writ small suggests that moral lessons are taught not only through sermons, great books, and serious study, but by personal example. Middle-class Americans think of morality in very personal rather than impersonal tones; it hardly matters what the formal rules are if ordinary people do not take it upon themselves to set moral examples in their own quiet ways. "I've never believed that one can explicitly teach values," as Brookline's Peter Hamilton put it. "Values are something you learn through induction. It's more that you absorb them as you go along by observing others and how they react to situations and what's the right thing to do." A. C. Stewart, formerly a football coach in Oklahoma, illustrated this point by suggesting that how teachers act is sometimes more important than what they say. "You can't escape that. You can have kids in class, within a week, they know basically what you feel and how you think, and you don't have to say a word. And so live it like you'd like to have other people live, and that energy is transferred." Many of the people with whom we spoke would appreciate the story told by the late Harvard political philosopher Judith Shklar about Montaigne. Attracted by one of the ordinary vices—misanthropy—Montaigne, she reminds us, could "valiantly ward it off by remembering personal friendships and the occasional hero of the moral life. Sustained by them, he was able to remain a self-reliant skeptic. Often touched by misanthropy, appalled by his fellow men, he maintained a moral balance." Middle-class Americans have more faith in other people than Montaigne, and they have few heroes of the moral life to celebrate, but they would appreciate both his respect for balance and his reliance on persons known to him as reminders of what is valuable in life.

Finally, morality writ small applies to both those who offer support to others and to those who receive it. From the perspective of the giver, this moral theory holds, one should never, in assuming responsibility for others, promise too much. If one is giving advice, one should do so tentatively; although it is a term of derision among Christian conservatives, the idea of the "Ten Suggestions" rather than the "Ten Commandments" is exactly the tone in which most middle-class Americans believe we ought to establish moral rules. If one is giving others financial assistance, it should be conditional, temporary, and understood as a gift; overpromising is to be avoided, not because of the expense involved, but because respect for balance and proportion suggests that even if one could deliver on an overpromise, one shouldn't make it in the first place. To insure that giving is appreciated, one should give to a restricted number and one should never give too much. By keeping morality modest, no one can escape its scope. Anyone, even those struggling to get by, can find a little bit extra for someone in desperate need.

In this moral world, modesty also binds the receiver. When the moral relationship is small in size, it can be shaped in such a way to fit the particular profile of the person in need. Advice, for example, is most likely to be accepted when it is based not on some general rule deemed applicable to all, but on the specific situation it is expected to remedy. Gifts accepted from close acquaintances that are also modest in size and scope, furthermore, enable the receiver to avoid any stigma associated with dependency. One should always say thank-you for a gift received, but not necessarily humble oneself in the process; a simple expression of gratitude is enough. For middle-class Americans, the ideal set of obligations are those in which people can monitor the reciprocal impacts of giving and getting, and only small-scale morality can achieve that objective. Americans want to see that their efforts at caring are noted: a reciprocity between giver and receiver, when more personal, is also more visible. They also want to insure that their moral concern is effective: a morality of modest proportions, they believe, is a morality under control.

Despite its obvious roots in the Jeffersonian origins of the United States, morality writ small is not purely a product of American values. The idea has a great deal in common with the notion of subsidiarity: the primarily European idea, rooted in Catholic social thought, that holds that social obligations should be carried out at levels closest to the actual people involved unless otherwise impossible. "What we do today is going to affect somebody down the line," we were told by Broken Arrow's Mrs. Behzadi. "The way I raise my child is definitely going to have an effect on some other people ... their husbands, their friends, their coworkers, so if you start from the bottom, then when you get to the top, it's a little easier." In a similar way, Toni Cartwright of Sand Springs believes that volunteer work in her neighborhood "fits into the local area and the state and how your state can work in with the United States." Subsidiarity means that if we care for those closest to us, we will be more likely to take care of those who are strangers to us. It also implies that if we do not take care of those closest to us, we will grow up to be moral monsters. Jim McLaughlin, for example, believes that people who take no responsibility for themselves must never have been taught responsibility as children: "If they're not trained in the home when they're small . . . , when they grow up they're going to do anything they want to do."

Everything that middle-class Americans appreciate about morality writ small is violated when government and politics become involved. By its very nature, government is large and impersonal. Its rules are meant to apply to all people at all times, regardless of their specific circumstances, making it morally inept. It is expensive, taxing people in very visible ways to support objectives that are mostly invisible to those paying for them. It is distant, located in a city and in a region of the country not fully trusted by people elsewhere. Corruption in its affairs is endemic. But none of these complaints, common as they are, get at what middle-class Americans perceive to be the true moral failings of politics and government. When government becomes involved in moral matters, which it inevitably does when its decisions influence how and in what ways people should lead their lives, morality comes to be writ large, and as it does, Americans are no longer sure they can trust it.

Middle-class Americans understand that in the modern world, government has to carry out obligations to people they do not, and will never, know; in that sense, they have come to recognize that morality writ large is necessary. But that does not mean that it has to be welcomed enthusiastically. The danger that follows when morality is writ too large is that those who carry out the actions of government, especially politicians, are transformed into people who lose a sense of the impact their actions have on others. There are four aspects of the way politicians act that stand in striking sharp contrast to the ways we act with our friends and neighbors: to capture and remain in power, they have to overpromise, become dependent on wealth, speak in loud rather than soft tones, and substitute ideology for common sense. When they do, a country filled with reasonable people comes to be governed by unreasonable politicians.

Cobb County's Brian Fischer was an enthusiast for President Bush's ideas about a "thousand points of light," an ideal that, in his opinion, reverberates with the best of American values. But he is unhappy with the way the notion developed. "The problem was that it was all politics," he told us. "It was probably a great idea, but there was no follow-through. It's just like everything else they say to get elected." The wide gap between people's expectations and what politicians usually do once in office led many Republican candidates for Congress in 1994 to put forth a "Contract with America" promising a new era in American politics.

As it turned out, these newly elected Republicans proved themselves too rashly extremist for the moderate sensibilities of most Americans, even many of those who voted for them. It was not only their specific actions that violated principles of morality writ small, but also their ideas about promising. Republicans surely thought that Americans, fed up with politics, wanted bold promises and determined statements to fulfill them. It was just as likely, however, that Americans would have preferred fewer promises, reasonable attempts to meet them, and honest explanations of why not all of them could be met. What is most interesting about the practice of promising in politics is how radically different it is from the practice of promising in closer-knit moral circles. We usually try to be reasonable with those for whom we care, fearing their disappointment if we offer more than we can deliver. But politicians appear to middle-class Americans to be habitual overpromisers, drunk with the idea of offering something to everyone and fooling hardly anyone when they blame the intransigence of the opposition for why they cannot deliver. By overpromising, politicians violate one of the key tenets of morality writ small, which is to be realistic in what you can expect to do for someone else.

Then there is the question of money. A run for office has become so expensive that its crass materialism violates a sensibility that seeks to balance financial concerns with such other values as loyalty or honesty. Ray Moore, a Sand Springs steelworker, gave a strong endorsement of government when we talked with him: "We have to support the government," he said. "It's not going to support itself." What troubled him was that "the election process . . . has gotten out of hand. You've got to have a million dollars to run for office now." It's not the prospect that large sums of money will serve as a source of corruption that bothers him so much as it is that large sums of money make those who raise it so different from people like him: "So a guy should be able to run, if he didn't have a dime and wanted to run." The demands of fund-raising are such that politicians, by definition, cannot possess a healthy dose of middle-class morality. If a prospective politician is not personally wealthy, he has to sell his integrity for dollars, a morally compromising situation that most Americans try to avoid in their personal lives. If he is personally wealthy, he can avoid that temptation, but then he is also, by definition, not middle class and therefore unable to understand both the financial and the moral squeeze in which so many middle-class families find themselves. Insatiable fund-raising is simply incompatible with the proper moral attitude toward money that middle-class Americans value in their own lives.

Politicians, even when supplied with funds, need to call attention to themselves and their ideas. To be heard, particularly in a media environment crammed with too many messages, they have to shout. When people talk about negative campaigning, it is not only the messages that they view as negative but also the tone: anything said too loudly, even if aggressively positive, is by definition negative. To get above the din, politicians begin to sound like everyone else who does not know you personally but is trying to tell you how to lead your life. Because they always emphasize the negative rather than the positive, the media belong firmly in the camp of the shouters. So do preachers who, instead of setting a moral example, become, in the words of Cobb County's Lila Stich, "the arm-waving kind of person."

But a special place of contempt is reserved for politicians, especially those with a propensity to pronounce quite loudly on the
right way to live. "We're all just individuals in a multitiered
process and only a few people can get to the moral or immoral
bully pulpit in Washington to pontificate," said Cobb's Foster
Rice. The key word here is "pontificate," a term that suggests
that those politicians who take it upon themselves to offer moral
advice have no particular moral standing to do so. To compen-
sate, they shout, and we, in turn, tune them out.

When the shouting becomes ideological, which it is bound
to do in order to call attention to itself, the messages offered are
even less likely to be positively received. "The conservative is
so angry at the liberal, and the liberals are so angry about the
conservatives," said Valda Sellers of Medford. "People just
aren't seeing each other as people . . . I just hate that." Why take
things so seriously? some of our respondents wondered. "Society will go on no matter what . . . ," Luis Garcia felt. "If the Republicans are in there, life will go on. Democrats get in, and it
will still go. It will be here long after we're gone. Good or bad,
conservative or liberal, it will make some people happy and it
will make some people sad." In our politics these days, added
Brian Fischer, every interest is represented by a group—even
"somebody like me, overweight, insurance guys, I'm sure we
have a constituency"—and we increasingly "seem to be beating
ourselves to death." This dislike for ideological politics is where
the intellectuals (and politicians) engaged in the culture war lose
touch with ordinary middle-class Americans. Just as there are
few if any pure traditionalists and pure modernists in middle-
class America, there are not very many liberals and conservatives. Ideologies cannot mobilize people behind a particular
vision of the world without emphasizing something negative,
for why else would we need a course correction? As DeKalb's
Nancy Elliott hears all the political talk, she admits to being
"fed up to my eyeballs in hearing so much negative [stuff] and
would like to see us take a more positive turn. I guess I'm a
positive person," she concludes, an attitude unlikely to make her
a soldier in any ideology's cause.

Convinced that the world of politics and government oper-
ates by the highly immodest vices of promising too grandly,
spending too much, speaking too loudly, and believing too infal-
libly, Americans, for moral sustenance, turn to an area below
politics—a realm of family, friends, and community underneath
(and generally out of sight) of government. There, the brutish
moral bearing so characteristic of what they dismiss as "politics"
plays little role. Below politics, reasonable people can continue
to be reasonable people. "If you sit down with people like you
are doing now and ask them to think through the issues,"
Mr. Fischer explained, "I think most people have their heads
straight, and most people under a calm circumstance will come
to the right conclusion." No wonder that, for so many middle-
class Americans, the world of personal ties counts for so much.
If that world were to disappear, so would the modest virtues as
they want them to be.

Middle-class Americans cannot help but contrast the behavior of those they know with those distant figures who appear to
them on the nightly news. And that is not a comparison favorable to the world of politics and government. For them, the
1960s slogan that the personal is the political is the exact opposite of the truth. Americans hate politics, not in spite of their
love for their private lives, but because they love their private
lives.

ABOVE POLITICS

There is a world above politics as well as a world below. What
Americans want in their close personal relationships—the
ability to trust that the others upon whom they rely will not become so corrupted by fame, money, power, or glamour that they
will lose touch with common sense—can, in theory, also be
found in those transcendental moral ideals that are presumed to
hold for all times. Biblical commandments, constitutional principles, the moral lessons taught by great literature or philosophy—these are things that no politician can corrupt because

they were here long before those who govern us were born and will continue to be here long after they are gone. When they search for moral codes by which the good life should be led, the world above politics offers as sharp a contrast to the failings of the world of Washington, D.C., as the world of neighbors and friends.

Yet, when they try to apply the lessons learned from this world above politics, middle-class Americans face a serious handicap. Timeless principles and universal commandments—the essence of morality traditionally understood—invariably uphold standards of the good in contrast to the bad around us. For that reason, these commandments force us to stand in judgment, insisting that we say no to our immediate desires for pleasure or reward for the sake of fidelity to a higher sense of right and wrong. Yet, middle-class Americans, as they have testified repeatedly, prefer to sit in the seat of nonjudgment. Reluctant to impose their value on others, they are committed to tolerance to such an extent that they have either given up finding timeless morality or would be unwilling to bring its principles down to earth if, by chance, they came across it.

Intellectuals who take the conservative side in the culture war tend to assume that Americans have succumbed too willingly to what they call cultural relativism or secular humanism to appreciate what is truly valuable in a world of transcendental truths. The Middle Class Morality Project found considerable evidence to support this claim. Despite their oft-professed religious faith—the General Social Survey in 1991 found that 57.2 percent of Americans agreed that "God's laws should decide right and wrong" compared with 21.4 percent who disagreed—middle-class Americans have never let God command them in ways seriously in conflict with modern beliefs; even the most faithful among them rely on liberal arguments involving free exercise in defense of a role for religion in public life. The idea of marriage as a sacred promise, pledged in the name of God, stands in sharp conflict with the application of cost-benefit reasoning to marital commitments. Old-fashioned ideals about love of country have given way to a more reflective and moderate kind of patriotism. Americans are wary about duties, and even though in principle they believe they have an obligation to help the unfortunate, in practice, they find much at fault with existing ways of doing so. At work and in their civic lives, people's ties to each other are increasingly instrumental, based less on a sense of loyalty and more on the utilitarian benefits such ties can offer. This tendency to resolve moral matters not by appealing to a transcendent world above everyday life, but instead to calculations of self-interest, even if more broadly understood, has enough validity that it rings true not only to conservatives, but also to writers such as Christopher Lasch or Robert Bellah and his colleagues in *Habits of the Heart*.

Yet, middle-class Americans also see much of value in the freedom given to them by the passing of a world of strict moral rules. Every indication suggests that they will continue to impose their individualism on their religious beliefs rather than the other way around. They are not about to relinquish the autonomy that family members, especially women, have achieved. It is difficult to imagine middle-class Americans returning to the days when patriotism meant blind faith in one's country and its leaders. When forced to choose between authority and freedom, most middle-class Americans are persuaded that the freedom they enjoy in their private lives is too appealing to be surrendered for the sake of abstract moral principles that do not seem fully in accord with how they want to lead their lives.

A commonly heard complaint about life in contemporary America is that, as William Bennett puts it, "we are . . . living in an era in which it has become increasingly unfashionable to make judgments on a whole range of behaviors and attitudes," with the consequences that America faces "unilateral moral disarmament, as harmful in the cultural realm as its counterpart is in the military." People who worry about this disappearance of a strong sense of right and wrong cast their eyes upon schools that have lowered academic standards and no longer make judgments about students' character, pornographers who exploit any avenues available to them to ply their wares, welfare programs that subsidize and encourage illegitimacy, cultural elites who

transform their secular ideology into constitutional principles
for the entire nation, criminals so unrestrained by dictates of
conscience that they have turned into superpredators, women
who consider abortion the way they consider a facial, and gay
marriages that undermine the biological basis of the family.
Only by turning to the moral wisdom contained in the world's
great religious and literary traditions, they conclude, can Americans once again be able to make the necessary distinction
between doing the right thing and doing the convenient thing.

Based on the interviews conducted by the Middle Class Morality Project, I am convinced that those who speak this way are
in one sense correct: Americans do feel that they have lost the
distinction between right and wrong and desperately want it
back. But I disagree with their conclusion that this is necessarily
a bad thing, for middle-class Americans no longer believe that
right and wrong provide unerring guidelines for informing them
about how to lead their lives. A few of those with whom we
spoke express themselves in what could be called a postmodern
voice, finding traditional conceptions of morality not to be universal and timeless but rather nakedly partisan efforts by powerful groups to impose their conception of the good life on the less
powerful: "I don't believe in objective moral truth, that there is
a set standard," as Bea Cohen of Cobb County put it. But this is
truly a minority position in middle-class America. Far more
common are professions of loyalty to the essential truths of
transcendental moral principles combined with determined revi-
sions of them to account for contemporary circumstances. It
is not that people are skeptical of the old virtues, for they do
not share the postmodernist's hermeneutics of suspicion. Instead, they hold such truths to be sacred, but not so sacred that
they should be inflexible. Rules are not meant to be broken, for
down that path lies anarchy. But they are made to be bent,
for down that path lies modernity.

Middle-class Americans can best be described as engaging in
moral *bricolage*. When he used that term, the anthropologist
Claude Lévi-Strauss emphasized the way "primitive" tribes as-
sembled their mythological beliefs out of already existing mate-

rials lying here and there around them, in contrast to modern engineers who develop a plan and adopt or develop materials to fit it. When faced with a situation that requires moral choice, middle-class Americans look around them for what they can use. Interestingly enough, they assemble their morality from exactly those places from which conservatives believe morality ought to come. Most Americans know at least a few stories from the Bible, have some sense of the Constitution's basic principles, remember stories read to them as children, have become familiar with other stories as they bring up their own children, and understand such crucial episodes in American history as the Civil War, the Great Depression, World War II and the struggle against totalitarianism, and the civil rights movement. From all these sources, they distill their moral principles. True, those principles do not have the logical consistency and theoretical elegance of the great moral philosophers, nor the sense of tragic limitations emphasized by many religious and political traditions. But by using what is available, they do their best. Few of our respondents were as well read as Chad Noone of Brookline, but even he was eclectic in how he picked his moral ideals:

> Every book like the Bible has got a certain set of morals, you know, and like in a less religious tone. . . . Philosophers, they set up a scale of moral law—I forget his name but whatever, the guy that tried to define morality as a sense of obligation . . . —Immanuel Kant, something like that. . . . You could bring in Gandhi and all that, I think would be an excellent example.

From this myriad set of sources, Americans develop a hybrid language for speaking about moral obligation. The words they use to express their support for individual freedom and the moral equality and dignity of all people are not just random noise: these commitments, which they know that not all people around the world share, represent the hard moral truths brought home to them by the triumphs and tragedies of their civilization. But such moral truths, as venerable as they may be, cannot always tell us what to do about a relative dying of AIDS, a daughter who needs an abortion, an inner-city resident on welfare, prayer in the schools, or loyalty to one's job. "There's morals and there's morals," as Lisa Andrews of Eastlake put it, and it is not always clear which apply when. "I don't know how we can teach morals as such because it's the fiber of you, and what is socially acceptable in some families is not socially acceptable in another," said Barbara Tompkins of Broken Arrow. "One of my students was a thirty-six-year-old homosexual and I loved him dearly. He's a fine human being. So again we come back to morals: how are we going to narrow it down? Who teaches the morals?" In the face of actually existing moral dilemmas, middle-class Americans discover that the conservative insistence on timeless notions of right and wrong fails them. When conservative intellectuals write on moral matters, if Robert Bork is at all representative, they often do so in a tone so harsh in its judgment, so intemperately negative of the modern condition, so distrustful of ordinary human beings, so vehement in its insistence on one and only truth, so ideological in its style of argumentation, and so seemingly unaware that even good morals can have bad consequences, that their message loses its resonance for real people in real world situations. If that is what a belief in right and wrong entails, many middle-class Americans would conclude, then perhaps it is better to find another way of thinking about right and wrong.

Such an approach to right and wrong has obvious implications for how middle-class Americans understand religion. "For most people," writes Bork, "only revealed religion can supply the premises from which the prescriptions of morality can be deduced." If he is right on this point, then he is also right when he claims that our turning away from revealed religion is due to modernity, since such forms of religion have not been especially successful in meeting the competition from consumer capitalism. It follows that, to recapture religion as the source of moral judgment, people will need to reject a good deal of the modern world around them, including, as it turns out, much of religion as it is actually practiced. For religion itself, as another conservative intellectual, Irving Kristol, has written, made a mistake by "surrendering to the spirit of modernity at the very moment when modernity itself is undergoing a kind of spiritual collapse." Suggesting that our increasing secular society has lost sight of orthodoxy and its notions of original sin and "a somewhat stoical temper toward the evils of the world," Kristol concludes that a return to orthodoxy—whose function "is to sanctify daily life and to urge us to achieve our fullest human potential through virtuous practices in our daily life, whether it be the fulfillment of the law in Judaism or Islam or *imitatio Christi* in Christianity"—could not help but have positive consequences for our society.

It is perfectly appropriate for anyone to write about the benefits of religious faith for themselves, or even to make an argument that the world would be better off if others shared their religious convictions. But it is another thing entirely to make an empirical claim, as Robert Bork does, that "most people" prefer revealed religion or for Kristol to claim—again, as in empirical proposition—that "young people do not want to hear that the church is becoming more modern." As sociology, these claims simply have no support; indeed, conservative intellectuals recognize that they have no support when they argue that the modern world is going to hell, for if people were as deeply religious as they would like them to be, the world would not be on the way to perdition. Comparing what conservative intellectuals say about the rewards of orthodoxy with the pragmatic, nonjudgmental, and inclusive language in which middle-class Americans discuss matters of religious faith, it is not hard to reach the conclusion that as puzzling as the reluctance of those with whom we spoke to make judgments is, it is highly preferable to the view of those whose judgmentalism bends so little that it cannot take into account what it means to live in this world surrounded by other people.

All of which leads me to wonder how conservative intellectuals have gotten themselves into a situation in which their books, even when best-sellers, have so little impact on changing how ordinary people think of their moral obligations. I believe the answer to that question has been supplied in another context by, of all people, conservative intellectuals—especially Irving Kristol. Conservatives are not the first group of thinkers whose inflexible ideological commitments have led them to lose touch with common sense; liberals did it before them. Now conservative writers find themselves following the exact same path taken by those leftist intellectuals, doubly ironic because it was conservative writers who first pointed out, quite convincingly, how suicidal that path was.

The neoconservative critique of the evolution of contemporary liberalism runs roughly as follows. The liberalism of Franklin Delano Roosevelt and Harry Truman struck deep roots in America, neoconservatives argue, in part because its emphasis on economic and national security, and its avoidance of hot-button cultural issues, made it seem safe to middle-class Americans. But throughout the late 1960s, eventually culminating in the nomination of George McGovern, a new spirit began to rule American liberalism. Speaking the language of a cultural elite committed to tolerance, relativism, and personal and group identity, liberals separated themselves off from the traditional moral views of hardworking middle-class Americans, becoming, in the process, a "new class" committed to an "adversary culture" of collectivist values, therapeutic remedies, hostility to corporations, and even anti-Americanism.

Such interpretations of the emergence of a "new class" are not always empirically demonstrable, but they nonetheless contain an important truth, one nowhere better illustrated than by the left when it began to think about the question of welfare. In the 1980s and 1990s, liberals took perfectly acceptable ideas, such as the fact that we have obligations to the poorest among us, and turned them into notions of welfare rights or into attacks on the principle that people ought to be supported irrespective of how they act or think. A passionately argued version of this transformation can be found in a recent book by Herbert Gans. By using terms like "underclass" as a convenient label for behaviors viewed as undeserving—unwillingness to work, homelessness, a tendency to have babies when too young, addictions and propensities toward crime—we do not, in Gans's view, describe an actual picture of poverty but look for ways to turn our backs on our obligations to the poor. But since the distinction between the deserving and the undeserving poor is so strongly held in this country, Gans was criticized for presuming to proclaim the moral high ground in ways that wind up dismissing as unworthy of respect the deepest moral beliefs of ordinary people. On this point, the theorists of the new class are right to suggest that liberal intellectuals find themselves arguing for positions far afield from what most Americans would consider common sense.

But then what are we to make of the fact that conservative writers treat people's views about religion in the same way liberals treat their ideas about welfare? At first, such writers argued that Americans were a religious people alienated from the secular, relativistic views of the policy establishment, certainly a perfectly reasonable thing to argue. But then the very thinkers who emphasized the split between policy elites and ordinary American sentiment, such as Kristol, equated a need to believe with a rejection of such benefits of the contemporary world as individualism. Yet, the very religious revival he correctly anticipated turned out, instead, to be one more ingenious way Americans discovered to live with personal autonomy. The right's idea that one's belief in God should furnish a set of absolutes that determines one's position on the political issues of the day is as incomprehensible to most middle-class Americans as the left's disdain for discipline and personal responsibility, as if, once again, only an intellectual could be so out of touch with real world experience. New class intellectuals and cultural elites know no ideology; one can find them on the right as easily as one can find them on the left.

Intellectuals, myself included, are often made uncomfortable by the libertarianism of the American middle class because such libertarianism always seems to cut two ways. Americans appreciate the freedom to work as they want and where they want: unlike those living in Eastern and Central Europe, they have not experienced state socialism followed by heady days of laissez-faire anarchy, but they have in recent years seen corporate

downsizing, governmental retrenchment, and other transformations of the nation's political economy that have undermined the
security so central to the worldview of their parents. While such
changes are bound to produce anxiety, many middle-class
Americans also view them opportunistically. Their commitment
to freedom in the economic realm means that they have a chance
to determine for themselves where they will end up in life.

The same appreciation of freedom extends to the moral
realm, a lesson perhaps better appreciated in Eastern Europe—
where the state tried to control the churches just as it did the
economy—than here. Americans are as concerned about the decline in traditional sources of morality as they are with political
and economic liberalization, but they respond to the weakening
of an absolute sense of right and wrong opportunistically as
well; if morality can no longer be derived from forces above and
beyond their control, they will make their own morality and do
the best with it they can. Would they, if they had the choice, give
up their newfound moral freedom if a stronger adherence to
right and wrong were available to them? The question is as irrelevant as asking whether they would prefer family farms to
mechanized agriculture. Let intellectuals ponder such questions,
would be their response. We just want to get on with making the
best moral lives for ourselves we can.

Conservative intellectuals have a particularly hard time dealing with the fact that the libertarianism they appreciate in the
economic realm has consequences that they perceive as perni-
cious in the moral realm. Despite prodigious efforts by writers
such as Michael Novak to find moral virtue in capitalist beliefs
and practices, Daniel Bell was right to point out two decades ago
that culture is too integrated with economics for freedom in the
one realm not to have spillover effects in the other. Make your
choice and get on with it, one wants to advise conservative intellectuals. If you like economic freedom so much, learn to live
with the fact that people simply will not tie themselves down, at
least in any meaningful way, to forms of absolutist moral belief
that prevent them from making their own judgments about
themselves and others. But if on the other hand you want to be a

party of morality, you will have to at some point condemn the capitalist mentality you otherwise so admire. It is not, and has probably never been, the left that is primarily responsible for the moral anarchy you see everywhere around you; if fault must be found, the truly important "new class" is actually one of the oldest classes we have: a business class, for which nothing, and certainly not morality, has ever been sacred.

Much the same dilemma confronts the left, but of course in reverse. If one believes that a society is better off when, instead of condemning homosexuals or welfare mothers for violating fixed standards of morality, it acknowledges the freedom of individuals to construct their own identity, one will have a hard time preventing them from enjoying the freedom of the market as well. The right to privacy so often invoked by the left cannot be split into a realm of the personal, which is presumed good, and a realm of the economic, which is presumed bad. The personal and the economic, after all, usually find themselves linked: gay identity developed inseparably from quite commercial bathhouses run to make profits for their owners, sexual liberation inevitably brings with it the (evidently lucrative) business of pornography, and a woman's right to an abortion eventually led to clinics offering such services for a fee. If the left wants to be the party of moral libertarianism, it cannot be long before it will have to dismiss its long-standing desire to plan and regulate the economy. If it instead insists that the private actions taken in the economy have implications for everyone else so important that we have a moral stake in their regulation, it will also have to conclude that private actions taken in the realm of sexuality and identity are also available to moral scrutiny by the public at large.

Because respect for moral freedom and nonjudgmentalism cut so deep in middle-class America, both left and right, to the degree that they seek political popularity, are more likely to swing to their libertarian than to their communitarian side. That, in turn, will arouse the passion with which critics find fault with the individualism of middle-class culture. What should we make of these periodic efforts to condemn the middle class for its lack of interest in transcendental truths? Whether the critique of America's moral culture comes from conservatives such as Bork or those with impossible to classify political views such as Christopher Lasch, it is often written in doomsday language, as if the day of reckoning is about to arrive yesterday. Yet, the popularity of jeremiads is the best argument against their prescriptions; since they have been around since the Puritans, America obviously has survived long enough for each generation to discover a new reason to question whether society can survive. I do not mean to be facetious here: critics like Lasch have had valuable things to say about both America's fascination with hedonism and its all-too-quick reliance on therapeutic "cures." Because middle-class Americans cannot find a sacred realm above politics from which they can deduce a strong sense of right and wrong, their ability to glimpse a world richer in meaning and human purpose is weakened. America's moral libertarianism does indeed create a situation that, as Émile Durkheim feared, can be characterized as "moral mediocrity."

But such a critique goes just so far; only a society that takes freedom for granted can worry about whether there is too much of it. As distraught as one may be to live in a morally mediocre society (and I admit to finding it a less than uplifting experience), there are benefits that should never be ignored. We live, after all, in a democracy, one, moreover, that has come to be characterized by increasingly diverse religious faiths, ethnic and racial heterogeneity, and, not surprisingly, a wide variety of conceptions about how to lead the good life. Democracies often do not survive under such conditions; buffeted by ideological controversy and moral division, they are unable to sustain the arts of compromise and bargaining that make democratic stability possible. Writing in the aftermath of this century's experiences with totalitarianism and war, a number of political thinkers in the 1950s and 1960s concluded that popular passions could be so disruptive of stability that political parties and political elites were required to dampen ideological enthusiasm. From such a perspective, the successful political system was one that generated leaders more appreciative of the virtues of moderation than the people who elected them. Such leaders, committed to commonly agreed upon rules of the game, would protect democracy from its worst populistic instincts.

I urge anyone put off by the nonjudmental way in which middle-class Americans describe their sense of modest virtues to compare how they think with the ways politicians express themselves these days. Listening in particular to the Republican firebrands who were elected to the House of Representatives in 1994 and the Senate in 1996, one senses that the conditions necessary for democratic stability now are the exact opposite of the way they were in the 1950s. Once political scientists put their faith in political parties and political leadership to channel popular enthusiasm, but the parties are more partisan then ever and the leadership more dedicated to scoring ideological points than to governing the country. Under such conditions, popular sentiment is necessary to curb the excesses of democratic elites, not the other way around. There is a virtue in modest virtue. By its very reasonableness, morality writ small—however mundane, unheroic, local, circumstantial, anecdotal, personal, and secular it may be—can help sustain a political system whose leaders aspire to moral purity, but whose actions threaten the very society trying to achieve it.

THE NEW MIDDLE-CLASS MORALITY

Morality writ small will always be disappointing to those who want either right or wrong, freedom or order. Because middle-class Americans do make distinctions—such as the ones between good and bad immigrants and the deserving and undeserving poor—their views will be dismissed by those who interpret such distinctions as a way to impose middle-class values on those who do not, and should not, share them. But because middle-class Americans also believe that everyone should have a second chance, that distinctions are made to be fudged, and that what others do is usually none of our business, their views are easily condemnable by those certain that hierarchy and obedience are requirements of social order. In some sense, such critics on both sides are correct: middle-class morality is not meant to please. It is instead meant to work, something that cannot be said with great confidence about either strict civil libertarianism on the one hand or religious and moral orthodoxy on the other.

But can morality writ small actually work in a modern society in which the fates of all are inextricably linked? Like most of the "big" questions our society faces, there is no easy answer to this one. The Middle Class Morality Project discovered maturity and moderation in middle-class America, virtues at odds with some of the more negative treatments of what it means to be middle class. But to recognize this is not to accept the viewpoints of our respondents as a new form of revealed truth; flattering the vanity of the middle class strikes me as little different than scolding it for its narcissism and individualism. For one thing, we report only on people's beliefs and have little to say about whether their actual behavior lives up to those beliefs; it certainly would come as no surprise if they did not. For another, there are aspects of morality writ small that are troublesome; to know middle-class morality is not to love it. Here is my own short list of what I found problematic in the views expressed to me by the respondents to the Middle Class Morality Project.

For all its pragmatism, there is a romantic nostalgia in middle-class morality that sometimes undercuts its seriousness. In moral matters, small is not always wise. As much as I came to appreciate the sense of reciprocity and the need for control implicit in notions of morality writ small, we cannot treat those whose relationship to us is distant and indirect the same way we treat those with whom we share streets and playgrounds. We ought to think of morality writ small as a parable, reminding us of what, in a world of big government, we often forget: that no one ought to presume that they can receive the help of others without obligating themselves to be worthy of that help. But we would be wrong to take morality writ small as the actual model for how public policies (such as welfare) ought to be financed and administered. To the degree that middle-class Americans apply their belief in small-scale morality as a guide to what should happen in politics, they succumb to a romantic vision of society quite at odds with the one in which they actually live.

There is, therefore, something myopic in the middle-class distrust of government. Government has been good to middle-class Americans, providing them, with reasonable efficiency, all those benefits that they now claim by right. No genius is required to realize that such benefits cannot be manufactured out of thin air but must be paid for in taxes. By constantly finding fault with government, even while demanding the benefits it provides, middle-class Americans have introduced an untenable instability into American life, which serves the interests of none but demagogues. If middle-class Americans were as realistic about what government can (and cannot) do as they are about finding their own paths between tradition and modernity on matters of religious belief or family form, they might find the same kind of balance in politics that they seek for business. Those with whom I spoke generally were able to see the world as it really is. The fact that government is a necessity in the modern world is the one great exception to that generalization.

Equally as unattractive about middle-class morality is a level of self-pity that sits uncomfortably with the moral maturity my respondents demonstrated in so many of their reflections. Listening to what they had to say about materialism, especially as it affected their children, serves as the most striking example. I never thought I would be in the position of wanting to remind people of Nancy Reagan's great truism, yet an all but uncontrollable desire to remind people with whom I talked to "just say no" was all I could think about as they denounced television and worried about expensive sneakers. Chronic complaining is one of the least attractive features of middle-class morality. Parents have a lot to fear for their children, but they also have more power to do something about those fears than they seem to realize. They can, for one thing, set an example by watching less television if they think their children watch too much. If materialism bothers you, earn less and buy less. As one of our respondents, Cobb County's Judy Vogel, put it, "Now I'm sorry, I don't see why you can't live in a one-hundred-fifty-thousand-dollar house as opposed to a three-hundred-thousand-dollar house and afford to run your life. If the child was the priority, then different decisions would be made. You can't have it all." It is even possible that one parent—and maybe even the mother—might decide to put her career on hold for the sake of the children. There is no law in this country against taking back your kids from the forces that many parents (quite properly) see arrayed against them. The amount of choice middle-class Americans have introduced into the family is a healthy development. But it also means that they have to live with the responsibility such choice entails, including the choice to live with fewer choices.

Not very pretty as a personal disposition, self-pity can be downright dangerous in politics. The public and the politicians, for all their distrust of each other, have a mutual interest in encouraging middle-class self-pity. For middle-class people themselves, being mad as hell confirms their indignant sense that they are always acted upon. But whatever relief self-pity provides is bound to be temporary, for the notion of being acted upon is passive, a confession that the anger motivating the pity need not be taken seriously. Unlike concrete demands, such as for better schools or child care or policies to deter crime, the demands that arise out of self-pity call for symbolic redress. That is why politicians, for all their promises to do something about middle-class anger, never seem to do anything concrete to relieve it. In an odd way, they are comfortable with a discomforted middle class. Encouraging middle-class self-pity lets them off the hook. Seeing an opportunity to appeal to voters without having to promise much of anything, they can praise the narcissistic sides of middle-class morality while ignoring the sense of moderation that is most attractive about it.

Hoping to arouse enough anger to get themselves elected, but not so much anger that they will be swept away in the backdraft, politicians play a dangerous game with public opinion, as if people's deep moral convictions about the world can be turned on today only to be turned off tomorrow. No wonder that so many citizens are just as frustrated by being pandered to as they are by being ignored. Whether politicians are patting them on the back for their wisdom or working behind their backs out of arrogance, they are never up front. Listening to politicians in America talk about cynicism is a bit like watching the beer industry's warnings about drinking and driving; their words convey concern, but the subtle import of their message is to encourage the very behavior that appears to concern them.

When the general public responds to the cynicism of politicians by cultivating a cynicism of its own, it illustrates yet another unpleasant feature of middle-class morality: a perverse pleasure in powerlessness. Participants in the culture war will pander to those feelings of powerlessness. Those on the left will insist that business has all the power, and if the anger were only directed there, and not to government, people would be justified in expressing it. Those on the right feel that liberals have all the power, especially through their control of the educational and therapeutic institutions of society, which in turn leads them to justify efforts by angry people to withdraw from the official institutions of society in favor of ones associated with traditional ideals of order, discipline, and faith.

I find neither version of the powerlessness story all that persuasive. At some level, of course, big business, big government, and big educational bureaucracies are impervious to popular input; the organized nearly always beat back the unorganized. But it is also true that neither democracy nor capitalism can survive for long unless it takes account of the discontents of ordinary people. An attitude of injured self-pity gives the middle class all it needs to avoid taking responsibility for its own condition, an odd response given the value that middle-class Americans, when they talk about such issues as welfare, attach to each person's taking responsibility for his or her own actions. Unlike many on the left, I do not view this emphasis on personal responsibility as an excuse to avoid supporting welfare or other programs designed to help the poor; it is common sense, the best of middle-class morality, to recognize that dependency breeds irresponsibility. But it does strike me as odd that people who believe so much in personal accountability seem to take so little responsibility for what they see as wrong with their society. Just as people get the media they deserve, the government they choose is the government they get. If Americans do not like the flood of money that alienates them so much from their political system, the ideological and negative campaigning, the politicians who condescend to them, they can elect others of a different ilk.

All this may explain why, for all the complaining I heard from time to time in my interviews, I was so gratified to hear voices like those of Jane Sargent, a Cobb County hospital administrator. Mrs. Sargent recognizes that the radical agenda of the Republican Party will inevitably scare people, but maybe, she goes on, we need to be scared. She would have us rethink our assumptions about the way things have to be: "I see us, as a society, continuing to attack problems and trying to solve problems like welfare reform by just hitting the brick wall harder. I mean, it's almost as if we say, 'Well, just a little harder. Just one more time.' That won't work. I think we need to take some risks." One does not have to agree with her politics to appreciate her willingness to experiment, an attitude that, however much it is supposed to represent the American character, seems remarkably missing from those who spend most of their time denouncing politicians. "I wish," she told us, "more people would recognize [that] we can't just stand back and whine about the way things are and whine about how terrible the changes will be. We've got to move forward and trust that we can do that and get to a solution eventually." If more middle-class Americans thought the way she does, there would be less tendency for Americans to talk about their government as if it were a foreign government. A people who have shown such success in finding their own way to God and in making their own kinds of families, if they applied the same energy and determination to their country, might finally bridge the gap between their positive feelings about their private lives and their negative views of their public lives. After all, in a democracy, the one has something to do with the other.

Whatever I think about the worldviews of those with whom I spoke, they are not likely to change. It is not, when all is said and done, whether their views are attractive or unattractive, practical or idealistic, liberal or conservative that matters. What does matter is that there has emerged a *new* middle-class morality in America that bears little relationship to the way that term has been used in the past. Worried that middle-class morality is a code-word for outdated Victorian ideals that were intrusive and punitive (at least in the novels of Sinclair Lewis and Sherwood Anderson), the left fears the return of a worldview hostile to women, minorities, and homosexuals. Worried that postmodern society has no place for the sacred and the meaningful, the right imagines middle-class morality as a corrective to secular humanism. But the new middle-class morality—with the conspicuous exception of its view of homosexuality—is more accommodating, pluralistic, tolerant, and expansive that either side has recognized.

Middle-class morality is what it is because it has no politics. It is an outlook on the world that grows up from personal experience, not down from ideological commitment. But the fact that middle-class Americans do not like their morality corrupted by politics does not mean that their morality is irrelevant to politics. On the contrary, the middle-class Americans with whom I spoke have much to offer American intellectuals and policymakers as they deal with a society undergoing significant moral transformation. All too often those who write about and act upon politics do so convinced that they have a superior truth that the less enlightened need to hear. Perhaps it is time for them to get as they give. Here, I believe, is what middle-class Americans would tell both the left and the right if they wrote the book about ordinary people leading ordinary lives that Judy Vogel hopes that someday will be written.

To critics of a conservative bent, middle-class Americans would say something like this: You were right, and Americans should always be in your debt, for your warnings against the direction in which our country was headed in the 1970s and 1980s. American liberalism has lost touch with common sense in its disdain for the victims of crime, its extremism on behalf of separation of church and state, its denigration of the work ethic, its celebration of hedonism over discipline, its turn against meritocracy, its pursuit of an equality of results rather than of opportunities, its excessive reliance on government—in short, its contempt for those middle-class values that we hold so dear. But your accomplishments will fail, not only for you but the country as well, if you say, as novelist and Republican speechwriter Mark Helprin said, that "conservatives are counterrevolutionaries by right," since America has become a place "in which individual rights have become group rights, in which responsibility has become entitlement, marriage has become divorce, birth has become abortion, medicine has become euthanasia, homosexuality is a norm, murder is neither a surprise nor necessarily punishable, pornography is piped into almost every home, gambling is legal, drugs are rife, students think Alaska is an island south of Los Angeles, and mothers of small children are sent off to war with great fanfare and pride." It is not a counterrevolution we are after, they would respond; we want the moral scales balanced, not loaded down to one side. We continue to like what conservatives have to say, but we hate the way you say it. If you start talking, as some of you have, about "whether we have reached or are reaching the point where conscientious citizens can no longer give moral assent to the existing regime," you will be consigned to the margins of society where you belong.

To liberals and leftists, the message would be equally blunt. In their extremism, conservatives are giving you a chance to reclaim some of the ground you lost by turning your backs on our moral worldviews. That could be good news, not only for you but also for the country, because you on the left have properly emphasized how the fate of any one person in this country is always tied to the fate of others. But early indications suggest that at least some of you are losing your opportunity. In particular, your insistent, almost pathological, fear of understanding the importance of personal responsibility astonishes us. When we raise concerns about illegitimacy, welfare dependency, or excessive abortion, you often respond, as legal scholar Linda McClain does, that such concerns reflect the fact that we have a "problematic gender ideology" and are susceptible to "troublesome stereotypes about people in poverty," as if any ideology but your own extremely rarefied and impractical one must be considered problematic. And if we should worry about a society in which criminals are out of control and fear for the safety of our children, our neighbors, and ourselves, when you counter, as political scientist James Morone does, that such concerns reflect only a "popular anxiety" in which "criminal delinquents make an ominous predatory other" and "fit neatly into a picture of American troubles that conservatives framed long ago," we simply part company with you. By dismissing our fears about declining morality out of hand, you fail to recognize that middle-class morality is not necessarily opposed to the values of inclusion and equality that you currently profess. Furthermore, as sympathetic as we are to equality and inclusion, we remain hostile to quotas and preferences, as well as to efforts to promote respect for groups or ideas that have not worked hard enough to achieve that respect. If you are ever to be taken seriously by us again, you have to scale down your belief in morality writ large. We do not share your faith in active government, but we can accept some role for government so long as its outcomes are not dictated and its reach never extended too far. Trust us more, and maybe we will trust you more. We happen to have our own ideas about how we ought to lead our lives, so when you stubbornly substitute yours for ours, you can hardly expect us to support your agenda.

"I think the American dream is alive and well, and I think I could sell the American dream to my kids through myself," we were told by one of the most optimistic of the people with whom we spoke, Henry Johnson:

> This stuff about working hard and being morally sound and the more you give the more you receive and if you work hard you will achieve and things will come to you—I think those are all things that are not fantasies. Those things can happen

and, through my own experiences, those things have happened. . . . Like I said, I believe in the American dream, I do.

"Wow, that was good; quote him on that," Mr. Johnson's
wife interjected as he paused for breath, which is pretty much
how we felt, too. If there is anyone to whom both conservatives
and liberals need to learn how to talk, it is to someone like Mr.
Johnson. Because he is black, he knows the importance of liberal
goals such as equality and social justice and he is unafraid of relying on government to achieve them. But because he is successful, forward-looking, and thoroughly middle class in his
outlook, he understands as well the importance that conservatives assign to hard work, discipline, and moral grounding. So
long as there are people like him in this country—and the Middle Class Morality Project has found many of them—it is hard
to take seriously the notion that America is in moral peril.

Rachel Benjamin, the Brookline dentist, like Henry Johnson, is very optimistic for her country. Because she knows so
many Jewish people from the former Soviet Union and Israel,
she also knows what can happen when morality is writ too large.
Compared with the countries they come from, she rightly points
out that "it's not absolute chaos here." What bothers her most
about her friends from abroad is how certain they are that they
are right; "I see us," she says of America, "as more reasonable."
In this country, "we're a little more wishy-washy, because we are
trying . . . to evaluate issues on a more complex level."

What Dr. Benjamin finds valuable about America—"wishy-
washy" is as good a term as any—is inevitably problematic as a
moral outlook; middle-class Americans might be better off with
a little more Kantian backbone in their moral assembly kit. But
intellectuals who write about America's moral condition might
also be more persuasive if they listened to people like Dr. Benjamin. A lot has happened to the American middle class over the
past three decades. Lifetime economic security is a thing of the
past. Political scandals and disappointments have seemingly
never ceased. Wars have been lost—and won. The nation's bor-

ders no longer seem secure. The idea that this is a Christian nation, blessed by one particular God, no longer describes the reality of the country's religious belief. Disagreements have broken out over how to achieve the goals of equality, social justice, inclusion, and liberty. But through it all, middle-class morality has survived. However wishy-washy it may be, that is as good a reason as any for concluding that, in moral matters, the American middle class might know something about what is on its mind.

ONE NATION, AFTER ALL

The single most important difference between the practitioners of the morality writ small so prevalent in middle-class America and the morality writ large so characteristic of ideological politics is this: the former want to believe that we can become one nation, after all. And they worry that the ideological proclivities of extremists of left and right will make us two nations—or more—in spite of ourselves.

The phrase "two nations" comes from a novel written by the nineteenth-century British Prime Minister Benjamin Disraeli. Although used most recently in America to discuss our racial divide, the "two nations" concept has been historically associated with class, not race. Indeed nineteenth-century Britain was so divided between a working-class living in squalor and an upper-class accustomed to privilege that Disraeli was correct to suggest that each class was, to the other, a foreign country.

America, at least in the minds of most Americans, is not Britain; the possibility that our society might also become hopelessly divided by class is not greeted cheerfully. When we become preoccupied with what I have called the middle-class withdrawal symptom—the tendency of middle-class Americans to flee from their obligations to the poor and downtrodden— we usually forget that the idea of the middle class was once attractive, not because it symbolized privilege, but because it represented equality. The best way to insure that we would never become the two nations of rich and poor was to make ourselves one nation of those in the middle.

Obviously we have not, in an economic sense, succeeded in that endeavor. However one resolves the hotly contested debate over the size of the American middle class, some significant number of Americans will not be in it. If you live in poverty, it hardly matters whether 50 percent or 75 percent of the rest of the country is middle class; you still live in poverty. Despite reductions in the rate of unemployment and a stock-market boom that has produced record numbers of millionaires, moveover, almost no one projects that the future will resemble the go-go years after World War II. For all the wealth generated in America in recent years, economic security, once the very definition of the middle-class way of life, is unlikely to return to our shores.

Yet the very insecurity that has come to characterize middle-class life may make us more of one nation than ever before. Because I have not studied the attitudes of the working poor, the unemployed, or the very rich, I cannot, of course, speak to whether the kinds of modest virtues I found among middle-class Americans can be found among all Americans, especially those who live below middle-class standards. But it would not surprise me if Irving Kristol's argument that the American working class is fiercely attached to bourgeois values were proven to be correct. Rare are the blue-collar workers who do not share more than one job within a family to elevate their income to middle-class standards. And rarer still are the middle managers of impeccable middle-class income who have not felt at least some of the uncertainty once experienced by primarily blue-collar workers. Despite obvious differences in income, stock-market participation, home ownership, and income, a middle-class *mentalité* has become increasingly ubiquitous in America. At a time when intellectuals have become preoccupied with race and gender, we are becoming a society unified, at least in our moral outlook, by class.

Although I cannot speak with certainly about all Americans, I am persuaded from the results of this study that there is little truth to the charge that middle-class Americans, divided by a culture war, have split into two hostile camps. Middle-class Americans, in their heart of hearts, are desperate that we once again become one nation. From a middle-class point of view, the ideal society would be one in which everyone—immigrants, minorities, the poor—would uphold middle-class values so that someday they might obtain middle-class incomes. That is another way of saying that their solution to class inequality is to insist on moral equality. One of the reasons the left has had trouble sinking deep roots into American culture is that it has persistently denied this moral ideal of one nation. The left's approach to welfare, for example, implicitly accepted the idea that there would exist a permanent class of dependent people—a nation within the nation, if you will—of individuals whose fortunes would not be under their own control. It would be difficult to imagine a conception more at odds with the middle-class belief in one nation, although affirmative action—by positing the legal existence in America of the five nations of whites, blacks, Asians, Native-Americans, and Hispanics—probably surpasses it. The American left has been most successful when, as during the New Deal, it could claim to speak for the one nation we ought to be. It fails whenever it breaks up into its constituent parts.

In the oddest of political twists and turns, the right is now engaged in undermining the ideal of one nation as systematically as the left. If Irving Kristol was correct to argue that working-class Americans share middle-class values, then nothing could be more detrimental to the hopes of the Republican Party for majority status than efforts to reward the very wealthy at the expense of working-class and lower-middle-class Americans. If welfare once sheltered the poor from middle-class values, Republicans are attempting to shelter the rich from such rock-ribbed middle-class moral ideals as personal responsibility, reciprocity, and generosity. It is not my intention in this book to make policy recommendations, but if the Republicans wanted to convince middle-class Americans that they speak to their dreams, they would be curbing the influence of money in campaigns, insuring that special interests have no special access, and insisting that everyone pay their fair share of taxes. Creating a nation within the nation of luxury-box sitting, tax-avoiding, and influence-peddling Americans hardly seems the appropriate path to long-term popularity. The middle-class withdrawal symptom has been greatly exaggerated. The upper-class withdrawal symptom is truly to be feared. It would be ironic indeed if the middle-class ideal of one nation survived the left's romanticism only to fall victim to the right's cynicism.

Against such a possibility, there is much to be admired in middle-class morality. The people who have spoken in this book have no monopoly on virtue. But they do understand that what makes us one nation morally is an insistence on a set of values capacious enough to be inclusive but demanding enough to uphold standards of personal responsibility. By combining traditional ideals with modern realities, even if in ways discordant to intellectuals and ideologues, middle-class morality offers the best formula for making the United States the one nation economically it already is morally.

NOTES

Chapter I: Middle Class at Middle Age

1 **"America has been dominated":** Seymour Martin Lipset, *American Exceptionalism: A Double-Edged Sword* (New York: Norton, 1996), 32.

1 **According to the General Social Survey:** Data from the General Social Survey were downloaded from the home page of the Inter-University Consortium for Political and Social Research: http://www.icpsr.umich.edu/gss. The suggested reference is James Allen Davis and Tom W. Smith, *General Social Surveys, 1972–1994* [machine-readable data file] (Chicago: National Opinion Research Center, 1994). GSS data are available in two forms: trends, for questions asked every year, and statistics, for questions asked occasionally. I will be citing data by referring either to trends or statistics and then giving the mnemonic that describes the question. For this question, see GSS, Trends, CLASS.

1 **a CBS News/*New York Times* poll:** "How We Classify Ourselves," *American Enterprise* 4 (May–June 1993): 82.

2 **When President Clinton in 1995:** U.S. Congress. Senate Committee on Finance. *Middle-Income Tax Proposals: Hearings Before the Committee on Finance, U.S. Senate, 104th Congress, First Session* (Washington, D.C.: Government Printing Office, 1995).

2 **Asked in 1993 how much income:** "How We Classify Ourselves," *American Enterprise* 4 (May–June 1993): 84.

3 **By that definition, Judy Vogel:** A fuller account of how people were selected to be interviewed for this study follows later in this chapter.

6 **Writing during the 1980s:** Bennett Harrison and Barry Bluestone, *The Deindustrialization of America* (New York: Basic Books, 1982) and "The Growth of Low-Wage Employment," *American Economic Review* 78 (May 1988), 124–28.

6 **others challenged the data:** Marvin H. Kosters and Murray N. Ross, "A Shrinking Middle Class?," *Public Interest* 90 (Winter 1988): 3–27.

6 **which in turn prompted:** Lawrence Mishel, "Better Jobs or Working Longer for Less: An Evaluation of the Research of Marvin Kosters and Murray Ross on the Quality of Jobs," Working Paper #101, Economic Policy Institute, July 1988.

6 **a "hollowing out" of middle-class jobs:** Frank Levy and Richard J. Murnane, "U.S. Earnings Levels and Economic Inequality: A Review of Recent Trends and Proposed Explanations," *Journal of Economic Literature* XXX (September 1992): 1371.

7 **A more recent study:** Edward N. Wolff, *Top Heavy: A Study of the Increasing Inequality of Wealth in America* (New York: The Twentieth Century Fund, 1995). See also Sheldon Danzger and Peter Gottschalk, *America Unequal* (Cambridge: Harvard University Press, 1995).

7 **That conclusion has also been challenged:** John H. Hinderaker and Scott W. Johnson, "Wage Wars," *National Review* XLVIII (April 22, 1996): 34–38. See

also Amity Shales, "Doom, Gloom, and the Middle Class," *Commentary* 101 (February 1996): 19–24.

7 **However the statistics are interpreted:** For balanced views of the data, see Michael Horrigan and Steven Hauger, "The Declining Middle Class: A Sensitivity Analysis," *Monthly Labor Review* 111 (May 1988): 3–13; Robert Lawrence, "Sectoral Shifts and the Size of the Middle Class," *Brookings Review* 3 (Fall 1984): 3–11; Katherine L. Bradbury and Lynn E. Browne, "New England Approaches the 1990s," *New England Economic Review* (January/February 1988): 30–45; and Elia Kacapyr, "Are You Middle Class?," *American Demographics* 18 (October 1996): 31–35.

7 **Devoting an unusually large number of pages:** This series began with Louis Uchitelle and N. R. Kleinfeld, "On the Battlefields of Business: Millions of Casualties," *New York Times*, March 3, 1996, A-1, and ended with David E. Sanger and Steve Lohr, "A Search for Answers and Avoid the Layoffs," *New York Times*, March 9, 1996, 1. The entire series has been published in a book: *The Downsizing of America* (New York: Times Books, 1996).

7 **But in the 1990s that picture:** Juliet Schor, *The Overworked American: The Unexpected Decline of Leisure* (New York: Basic Books, 1991). For a critique of her analysis, see Kristin Roberts and Peter Rupert, "The Myth of the Overworked American," Economic Commentary Series (Federal Reserve Bank of Cleveland), January 15, 1995, as cited in Robert J. Samuelson, *The Good Life and Its Discontents: The American Dream in an Age of Entitlement* (New York: Times Books, 1995), 273. For another important critique of the idea that Americans have insufficient amounts of time, see John Robinson and Geoffrey Godbey, *Time for Life: The Surprising Ways Americans Use Their Time* (University Park, PA: Pennsylvania State University Press, 1997).

7 **Both spouses now worked to keep up:** Alice S. Rossi, "The Future in the Making: Recent Trends in Work-Family Interface," *American Journal of Orthopsychiatry* 63 (April 1993): 166–76.

8 **Long commuting hours:** Meni Koslowski, *Commuting Stress: Causes, Effects, and Methods of Coping* (New York: Plenum Press, 1995), and Peter G. Hall, *Managing the Suburban Commute: A Cross National Comparison of Three Metropolitan Areas* (Berkeley: Institute of Urban and Regional Research, 1993). On day care: Julia Wrigley, *Other People's Children: An Intimate Account of the Dilemmas Facing Middle Class Parents and the Women They Hire to Raise Their Children* (New York: Basic Books, 1995), and William Michaelson, "Childcare and the Daily Routine," *Social Indicators Research* 23 (December 1990): 353–66. On schools: The Harwood Group for the Kettering Foundation, "Halfway Out the Door: Citizens Talk about Their Mandate for Public Schools," The Kettering Foundation, January 1995.

8 **"the age of entitlement":** Samuelson, *The Good Life and Its Discontents*, 208, 188–204. See also Philip Longman, *The Return of Thrift: How the Collapse of the Middle Class Welfare State Will Reawaken Values in America* (New York: Free Press, 1996).

8 **they also were financing their personal lifestyles:** Joseph Nocera, *A Piece of the Action: How the Middle Class Joined the Money Class* (New York: Simon and Schuster, 1994).

8 **Indicative is a 1995 poll:** Cited in Urie Bronfenbrenner, Peter McClelland, Elaine Wethington, Phyllis Moen, and Stephen J. Ceci, *The State of Americans* (New York: Free Press, 1996), 52.

8 **Surveys from a wide variety of sources:** Both surveys are cited in Susan Tolchin, *The Angry American: How Voter Rage Is Changing the Nation* (Boulder, CO: Westview Press, 1996), 8, 51.

10 **"it is only the common people":** Irving Kristol, "About Equality," in *Neo-Conservatism: Selected Essays, 1949–1995* (New York: Free Press, 1995), 168, 171, 172.

11 **Contemporary American conservatism:** For a reasonably representative sam-

pling of views to this effect, see Mark Gerson, ed., *The Essential Neo-Conservative Reader* (New York: Addison-Wesley, 1996), and Neal Kozodoy, ed., *What to Do About . . . : A Collection of Essays from* Commentary *Magazine* (New York: Regan Books, 1995).

11 **American intellectuals and activists on the left:** Robert D. Johnston, "From Yeoman to Yuppie: The Demonization of the American Middle Class," presented at the American Historical Association Annual Meeting, December 1990.

12 **"The nervous, uphill financial climb":** Barbara Ehrenreich, *Fear of Falling: The Inner Life of the Middle Class* (New York: Pantheon, 1989), 250. Another effort to diagnose the conservative sickness of the American middle class in this period is Benjamin DeMott, *The Imperial Middle: Why Americans Can't Think Straight About Class* (New York: Morrow, 1990).

12 **Using one of the most emotionally laden terms:** Robert Reich, *The Work of Nations: Preparing Ourselves for 21st Century Capitalism* (New York: Vintage, 1992), 268. My emphasis.

14 **The culture war, in his view:** Christopher Lasch, *The Revolt of the Elites and the Betrayal of Democracy* (New York: Norton, 1995).

14 **In a similar way:** Michael Lind, *The Next American Nation: The New Nationalism and the Fourth American Revolution* (New York: Free Press, 1995).

14 **Scholars have been writing about:** Donald Warren, *The Radical Center: Middle Americans and the Politics of Alienation* (Notre Dame: University of Notre Dame Press, 1978); Herbert J. Gans, *Middle American Individualism: The Future of Liberal Democracy* (New York: Free Press, 1988).

15 **asked whether a person who works hard:** "How We Classify Ourselves," *American Enterprise* 4 (May–June 1993): 87.

16 **"was simply a few modest adjustments":** William G. Mayer, *The Changing American Mind: How and Why American Public Opinion Changed Between 1960 and 1988* (Ann Arbor: University of Michigan Press, 1992), 109–10.

16 **A number of books by distinguished sociologists:** See especially James Davison Hunter, *Culture War: The Struggle to Define America* (New York: Basic Books, 1991), and *Before the Shooting Starts: Searching for Democracy in America's Culture War* (New York: Free Press, 1994).

16 **other studies have appeared:** Paul DiMaggio, John Evans, and Bethany Bryson, "Have Americans' Social Attitudes Become More Polarized?," *American Journal of Sociology* 102 (November 1996): 690–755, and John Evans, " 'Culture Wars' or Status Group Ideology as the Basis of U.S. Moral Politics," *International Journal of Sociology and Social Policy* 16, no.1-2 (1996): 15–34.

17 **I even published an article:** Alan Wolfe, "Middle Class Moralities," *Wilson Quarterly* XVII (Summer 1993): 49–64.

17 **Ethnographic reports concentrate:** Herbert J. Gans, *The Levittowners: Ways of Life and Politics in a New Suburban Community* (New York: Vintage Books, 1967), and Jonathan Rieder, *Canarsie: The Jews and Italians of Brooklyn Against Liberalism* (Cambridge: Harvard University Press, 1985).

17 **Ever since a team of sociologists:** Robert S. Lynd and Helen Merrell Lynd, *Middletown: A Study in Contemporary American Culture* (New York: Harcourt, Brace and Co., 1929), and Robert S. Lynd and Helen Merrell Lynd, *Middletown in Transition* (New York: Harcourt, Brace and Co., 1937). See also Theodore Caplow et al., *Middletown Families: Fifty Years of Change and Continuity* (Minneapolis: University of Minnesota Press, 1982). For a recent example in this tradition, see Kathryn Marie Dudley, *The End of the Line: Lost Jobs, New Lives in Postindustrial America* (Chicago: University of Chicago Press, 1994).

18 **"a vague sense of dissatisfaction":** Katherine Newman, *Falling from Grace: The Experience of Downward Mobility in the American Middle Class* (New York: Free Press, 1988), 24.

18 **the National Election Study:** The National Election Study was also downloaded

from the home page of the Inter-University Consortium for Political Research at the University of Michigan. The formal citation is: Stephen J. Rosenstone, Donald R. Kinder, Warren E. Miller, and the National Elections Studies, *American National Election Study 1994: Post-Election Survey* [enhanced with 1992 and 1993 data] [computer file] (Ann Arbor: Inter-University Consortium for Political Research, 1995). I will be citing data by indicating the variable number of the question asked.

18 **They have, furthermore, been supplemented:** The Pew Research Center for the People and the Press, "The Diminishing Divide: American Churches, American Politics," June 25, 1996; James Davison Hunter and Carl Bowman, *The State of Disunion: 1996 Survey of American Political Culture* (Ivy, VA: In Medias Res Educational Foundation, 1996). References to the Hunter and Bowman survey throughout this book will be called the Post-Modernity Project.

18 **And election returns are notorious:** An especially insightful attempt to capture the mood of America through an analysis of recent electoral data is Stephen C. Craig, ed., *Broken Contract: Changing Relationships Between Americans and Their Government* (Boulder, CO: Westview, 1996).

19 **It is a less known fact:** William P. O'Hare, "A New Look at Poverty in America," *Population Bulletin* 51 (September 1996): 14.

19 **"Racial prejudice played a role":** David Rusk, *Cities Without Suburbs* (Baltimore: Johns Hopkins University Press for the Woodrow Wilson Center, 1993), 29.

19 **"a deep antagonism toward the nation's poor":** David L. Kirp, John P. Dwyer, and Larry A. Rosenthal, *Our Town: Race, Housing, and the Soul of Suburbia* (New Brunswick: Rutgers University Press, 1995), 5.

20 **Gans also writes of:** Herbert Gans, *The War Against the Poor: The Underclass and Anti-Poverty Policy* (New York: Basic Books, 1995), 2, 7, 76.

20 **the example of Mount Laurel, New Jersey:** For an additional account of the controversies around Mount Laurel, see Charles Haar, *Suburbs Under Siege: Race, Space, and Audacious Judges* (Princeton: Princeton University Press, 1996).

20 **"the dominant ideology is privatism":** Evan MacKenzie, *Privatopia: Homeowner Association and the Rise of Residential Private Government* (New Haven: Yale University Press, 1994), 177. Also relevant is Edward J. Blakely and Mary Gail Snyder, *Fortress America: Gated and Walled Communities in the United States* (Washington, D.C.: The Brookings Institution, 1997). For a description of one such community, Bear Creek in Washington State, see Timothy Egan, "Many Seek Security in Private Communities," *New York Times*, September 13, 1995, A1.

20 **There, according to liberal critics:** MacKenzie, 186; Reich, 268–81.

20 **as conservative journalist Tom Bethell has written:** Tom Bethell, "Losing the War," *American Spectator*, February 1997, 20.

21 **Americans invariably choose places to live:** Philip H. Rees, "Residential Patterns in American Cities," The University of Chicago, Department of Geography, Research Paper #189 (1979), cited in Howard Husock, "Standards versus Struggle: The Failure of Public Housing and the Welfare State Impulse," *Social Philosophy and Policy* 14 (Summer 1997): 69–94.

22 **Magazines such as *Worth*:** Jane Berentson, "The Richest Towns," *Worth*, 6 (July–August 1997): 80–94.

22 **1990 census data are:** I downloaded median family income data from the census's homepage: http://www.census.gov.

23 **"I won't stand for a Brookline education":** Gans, *The Levittowners*, 88.

23 **home of the first country club in the United States:** Kenneth T. Jackson, *Crabgrass Frontier: The Suburbanization of the United States* (New York: Oxford University Press, 1985), 98.

23 **a bitter fight over Western civilization:** As recounted in Richard Bernstein, *Dictatorship of Virtue: Multiculturalism and the Battle for America's Future* (New York: Knopf, 1994), 235–91.

23 In their book *The Bell Curve*: Richard J. Herrnstein and Charles Murray, *The Bell Curve: Intelligence and Class Structure in American Life* (New York: Free Press, 1994), 517.

23 moved to places like Medford: Herbert Gans, *The Urban Villagers: Group and Class in the Life of Italian-Americans* (New York: Free Press, 1962).

23 the busing controversies that dominated Boston: Ronald P. Formisano, *Boston Against Busing: Race, Class, and Ethnicity in the 1960s and 1970s* (Chapel Hill: University of North Carolina Press, 1991), and J. Anthony Lukas, *Common Ground: A Turbulent Decade in the Lives of Three American Families* (New York: Knopf, 1985).

24 who became Reagan conservatives: Stanley B. Greenberg, *Middle Class Dreams: The Politics and Power of the New American Majority* (New York: Times Books, 1995), 23–54.

24 children of immigrants who turned to the right: Samuel Freedman, *The Inheritance: How Three Families and America Moved from Roosevelt to Reagan and Beyond* (New York: Simon and Schuster, 1996).

24 the largest increase in black suburbanization: William H. Frey, "Minority Suburbanization and Continued 'White Flight' in U.S. Metropolitan Areas," *Research in Community Sociology* 4 (1994): 30–31; Carol J. DeVita, "The United States at Mid-Century," *Population Bulletin* 50 (March 1996): 10.

24 the U.S. Supreme Court ruled: Peter Applebome, "Passage of Time Blurs the Lines in Busing Case: Mixed Emotions Greet Court Decision," *New York Times*, April 2, 1992, A14.

24 Southeast DeKalb contains many successful: "Atlanta has been the number one location choice for African-American executives throughout the 1980s and 1990s, with a 23% black 'in-migration' rate between 1985–1990." Laura Nash, "Atlanta's Business Culture: Reexamining Corporate Civic Responsibility," published by Boston University Institute for the Study of Economic Culture, July 1996, 4.

24 the most conservative county in America: Peter Applebome, "Conservatism Flowering among the Mall," *New York Times*, August 1, 1994, A1.

24 That distinction was conferred upon it: "Olympic Officials Try to Cool Dispute about Homosexuality," *New York Times*, May 1, 1994, 29; Ronald Smothers, "Olympic Torch Relay Will Skip Atlanta Suburb That Condemned Gay Life," *New York Times*, April 20, 1996, 7; Peter Applebome, "Vote in Atlanta Suburb Condemns Homosexuality," *New York Times*, August 12, 1993, 16.

25 most violent racial disturbances: Scott Ellsworth, *Death in a Promised Land: The Tulsa Riot of 1921* (Baton Rouge: Louisiana State University Press, 1982).

25 charismatic Pentecostal megachurches: On the phenomenon of the American megachurch, see Charles Trueheart, "Welcome to the Next Church," *Atlantic Monthly* 278 (August 1996): 37–58.

26 as an ethnic group about to make: Peter Skerry, *Mexican-Americans: The Ambivalent Minority* (New York: Free Press, 1993).

26 by one estimate: Gregory Rodriquez, "The Emerging Latino Middle Class" (Institute for Public Policy, Pepperdine University, October 1996), 1, 6, 7.

27 one of the first writers to use: Richard Louv, *America II* (Los Angeles: J. A. Tarcher, 1983), 79–83. See also MacKenzie, 15.

27 Themes of generational selfishness: Philip Longman, *Born to Pay: The New Politics of Aging in America* (Boston: Houghton Mifflin, 1987).

33 a concern with middle-class values: William H. Whyte, *The Organization Man* (New York: Simon and Schuster, 1956); Betty Friedan, *The Feminine Mystique* (New York: Norton, 1963); Max Weber, *The Protestant Ethic and the Spirit of Capitalism*, Talcott Parsons, trans. (New York: Scribners, 1958).

33 all that much investigation: One exception is Michèle Lamont, *Money, Morals, and Manners: The Culture of the French and the American Upper Middle Class* (Chicago: University of Chicago Press, 1992).

33 and it was in Polish: Maria Ossowska, *Bourgeois Morality*, G. L. Campbell, trans. (London: Routledge and Kegan Paul, 1986).

33 **people far removed from their own experience:** Among the best examples of such studies are Mitchell Duneier, *Slim's Table: Race, Respectability and Masculinity* (Chicago: University of Chicago Press, 1992), and Francie Ostrower, *Why the Wealthy Give: The Culture of Elite Philanthropy* (Princeton: Princeton University Press, 1995).

34 **number of concrete sociological studies:** Newman, 58, citing Mark Baldassare, *Trouble in Paradise: The Suburban Transformation of America* (New York: Columbia University Press, 1968), and M. P. Baumgartner, *The Moral Order of a Suburb* (New York: Oxford University Press, 1988).

36 **There is, in fact, a moral revival taking place:** Robert Westbrook and Richard Fox, eds., *In Face of the Facts: Moral Inquiry and American Scholarship* (New York and Washington, D.C.: Cambridge University Press and the Woodrow Wilson Center Press, 1998).

Chapter II: Quiet Faith

39 **critics wondered:** James Hudnut-Beumler, *Looking for God in the Suburbs: The Religion of the American Dream and Its Critics, 1945–1965* (New Brunswick: Rutgers University Press, 1994).

39 **accommodations with material things:** R. Laurence Moore, *Selling God: American Religion in the Marketplace of Culture* (New York: Oxford University Press, 1994).

40 **"The vogue of Van Gogh":** Will Herberg, *Protestant-Catholic-Jew: An Essay in American Religious Sociology* (Garden City: Anchor Books, 1960), 59. A new, completely revised edition.

40 **liberal Protestants:** Gibson Winter, *The Suburban Captivity of the Churches: An Analysis of Protestant Responsibility in the Expanding Metropolis* (Garden City: Doubleday, 1961).

40 **conservative Protestants:** Peter L. Berger, *The Noise of Solemn Assemblies: Christian Commitment and the Religious Establishment in America* (Garden City: Doubleday, 1961).

40 **Jews, the most upwardly mobile:** Hillel Levine and Lawrence Harmon, *The Death of an American Jewish Community: The Tragedy of Good Intentions* (New York: Free Press, 1992); Albert J. Gordon, *Jews in Suburbia* (Boston: Beacon Press, 1959), 244–45; Marshall Sklare and Joseph Greenbaum, *Jewish Identity on the Suburban Frontier: A Study of Group Survival in the Open Society* (New York: Basic Books, 1987), 306–7.

40 **Catholics tended to live:** Alan Ehrenhalt, *The Lost City: Discovering the Forgotten Virtues of Community* (New York: Basic Books, 1995); John T. McGreevy, *Parish Boundaries: The Catholic Encounter with Race in the Twentieth Century Urban North* (Chicago: University of Chicago Press, 1996).

40 **when the rates of those leaving:** Joseph J. Casino, "From Sanctuary to Involvement: A History of the Catholic Parish in the Northeast," in Jay P. Dolan, ed., *The American Catholic Parish: A History*, vol. 1 (New York: Paulist Press, 1987), 91–92.

40 **"mighty challenge":** Jay P. Dolan, *The American Catholic Experience: A History from Colonial Times to the Present* (Garden City: Doubleday, 1985), 358.

41 **church membership reached its peak:** Robert Wuthnow, *The Restructuring of American Religion: Society and Faith Since World War II* (Princeton: Princeton University Press, 1988), 159.

41 **the American belief in belief:** Ronald F. Thiemann, *Religion in Public Life: A Dilemma for Democracy* (Washington, D.C.: Georgetown University Press, 1996).

42 **Christian nation:** Cited in Kenneth Karst, *Law's Promise: Law's Expression: Visions of Power in the Politics of Race, Gender, and Religion* (New Haven: Yale University Press, 1993), 6.

42 **what sociologists called "civil religion":** Robert N. Bellah, *The Broken Covenant: American Civil Religion in a Time of Trial* (New York: Seabury Press, 1975), 3.

42 **Not all Jews followed:** Herbert M. Danzger, *Returning to Tradition: The Contemporary Revival of Orthodox Judaism* (New Haven: Yale University Press, 1989); Lynn Davidman, *Tradition in a Rootless World: Women Turn to Orthodox Judaism* (Berkeley and Los Angeles: University of California Press, 1991). In the New York suburbs, areas of Rockland County, particularly around New City, became the locus of Orthodox Jewish suburbanization.

42 **Catholics surpassed Protestants:** McGreevy, 80; Gene Burns, *The Frontiers of Catholicism: The Politics of Ideology in a Liberal World* (Berkeley and Los Angeles: University of California Press, 1992), 99.

42 **"white Catholics are now very much part":** Barry A. Kosmin and Seymour P. Lachman, *One Nation Under God: Religion in Contemporary American Society* (New York: Harmony Books, 1993), 256.

42 **skipped over the city:** Mirta Ojito, "Immigrants' New Road Leads to Suburbia," *New York Times*, September 30, 1996, B1.

42 **growth in conservative Protestant sects:** Dean M. Kelley, *Why Conservative Churches Are Growing* (New York: Harper, 1977).

43 **As the religious schism became:** Wuthnow, 132–72; James Davison Hunter, *Culture Wars: The Struggle to Define America* (New York: Basic Books, 1991).

43 **formation and funding:** *Rosenberger v. Rector and Visitors of the University of Virginia et al.* 115 S.Ct. 2510. The Court had clearly been influenced by Michael McConnell, "Accommodation of Religion," in Philip B. Kurland, ed., *The Supreme Court Review: 1995* (Chicago: University of Chicago Press, 1988), 1–60, and "Religious Freedom at the Crossroads," in Geoffrey Stone, ed., *The Bill of Rights* (Chicago: University of Chicago Press, 1992), 115–94.

43 **the Christian Coalition was formed:** Ralph Reed, *Active Faith: How Christians Are Changing the Soul of American Politics* (New York: Free Press, 1996).

43 **leading some on the left:** Jim Wallis, *Who Speaks for God? An Alternative to the Religious Right* (New York: Delacorte, 1996).

43 **America's first culture war:** Robert T. Handy, *Undermined Establishment: Church-State Relations in America, 1880–1920* (Princeton: Princeton University Press, 1991); Isaac Kramnick and R. Laurence Moore, *The Godless Constitution: The Case Against Religious Correctness* (New York: Norton, 1996).

43 **making sweeping rulings:** Elizabeth Mensch and Alan Freeman, *The Politics of Virtue: Is Abortion Debatable?* (Durham, NC: Duke University Press, 1993).

44 **Americans stand out for:** Andrew Greeley, *Religion Around the World: A Preliminary Report* (Chicago: National Opinion Research Center, 1991), 39, cited in Seymour Martin Lipset, *American Exceptionalism: A Double-Edged Sword* (New York: Norton, 1996), 61.

44 **polling data regularly yield:** The Pew Research Center for the People and the Press, "The Diminishing Divide: American Churches, American Politics," June 25, 1996, 10–11; *American Enterprise* 5 (September/October 1994): 90; Tom W. Smith, "The Polls: Religious Beliefs and Behaviors and the Televangelist Scandals of 1987–88," *Public Opinion Quarterly* 56 (Fall 1992): 367; Pew Center, 11; Smith, 367–71; GSS, Trends, ATTEND. Similar findings are reported in the National Election Study: 13 percent said that "the Bible is a book written by men and is not the word of God," compared with 38 percent who indicated that "the Bible is the word of God and is to be taken literally, word for word," and 45.6 percent who said that "the Bible is the word of God, but not everything in it should be taken literally, word for word." NES VAR 1047.

45 **Even if we accept:** C. Kirk Hadaway, Penny L. Marler, and Mark Chaves, "What the Polls Don't Show: A Closer Look at U. S. Church Attendance," *American Sociological Review* 58 (December 1993): 741; Jeffery Haddon and C. E. Swann,

Prime-Time Preachers: The Rising Power of Televangelism (Reading, MA: Addison-Wesley, 1981), 44–67.

45 **church attendance is higher:** Steve Bruce, *Religion in the Modern World: From Cathedrals to Cults* (Oxford and New York: Oxford University Press, 1996), 129.

46 **Comparative survey data reported:** Ronald Inglehart, *1990 World Values Survey* (Ann Arbor: Institute for Social Research, 1990), cited in Lipset, 64.

50 **What is it that makes so many:** For a similar finding, see Theodore Caplow, Howard M. Bahr, and Bruce A. Chadwick, *All Faithful People: Change and Continuity in Middletown's Religion* (Minneapolis: University of Minnesota Press, 1983), 98.

51 **In his study of the way:** Robert Wuthnow, *Poor Richard's Principle: Rediscovering the American Dream Through the Moral Dimension of Work, Business, and Money* (Princeton: Princeton University Press, 1996), 312.

56 **as a result of the televangelist:** Smith, 364–65.

58 **Sociologists believe that levels of education:** Wuthnow, *The Restructuring of American Religion,* 169.

59 **one 1996 survey gave Robertson:** Pew Research Center, 7.

59 **another showed that Robertson's name:** Post-Modernity Project, tables 15.A–15.P.

59 **while it is undoubtedly true:** Pew Research Center, 1–6.

59 **among them there is anything but consensus:** Nancy J. Davis and Robert V. Robinson, "Religious Orthodoxy in American Society: The Myth of a Monolithic Camp," *Journal for the Scientific Study of Religion* 35 (September 1996), 229–45.

59 **more Americans disagree with the statement:** Post-Modernity Project, table 16.M.

60 **Cathedral at Chapel Hill:** This church is the subject of a doctoral dissertation. See Scott L. Thumma, *The Kingdom, the Power, the Glory: The Megachurch in Modern American Society* (Candler School of Theology, Emory University, 1996).

60 **Bakker would publish a book:** Jim Bakker, *I Was Wrong* (Nashville: Thomas Nelson, 1996).

61 **marrying outside their faith:** Egon Mayer, *Love and Tradition: Marriage Between Christians and Jews* (New York: Plenum Press, 1985).

61 **the faith that fit them best:** This tendency of Americans to pick their own religious faith led to the development of rational choice approaches to religion. See Roger Finke and Rodney Stark, *The Churching of America 1576–1990: Winners and Losers in Our Religious Economy* (New Brunswick: Rutgers University Press, 1992).

61 **immigration brought with it:** R. Stephen Warner, "Work in Progress Toward a New Paradigm for the Sociological Study of Religion in the United States," *American Journal of Sociology* 98 (March 1993): 1044–93, and the essays in R. Stephen Warner and Judith G. Wittner, eds., *Congregations as Cultural Spaces: Immigration, Ethnicity, and Religion in the United States* (Philadelphia: Temple University Press, forthcoming).

64 **One answer to this question:** Amy Gutmann and Dennis Thompson, *Democracy and Disagreement* (Cambridge: The Belknap Press of Harvard University Press, 1996).

66 **religion in the public square:** Richard John Neuhaus, *The Naked Public Square* (Grand Rapids, MI: Eerdmans, 1984).

67 **in places such as Springfield, Massachusetts:** N. J. Demerath III and Rhys H. Williams, *A Bridging of Faiths: Religion and Politics in a New England City* (Princeton: Princeton University Press, 1992), 100.

68 **In the wake of a Supreme Court ruling:** *Employment Division, Department of*

Human Resources v. Smith, 494 U.S. 872 (1990). For an analysis, see Jesse Chopper, *Securing Religious Liberty: Principles for Judicial Interpretation of the Religious Clauses* (Chicago: University of Chicago Press, 1995).

72 **Christianity requires the love:** Keith Hartman, *Congregations in Conflict: The Battle Over Homosexuality* (New Brunswick: Rutgers University Press, 1996).

73 **according to the Post-Modernity Project's poll:** Post-Modernity Project, table 42.A.

74 **According to the General Social Survey:** GSS, Statistics, HOMOSEX1. See also Tom W. Smith, "The Polls: The Sexual Revolution," *Public Opinion Quarterly* 54 (Fall 1990): 424. For similar results, see *Public Opinion* 10 (July/August 1987): 27.

74 **involving matters of privacy:** Americans are more likely to allow homosexuals to speak or to permit gay books in libraries than not; GSS, Statistics, SPKHOMO, LIBHOMO. In 1987, slightly more Americans thought that homosexual relations between consenting adults in the privacy of their own homes should be legal than believed it should be illegal. Smith, "The Polls: The Sexual Revolution," 424.

75 **it is clear from General Social Survey data:** GSS, Trends, COLHOMO.

79 **large majorities in America support:** Theresa F. Rogers, Eleanor Singer, and Jennifer Imperio, "The Polls: AIDS, an Update," *Public Opinion Quarterly* 57 (Spring 1993): 109, 111–12.

80 **by 92 percent compared with 82 percent:** *Public Opinion* 10 (January/February 1988): 31.

81 **At the present time, Americans:** Pew Research Center, 65. See also Post-Modernity Project, table 42.B, for roughly similar results. A 1988 GSS question showed 77.6 percent disagreeing and 12.5 percent agreeing that gays should have the right to marry. GSS, Statistics, MARHOMO.

81 **It certainly has not escaped the attention:** Thomas C. Reeves, "Not So Christian America," *First Things* 66 (October 1996): 16–21, and *The Empty Church: The Suicide of Liberal Christianity* (New York: Free Press, 1996).

83 **as few as 23 percent:** Smith, "The Polls: Religious Beliefs and Behaviors and the Televangelist Scandals of 1987–88," 367.

83 **a 1987 Gallup poll:** *Public Opinion* 10 (July/August 1987): 23.

85 **A generation ago, Will Herberg:** *Protestant-Catholic-Jew* 89.

85 **as the General Social Survey phrases:** GSS WORLD1.

Chapter III: The Culture War Within

92 **well over 60 percent of Americans:** Bruce A. Chadwick and Tim B. Heaton, *Statistical Handbook on the American Family* (Phoenix, AZ: The Oryx Press, 1992), 21, 54; GSS, Trends, SATFAM. However, as Norval Glenn argues, the percentage of people in satisfactory marriages after ten years has probably declined in the United States. Norval D. Glenn, "The Recent Trend in Marital Success in the United States," *Journal of Marriage and the Family* 53 (May 1991): 261–70.

92 **Roughly similar percentages:** Roper Organization for Virginia Slims, *American Enterprise* 4 (September/October 1993): 91.

92 **the proportion of those who believe:** GSS, Trends, MARHAPPY.

92 **the Western moral tradition:** For recent treatments of these issues, see Diana Tietjens, Kenneth Kipnist, and Cornelius F. Murphy, Jr., *Kindred Matters: Rethinking the Philosophy of the Family* (Ithaca: Cornell University Press, 1993).

92 **there is *Ozzie and Harriet*:** Critics of the "Ozzie and Harriet" model include Stephanie Coontz, *The Way We Never Were: American Families and the Nostalgia Trap* (New York: Basic Books, 1992), Judith Stacey, *In the Name of the*

Family: Rethinking Family Values in the Postmodern Age (Boston: Beacon Press, 1996), and Rosalind L. Barnett and Caryl Rivers, *She Works/He Works: How Two Income Families Are Happier, Healthier, and Better Off* (San Francisco: HarperCollins, 1996), the first chapter of which (pp. 1–8) is called "Ozzie and Harriet Are Dead." For the opposite point of view, but one that uses the same metaphor, see Daniel D. Polsby, "Ozzie and Harriet Had It Right," *Harvard Journal of Law and Public Policy* 18 (Spring 1995), 531–36.

92 **there is** *Murphy Brown*: Barbara DaFoe Whitehead, "Dan Quayle Was Right," *Atlantic* 271 (April 1993): 47–84, and Dan Quayle and Diane Medved, *The American Family: Discovering the Values That Make Us Strong* (New York: HarperCollins, 1996). For treatments along similar lines, see James Q. Wilson, "The Family Values Debate," *Commentary* 95 (April 1993): 24–31; Maggie Galagher, *The Abolition of Marriage: The Way We Destroy Lasting Love* (Washington, D.C.: Regnery, 1996), and Barbara DaFoe Whitehead, *The Divorce Culture* (New York: Knopf, 1997).

92 **Even when social scientists mobilize:** On that debate, see David Popenoe, "American Family Decline, 1960–1990," *Journal of Marriage and the Family* 55 (August 1993): 527–42, and Judith Stacey, "Good Riddance to 'The Family,'" *Journal of Marriage and the Family* 55 (August 1993): 545–47.

92 **The questions in the debate:** For a treatment of many of these themes from a perspective that argues that many of the changes facing the family, especially divorce, are harmful, see David Popenoe, Jean Bethke Elshtain, and David Blankenhorn, eds., *Promises to Keep: Decline and Renewal of Marriage in America* (Lanham, MD: Rowman and Littlefield, 1996).

94 **fatherhood is central to the raising:** David Popenoe, *Life Without Father: Compelling New Evidence That Fatherhood and Marriage Are Indispensable for the Good of Children and Society* (New York: Martin Kessler Books of the Free Press, 1996); David Blankenhorn, *Fatherless America: Confronting Our Most Urgent Social Problem* (New York: Basic Books, 1995).

95 **what sociologist Judith Stacey calls:** Judith Stacey, *Brave New Families: Stories of Domestic Upheaval in Late Twentieth Century America* (New York: Basic Books, 1990), 16–19. See also Stephanie Coontz, *The Way We Really Are: Coming to Terms with America's Changing Families* (NewYork: Basic Books, 1997).

96 **Of those surveyed:** GSS, Statistics, FEJOBIND; Post-Modernity Project, table 6.A. A similar survey found only 19 percent of the American population agrees with the statement: "Society made a mistake in encouraging so many women with families to work," while 76 percent agreed with the statement: "Society has been improved because women are now represented in the workplace." Pew Research Center for the People and the Press, "The Diminishing Divide: American Churches, American Politics," June 25, 1996, 67.

96 **Such attitudes have produced changes:** For Europe, see Duane F. Alwin, Michael Braun, and Jacqueline Scott, "The Separation of Work and the Family: Attitudes Towards Women's Labor Force Participation in Germany, Great Britain, and the United States," *European Journal of Sociology* 8 (May 1992): 13–37. The consequences of these transformations for America are discussed in Daphne Spain and Suzanne M. Bianchi, *Balancing Act: Motherhood, Marriage, and Employment Among American Women* (New York: Russell Sage Foundation, 1996).

96 **strategic picking between various:** Kathleen Gerson, *Hard Choices: How Women Decide About Work, Career, and Motherhood* (Berkeley and Los Angeles: University of California Press, 1985).

100 **On few other issues in America:** Arland Thorton, "Changing Attitudes Toward Family Issues in the United States," *Journal of Marriage and the Family* 51 (November 1989): 873–93.

103 **over 80 percent of the American population:** *American Enterprise* 3 (July/August 1992): 101.

103 **49.5 percent of GSS respondents:** GSS, Statistics, SINGLPAR.

104 **African-American middle-class families:** On gender relations among African-Americans, see Orlando Patterson, "The Crisis of Gender Relations Among African-Americans," in Anita Fay Hill and Emma Coleman Jordon, eds., *Race, Power, and Gender in America: The Legacy of the Hill-Thomas Hearings* (New York: Oxford University Press, 1995), 56–104.

107 **If people were more attuned:** David Gelenter, "Why Mothers Should Stay Home," *Commentary* 101 (February 1996): 25–28.

109 **Arguing that two-career families:** Barnett and Rivers, *She Works/He Works,* passim.

111 **What the sociologists:** Peter and Brigitte Berger, *The War Over the Family: Capturing the Middle Ground* (Garden City: Anchor Books, 1983).

111 **Children, those of this persuasion believe:** Jacob Joshua Ross, *The Virtues of the Family* (New York: Free Press, 1994), 261–62.

112 **Feminists accept the same analysis:** Katha Pollit, "Utopia Limited," *Nation* 263 (July 29/August 5, 1996): 9.

112 **Families have not weakened:** Steven Mintz and Susan Kellogg, *Domestic Revolutions: A Social History of American Family Life* (New York: Free Press, 1988).

112 **Jon Katz:** Jon Katz, *The Last Housewife* (New York: Bantam Books, 1996).

113 **Even women whose religious beliefs:** Nancy Tatom Ammerman, *Bible Believers: Fundamentalists in the Modern World* (New Brunswick: Rutgers University Press, 1987), 136.

113 **"Majorities may claim":** Daniel Yankelovich, *New Rules: Searching for Fulfillment in a World Turned Upside Down* (New York: Random House, 1981), 104.

114 **Things might be easier:** Arlie Hochschild with Anne Machung, *The Second Shift* (New York: Viking, 1989).

116 **these are the words middle-class Americans:** For background, see David Elkind, *Ties That Stress: The New Family Imbalance* (Cambridge: Harvard University Press, 1994).

117 **as difficult as it may be:** My findings on this point overlap with those of Robert Wuthnow, *Poor Richard's Principle: Rediscovering the American Dream Through the Moral Dimension of Work, Business, and Money* (Princeton: Princeton University Press, 1996). See also Robert Wuthnow, ed., *Rethinking Materialism: Perspectives on the Spiritual Dimension of Economic Behavior* (Grand Rapids, MI: Eerdmans, 1995).

119 **Both of them know full:** Daniel J. Monti, *Wannabe: Gangs in Suburbs and Schools* (Cambridge, MA: Basil Blackwell, 1994).

119 **Surveys undertaken by:** L. D. Johnston, P. M. O'Malley, and J. C. Bachman, *National Survey Results in Drug Use from the Monitoring the Future Study, 1975–1995.* Vol. 1: *Secondary School Students* (NIH Publication No. 97-4139). (Rockville, MD: National Institute of Drug Abuse, 1996).

119 **Asked in 1994:** *American Enterprise* 6 (November/December 1995): 104.

120 **84 percent of the American people:** *Public Opinion* 9 (September/October 1986): 37.

120 **according to a 1985 poll:** *Public Opinion* 9 (September/October 1986): 39.

120 **Kristin Luker, studying sexual behavior:** Kristin Luker, *Dubious Conceptions: The Politics of Teenage Pregnancy* (Cambridge: Harvard University Press, 1996), 93.

121 **Like populists in America:** Michael Lind, *The Next American Nation: The New Nationalism and the Fourth American Revolution* (New York: Free Press, 1995).

121 **A third approach:** Christopher G. Ellison, John P. Bartowski, and Michelle L. Segal, "Do Conservative Protestant Parents Spank More Often? Further Evidence from the National Survey of Families and Households," *Social Science Quarterly* 77 (September, 1996): 663–73, and Christopher G. Ellison and

Darren M. Sherkat, "Conservative Protestantism and Support for Corporal Punishment," *American Sociological Review* 58 (February 1993): 131–44.

122 **And for all the attraction:** Duane F. Alwin, "Changes in Qualities Valued in Children in the United States, 1964–1984," *Social Science Research* 18 (1989): 203–14, and Duane F. Alwin, "From Obedience to Autonomy: Changes in Traits Desired in Children, 1924–1978," *Public Opinion Quarterly* 52 (Spring 1988): 33–52.

125 **Conservatives in particular:** One book that brings many of these themes together is Dana Mack, *The Assault on Parenthood: How Our Culture Undermines the Family* (New York: Simon and Schuster, 1997).

125 **Conservatives blame such failure:** This is true of Mack's account (p. 12).

125 **"two distinct political cultures":** Mack, 232–33.

128 **John Rawls's 1971 book:** John Rawls, *A Theory of Justice* (Cambridge: Harvard University Press, 1971).

128 **Susan Moller Okin:** Susan Moller Okin, *Justice, Gender, and the Family* (New York: Basic Books, 1989).

128 **The most detailed criticism:** Michael Sandel, *Liberalism and the Limits of Justice* (Cambridge: Cambridge University Press, 1982).

128 **Taking on the question:** Alasdair MacIntyre, *After Virtue* (South Bend, IN: University of Notre Dame Press, 1981).

129 **The importance assigned by:** Okin, 41–73.

129 **Philip Selznick's:** Philip Selznick, *The Moral Commonwealth: Social Theory and the Promise of Community* (Berkeley and Los Angeles: University of California Press, 1992), 387–427.

129 **Even John Rawls himself:** John Rawls, *Political Liberalism* (New York: Columbia University Press, 1993).

Chapter IV: Mature Patriotism

133 **What other nation:** Seymour Martin Lipset, "The Sources of the Radical Right," in Daniel Bell, ed., *The Radical Right* (Garden City: Doubleday Anchor, 1963), 320.

133 **This disposition was brought out:** Elizabeth Hann Hastings and Philip K. Hastings, eds., *Index to International Public Opinion 1994–95* (Westport, CT: Greenwood Press, 1996), 631.

134 **Recent trends in international:** Kenicki Omae, *The End of the Nation State: The Rise of Regional Economies* (New York: Free Press, 1995). See also Jean Marie Guehenno, *The End of the Nation State*, Victoria Elliot, trans. (Minneapolis: University of Minnesota Press, 1995).

137 **Immigration has become:** Recent contributions to that debate include Chilton Williamson, *The Immigrant Mystique: America's False Conscience* (New York: Basic Books, 1996); Roy Beck, *The Case Against Immigration: The Moral, Economic, Social and Environmental Reasons for Reducing U.S. Immigration Back to Traditional Levels* (New York: Norton, 1996); Sanford J. Unger, *Fresh Blood: The New American Immigrants* (New York: Simon and Schuster, 1995); Margaret Mahler, *American Dreaming: Immigrant Life on the Margins* (Princeton: Princeton University Press, 1995); Peter Brimelow, *Alien Nation: Common Sense about America's Immigration Disaster* (New York: Random House, 1995); Georgie Anne Geyer, *Americans No More: The Death of Citizenship* (New York: Atlantic Monthly Press, 1996); Nicholas Mills, ed., *Arguing Immigration: Are New Immigrants a Wealth of Diversity or a Crushing Burden?* (New York: Simon and Schuster, 1994); Vernon M. Briggs, Jr., *Mass Immigration and the National Interest.* 2nd ed. (Armonk, NY: M. E. Sharpe, 1996); and Peter D. Salins, *Assimilation, American Style* (New York: Basic Books, 1996).

138 **According to a 1995 Gallup:** George Gallup, Jr., *The Gallup Poll: Public Opinion 1995* (Wilmington, DE: Scholarly Resources, Inc., 1996), 207. Future references to Gallup polls in this book will cite the year of the annual report.

138 **Historically, Americans have always:** Rita James Simon, *Public Opinion and Immigration: Print Media Coverage 1800–1980* (Lexington, MA: Lexington Books, 1985), and Rita James Simon and Susan H. Alexander, *The Ambivalent Welcome: Public Opinion and Immigration* (Westport, CT: Praeger, 1993).

138 **before undergoing a resurgence:** Edwin Harwood, "American Public Opinion and U.S. Immigration Policy," *Annals of the American Academy of Political and Social Science* 487 (September 1986): 201–12.

138 **At best, the new act:** Katherine Donato, Jorge Durand, and Douglas Massey, "Stemming the Tide? Assessing the Deterrent Effects of the Immigration Reform and Control Act," *Demography* 29 (May 1992): 139–57.

138 **By one account:** *American Enterprise* 6 (March/April 1995): 104. A 1996 poll showed that 51 percent thought immigration should be decreased, compared with 4 percent for increased, and 45 percent for keeping immigration at current levels: Post-Modernity Project, table 40.A.

138 **polling for the Pew:** Pew Research Center for the People and the Press, "The Diminishing Divide: American Churches, American Politics," 67; *Gallup Poll: 1995*, 207; GSS, Statistics, IMMFARE.

139 **Despite efforts by social scientists:** Thomas J. Espenshade, "Unauthorized Immigration to the U.S.," *Annual Review of Sociology* 21 (1995): 195–216.

139 **"a widespread populist backlash":** Unger, 372. See also Roberto Suro, *Watching America's Door: The Immigration Backlash and the New Policy Debate* (New York: Twentieth Century Fund, 1996).

141 **Because education is invariably:** Thomas Espenshade and Charles A. Calhoun, "An Analysis of Public Opinion Toward Undocumented Immigration," *Population Research and Public Policy Review* 12 (1993): 189–224; Jack Citron, Beth Reingold, and Donald P. Green, "American Identity and the Politics of Ethnic Change," *Journal of Politics* 52 (1990): 1124–54.

141 **Despite evidence that:** Roger D. Waldinger, *Still the Promised City? African-Americans and the New Immigrants in Postindustrial New York* (Cambridge: Harvard University Press, 1996). According to the 1994 General Social Survey, 74 percent of blacks believed it was likely that immigration would make it hard for America to be unified compared with 67 percent of whites. See Susan Mitchell, *The Official Guide to American Attitudes: Who Thinks What About the Issues That Shape Our Lives* (Ithaca, NY: New Strategist Publishers, 1996), 159. On the other hand, 10 percent of blacks thought immigration should be increased compared with 5 percent of whites: Mitchell, 153. Hunter's data show blacks marginally more hostile to immigration than whites: Post-Modernity Project, table 40.A.

141 **Anthropologists have long been interested in borders:** Victor Turner, *The Ritual Process: Structure and Anti-Structure* (Chicago: Aldine, 1969).

143 **Despite the widespread unpopularity:** *Gallup Poll: 1995*, 244.

147 **73 percent of them would oppose:** *Gallup Poll: 1995*, 207.

149 **black Americans support such programs:** Donald R. Kinder and Lynn M. Sanders, *Divided by Color: Racial Politics and Democratic Ideals* (Chicago: University of Chicago Press, 1996), 30. See also Louis Bolce, Gerald De Maio, and Douglas Muzzio, "Blacks and the Republican Party: The Twenty Per Cent Solution," *Political Science Quarterly* 107 (Spring 1992): 63–80.

151 **who were concerned that anti-immigrant:** If anything, slightly more Americans of Mexican and Puerto Rican background agree or strongly agree that America has too many immigrants. See Rodolfo O. de la Garza, Louis DeSipio, F. Chris Garcia, John Garcia, and Angelo Falcon, *Latino Voices: Mexican, Puerto Rican and Cuban Perspective on American Politics* (Boulder, CO: Westview, 1992), 101.

152 **those who believe that a country:** For the former view, see Michael Walzer, *Spheres of Justice* (New York: Basic Books, 1983), and for the latter, see John A. Scanlon and O. T. Kent, "The Force of Moral Arguments for a Just Immigration Policy in a Hobbesian Universe," in Mark Gibney, ed., *Open Borders?*

Closed Societies? The Ethical and Political Issues (Westport, CT: Greenwood Press, 1988), 61–107. Also relevant is Warren Schwartz, ed., *Justice in Immigration* (New York: Cambridge University Press, 1995), and David Jacobsen, *Rights Across Borders: Immigration and the Decline of Citizenship* (Baltimore: Johns Hopkins University Press, 1996).

152 **There is a school of thought:** Michèle Lamont and Marcel Fournier, eds., *Cultivating Differences: Symbolic Boundaries and the Making of Inequality* (Chicago: University of Chicago Press, 1992).

152 **From such a perspective:** For an argument along these lines see Bonie Honig, "Ruth, The Model Emigrée: Mourning and the Symbolic Politics of Immigration," *Political Theory* 25 (February 1997): 112–36.

153 **"the most important lesson":** George F. Borjas, "The Economics of Immigration," *Journal of Economic Literature* 32 (December 1994): 1668. See also George F. Borjas, Richard B. Freeman, and Lawrence F. Katz, "Searching for the Effect of Immigration in the Labor Market," National Bureau of Economic Research, Working Paper 5454, 1996.

154 **In the way multiculturalism:** The best example of what the debate is about is contained in Charles Taylor, *Multiculturalism and the Politics of Recognition* (Princeton: Princeton University Press, 1992).

154 **when given a series:** GSS, Statistics, OBVOT, OBVOL, OBJURY, OB911, OBENG, OBKNOW, OBMEPAX, OBMEWAR, OBFEPAN, OBFEWAR.

155 **That helps explain why:** GSS, Statistics, ENGOFFCL. For roughly similar findings, somewhat more favorable to making English the country's official language, see Post-Modernity Project, table 10.S.

155 **Groups such as U.S. English:** For a defense of U.S. English, see Gary Imhoff, "The Position of U.S. English on Bilingual Education," *Annals of the American Academy of Political and Social Science* 508 (March 1990): 48–61. For a critique, see James Crawford, *Hold Your Tongue: Bilingualism and the Politics of English Only* (Reading, MA: Addison-Wesley, 1992).

155 **state measures, such as California's:** Jack Citron, "Language Politics and American Identity," *Public Interest* 99 (Spring 1990): 103.

156 **hostility to bilingualism:** Citron, Reingold, and Green, passim. Opposition to illegal immigration in general can be explained by symbolic politics: Espenshade and Calhoun, passim.

156 **Bilingualism is one of those issues:** The Ramirez study, commissioned by the U.S. Department of Education, showed that while there was no difference between short-term bilingualism and English immersion with respect to academic achievements, long-term programs did have positive effects: J. David Ramirez et al., *Executive Summary Final Report: Longitudinal Study of Immersion Strategy, Early Exit, and Late Exit Transitional Bilingual Education Programs for Language-Minority Children* (San Mateo, CA: Aguirre International, submitted to U.S. Department of Education, 1990), as cited in L. Scott Miller, *An American Imperative: Accelerating Minority Educational Advancement* (New Haven: Yale University Press, 1995), 263. For a critique of the effectiveness of such programs, see Christine H. Rossell and Keith Baker, *Bilingual Education in Massachusetts: The Emperor Has No Clothes* (Boston: Pioneer Institute, 1996).

156 **Some claim that bilingualism:** See, for example, Colin Baker, *Foundations of Bilingual Education and Bilingualism* (Clevedon: Multicultural Matters, Ltd., 1996).

156 **Others suggest that all immigrants:** Alejandro Portes and Rubén Rumbaut, *Immigrant America: A Portrait* (Berkeley and Los Angeles: University of California Press, 1990), 221. See also Alejandro Portes and Richard Schauffler, "Language and the Second Generation: Bilingualism Yesterday and Today," in Alejandro Portes, ed., *The New Second Generation* (New York: Russell Sage Foundation, 1996), 8–29.

157 **despite strong support for making:** GSS, Statistics, ENGBALLT, BILINGED.

157   a 1987 poll taken: Citron, 105.
159   perhaps reflecting the fact: Michael W. Link and Robert W. Oldendick, "So-
      cial Construction and White Attitudes Toward Equal Opportunity and Multi-
      culturalism," *Journal of Politics* 58 (February 1996): 146–68.
163   Herbert Gans once coined: Herbert Gans, "Symbolic Ethnicity: The Future
      of Ethnic Groups and Cultures in America," *Ethnic and Racial Studies* 12
      (January 1979): 1–20.
163   "The national community's fate": David Hollinger, *Post-Ethnic America: Be-
      yond Multiculturalism* (New York: Basic Books, 1995), 157.
164   nearly all versions of liberal: Stephen Holmes, *Passions and Constraints*
      (Chicago: University of Chicago Press, 1995), 39.
164   "a morally irrelevant characteristic": Martha C. Nussbaum, with others, *For
      Love of Country: Debating the Limits of Patriotism* (Boston: Beacon Press,
      1996), 5.
164   Although there has been a rebirth: Michael Walzer, *What Does It Mean to Be
      an American?* (New York: Marsilo, 1992).
165   Such divisions persist: *Gallup Poll: 1993*, 228.
168   Tempered by so many disappointments: According to NES data, 31.8 percent
      of Americans, in 1964, said that government pays a good deal of attention to
      what the people think, compared with 12.2 percent in 1992; see Stephen C.
      Craig, *The Malevolent Leaders: Popular Discontent in America* (Boulder, CO:
      Westview Press, 1993).
170   There has, in fact, been: GSS, Trends, USINTL.
170   A comprehensive review of polling: Alvin Richman, "American Support for
      International Involvement: General and Specific Components of Post-Cold
      War Changes," *Public Opinion Quarterly* 60 (Summer 1996): 305–21. Another
      survey of the surveys indicates that although the proportion of those who
      thought the United States should take an active part in world affairs
      dipped to as low as 61 percent in the 1970s and 1980s, in more recent years, it
      was at about the same percentage (73 percent) as it was during World War II:
      American Enterprise (March–April 1993): 95.
170   66.1 percent disagree with the statement: NES, VAR 1019; *Gallup Poll: 1993*,
      239–40.
171   71 percent want to reduce it: *Gallup Poll: 1995*, 201.
172   the Post-Modernity Project's: Post-Modernity Project, tables 44.A–AA.
174   Polling data indicate: Gallup poll data, for example, found that 70 percent of
      immigrants believed that "your children will have better opportunities in the
      U.S. than you have had." *Gallup Poll: 1995*, 235.
176   serious students of American history: Arthur M. Schlesinger, Jr., *The Dis-
      uniting of America: Reflections on a Multicultural Society* (New York: Norton,
      1992).

Chapter V: Suburbia's Changing Moral Story

181   Demographers interested in residential: Everett Lee, "A Theory of Migra-
      tion," *Demography* 3 (1966): 47–57.
181   The particular shape and location: Clifford E. Clark, Jr., "Ranch-House Sub-
      urbia: Ideals and Realities," in Lary May, ed., *Recasting America: Culture and
      Politics in the Age of Cold War* (Chicago: University of Chicago Press, 1989),
      171–91.
182   reveal our hidden assumptions: Gwendolyn Wright, *Building the American
      Dream: A Social History of Housing in America* (New York: Pantheon, 1981);
      Dolores Hayden, *Redesigning the American Dream: The Future of Housing,
      Work, and Family Life* (New York: Norton, 1984); Margaret Marsh, *Suburban
      Lives* (New Brunswick: Rutgers University Press, 1990).
182   if we read between the lines: Constance Perrin, *Belonging to America: Reading
      Between the Lines* (Madison: University of Wisconsin Press, 1988).

182 **the choice of suburbia:** Robert Fishman, *Bourgeois Utopias: The Rise and Fall of Suburbia* (New York: Basic Books, 1987).

182 **what Justice William O. Douglas:** *Village of Belle Terre v. Borass*, 416 U. S. 1 (1974), cited in David L. Kirp, John P. Dwyer, and Larry A. Rosenthal, *Our Town: Race, Housing, and the Soul of Suburbia* (New Brunswick: Rutgers University Press, 1995), 80.

182 **resembles South African apartheid:** Douglas A. Massey and Nancy Denton, *American Apartheid* (Cambridge: Harvard University Press, 1993).

183 **than by a Connecticut Supreme Court:** *Sheff v. O'Neill*, 238 Conn. 1 (1996). For background, see J. C. Brittain, "Educational and Racial Equity Toward the Twenty-first Century: A Case Experiment in Connecticut," in Herbert Hill et al., *Race in America: The Struggle for Equality* (Madison: University of Wisconsin Press, 1993), 167–83.

183 **are also increasingly becoming:** See Kevin M. Fitzpatrick and John R. Logan, "The Aging of the Suburbs," *American Sociological Review* 50 (February 1985): 106–17, and Diane Crispell and William H. Frey, "American Maturity," Special Report, *American Demographics* 15 (March 1993): 31–40.

183 **represents the retreat:** For a summary (and criticism) of the literature that makes this point, see Brett W. Hawkins and Stephen L. Percy, "On Anti-Suburban Orthodoxy," *Social Science Quarterly* 72 (September 1991): 478–90.

183 **"The very last thing":** Kirp, Dwyer, and Rosenthal, 6. See also Michael Danielson, *The Politics of Exclusion* (New York: Columbia University Press, 1976), 49.

183 **many people will give what:** Timur Kuran, *Private Truths, Public Lies: The Social Consequences of Preference Falsification* (Cambridge: Harvard University Press, 1995).

185 **The percentage of African-Americans:** Carol J. DeVita, "The United States at Mid-Decade," *Population Bulletin* 50 (March 1996): 10.

185 **the average income of black:** William P. O'Hare and William H. Frey, "Booming, Suburban, and Black," *American Demographics* 14 (September 1992): 30–38.

186 **Rates of suburbanization:** DeVita; see also Karen DeWitt, "Wave of Suburban Growth Is Being Fed by Minorities," *New York Times*, August 15, 1994, A1.

186 **research undertaken by the public policy:** Urban Neighborhoods Study Group, "Research Proposal: Field Network Study of Working-Class and Middle-Class Urban Neighborhoods," Nelson A. Rockefeller Institute of Government, State University of New York at Albany, November 9, 1994. See also Michael E. Porter, "The Rise of the Urban Entrepreneur," *INC* (May 1995): 104–19. My thanks to Jan Rosenberg for providing these citations.

186 **black middle-class suburbs:** Douglas S. Massey and Nancy Denton, "Suburbanization and Segregation in U.S. Metropolitan Areas," *American Journal of Sociology* 94 (November 1988): 592–626; John R. Logan, "Racial Segregation and Racial Change in American Suburbs, 1970–1980," *American Journal of Sociology* 89 (January 1984): 874–88; Richard D. Alba and John R. Logan, "Minority Proximity to Whites in Suburbs: An Individual-level Analysis of Segregation," *American Journal of Sociology* 98 (May 1993): 1388–1427.

186 **notoriously color-conscious:** Charles Abrams, *Forbidden Neighbors: A Study of Prejudice in Housing* (New York: Harper, 1955).

186 **"have a right to live":** Benjamin I. Page and Robert Y. Shapiro, *The Rational Public: Fifty Years of Trends in Americans' Policy Preferences* (Chicago: University of Chicago Press, 1992), 74.

187 **"an exodus from central cities":** William O'Hare, as cited by Seymour Martin Lipset, *American Exceptionalism: A Double-Edged Sword* (New York: Norton, 1996), 135.

187 **Since the 1970s:** Brett W. Hawkins and Stephen L. Percy, "On Anti-Suburban Orthodoxy," *Social Science Quarterly* 72 (September 1991): 480.

191 **"the lost city":** Alan Ehrenhalt, *The Lost City: Discovering the Forgotten Virtues of Community in the Chicago of the 1950s* (New York: Basic Books, 1995).

192 **Children, especially young children:** David P. Varady, "Influences on the City-Suburban Choice: A Study of Cincinnati Home-Buyers," *Journal of the American Planning Association* 56 (Winter 1990): 22–40.

192 **"one of the widest issue gaps":** Mark J. Penn, "Rebuilding the Vital Center 1996: Post-Election Voter Survey" (Washington, D.C.: Democratic Leadership Council, 1996), 7.

193 **a world bifurcated:** William H. Frey, "The New Urban Revival in the United States," *Urban Studies* 30 (May 1993): 741–74.

194 **"leaves untouched the largest":** Charles R. Lawrence III, "If He Hollers Let Him Go: Regulating Racist Speech on Campus," in Mari J. Matsuda, Charles R. Lawrence III, Richard Delgado, and Kimberlè Williams Crenshaw, eds., *Words That Wound: Critical Race Theory, Assaultive Speech, and the First Amendment* (Boulder, CO: Westview Press, 1993), 63. See also Gary Orfield, "Housing and the Justification of School Segregation," *University of Pennsylvania Law Review* 143 (May 1995): 1397–1406.

195 **According to the conservative publicist:** Myron Magnet, *The Dream and the Nightmare: The Sixties Legacy to the Underclass* (New York: Morrow, 1993).

196 **contemporary conservatives attach:** George Lakoff, *Moral Politics* (Chicago: University of Chicago Press, 1996), 65–107.

196 **Beware, therefore, anyone preaching:** James Morone, "The Corrosive Politics of Virtue," *American Prospect* 26 (May/June 1996): 30–39.

196 **Surveys indicate that public:** Steven Teles, *Whose Welfare? AFDC and Elite Politics* (Lawrence: University Press of Kansas, 1996), 43.

197 **This suggests that opposition:** Martin Gilens, " 'Race Coding' and White Opposition to Welfare," *American Political Science Review* 90 (September 1996): 593–604, and "Racial Attitudes and Opposition to Welfare," *Journal of Politics* 57 (November 1995): 994–1014.

197 **roughly 57 percent of the American:** R. Kent Weaver, Robert Y. Shapiro, and Lawrence R. Jacobs, "The Polls: Welfare," *Public Opinion Quarterly* 59 (Winter 1995): 615–16.

197 **According to the General Social Survey:** GSS, Statistics, WELFARE5, WELFARE2, and WELFARE1.

197 **48 percent were opposed:** Post-Modernity Project, table 10.J.

197 **Americans make a sharp distinction:** Jeffrey Will, "The Dimensions of Poverty: Public Perceptions of the Deserving Poor," *Social Science Research* 22 (1993): 322–23; Tom Smith, "That Which We Call Welfare by Any Other Name Would Smell Sweeter," *Public Opinion Quarterly* 51 (Spring 1987): 75–83.

197 **Almost two-thirds of the American:** Weaver, Shapiro, and Jacobs, 620.

202 **"the revolution of rising":** Daniel Bell, *The Cultural Contradictions of Capitalism* (New York: Basic Books, 1976).

202 **their language is filled:** Mary Ann Glendon, *Rights Talk: The Impoverishment of Political Discourse* (New York: Free Press, 1991).

204 **"I'm one of the undeserving poor":** *Four Plays by George Bernard Shaw*, introduction by Louis Kronenberger (New York: Modern Library, 1953), 252.

204 **Ever since, liberal social critics:** For some examples, see Doug A. Timmer, "Homelessness as Deviance: The Ideology of the Shelter," *Free Inquiry in Creative Sociology* 16 (November 1988): 163–70; Paula K. Speck, "Underworld: Sexual Satire in Three Latin American Novelists," *New Scholar* 8 (1982): 235–44; Richard V. Ericson, "Penal Psychiatry in Canada: The Method of Our Madness," *University of Toronto Law Journal* 26 (1976): 17–27.

204 **The distinction between the deserving:** Michael Katz, *The Undeserving Poor: From the War on Poverty to the War on Welfare* (New York: Pantheon, 1989); Joel Handler and Yaheskel Hasenfeld, *The Moral Construction of*

Poverty: Welfare in America (Newbury Park, CA: Sage Publications, 1991); and Herbert J. Gans, *The War Against the Poor: The Underclass and Anti-Poverty Policy* (New York: Basic Books, 1996).

205 **"a convenient lightning rod":** Kristin Luker, *Dubious Conceptions: The Politics of Teenage Pregnancy* (Cambridge: Harvard University Press, 1996), 106.

205 **For Linda McClain:** Linda C. McClain, " 'Irresponsible' Reproduction," *Hastings Law Journal* 47 (January 1996): 339–453.

206 **roughly two-thirds of the American population:** GSS, Trends, PILLOK; Post-Modernity Project, table 6.D.

206 **Despite the fact that the 1960s:** Forty-two percent of Americans thought it should be legal to have children without getting married compared with 12 percent in 1970, while 45 percent believed that premarital sex is immoral in the latter year compared with 59.5 percent in the former: Tom W. Smith, "The Polls: The Sexual Revolution," *Public Opinion Quarterly* 54 (Fall 1990): 422.

206 **"a small, fairly constant":** Luker, *Dubious Conceptions*, 39.

209 **among those who have had:** Teles, 58–59, citing Nancy Goodban, "The Psychological Impact of Being on Welfare," *Social Service Review* 59 (September 1985): 403–22; Susan Popkin, "Welfare: Views from the Bottom," *Social Problems* 37 (February 1990): 64–79; and Christopher Jencks and Kathryn Edin, "The Real Welfare Problem," *American Prospect* (Spring 1990): 31.

210 **"strong and still growing":** Howard Schuman, Charlotte Steeh, and Lawrence Bobo, *Racial Attitudes in America: Trends and Interpretations* (Cambridge: Harvard University Press, 1985), 206. See also Tom W. Smith and Paul B. Sheatsley, "American Attitudes Toward Race Relations," *Public Opinion* 7 (October/November 1984): 50–53.

210 **there are no signs:** Charlotte Steeh and Howard Schuman, "Young White Adults: Did Racial Attitudes Change in the 1980s?," *American Journal of Sociology* 98 (September 1992): 340–67.

210 **"a huge racial rift":** Donald R. Kinder and Lynn M. Sanders, *Divided by Color: Racial Politics and Democratic Ideals* (Chicago: University of Chicago Press, 1996), 20.

210 **"blacks and whites inhabit":** Lee Seligman and Susan Welch, *Black Americans' Views of Racial Inequality: The Dream Deferred* (Cambridge: Cambridge University Press, 1991), 65.

210 **"African-Americans increasingly believe":** Jennifer Hochschild, *Facing Up to the American Dream: Race, Class, and the Soul of the Nation* (Princeton: Princeton University Press, 1995), 55.

211 **among middle-class African-Americans:** Joe R. Feagin and Melvin P. Sikes, *Living with Racism: The Black Middle Class Experience* (Boston: Beacon Press, 1994).

212 **discrimination, they are fully aware:** Seventy-three percent of GSS respondents in 1990 thought that blacks were discriminated against in jobs "a lot" or "some" compared with 26.1 percent who thought "only a little" or "not at all." GSS, Statistics, BLKJOBS. For an interpretation contrary to mine, which argues that "whites simply do not acknowledge the persisting prejudice and discrimination that are so obvious to blacks," see Seligman and Welch, 65.

212 **The language of accusation:** Von Bakanic, "I'm Not Prejudiced, But . . . : A Deeper Look at Racial Attitudes," *Sociological Inquiry* 65 (Winter 1995): 67–86.

214 **according to some polls:** Hochschild, 72.

215 **the 1986 National Election Study:** Kinder and Sanders, 17; Charlotte Steeh and Maria Krysan, "The Polls—Trends, Affirmative Action and the Public, 1970–1995," *Public Opinion Quarterly* 60 (Spring 1996): 135.

215 **whites are against affirmative action:** Jack Citron, "Affirmative Action in the Court of Public Opinion," *Public Interest* 122 (Winter 1996): 43.

217 **Survey researchers have discovered:** Larua Stocker, "Understanding White Resistance to Affirmative Action: The Role of Principled Commitments and

Racial Prejudice," in Jon Hurwitz and Mark Peffley, eds., *Perception and Prejudice: Race and Politics in the United States* (New Haven: Yale University Press, forthcoming).

217 **Even whites who say:** Steeh and Krysan, 134.

219 **Americans believe in both:** Lipset, 128–31.

220 **"a considerable convergence":** Steeh and Krysan, 136.

221 **"that bear unambiguously":** Kinder and Sanders, 9.

221 **And when they do disagree:** Paul M. Sniderman and Thomas Piazza, *The Scar of Race* (Cambridge: Harvard University Press, 1993).

221 **Finally, as a *Wall Street Journal*:** Gerald F. Seib and Joe Davidson, "Whites, Blacks Agree on Problems: The Issue Is How to Solve Them," *Wall Street Journal*, September 29, 1994, A1.

222 **whether he meant that affirmative:** Richard D. Kahlenberg, *The Remedy: Class, Race, and Affirmative Action* (New York: Basic Books, 1996).

223 **Since the Kerner Commission:** U.S. National Advisory Commission on Civil Disorders, *Report of the National Advisory Commission on Civil Disorders* (New York: Bantam, 1968).

223 **The titles of such books:** Besides works already cited in this chapter, I am referring to Tom Wicker, *Tragic Failure: Racial Integration in America* (New York: Morrow, 1996); Martin Carnoy, *Faded Dreams: The Politics and Economics of Race in America* (New York: Cambridge University Press, 1994); Derrick A. Bell, *Faces at the Bottom of the Well*, and Richard Delgado, *The Coming Race War, and Other Apocalyptic Tales of America after Affirmative Action and Welfare* (New York: New York University Press, 1996); Andrew Hacker, *Two Nations: Black and White, Separate, Hostile, Unequal* (New York: Ballantine Books, 1992).

223 **This is not the place:** Stephen Thernstrom and Abigail Thernstrom, *America in Black and White: One Nation, Indivisible* (New York: Simon and Schuster, 1997).

224 **the "streetwise" men and women:** The term comes from Elijah Anderson, *Streetwise: Race, Class, and Change in an Urban Community* (Chicago: University of Chicago Press, 1990).

225 **toward fearful encounters:** Craig St. John and Tamara Heald-Moore, "Fear of Black Strangers," *Social Science Research* 24 (September 1995): 262–80.

227 **"a culture of paranoia";** Homi Bhabha, "Bombs Away in Front-Line Suburbia," in Roger Silverstone, ed., *Visions of Suburbia* (London and New York: Routledge, 1997), 299–300.

Chapter VI: Ordinary Duties

228 **Robert Moses, the man whose plans:** Marshall Berman, *All That Is Solid Melts into Air: The Experience of Modernity* (New York: Simon and Schuster, 1982), 290–312.

230 **The most widely discussed:** See the following articles by Robert Putnam, "Bowling Alone," *Journal of Democracy* 6 (January 1995): 65–78; "Tuning In, Tuning Out: The Strange Disappearance of Social Capital in America," *P.S.: Political Science and Politics* 28 (Winter 1995): 1–20; "The Strange Disappearance of Civic America," *American Prospect* 24 (Winter 1996): 34–48; and Robert Putnam, "Bowling Alone Revisited," *Responsive Community* 5 (Spring 1995): 18–33.

230 **Survey data provide support:** GSS, Trends, TRUST.

230 **according to the GSS:** GSS, Statistics, SELFIRST.

231 **Trust, we have been told:** Francis Fukuyama, *Trust: The Social Virtues and the Creation of Prosperity* (New York: Free Press, 1995).

231 **a political system characterized:** Ronald Inglehart, "Trust, Well-Being and Democracy." A paper presented at the Conference on Trust and Democracy, Georgetown University, November 7–9, 1996.

231 **journalists and political commentators:** See the series of articles in the *Washington Post* on this subject that began with Richard Morin and Dan Balz, "Americans Losing Trust in Each Other and Institutions: Suspicion of Strangers Breeds Widespread Cynicism," *Washington Post*, January 28, 1996, and ended with David S. Broder, "Cure for the Nation's Cynicism Eludes Its Leaders," *Washington Post*, February 4, 1996.

232 **lies behind the withdrawal:** Besides the work of Putnam, see Jean Bethke Elshtain, *Democracy on Trial* (New York: Basic Books, 1995), and Michael J. Sandel, *Democracy's Discontent: America in Search of a Public Philosophy* (Cambridge: Harvard University Press, 1996).

232 **in my book *Whose Keeper?*:** Alan Wolfe, *Whose Keeper? Social Science and Moral Obligation* (Berkeley and Los Angeles: University of California Press, 1989).

232 **subject to considerable:** For examples from many directions, see Nicholas Lemann, "Kicking in Groups," *Atlantic Monthly* 277 (April 1996): 22–26; Michael Schudson, "What If Civic Life Didn't Die?" *American Prospect* 25 (March–April 1996): 17–20; Everett C. Ladd, "The Data Just Don't Show Erosion of America's Social Capital," *Public Perspective* 7 (June/July 1996): 1; John Clark, "Shifting Engagements: Lessons from the 'Bowling Alone' Debate," *Hudson Brief Paper 196* (Indianapolis: Hudson Institute, October 1996); George Petticino, "Civic Participation and American Democracy: Civic Participation Alive and Well in Today's Environmental Groups," *Public Perspective* 7 (June/July 1996): 27–30; and Robert J. Samuelson, " 'Bowling Alone' Is Bunk," *Washington Post*, April 10, 1996, A19. There is also an implicit criticism of Putnam's thesis in the finding that newer forms of civic associations have replaced older ones; see Sidney Verba, Kay Lehman Schlozman, and Henry E. Brady, *Voice and Equality: Civic Voluntarism in America* (Cambridge: Harvard University Press, 1995).

234 **people as the leading social:** William H. Whyte, Jr., *The Organization Man* (New York: Simon and Schuster, 1956).

234 **Whyte took as his texts:** Elton Mayo, *The Human Problems of an Industrial Civilization* (New York: Macmillan, 1933); W. Lloyd Warner, *Democracy in Jonesville: A Study of Quality and Inequality* (New York: Harper, 1949); and Frank Tannenbaum, *A Philosophy of Labor* (New York: Knopf, 1955).

234 **Free-floating fluidity:** William Kornhauser, *The Politics of Mass Society* (Glencoe: Free Press, 1959). See also Daniel Bell, "America as a Mass Society: A Critique," in *The End of Ideology: On the Exhaustion of Political Ideas in the Fifties* (Glencoe: Free Press, 1960), 21–38.

235 **as Samuel Freedman's account:** Samuel Freedman, *The Inheritance: How Three Families and America Moved from Roosevelt to Reagan and Beyond* (New York: Simon and Schuster, 1996).

235 **According to many social:** Seymour Martin Lipset, James A. Trow, and James S. Coleman, *Union Democracy: The Internal Politics of the International Typographers Union* (Glencoe: Free Press, 1956).

235 **The decline of union members:** U.S. Bureau of the Census, *Statistical Abstract of the United States: 1995* (Washington, D.C.: Government Printing Office, 1995), 443. For an explanation emphasizing the changing structure of the labor force, see C. Timothy Koeller, "Union Activity and the Decline in American Trade Union Membership," *Journal of Labor Research* 15 (Winter 1994): 19–32.

235 **institutions of civil society:** Putnam includes declining union membership as an example of the disappearance of civic America in most of the published versions of this thesis.

237 **to be shared by conservative:** Stephen Hart, *What Does the Lord Require? How American Christians Think about Economic Justice* (New York: Oxford University Press, 1992), 5.

239 **described in one account:** Bennett Harrison, *Lean and Mean: The Changing*

Landscape of Corporate Power in the Age of Flexibility (New York: Basic Books, 1994).

241 **the percentage of those:** *American Enterprise* 6 (January/February 1995): 106.

241 **A second way:** Diane Burden and Bradley Googins, *Balancing Job and Home-life Study: Managing Work and Family Stress in Corporations* (Boston: Boston University School of Social Work, 1987).

243 **In a book published:** Arlie Russell Hochschild, *The Time Bind: When Work Becomes Home and Home Becomes Work* (New York: Metropolitan Books, 1997).

245 **The argument by economists:** Daniel Fischel, *Payback: The Conspiracy to Destroy Michael Milken and His Financial Revolution* (New York: Harper-Business, 1995). For an argument to the effect that boards of directors have more discretion in matters of business restructuring than laissez-faire theorists acknowledge, see Michael Useem, "Business Restructuring, Management Control, and Corporate Organization," *Theory and Society* 19 (December 1990): 681–707.

247 **"high-status life":** Richard P. Coleman and Lee Rainwater, *Social Standing in America: New Dimensions of Class* (New York: Basic Books, 1978), 139.

247 **according to a Roper poll:** Cited in Irwin M. Stelzer, "Are CEOs Overpaid?," *Public Interest* 126 (Winter 1997): 26.

247 **If they had read:** Joseph Schumpeter, *Capitalism, Socialism, Democracy* (New York: Harper, 1942).

247 **Economists who espouse:** Michael Jensen and Kevin J. Murray, "Performance Pay and Top-Management Incentives," *Journal of Political Economy* 98 (April 1990): 225–64.

248 **But they don't have:** See George Brockway, "Executive Salaries and Their Justification," *Journal of Post-Keynesian Economics* VII (Winter 1984–85): 175.

249 **Putting aside the empirical:** For the former position, see David M. Gordon, *Fat and Mean: The Corporate Squeeze of Working Americans and the Myth of Managerial "Downsizing"* (New York: Free Press, 1996), and Ralph Estes, *The Tyranny of the Bottom Line: Why Corporations Make Good People Do Bad Things* (San Francisco: Berrett-Koehler, 1996); for the latter, see John M. Hood, *The Heroic Enterprise: Business and the Common Good* (New York: Free Press, 1996).

250 **at least in the account of:** Betty Friedan, *The Feminine Mystique* (New York: Norton, 1963).

253 **"only a slight decline":** John F. Helliwell and Robert D. Putnam, "Correction," circulated by the authors.

253 **Sociologists know that:** C. Kirk Hadaway, Penny L. Marler, and Mark Chaves, "What the Polls Don't Show: A Closer Look at U.S. Church Attendance," *American Sociological Review* 58 (December 1993): 741–52.

257 **To the degree that we look:** This is the subject of the doctoral dissertation written by Maria Poarch as part of the Middle Class Morality Project. Maria T. Poarch, "Civic Life and Work: A Qualitative Study of Changing Patterns of Sociability and Civic Engagement in Everyday Life," Ph.D. dissertation, Department of Sociology, Boston University, 1997.

257 **One of the sharpest criticisms:** Katha Pollitt, "For Whom the Ball Rolls," *Nation*, April 15, 1996, 9.

257 **in subsequent formulations:** "Strange Disappearance of Civic America," 670–71.

258 **"although most discussions of civic":** Clark, "Shifting Engagements," 11.

259 **In *The Theory of Moral Sentiments*:** For more on this point, see Allan Silver, " 'Two Different Sorts of Commerce'—Friendship and Strangership in Civil Society," in Jeff Weintraub and Krishan Kumar, eds., *Public and Private in Thought and Practice: Perspectives on a Grand Dichotomy* (Chicago: University of Chicago Press, 1997), 43–74.

259 **a case could be made:** Arlie Hochschild, *The Managed Heart: Commercial-*

ization of Human Feeling (Berkeley and Los Angeles: University of California Press, 1983).

261 **often pictured as exemplifying:** John Steadman Rice, *A Disease of One's Own: Psychotherapy, Addiction, and the Emergence of Co-Dependency* (New Brunswick: Transaction, 1996).

263 **Social critics—skeptical:** Christopher Lasch, *The Culture of Narcissism: American Life in an Age of Diminishing Expectations* (New York: Norton, 1978); Robert Bellah et al., *Habits of the Heart: Individualism and Commitment in American Life* (Berkeley and Los Angeles: University of California Press, 1985).

265 **The political philosopher Judith Shklar:** Judith Shklar, *Ordinary Vices* (Cambridge: Harvard University Press, 1984).

269 **"It is quite clear":** Coleman and Rainwater, 314.

Chapter VII: Morality Writ Small

275 **"Americans . . . do indeed share":** The Post-Modernity Project, University of Virginia, *The State of Disunion: 1996 Survey of American Political Culture* (Ivy, VA: In Medias Res Educational Foundation, 1996), vol. 1, p. 11.

276 **"one quarter of the population":** Ibid, p. 70.

282 **"Throughout most of this century":** Daniel Yankelovich, *New Rules: Searching for Fulfillment in a World Turned Upside Down* (New York: Random House, 1981), 230.

283 **"large chunks of the moral life":** Robert H. Bork, *Slouching Towards Gomorrah: Modern Liberalism and American Decline* (New York: ReganBooks, 1996), 4, 12.

283 **I write very opinionated essays:** Those who are not familiar with those essays will find many of them collected in Alan Wolfe, *Marginalized in the Middle* (Chicago: University of Chicago Press, 1996).

285 **chaired by William Bennett:** The author testified to the Bennett-Nunn Commission in January 1997 on the themes discussed in this book.

285 **I wanted to join:** Michael Sandel, "Making Nice Is Not the Same as Doing Good," *New York Times*, December 29, 1996, 9.

286 **An astonishingly high:** GSS, Trends, ANOMIA7. Sixty-nine percent agreed with the statement that "most elected officials don't care what people like you think" compared with 31 percent who disagreed: Post-Modernity Project, table 16.A. See also Stephen C. Craig, *The Malevolent Leaders: Popular Discontent in America* (Boulder, CO: Westview Press, 1993).

287 **"I am optimistic":** Cited in Seymour Martin Lipset, *American Exceptionalism: A Double-Edged Sword* (New York: Norton, 1996), 287; GSS, Statistics, HAPUNHAP.

287 **to create an "optimism gap":** The Pew Research Center for the People and the Press, "The Optimism Gap Grows," press release, January 17, 1997, 3.

289 **Political scientist Eric Uslander:** Eric M. Uslaner, "Social Capital, Television, and the 'Mean World': A Discourse on Chickens and Eggs," prepared for presentation at the Annual Meeting of the American Political Science Association, August 28–September 1, 1996.

291 **"Often touched by misanthropy":** Judith Shklar, *Ordinary Vices* (Cambridge: Harvard University Press, 1982), 225.

298 **Despite their oft-professed:** GSS, Statistics, GODRIGHT.

299 **that it rings true:** Christopher Lasch, *The Culture of Narcissism: American Life in an Age of Diminishing Expectations* (New York: Norton, 1978), and *Haven in a Heartless World* (New York: Basic Books, 1977); Robert Bellah, et al., *Habits of the Heart* (Berkeley and Los Angeles: University of California Press, 1985).

299 **"we are . . . living in an era":** William J. Bennett, "The Children," in Neal Kozodoy, ed., *What to Do About . . . : A Collection of Essays from* Commentary *Magazine* (New York: ReganBooks, 1995), 5–6.

299 **People who worry:** For samplings of views like these, see Chester Finn, "The Schools," in Kozodoy, 100–120; Dana Mack, *The Assault on Parenthood: How Our Culture Undermines the Family* (New York: Simon and Schuster, 1997); John DiIulio, "The Coming of the Super-Predators," *Weekly Standard* 1 (November 27, 1995): 23–28; William Tucker, "The Moral of the Story," *American Spectator* 29 (October 1996): 119–24; Russell Hittinger, "A Crisis of Legitimacy," *First Things* 67 (November 1996): 25–29; and Hadley Arkes, "A Culture Corrupted," *First Things* 67 (November 1996): 30–33.

300 **When he used that term:** Claude Lévi-Strauss, *The Savage Mind* (Chicago: University of Chicago Press, 1962), 16–33.

302 **"For most people . . . only":** *Slouching Towards Gomorrah*, 278.

303 **"surrendering to the spirit":** Irving Kristol, "Christianity, Judaism, and Socialism," in *Neo-Conservatism: Selected Essays, 1945–1995* (New York: Free Press, 1995), 440, 431, 432.

303 **"young people do not want to hear":** *Neo-Conservatism*, 441.

304 **But throughout the late 1960s:** See, for example, Ronald Radosh, *Divided They Fell: The Demise of the Democratic Party, 1964–1996* (New York: Free Press, 1996). For another account, see Stephen Gillon, *The Democrat's Dilemma: Walter F. Mondale and the Legacy of Liberalism* (New York: Columbia University Press, 1992).

304 **becoming, in the process:** Stanley Rothman, Althea K. Nagai, and Robert Lerner, *American Elites* (New Haven: Yale University Press, 1996). See also Paul Hollander, *Anti-Americanism: Critiques at Home and Abroad, 1965–1990* (New York: Oxford University Press, 1992). In the interests of full disclosure, I should add that Hollander includes me as one of his anti-American intellectuals (p. 53).

304 **not always empirically:** Lerner, Nagai, and Rothman do take pains to verify their analysis empirically. Earlier versions of "new class" theory did not always do so convincingly; on this point, see Steven G. Brint, *In an Age of Experts: The Changing Role of Professions in Politics and Public Life* (Princeton: Princeton University Press, 1994).

304 **A passionately argued version:** Herbert J. Gans, *The War Against the Poor: The Underclass and Anti-Poverty Policy* (New York: Basic Books, 1996), 71.

305 **Gans was criticized:** John DiIulio, "Liberalism's Last Stand?," *Public Interest* 122 (Winter 1996): 119–24.

306 **Despite prodigious efforts:** Michael Novak, *The Spirit of Democratic Capitalism* (New York: Simon and Schuster, 1982); Daniel Bell, *The Cultural Contradictions of Capitalism* (New York: Basic Books, 1976).

307 **The personal and the economic:** For a further elaboration of this point, see my essay "Whose Body Politic?," *American Prospect* 12 (Winter 1993): 99–108.

308 **"moral mediocrity":** Émile Durkheim, *The Elementary Forms of the Religious Life*, Karen E. Fields, trans. (New York: Free Press, 1995), 429.

308 **Writing in the aftermath:** For a typical expression of this point of view, Committee on Political Parties, American Political Science Association, *Toward a More Responsible Two Party System* (New York: Rinehart, 1950).

316 **"conservatives are counter-revolutionaries":** Mark Helprin, "To Fight for Principle," *Wall Street Journal*, January 15, 1997, A16.

316 **"whether we have reached":** "The End of Democracy? The Judicial Usurpation of Politics," *First Things* 67 (November 1996): 18.

317 **"problematic gender ideology":** Linda C. McClain, " 'Irresponsible' Reproduction," *Hastings Law Journal* 47 (January 1996), 342.

317 **"criminal delinquents make":** James Morone, "The Corrosive Politics of Virtue," *American Prospect* 26 (May–June 1996), 33.

319 **The phrase "two nations":** Benjamin Disraeli, *Sybil, or, The Two Nations* (London: H. Colburn, 1845).

319 **Although used most recently:** Andrew Hacker, *Two Nations: Black & White, Separate, Hostile, Unequal* (New York: Scribner's, 1992).

INDEX